MW01000584

WILSON'S WAR

WILSON'S
WAR

HOW WOODROW WILSON'S GREAT BLUNDER
LED TO HITLER, LENIN, STALIN,
AND WORLD WAR II

JIM POWELL

CROWN
FORUM
NEW YORK

Copyright © 2005 by Jim Powell

Published in the United States by Crown Forum, an imprint of the Crown Publishing
Group, a division of Random House, Inc., New York.
www.crownpublishing.com

CROWN FORUM and the Crown Forum colophon are trademarks of
Random House, Inc.

Library of Congress Cataloging-in-Publication Data
Powell, Jim, 1944–
Wilson's war: how Woodrow Wilson's great blunder led to Hitler, Lenin, Stalin, and
World War II / Jim Powell.
Includes bibliographical references and index.
1. Wilson, Woodrow, 1856–1924. 2. United States—Foreign relations—1913–1921.
3. World War, 1914–1918—Causes. 4. World War, 1914–1918—United States. 5. World
War, 1914–1918—Diplomatic history. 6. World War, 1939–1945—Causes. I. Title.
E768.P75 2005
327.73'009'041—dc22
2004021472

ISBN 1-4000-8236-6

Printed in the United States of America

Design by Leonard Henderson

10 9 8 7 6 5 4 3 2 1

First Edition

To Madeline, Frank, Marisa, Justin, Kristin, and Rosalynd

CONTENTS

WILSON'S WAR

ARROGANCE AND POWER

P<small>RESIDENT</small> <small>WOODROW</small> <small>WILSON,</small> according to the conventional view, was a great "progressive," a president who showed how the United States can do good by intervening in the affairs of other nations.

"I am in complete sympathy with Wilson's broad program and with his vision for the future," wrote diplomatic historian Thomas A. Bailey. "He spoke with unchallengeable realism when he said that isolationism had been repealed by the forces of history; he spoke with prophetic vision when he said that if we did not set up an agency to prevent war, another and more terrible holocaust would engulf the next generation."[1] Arthur S. Link, long a guardian of Wilson's reputation, credited him with helping to "lay the foundations of a new world order."[2]

The conventional view must be challenged, because Wilson made a decision that led to tens of millions of deaths. Far from helping "make the world safe for democracy," as he claimed, he contributed to the rise of some of the most murderous dictators who ever lived. No other U.S. president has had a hand—however unintentional—in so much destruction. Wilson surely ranks as the worst president in American history.

Wilson's fateful decision was for the United States to enter World War I. This had horrifying consequences.

First, American entry enabled the Allies—principally Britain and France—to win a decisive victory and dictate harsh surrender terms on the losers, principally Germany.

1

Until the United States entered the war, which had begun in August 1914, it was stalemated. The British and French together always had more soldiers on the Western Front than the Germans, but the Germans had smarter generals and more guns.[3] The British navy maintained a blockade that prevented the Germans from importing just about anything, including food, and the Germans had no way to invade England. Both sides suffered millions of fatalities, and their fighting forces were weary. Neither side had the capacity to dictate harsh terms to the other.

After two years of war, there was increasing support for peace on both sides. In Russia, as early as the summer of 1915, there were widespread protests against the war.[4] Wilson repeatedly offered his services as a mediator for peace, but as historian Barbara Tuchman noted, "The talk exasperated the Allies. It was not mediation they wanted from America but her great, untapped strength."[5] In December 1916, the Germans proposed peace talks, but they wanted to retain the French and Belgian territory they occupied, and the idea was rejected; the British and French anticipated that the United States would enter the war and enable them to win a decisive victory that would avoid compromise with the Germans. Politicians on both sides knew they would be toppled if they couldn't brag about territorial gains and if it became obvious that millions of people had died for nothing. In February 1917, the Hapsburg emperor Karl I pursued peace negotiations with the British and French, aimed at getting Austria-Hungary out of the war even if their ally Germany continued fighting, but Italy objected. If the United States had stayed out, the British and French would have been under more pressure to compromise. There probably would have been a negotiated settlement.

American entry in the war undermined efforts to develop a viable German republic. German generals Paul von Hindenburg and Erich von Ludendorff, who controlled the military and the government, recognized that the individual who carried out the surrender—by signing the armistice agreement—would be hated. They resigned, and the king, Kaiser Wilhelm II, abdicated. These men didn't want their fingerprints on the Armistice. A republic was declared on November 9, and the thankless task of signing the Armistice fell to Matthias Erzberger, a civilian and leader of the Catholic Centre Party, who had spoken out for peace. The humiliating list of surrender terms included a shocker: the British naval blockade would continue indefinitely even though the German soldiers had stopped fighting, and German children were starving to death. The newborn German republic, not the military, was discredited by the Armistice. Erzberger was later murdered as one of the "November criminals."

Having enabled the French and British to win the war, Wilson imagined that he could persuade them to agree on a peace settlement according to the high-minded principles he outlined in his January 18, 1918, "Fourteen Points" speech before a joint session of Congress—principles including self-determination for peoples, freedom of the seas, and no more secret treaties. But at the Paris Peace Conference, beginning in January 1919, Wilson participated in secret diplomacy—from which the Germans were excluded—and an old-fashioned scramble among victors for the spoils of war.

Wilson failed to stop French prime minister Georges Clemenceau. Known as "the Tiger," Clemenceau was determined to avenge Germany's defeat of France in 1870—a war France had started—and the loss of 1.3 million Frenchmen during World War I. Clemenceau got the notorious "war guilt" clause (Article 231) claiming that Germany was 100 percent responsible for the war, and he made sure the treaty obligated Germany to pay huge reparations and surrender a long list of assets including coal, trucks, guns, and ships—private property as well as property of the German government.[6]

Despite Wilson's professed ideals about self-determination, he didn't stop the Allies from dividing German colonies among themselves. Neither the British nor the French were about to dismantle their colonial empires. The British Empire expanded by taking over the former German colonies of Tanganyika and part of Togoland and the Cameroons. Belgium and South Africa divided the rest of Germany's holdings in Africa. To bribe Italy to enter the war on their side, the British and French had signed the secret Treaty of London (1915), which promised the Italians war spoils in Austria-Hungary, the Balkans, Asia Minor, and elsewhere, and the Italians wanted it all; they were outraged to find that the British and French planned on giving them little.[7] The Japanese demanded Chinese territory and a statement affirming racial equality, and while they didn't get those things, they ended up receiving German assets in China's Shantung province, including a port, railroads, mines, and submarine cables.[8]

Maybe the Germans deserved to be treated as they had treated others, but the harsh surrender terms, made possible by American entry in the war and enshrined in the Treaty of Versailles, further discredited the German republic and triggered a dangerous nationalist reaction. Many Germans became convinced that armed force was ultimately the only way to make up for "the shame of Versailles." A year after the signing of the Versailles Treaty, former German corporal Adolf Hitler took over the tiny German Workers Party, transformed it into the National Socialist German Workers Party, and began recruiting thousands of members by denouncing the treaty, Jews, and Bolsheviks. As far as Bolsheviks were concerned, one might say that Hitler found one of his most politically useful adversaries thanks to Woodrow Wilson. Among Hitler's early recruits, becoming Nazis in 1922, were Joseph Goebbels, who was to play a vital role orchestrating Nazi propaganda and mass rallies; and Rudolf Hoess, who was to manage the extermination of Jews at Auschwitz.

The reparations bill, which the Allies presented to the Germans in 1921, created powerful incentives for the Germans to inflate their currency and try paying their debts with worthless marks. Reparations weren't the only factor in the ruinous runaway inflation—the Germans were trying to maintain a deficit-ridden welfare state, including government-run sausage factories, at the same time—but unquestionably reparations added incentives to inflate. It was no coincidence that the German inflation was worse than any other inflation following World War I. Before the war, marks were being exchanged at the rate of 4.2 per U.S. dollar, and by the end of 1923 the rate was about 4 trillion marks per dollar.[9] The inflation wiped out life savings, made a mockery of honest contracts, disrupted production, devastated rich and poor, young and old, men and women.

Hitler effectively appealed to these bitter people, whom he referred to as "starving billionaires." In a speech he gave during the summer of 1923, he told a story that illustrated the agony of inflation: "We have just had a big gymnastic festival in Munich . . . athletes from all over the country assembled here. That must have brought our city lots of business, you think. Now listen to this: There was an old woman who sold picture postcards. She was glad because the festival would bring her plenty of customers. She was beside herself with joy when sales far exceeded her expectations. Business had been good—or so she thought. But now the old woman is sitting in front of an empty shop, crying her eyes out. For with the miserable paper money she took in for her cards, she can't buy a hundredth of her old stock. Her business is ruined, her livelihood absolutely destroyed. She can go begging. And the same despair is seizing the whole people. We are facing a revolution."[10]

Near the climax of the inflation, November 8, 1923, Hitler made his first attempt to seize power, in a Munich beer hall where German government officials had gathered. Present for the "Beer Hall Putsch" were men who were to become key collaborators in the Nazi regime: Rudolf Hess (not to be confused with Rudolf Hoess) served as Hitler's personal secretary and deputy (Hitler dictated the manuscript for his book *Mein Kampf* to Hess); Ernst Röhm, a street brawler who was an army captain during World War I, helped organize the *Sturmabteilung* (SA)—the brown-shirted Stormtroopers who formed Hitler's first private army; Gregor Strasser was another key figure in the SA; Wilhelm Frick was a lawyer who for a while headed Hitler's private armies and drafted laws for the Nazi regime; Hermann Göring, an ace fighter pilot, became a leader of the SA and later head of armed forces in Nazi Germany; Heinrich Himmler headed the Gestapo and the black-shirted *Schutzstaffel* (SS) secret police forces, set up the first Nazi concentration camp, and planned the Holocaust.

Suppose, for a moment, that Germany had won the land war on the Western Front. How bad might that have been? The Germans showed they could be tough in the Treaty of Brest-Litovsk (March 3, 1918). As a condition for ending the war on the Eastern Front, it provided that Germany would gain large chunks of the Russian empire—including Ukraine, Georgia, Finland, and the Baltic states. These territories, though, had non-Russian peoples who had long yearned to be free from Russian control. If the Germans had won on the Western Front, presumably they would have acquired territory their soldiers occupied in France and Belgium. This probably would have amounted to less than the German territory seized by the French

conqueror Napoleon Bonaparte a century earlier. The rivalry between the French and Germans had been going on for a long time,
and one wonders why American lives should have been sacrificed
when the French and Germans got into another war.

The Germans probably wouldn't have been able to enjoy their
victory for long. Although German submarines had threatened to cut
off Britain from imported food and war materials, the British countered with the convoy system; from May 1917 to November 1918
there were 1,134 convoys protecting 16,693 merchant ships, and reportedly 99 percent delivered the goods.[11] Britain would have retained
its independence, protected by its navy, which would have continued
the hunger blockade against Germany. In all likelihood, Germany
would have become bogged down in endemic conflicts along the vast
frontier with Russia, complicated by nationalist rebellions in the
wreckage of Germany's ally, Austria-Hungary. All this probably
would have proven too much for the war-weary German army, which
was already struggling to put down mutinies. Such an outcome
would surely have been preferable to what did happen, namely the
rise of Hitler, World War II, and the Holocaust.

Ironically, despite Wilson's high-minded ideals, when entering
World War I he joined the side that placed a lower value on human
life. British and French generals were notorious for squandering
human lives—as many as 19,240 in a single day, and hundreds of
thousands in a single battle. The British and French wanted American bodies to order out of the trenches into enemy machine-gun fire,
replacing British and French bodies that had been thrown away in
battle. At every turn the British and French resisted the idea that
American soldiers should be under American command. They wanted
American soldiers under the same generals responsible for so much
mindless slaughter. Almost half of American soldiers were transported to Europe in British ships, and the British relentlessly tried to
break up American command units, so they could claim the soldiers
would have no choice but to go into British command units and serve
under British generals.

Historian John Mosier cited one of General Douglas Haig's many
blunders: "advancing in long rows at a walk was suicidal, but that was
the plan. On 1 July 1916, the British infantry—all 100,000 of them—

climbed out of their trenches in four distinct waves, and began to advance across to the other side. The German machine gunners could hardly believe their eyes. In two years of fighting they had never seen anything like it. As one German who was there wrote: 'We were surprised to see them walking. We had never seen that before. . . . When we started to fire we just had to load and reload. They went down in their hundreds. We didn't have to aim, we just fired into them.'"[12]

By contrast, because the Germans were outnumbered on the Western Front, they were more inclined to conserve soldiers and make tactical retreats to locations that could be more easily defended. British and French generals repeatedly misinterpreted such tactical retreats as weakness. They kept hoping for one big battle that might enable them to win the war, for which they committed all possible resources, whereas the Germans generally focused on smaller, more attainable, less risky objectives. German fatalities were almost always much lower than British and French fatalities. Mosier explained, "If the choice was between the probability of fatally weakening the army on the chance of a great victory, or preserving it intact for a long war, the correct decision was preservation."[13]

Wilson's decision to enter World War I had terrible consequences not only in Germany but also in Russia: the November 1917 Bolshevik coup. It's important to realize that the Bolsheviks had difficulty seizing power. Lenin failed three times between April and July 1917.[14] He never had much popular support. In elections for the Constituent Assembly, the Bolsheviks didn't receive more than a quarter of the votes. They needed everything in their favor, and Wilson's decision made a difference.

Of course, the initial mistake was made by the Russian Czar Nicholas II, who decided to enter the war in 1914. It led to millions of Russian casualties, drained the country's finances, generated devastating inflation, caused pervasive shortages, and discredited the government and the army. Despite Russia's deterioration, Britain and France pressured the Russians to stay in the war, so that substantial German forces would continue to be tied up on the Eastern Front. The last thing Britain and France wanted was for Russia to make a separate peace with Germany and thereby enable the Germans to transfer forces to the Western Front.

Following the spontaneous revolution and abdication of the czar in February 1917, Wilson's ambassador in Petrograd, David R. Francis, congratulated the Provisional Government "that the great Russian people have joined the powerful democracies who are struggling against autocracy [Germany]." Wilson authorized Francis to offer the Provisional Government $325 million of credits—equivalent to almost $4 billion today—provided it agree to stay in the war.[15] This was a modest sum compared with what Russia had already spent on the war, and because of Russia's worsening crisis, it came too late to do much good, but the Provisional Government was broke, and it accepted the deal. Republican lawyer and former secretary of state Elihu Root led an American mission to Russia, underscoring Wilson's terms: "No fight, no loans."

Root returned to the United States in August 1917 and filed a report that, as Wilson's secretary of state, Robert Lansing, summarized it, "showed great confidence in the existing Government of Russia and in its determination and ability to continue the war." Lansing was skeptical because he thought Alexander Kerensky, head of the Provisional Government, invited trouble by compromising too much with radicals. Lansing didn't see continuing the war as a problem for Russia.[16]

Wilson disregarded the fact that ordinary Russians had nothing to gain from whatever happened on the Western Front, which was his sole concern. He was blissfully unaware of Russia's disintegration, which had been under way since 1916. The Bolsheviks benefited from deteriorating conditions brought on or aggravated by the war, because they were the only ones on the Russian political scene advocating withdrawal. The longer Russia stayed in the war, the more disgruntled people became, and the weaker the army. Lenin's slogan was "Peace, Land and Bread." Lenin himself said, "Our revolution was born of the war."[17] By the fall of 1917 the Russian army collapsed, and there wasn't anything left to defend the Provisional Government.

Russian expert and Pulitzer Prize–winning historian George F. Kennan observed with characteristic understatement, "It may be questioned whether the United States government, in company with other western Allies, did not actually hasten and facilitate the failure of the Provisional Government by insisting that Russia should continue the war effort, and by making this demand the criterion for its support. In asking the leaders of the Provisional Government simultaneously to consolidate their political power and to revive and continue participation in the war, the Allies were asking the impossible."[18]

Biographer Robert Service observed that "Lenin had been given his chance because of the wartime economic dislocation, administrative breakdown and political disarray."[19] Lenin seized power on October 25 (old Russian calendar, November 7 by the Western calendar). Lenin was more single-minded and ruthless than any of his rivals, and he understood he would probably be overthrown if he didn't consolidate power fast. On December 20, 1917, he established the All-Russian Extraordinary Commission, the secret police better known as Cheka that was to be a model adopted by Hitler and other mass murderers. Lenin ordered the assassination of rivals, had "unreliable elements" imprisoned in concentration camps, and launched a reign of terror.

Lenin understood, too, the urgency of getting Russia out of World War I. He dispatched Leon Trotsky, People's Commissar of External Affairs, to negotiate with the Germans at Brest-Litovsk, the town closest to the Eastern Front. Because the Germans demanded big territorial concessions, Trotsky wanted to stall the proceedings and hope for something "neither war nor peace." But Lenin was concerned that the Germans would end up demanding even more. The Germans resumed fighting and advanced to within 400 miles of Petrograd. The Treaty of Brest-Litovsk was signed on March 3, 1918. Lenin, however, was afraid of having his name on the treaty since the concessions would make it unpopular among many Russians. He had one of his comrades, Central Committee member Grigori Sokolnikov, do the dirty deed.

"If Lenin had not won the debate," observed Robert Service, "there is little doubt the Central Powers would have concluded that the Bolsheviks were no longer of any use to them. The result would have been the occupation of the Russian heartland and the collapse of the October Revolution."[20] So the peace that could have saved the Provisional Government ended up securing Bolshevik power.

Ironically, Lenin went on to launch a civil war aimed at crushing "White Russians," dissident minorities, and other political opponents.

After Lenin's death on January 21, 1924, his comrade Joseph Stalin outmaneuvered rivals to seize power and commit an unprecedented number of mass murders. We wouldn't have had Stalin without Lenin, and Lenin probably would have been a forgotten man if Woodrow Wilson hadn't pressured and bribed the Provisional Government to stay in World War I.

The result was seven decades of Soviet communism. Historian R. J. Rummel estimated that "61,911,000 people, 54,769,000 of them citizens, have been murdered by the Communist party—the government—of the Soviet Union. . . . Old and young, healthy and sick, men and women, and even infants and the infirm, were killed in cold blood. They were not combatants in civil war or rebellions and they were not criminals. Indeed, nearly all of them were guilty of nothing.

"Some were from the wrong class," Rummel continued: "bourgeoisie, land owners, aristocrats, kulaks. Some were from the wrong nation or race: Ukrainians, Black Sea Greeks, Kalmyks, Volga Germans. Some were from the wrong political faction: Trotskyites, Mensheviks, Social Revolutionaries. Or some were just their sons and daughters, wives and husbands, or mothers and fathers. Some were those occupied by the Red Army: Balts, Germans, Poles, Hungarians, Rumanians. Then some were simply in the way of social progress, like the mass of peasants or religious believers. Or some were eliminated because of their potential opposition, such as writers, teachers, churchmen, the military high command, or even high and low Communist party members themselves.

"Part of this mass killing was genocide," Rummel added, "as in the wholesale murder of hundreds of thousands of Don Cossacks in 1919, the intentional starving to death of about 5,000,000 Ukrainian peasants in 1932–33, or the deportation to death of 50,000 to 60,000 Estonians in 1949. Part was mass murder, as of the wholesale extermination of perhaps 6,500,000 kulaks (in effect, the better-off peasants and those resisting collectivization) from 1930 to 1937, the execution of perhaps a million party members in the Great Terror of 1937–38, and the massacre of all Trotskyites in the forced labor camps. Moreover, part of the killing was so random and idiosyncratic that journalists and social scientists have no concept for it, as in hundreds of thousands of people being executed according to pre-set government quotas."[21]

Events in Russia had a dynamic impact on Germany. As historian Richard Pipes observed, "Had it not been for the Russian Revolution, there very likely would have been no National Socialism; probably no Second World War and no decolonization; and certainly no Cold War, which once dominated our lives."[22]

What might have happened in Russia if the United States had stayed out of World War I? As a genuine neutral, the United States surely wouldn't have pressured and bribed the Russians to stay in. Perhaps, with the more objective viewpoint of a neutral power, the United States would have responded to the signs of deterioration by encouraging the Russians to leave the war before things got worse.

If American representatives had been less enthusiastic about socialism, they would have been concerned about the news coming out of Russia. Pipes observed that "Woodrow Wilson seems to have believed that the Bolsheviks truly spoke for the Russian people and formed a detachment of that grand international army that he imagined advancing toward universal democracy and eternal peace.... Every message which the U.S. government transmitted to the Bolshevik authorities in the early months of 1918 conveyed the sense that Washington took at face value the Bolsheviks' professions of democratic and peaceful intentions and ignored their calls for world revolution."[23]

On August 23, 1939, Hitler and Stalin agreed that they wouldn't go to war against each other and that they would divide Poland and the Baltic states between them. The resulting pact, signed by German foreign minister Joachim von Ribbentrop and Soviet foreign minister Vyacheslav Molotov, assured Hitler that he could launch a war in the west without being concerned about a war in the east—with the Soviets. Hitler invaded Poland a week later, and World War II was under way.

Stalin, of course, survived that conflict, expanded into Eastern Europe, and launched a Cold War that continued for more than five decades until the Soviet Union collapsed. Without Stalin, we probably wouldn't have had the arms buildup, the subversion of regimes around the world, and the rest of the Cold War as it developed.

Nothing Wilson did could avert the consequences of his decision to enter World War I. His fabled crusade to establish the League of Nations accomplished little. He claimed it would help prevent future wars, but he never seems to have thought through the inherent limitations and contradictions of the scheme. Charter members of the League of Nations included the winners of World War I and their friends—countries that hadn't been fighting one another. Supposedly the big breakthrough idea was that the charter members would swear to a "Covenant" affirming that they would continue to not fight one another. Member nations agreed to join in defending a member nation from attack. Consequently the League amounted to just another alliance, and if all members fulfilled their obligations, an attack on one member nation would lead to a big war involving all member nations. This, of course, is how a 1914 assassination in a Balkan town led to World War I!

Notably excluded from the League of Nations were the supposed troublemakers, the losers of World War I—Germany, Austria, Hungary, and Turkey. One of the Allies, Russia, wasn't in the League of Nations either. By imposing humiliating penalties on the losers, the Treaty of Versailles, of which the League of Nations was a part, provided powerful incentives to get revenge at the earliest opportunity. Hence the widespread view that World War I and the Treaty of Versailles set the stage for World War II.

Wilson complained that the U.S. Senate, by rejecting the Treaty of Versailles and keeping America out of the League of Nations, prevented the world body from fulfilling its peacemaking potential. But if the League couldn't function without the United States, it never was more than a way of tapping American taxpayers and soldiers to solve the problems of the world.

What about the provocations that led Wilson to ask Congress for a declaration of war against Germany? There were two. The first was the announcement, by Admiral Alfred von Tirpitz on February 1, 1917, that Germany would resume submarine warfare against all shipping in the North Atlantic. Germany did this because the European land war wasn't going anywhere, and the British naval blockade was preventing Germans from getting food. Germany didn't have enough surface ships to rival the British navy, so the aim was to establish a blockade around Britain with submarines. They weren't more sinister than any other weapons of war, certainly no more sinister than Britain's surface ships. Nor was a blockade with submarines morally different from a blockade with surface ships. Wilson took the absurd position that Americans had a God-given right to travel in a war zone. Well, if anybody wants to venture into a war zone, that's their business, but they need to accept responsibility for the risks they're taking. As a practical matter, a war zone is best avoided.

The second provocation was the so-called Zimmermann Telegram. This was sent January 19, 1917, by German foreign minister Arthur Zimmermann to Germany's ambassador in Mexico, Heinrich von Eckhardt, suggesting that if—*if*—the United States declared war against Germany, Mexico might want to consider becoming an ally of Germany, for which Germany would provide financial support. Zimmermann offered "an understanding on our part that Mexico is to reconquer the lost territory in Texas, New Mexico, and Arizona." How Germany, embroiled in the European war, could conceivably help Mexico reconquer U.S. territory, Zimmermann didn't say. He suggested the possibility of Japan, an ally of Britain and France, becoming an ally of Germany and Mexico. The telegram, intercepted and decoded by British intelligence, was published in American newspapers on March 1, and it provoked a wave of anti-German feeling that propelled the United States into war.

Such complications didn't come out of the blue. Wilson seems to have alienated just about everybody in Mexico with a succession of bungled interventions. For thirty-five years, until 1911, the military leader Porfirio Díaz had ruled the country. He was overthrown by Francisco Madero, a wealthy owner of agricultural properties, when Díaz refused to permit honest elections. But in February 1913, Victoriano Huerta, a general in the government's army, had Madero assassinated and seized power for himself. Wilson, who had just begun his first term, remarked, "It would be an irony of fate if my administration had to deal chiefly with foreign affairs."[24] Wilson denounced Huerta and waded into the thickets of Mexican politics, determined to pick a decent leader for the Mexicans. Wilson refused to extend diplomatic recognition to Huerta, and he supported general Venustiano Carranza, who led the "Constitutionalist Revolution"—Wilson liked the sound of the word "constitutionalist." A misunderstanding involving a U.S. ship anchored in Mexican waters off Tampico became an insult against Mexico. Then Wilson dispatched American forces to seize Veracruz, inflaming Huerta as well as revolutionary leaders. Huerta was ousted in 1914, and Carranza seized power. He soon proved to be another tyrant, and Wilson offended him. Wilson found himself dealing with yet another adversary, the bandit and guerrilla leader Pancho Villa, who conducted an embarrassing raid into New Mexico in March 1916. Wilson dispatched general John Pershing and some 6,600 American soldiers to chase Villa around northern Mexico, but they couldn't catch him. Wilson fumed, "I am going to teach the Latin American republics to elect good men!"[25]

All this unnerved the British, who wanted somebody, anybody, to establish a stable regime in Mexico, so that business could function. At that time, Mexico supplied about a quarter of the world's oil, and the British navy got most of its oil from Mexico. Carranza denied receiving any proposal of an alliance from Germany, and Zimmermann couldn't get an answer from Carranza, either. Carranza was eventually overthrown, Villa was assassinated, and the saga continued, oblivious of Wilson's good intentions.

The consequences of Wilson's fateful decision to enter World War I played out long after he died in 1924, because of Hitler, Lenin, and Stalin. Those ruthless killers would not have come to power as they did if the United States had stayed out of the war. Their crimes are part of Wilson's story, ignored in Wilson biographies and history books. Wilson biographies, like other biographies, typically end with the subject's death. American history books focus on the ways World War I affected Americans; these books say little, if anything, about how Wilson's decision played out in Germany and Russia. Conversely, books about German and Russian history say little about Wilson, although they make clear the consequences of keeping Russia in the war and imposing vindictive surrender terms on Germany.

This is the first book attempting to tell how the consequences of Wilson's decision played out in both Germany and Russia. Moreover, Hitler and Stalin were the principal instigators of World War II, so that's a consequence of Wilson's decision—part of his story. After World War II, Stalin grabbed Eastern Europe and provoked the Cold

War, and Wilson's legacy continued. The Cold War involved two major hot wars—Korea and Vietnam—and the United States entered both in the Wilsonian tradition of trying to do good even when there wasn't a direct threat to America's national security. Wilson's shadow has loomed over the Middle East as well, since bitter adversaries were forced into a new nation—Iraq—thanks to the Versailles Treaty made possible by Wilson.

It's important to understand why things turned out the way they did, and what the United States might have done differently. Did Woodrow Wilson really botch the Versailles Treaty? Could any American president have overcome the determination of the French to avenge the huge casualties they suffered on their soil? Could some of the postwar problems have been avoided by doing a better job of redrawing the map of Europe? How important was the Allied decision to force their civilian leaders—rather than their generals—to accept responsibility for the surrender? How effective are we ever likely to be when intervening in the affairs of people far away, whose culture, language, and situation are very different from ours? What can we learn about the risks of intervening in other people's wars and trying to build other people's nations?

This book aims to answer these and many more questions. One thing is certain: we should focus less on a president's good intentions and more on the consequences of a president's actions.

1

HOW DID THAT MONSTROUS WAR HAPPEN?

WORLD WAR I MARKED the end of a glorious era, the most peaceful period in modern history. The last general European war had concluded a century earlier, in 1815, when the French emperor Napoleon Bonaparte was defeated and banished to a shabby house on St. Helena, a British-controlled island in the South Atlantic Ocean, about 1,140 miles west of South Africa.

The Napoleonic Wars helped convince several generations that war was an evil to be avoided. The dapper Corsican Napoleon had emerged as a military strongman amid the wreckage of the French Revolution. In 1799 and 1800 he led successful French military campaigns against Austro-Hungarian armies in Italy and Germany. In 1799 he seized power in a coup. He declared himself to be consul for life. He resolved to conquer Egypt, gain French territory in the Caribbean, and extend his influence throughout the Mediterranean. He annexed Piedmont and forced a more congenial government on the Swiss Confederation.

Napoleon established the first modern police state. He tapped Joseph Fouché, who had been educated for the clergy but had never taken his vows as a priest, to organize a secret police force. As a Jacobin during the French Revolution, Fouché had organized mass shootings. He developed Napoleon's spy network throughout Europe, and he arranged to have adversaries abducted and shot.

The nationalist fury that swept through Germany during the mid-twentieth century, providing political support for Hitler, began to develop after Napoleon humiliated the German-speaking people. He defeated the Austrian army at Austerlitz (1805) and crushed the Prussians at Jena (1806). Prussian generals turned out to be cowards, and the Prussian army quickly disintegrated. Prussia had built a system of forts that were expected to provide a sturdy defense, but they generally surrendered without much resistance.[1] Napoleon ordered that German-speaking states, including Bavaria, Württemberg, Baden, Hesse-Darmstadt, Nassau, and Berg, be combined to form the *Confédération du Rhin*—the Confederation of the Rhine. The French had already, in 1792, annexed territories west of the Rhine, notably Cologne and Mainz.

Napoleon dismissed corrupt old tyrants, an action that local people surely appreciated, but in many cases they were replaced by Napoleon's relatives, who became corrupt new tyrants. He imposed his *Code Napoléon* on conquered territories. Based on Roman law and some 14,000 decrees issued during the French Revolution, this was a simplified civil law code providing uniform rules for people to live by. Napoleon abolished the hodgepodge of feudal laws and customs. As historian J. M. Thompson noted, "The *Code Napoléon* contained less than 120,000 words and could be carried in the pocket."[2]

Some 100,000 of Napoleon's troops occupied Prussia at the nation's expense.[3] In 1807 he signed the Treaty of Tilsit with Russia, stripping Prussia of German-speaking provinces north and west of the lower Elbe River, and Polish provinces to the east.[4] Altogether, Prussian territory was cut from 89,120 square miles to 46,032. Napoleon demanded that the Prussian government pay him 140 million francs.[5] This amounted to a huge tax that devastated the economy. Making things worse was Napoleon's "Continental System," aimed at harming Britain by closing Europe's ports. The Continental System meant that Prussia couldn't earn its accustomed revenues from grain exports.

When Napoleon was paid off, he withdrew his forces from Prussia and turned his attention elsewhere, and the Prussian king pondered how his state might regain its place in the world. He was persuaded to name Karl vom Stein as chief minister. Stein was fascinated by Anne-Robert-Jacques Turgot, who had urged dramatic reforms on the last French king to possess absolute power, Louis XVI.

Stein persuaded Frederick William III to issue the Edict of Emancipation, in October 1807, which abolished feudal privileges and restrictions on the sale of land. In other words, he opened up property markets, erasing legal distinctions among aristocrats, merchants, or peasants. Stein also extended civil rights to Jews. He was convinced these reforms would unleash the energies of the people.

Prussia also reformed what was left of its army: ineffective officers were dismissed; junior officers were promoted on merit; army policies were adopted to improve efficiency. The long process of rebuilding got under way. The consequences of the Napoleonic Wars were devastating as they played out decades later in Prussia and throughout Europe.

The Napoleonic Wars themselves were bad enough. Historian Paul Johnson observed that the wars "set back the economic life of much of Europe for a generation. They made men behave like beasts, and worse. The battles were bigger and much more bloody. The armies of the old regimes were of long-service professional veterans, often lifers, obsessed with uniforms, pipe clay, polished brass, and their elaborate drill—the kings could not bear to lose them. Bonaparte cut off the pigtails, ended the powdered hair, supplied mass-produced uniforms and spent the lives of his young, conscripted recruits as though they were loose change. His insistence that they live off the land did not work in subsistence economies like Spain and Russia, where if the soldiers stole, the peasants starved. . . . Throughout Europe, the standards of human conduct declined as men and women, and their growing children, learned to live brutally."[6]

The savagery was shocking. Reporting on Napoleon's campaign in Spain, historian Antonina Vallentin wrote: "French corpses piled up in the mountain ravines. . . . Drunk with fury against the servants of Christ who preached hatred, the French soldiers sacked the churches, carried away the objects of veneration, profaned the House. The village priests slaughtered the French who sought refuge among them. Farms were left burning like torches when the French had passed by. The wounded and the ill were murdered as they were being taken from one place to another. The roads were strewn with denuded corpses; the trees were weighed down with the bodies of men hanged; blind hate was loosed against hate, a nameless terror roamed the deserted countryside, death came slowly through the most frightful mutilations."[7]

Napoleon's worst horrors occurred during the Russian campaign. In the spring of 1812, he assembled some 600,000 soldiers—his "Grand Army" including Prussians, Austrians, and Italians. They crossed the Niemen River, which flows from western Russia into the Baltic, and headed east in a front some 300 miles wide. Napoleon wanted a decisive battle that would force Czar Alexander I to become his subject, but the czar's forces harassed Napoleon's soldiers in skirmishes, then withdrew into the interior of the country, destroying fields, towns, and cities as they went, denying Napoleon the opportunity to replenish his supplies. The farther Napoleon advanced, the farther Russian forces withdrew, and the more devastation Napoleon encountered. His forces entered Smolensk, only to find it consumed by flames.

According to historian Christopher Herold, "The progress of his carriage along a road choked with limping cripples, stretchers, and ambulances set him into a somber mood. In Smolensk he passed carts loaded with amputated limbs. In the hospitals the surgeons ran out of dressings and used paper and birch bark fibers as substitutes; many of those who survived surgery died of starvation, for the supply service had virtually broken down. In addition to the battle casualties, hundreds of men fell victim to the Russian secret weapon, vodka, dying by the roadside from a combination of raw spirits and exposure. Such, it must be emphasized, was the condition of the Grand Army not during its tragic retreat but during its victorious advance."[8]

Although Napoleon's supply lines were stretched to the limit, he could see that his forces would disintegrate if they spent the winter in Smolensk. He decided they must continue on to Moscow. The September 1812 Battle of Borodino was among the few engagements—there were some 30,000 French casualties and 45,000 Russian casualties. On September 14, Napoleon reached the outskirts of Moscow with about 90,000 soldiers. He stopped advancing and waited for a Russian delegation to surrender, but they never came. By the time Napoleon actually entered Moscow, it was burning.[9]

French soldiers reveled in the riches they looted from the city, but they needed food. Foraging in the countryside yielded less and less. Their boots had worn out, and they had nothing else to wear. They didn't have winter clothing when the weather turned bitter cold in October. By then, Napoleon recognized that he had to retreat, and he headed for Smolensk. As his soldiers retreated, they were attacked by Cossack fighters and peasant guerrillas. One of Napoleon's generals, Philippe-Paul Ségur, recalled that "the earth was littered with battered helmets and breastplates, broken drums, fragments of weapons, shreds of uniforms, and blood-stained flags. Lying amidst this desolation were half-devoured corpses."[10]

The first heavy snowfall was on November 6. Ségur wrote, "Objects changed their shape; we walked without knowing where we were or what lay ahead, and anything became an obstacle. . . . Yet the poor wretches [Napoleon's soldiers] dragged themselves along, shivering, with chattering teeth, until the snow packed under the soles of their boots, a bit of debris, a branch, or the body of a fallen comrade tripped them and threw them down. Then their moans for help went unheeded. The snow soon covered them up and only low white mounds showed where they lay." Cossack fighters and peasant guerrillas massacred the stragglers, and Russian armies joined the rout. When Napoleon's Grand Army had been reduced to about 9,000, he went ahead to raise another army in an effort to suppress Germans and other rebellious nationalities.

One of the most eloquent French liberals, Benjamin Constant, denounced Napoleon: "Are we here only to build, with our dying bodies, your road to fame? You have a genius for fighting; what good is it to us? You are bored by the inactivity of peace. Why should your boredom concern us? Learn civilization, if you wish to reign in a civilized age. Learn peace, if you wish to rule over peaceful peoples. Man from another world, stop despoiling this one."[11]

Altogether, Napoleon's wars resulted in the deaths of some 2 million people.[12] Undoubtedly the memories of Napoleonic war horrors convinced many people that they should refrain from war. In September 1814, five months after Napoleon's first abdication, European foreign ministers met at the Congress of Vienna to negotiate history's most comprehensive and successful peace treaty.

LAISSEZ-FAIRE AND PEACE

Vivid memories of Napoleon's war horrors weren't the only reasons why the nineteenth century was comparatively peaceful. This was a period when the intellectual movement known as classical liberalism was in its heyday. Classical liberals cherished individual liberty, toleration, and peace, and to achieve these things they embraced constitutional limitations on government power.

These were radical ideas, because for centuries the prevailing view had been that private individuals couldn't be trusted to make their own choices. The fear was that if people were free to choose their church, or to buy and sell as they wished, there would be chaos. Hence it was thought that kings were needed to maintain order by enforcing religious and business monopolies. But by the 1700s it had become clear that government-enforced religious monopolies and business monopolies led to wars. Those who didn't agree with the church monopoly or the business monopoly had to fight or be crushed. As people grew weary of all the bloodshed, governments in Western Europe gradually let people make more of their own choices, and there was more peace. The movement toward a separation of church and state meant that Roman Catholics could go to their places of worship, and Lutherans, Congregationalists, Quakers, and Jews to theirs, and none of them had to fight about it. There was harmony. Similarly, a separation of the economy and the state meant that increasingly people could do business where and with whom they wished, and business conflicts didn't have to cause military conflicts. The battle cry of eighteenth-century French liberals like Jacques Turgot was *"Laissez faire!"* which meant "Let it be!" Classical liberals began to sweep away thousands of taxes, tariffs, restrictions, and special privileges that had kept people down.

Throughout Europe, people debated and adopted written constitutions. *The Spirit of the Laws* (1748) by Charles-Louis Secondat, Baron de Montesquieu, was an early discussion of constitutions that inspired America's founders to develop a modern constitution for a large country. Another influential Frenchman, Benjamin Constant, had witnessed the horrors of the French Revolution as well as the horrors of Napoleon. He recognized that for liberty to flourish, government power must be limited, whether it was exercised in the name of the king or of the people.

Ironically, although Britain didn't have a written constitution, its unwritten scheme, which evolved over the centuries, influenced people everywhere. According to historian Carleton J. H. Hayes: "The English system of government—with its full complement of a bill of rights, a king who reigned but did not rule, a parliament which levied the taxes and made the laws, and a ruling ministry responsible to the parliament—all this had been formally embodied in written constitutions in Spain, Portugal, Belgium, Italy, Greece, Austria and Hungary. In France, where there had been a plethora of written constitutions ever since the revolutionary days of 1791, the English system finally prevailed in the 'constitutional laws' of 1875, except that the titular head was a president instead of a king. Written constitutions obtained in other countries, but while they provided for parliaments and ministries more or less in the English fashion, they usually left the ministry responsible to the monarch rather than to the parliament."[13]

It was during the nineteenth century that the West became the first civilization to abolish slavery on its own initiative. Thomas Sowell observed that "although Western Europeans had for centuries enslaved principally the peoples of Eastern Europe and the Balkans, by the time the Western Hemisphere was discovered and conquered, Africa was one of the few remaining areas of the world where massive enslavement continued to be feasible. After still more centuries, however, the ideological contradiction between the European conception of freedom and the brutal reality of their enslavement of Africans began to produce, first in Britain and later in other European and European-offshoot nations, a growing political opposition to slavery as such—the first such mass opposition to this ancient institution in the history of the world. Because this moral opposition developed within countries with overwhelming military power and worldwide imperial hegemony, slavery came under growing pressure all over the planet—and was eventually destroyed by Europeans, despite opposition within their own ranks, as well as opposition and evasion by virtually every non-European civilization."[14]

During the nineteenth century, more than twenty Western societies abolished slavery without the kind of civil war that devastated the

United States. Among these were Argentina (1813), Colombia (1814), Chile (1823), Central America (1824), Mexico (1829), Bolivia (1831), British colonies (1840), Uruguay (1842), French colonies (1848), Danish colonies (1848), Ecuador (1851), Peru (1854), Venezuela (1854), Dutch colonies (1863), Puerto Rico (1873), Brazil (1878), and Cuba (1886).[15]

Support for free trade and peace grew hand-in-hand. One of the most crucial insights of classical liberal economists like Adam Smith was that nations could become more prosperous through trade rather than through conquest. It didn't matter where political borders might be drawn, as long as people were free to trade, invest, and travel. Adam Smith presented his case in *The Wealth of Nations* (1776), and it began to have an impact in Britain after the Napoleonic Wars. Smith's ideas inspired Manchester textile entrepreneurs Richard Cobden and John Bright, who led the movement to repeal the "corn laws"—tariffs on imported grain. The corn laws were abolished in 1846. Just as earlier champions of liberty had agitated for a separation of church and state, Cobden and his associates agitated for a separation of economy and state. By reducing if not eliminating trade restrictions, people on one side of a border had the same economic advantages as people on the other side. Neither side was penalized by tariffs, taxes, or other discriminatory measures. Free trade reduced the risks that economic disputes would escalate into political disputes and war.

Cobden and Bright were eloquent foes of colonialism and imperialism, a common source of conflict among nations. Cobden declared, "It will be a happy day when England has not an acre of territory in Continental Asia. But how such a state of things is to be brought about is more than I can tell. . . . For where do we find even an individual who is not imbued with the notion that England would sink to ruin if she were deprived of her Indian Empire? Leave me, then, to my pigs and sheep, which are not labouring under any such delusions."[16]

Meanwhile, in Bordeaux, France, journalist Frédéric Bastiat organized the Association for Free Trade, and he kept French people informed about what the British free traders were doing. Born in 1801, he had been a gentleman farmer in Mugron, absorbing the work of Adam Smith and Jean-Baptiste Say, who popularized Smith's ideas in France. Bastiat became a prolific pamphleteer, doing much of his work on the socially beneficial effects of trade. In 1845 he published *Cobden et la Ligue, ou l'Agitation Anglaise pour la Liberté des Échanges* [*Cobden and the League, or The English Agitation for Freedom of Trade*]. Bastiat issued a succession of clever satires, the most famous of which was about a petition from candlemakers who wanted the government to block competition from sunlight. Bastiat insisted that a country gained by opening its borders, even though other countries retained restrictions.

In July 1859, Bright gave a speech suggesting that England cut its military spending—much of which was to protect against a possible attack from France—and that both countries should liberalize trade to help promote peace. This, he declared, "would bring about a state of things which history would pronounce to be glorious."[17] Six months later, on January 23, 1860, a treaty was signed, liberalizing trade between the two countries. In December 1860, Cobden persuaded the French minister of the interior to abolish passports for English subjects, thereby achieving greater freedom of travel.[18]

The treaty had a dynamic impact. Between 1862 and 1866, the French negotiated trade liberalization treaties with the Zollverein (German customs union), Italy, Belgium, the Netherlands, Switzerland, Spain, Portugal, Sweden, Norway, the Papal States, and North German commercial cities. Most of these, in turn, liberalized trade with one another. Trade restrictions were reduced or eliminated on international waterways such as the Baltic and the North Sea channel (1857), as well as the Danube (1857), Rhine (1861), Scheldt (1863), and Elbe (1870) rivers. Even Russia lowered tariffs somewhat, in 1857 and 1868.[19] Because each treaty observed the "most favored nation" principle, it liberalized trade not only for the signatory nations, but for everyone else, as well. Never before in European history had people been able to go about their daily business so freely.

Britain continued to set an example. Prime Minister William Ewart Gladstone led a successful campaign to abolish more than a thousand—95 percent—of Britain's tariffs that remained after the abolition of the corn laws.[20] Gladstone cut Britain's income tax to 1.25 percent. Although he was less successful campaigning to stop British imperialism and give the oppressed Irish people self-government, it was remarkable that a British government leader would mount such a campaign at all. His biographer, H. C. G. Matthew, observed, "In offering freedom, representative government, free-trade economic progress, international co-operation through discussion and arbitration, probity in government and society generally, as the chief objectives of public life, and an ideology which combined and harmonized them, Gladstone offered much to the concept of a civilized society of nations."[21]

Classical liberal ideas prevailed through the 1860s in western Europe, and military conflicts were few and limited. There was substantial separation between the economy and the state. Political borders were more open than they had been before, and if private businessmen in one country wanted to do a deal in another country, they could negotiate directly with their counterparts. They weren't thwarted or discriminated against by regulations in the other country, so they didn't have any reason to be concerned about where the political borders happened to be. As long as governments stayed out of business, competition among private firms from different countries wasn't likely to have political consequences, any more than the success of imported Mercedes cars would be viewed as a national security threat today, even though it might mean less business for a U.S.-based car producer like General Motors.

INTELLECTUALS ATTACK LAISSEZ-FAIRE

There are always intellectual countercurrents, and attacks on laissez-faire began before it was at a peak.

The most explicit, influential case for government interference in the economy came from the German political activist Friedrich List (1789–1846). He had spent his early adult years helping to promote a German customs union as a way of retaliating against the British corn laws that prevented German farmers from selling their grain in Britain. List developed his ideas after a visit to the United States, where prevailing policy at the time was Henry Clay's high-tariff "American System," based on Alexander Hamilton's ideas about protecting domestic manufacturers at the expense of foreign competitors. In his *National System of Political Economy* (1841), List attacked free trade as a devious means for industrialized nations, especially Britain, to exploit backward nations. He believed the primary objective of economic policy should be to enhance national power. He claimed that backward nations could foster industrialization with high tariffs, thereby enhancing their national power. Some passages suggest that List favored expanding German-controlled territory and building a colonial empire. He had limited influence during his lifetime, but his book became a bible of economic nationalism. It was translated into English in 1856.

In *The Communist Manifesto* (1848), Karl Marx and Friedrich Engels denounced "that single, unconscionable freedom—Free Trade. In one word, for exploitation, veiled by religious and political illusions, it has substituted naked, shameless, direct, brutal exploitation." They advocated "the Communist abolition of buying and selling, of the bourgeois conditions of production, and of the bourgeoisie itself."[22]

British socialists founded the Fabian Society (1883), which relentlessly promoted the expansion of government power to remedy the perceived ills of laissez-faire. They wanted social welfare spending, nationalization of public utilities, credit, transportation, and mining, and they steadfastly opposed free trade. Playwright George Bernard Shaw, among the most famous of Fabians, urged people to "turn our backs on Adam Smith and Cobden, and confess that both the old Tories and modern Socialists are right, and that there is no salvation for the world in Free Contract and Free Trade."

Sidney Webb, perhaps the most prolific Fabian propagandist, revealed the collectivism underlying these views: "The perfect and fitting development of each individual is not necessarily the utmost and highest cultivation of his own personality, but the filling, in the best possible way, of his humble function in the great social machine. We must abandon the self-conceit of imagining that we are independent units, and bend our jealous minds, absorbed in their own cultivation, to this subjection to the higher end, the Common Weal."[23]

IMPERIALISM AND WAR

Otto von Bismarck did more than anyone else to begin turning the world away from the principles of laissez-faire, free trade, and peace.

Though he was considered a conservative, he saw that socialist ideas could help expand his government's power to strike at real or imagined adversaries, and he accelerated trends that exploded into World War I.

Bismarck was the prime minister of Prussia (1862-1890) and founder and first chancellor of the German Empire (1871–1890). Historian A. J. P. Taylor described him as "a big man, made bigger by his persistence in eating and drinking too much. He walked stiffly, with the upright carriage of a hereditary officer. Yet he had a small, fine head; the delicate hands of an artist; and when he spoke, his voice, which one would have expected to be deep and powerful, was thin and reedy—almost a falsetto—the voice of an academic, not of a man of action. Nor did he always present the same face to the world. He lives in history clean-shaven, except for a heady moustache. Actually he wore a full beard for long periods of his life; and this at a time when beards were symbols on the continent of Europe of the Romantic movement, if not of radicalism."[24]

He was born in Schönhausen, Prussia, April 1, 1815, the son of a minor landowning aristocrat. On his mother's side were government officials and academics. His mother pushed him to study law at the University of Göttingen, but he didn't do well. He spent some time at the University of Berlin, then went to work for the Prussian government. At the time, before unification, "Germany" consisted of many small states, the strongest of which was Prussia. He accepted the traditional view that the role of the government was to enforce order. He rejected the liberal idea that Britain was a good model for Prussia.

In 1849 Bismarck was elected to the Prussian Chamber of Deputies—one of the two parts of their Diet (legislature), meeting in Berlin. He came to resent Austria-Hungary's—the Hapsburg empire's—dominance of Central Europe. He became a defender of the Prussian monarchy and an advocate of Prussian supremacy. King Frederick William IV of Prussia named Bismarck as the Prussian representative at the federal Diet in Frankfurt. By 1859 Bismarck was Prussia's ambassador to Russia, and three years later he was Prussia's ambassador to France.

Meanwhile, Frederick William struggled with liberal members of the Chamber of Deputies, who demanded control over military expenditures. The king insisted that the military was his prerogative.

In 1862 he appointed Bismarck as Prussia's prime minister and for-eign minister, hoping that Bismarck would find a way to prevail. Bis-marck declared that a loophole in Prussia's constitution provided that if the king and Diet couldn't agree on a budget, previous spend-ing and taxing levels continued in force, and the king's ministers could make decisions until there was an agreement. For three years Bismarck used the opportunity to strengthen Prussia's military.

He declared, "Prussia's frontiers as laid down by the Vienna treaties are not conducive to a healthy national life; it is not by means of speeches and majority resolutions that the great issues of the day will be decided—that was the great mistake of 1848 and 1849—but by blood and iron." He maneuvered Austria-Hungary into a quick war that Prussia won in 1866. While he didn't seek terri-tory from Austria-Hungary, he annexed Hanover, Hesse-Kassel, Nassau, and Frankfurt—German territories that had fought against him. He established the North German Confederation. He worked to achieve a German free-trade area and joint military exercises among various German armies.

When, in 1869, the Spanish throne was offered to the Prussian king's cousin, the French emperor Napoleon III opposed this as a threat to his country, and he declared war on Prussia the following year. Prussia made quick work of France and annexed the provinces of Alsace and Lorraine, for which the French never forgave the Ger-mans. By January 1871, southern German territories joined the North German Confederation to form the German Empire. With these foreign policy successes, Bismarck trumped the liberals who had tried to control the government's budget. He became known as the "Iron Chancellor."

The German historian Heinrich von Treitschke, a professor at the government-controlled University of Berlin, declared that the mission of a powerful government was to expand its territory. He crusaded for Prussia to annex more territory. He wrote a friend that "only the good sword of the conqueror can unite these lands with the North." Bismarck launched Germany's overseas empire in 1884 by claiming Southwest Africa as a protectorate. Italy, Belgium, and other countries joined the scramble for territory.

Apparently, in just a few decades, the horrors of the Napoleonic

Wars had been forgotten, and more people began to dream about imperial glory. Britain had lost its American colonies but had developed trading posts in India, and after 1870 people wanted more. Randolph Churchill launched the "Primrose League" to promote imperialism in the name of securing overseas markets, finding outlets for excess population, and denying advantages to rivals.

Britain's Benjamin Disraeli promoted imperialism. A thin and dark-complexioned man, with long ringlets of black hair, for years he was known as a dandy who wore jeweled shirts and sported rings worn over his gloves.[25] He was born in December 1804, the son of a Jewish man of letters, but was later baptized into the Church of England. As Tory prime minister from 1874 to 1880, he defended the monarchy, the House of Lords, and the Church of England.

Disraeli spent more money on armaments. He got involved in the war between Russia and Turkey. He occupied Cyprus. He had British forces invade Transvaal, South Africa, and Kabul, Afghanistan. He guaranteed to protect three states on the Malay Peninsula.[26] He claimed about 200 Pacific islands. He acquired a controlling interest in the Suez Canal, a move that afforded more secure access to British India but became an eighty-year occupation of Egypt, including wars, big military expenditures, and political embarrassments.[27] Disraeli flattered Queen Victoria by naming her Empress of India, and she cherished the thought that the sun never set on the British Empire.

The French Republican premier, Jules Ferry, warned that if his country didn't gain imperial territory while it was still available, it would "descend from the first rank to the third or fourth." In 1881, Ferry seized territory in Africa and East Asia.

Advocates of imperialism cited the protectionist Friedrich List, who had declared: "Companies should be founded in the German seaports to buy lands in foreign countries and settle them with the German colonies; also companies for commerce and navigation whose object would be to open new markets abroad for German manufacturers and to establish steamship lines. . . . Colonies are the best means of developing manufactures, export and import trade, and finally a respectable navy."

Socialists blamed imperialism on capitalism. Yet conquerors pillaged the earth for centuries before anyone ever heard of free markets. Some of the highest living standards were recorded in countries like Norway, Sweden, and Denmark when those countries didn't have an empire. Countries without much investment capital, like Russia and Italy, eagerly pursued imperial glory. Germany exported capital only after it had established an overseas empire. Once colonies were acquired, European investments still flowed not to the colonies but to other prosperous countries—established markets. French investors, for instance, concentrated their efforts in Eastern Europe, Russia, and Argentina. Similarly, European countries continued to conduct an estimated three-quarters of their trade with one another. Poor colonial people simply couldn't afford to buy many European manufactured goods. Nor did many Europeans migrate to the colonies, especially those in the tropics. As a financial proposition, most colonies were losers, since there was little trade, and the cost of defending the colonies and building infrastructure was high. Imperialism was a competition for power and prestige, not wealth. British, French, and German imperial ambitions clashed in the Middle East, Africa, and Asia. Russia clashed with Japan.

TRADE WARS AND POLITICAL CONFLICTS

The reaction against free trade was strongest in the most backward, brutal, authoritarian regimes like Russia, which had never cut their tariffs much. Czar Alexander II ruled by imperial decree and police action. The czar reintroduced a secret police that dispatched dissenters to forced labor in Siberian mines. Officials encouraged the murder of Jews. In 1876 the czar raised tariffs 50 percent and demanded that they be paid in gold, throttling imports of coal, steel, machinery, and other manufactured goods.[28] Following his assassination in 1881, the new czar, Alexander III, intensified these authoritarian policies.

The same year in Spain, the Conservative premier, Antonio Canovas del Castillo, announced a new constitution that curtailed freedom of religion, of the press, and of association. He reasserted a high-tariff policy. Moreover, he introduced tariff discrimination—a schedule of lower tariffs for countries that signed reciprocal trade agreements, and a schedule of higher tariffs for everyone else. He

was driven from power following his violent repression of demonstrators, then returned in 1890. Two years later he successfully promoted a tougher tariff policy. Spain's railroad traffic, international
trade, and finance declined, bringing on an economic crisis that persisted through the 1890s.

When Italian states were unified in 1861, they adopted Piedmont's trade liberalization policy, but farmers agitated for higher
tariffs to prevent Italian consumers from buying cheaper food elsewhere. Since, as a result of higher tariffs, the cost of raw materials
rose, manufacturers wanted higher tariffs, too, and in 1878 Italy enacted higher tariffs for both agricultural commodities and manufactured goods.[29]

In 1881 French legislators abandoned the trade liberalization
treaty with Britain and raised tariff rates about 24 percent on manufactured goods and such agricultural commodities as sugar beets,
wheat, rye, barley, and flour.[30] The government subsidized shipping
and shipbuilding. The 1892 Méline tariff provided two tariff sched-
ules, much higher rates on products imported from "bad guys," and
lower rates on products imported from "good guys."[31]

By 1886 both France and Italy raised tariffs against each other's
products. The following year the Italian legislature raised tariffs to
about 60 percent and denounced trade liberalization treaties with
other countries. Italian prime minister Francisco Crispi demanded
that the French lower their tariffs on Italian silk, wine, olive oil, and
cattle. On December 19, 1887, indignant French legislators voted to
double tariffs against Italian products and imposed a 50-percent tariff on Italian goods that had previously been tariff-free. According to
one estimate, between 1887 and 1897 French exports to Italy fell 21
percent, and Italian exports to France plunged 57 percent.[32]

Ill will generated by these trade wars was a factor leading Italy
to join Germany in an alliance against France. Germany promised
Italy support against France in the struggle for African colonies. In
January 1888, Italy promised to provide military assistance in the
event of another war between France and Germany.

During the 1890s France got into a trade war with Switzerland,
which had no general tariffs before it adopted a federal constitution
in 1848, and had low tariffs until 1890. The Swiss demanded that the

French cut tariffs on sixty-two Swiss products, and when the French refused, the Swiss raised tariffs 90 percent against French products. The French retaliated by raising their already high tariffs another 50 percent against Swiss products. Between 1891 and 1894, Swiss exports to France fell about 35 percent, while French exports to Switzerland fell about 45 percent.

Meanwhile, German farmers and manufacturers pushed hard for higher tariffs to limit competition. Alarmed at the prospect of paying more for manufactured goods, farmers demanded high tariffs. On June 12, 1879, the German Reichstag—their legislature—approved high tariffs on textiles, iron, grain, and meat, while admitting industrial raw materials duty-free. From the standpoint of German government officials, the tariffs were intended to increase revenue. As biographer Emil Ludwig observed, "Protection was only a means for increasing the power of the state."[33]

The 1879 German tariff law, as well as revisions in 1885 and 1887, raised tariffs on Russian agricultural commodities.[34] The Russians retaliated by raising tariffs on German imports in 1881, 1886, and 1891. Then Russia offered not to raise its tariffs further against German products for a decade, but the Germans countered that Russian tariffs were already very high. The Germans demanded that Russian tariffs be rolled back to the levels prevailing in 1880. Russia countered by raising tariffs against German goods, Germany retaliated with 50-percent penalties against Russian goods, and Russia retaliated with 50-percent penalties on top of its high tariff rates. Historian Gordon A. Craig noted that the Russians "vented their feelings in the nationalist press in Moscow and the semi-official press in St. Petersburg."[35] It was during this trade war that Russia signed a military alliance with France against Germany.

Germany's high tariffs were a drain on the German economy as well. The gains of large German farmers, noted Craig, "were paid for by the ordinary German citizen and were made at the cost of technical progress. What happened in effect was that land remained in grain production (as late as 1902, 60 percent of cultivated land was used for this purpose) that might more profitably have been converted to cattle raising, dairy farming, and specialized production. Such conversion would probably have made Germany more vulnerable to blockade during the First World War, but that is hardly a good argument in favour of the grain tariff, particularly when one remembers its political and social significance."[36]

It was widely claimed that tariffs were needed to spur industrialization, but Germany had begun industrializing decades before high tariffs were enacted in 1879. Prussia had previously promoted modernization by enacting what was probably Europe's *lowest* tariff, in 1816. This formed the basis of the Zollverein, which evolved into central Europe's largest free-trade area. It stimulated growth by vastly expanding the market for Central European companies. German railroad construction accelerated in the 1840s, cutting the cost of Ruhr coal shipments 65 percent, and that certainly gave an important boost to German industry. Germany's main rail lines were completed by 1876, by which time tariffs had been reduced to less than 5 percent. Economic historian David Landes described how "the industrial centres of west Germany—Krefeld, Monschau, the Wuppertal in textiles, Solingen and Remscheid in metalwork—grew rapidly without assistance and gave rise to large firms of international reputation."[37]

In 1878 the British amateur chemists Richard Thomas and Sidney Gilchrist developed an ingenious process for removing phosphorus from iron, making it possible to produce significantly stronger steel; suddenly the high-phosphorus iron deposits in Germany, Luxembourg, and Belgium had enormous value. Alert German entrepreneurs licensed the Thomas-Gilchrist patents to begin production within a year. British steel companies continued using the Bessemer process, which suited the non-phosphoric iron ores mined in Britain and Spain. So Germany didn't owe its industrial strength to high tariffs.[38]

In any case, as Massachusetts Institute of Technology economic historian Charles P. Kindelberger noted: "Germany overtook Britain in real income per capita only in the 1960s, and not at all in the nineteenth century. A crude measure of growth is the percentage of employment in agriculture. By this yardstick Britain is still [1978] far ahead of Germany. Or perhaps one ought to measure not output so much as consumption; this favors Britain in the short run because of her smaller portion of income used for investment. One can take overall or per capita measures, or rates of exchange . . . or the growth of productivity per weighted index of factor inputs. Or capacity to transform, that is, to adapt to changes in economic variables. A less subtle measure would relate to economic power defined in some sense such as [R. G.] Hawtrey used—the ability to deliver firepower at a distance, a definition that peculiarly favored the insular position of Britain with her big navy. Or steel production. Or the rate of growth in competitive export markets. Or foreign lending. On each of these measures there will be somewhat different results. Germany never caught up with Britain in agriculture, textiles, shipping, or overseas banking."[39]

Trade wars proliferated during the 1890s. Germany waged a five-year trade war with Spain. Off and on, Germany slapped tariffs on Canadian goods. The United States retaliated repeatedly against Brazil and Cuba as well as European countries.

After 1900, more and more nations adopted higher tariffs, partially to appease their own interest groups clamoring for protection and partially to use as bargaining chips when negotiating tariff reduction deals with other nations. By 1904, according to economic historian John H. Clapham, average tariffs were 25 percent in Germany, 27 percent in Italy, 34 percent in France, 35 percent in Austria, 73 percent in the United States, and 131 percent in Russia.[40] All this generated ill will that undoubtedly figured in political and ultimately military conflicts.

The only nations disregarding the protectionist trend were Britain, Belgium, and the Netherlands.[41] Free-trade Britain remained enviably strong in 1914. Britain dominated global shipping and insurance. Germany as well as other industrializing countries bought more goods directly from suppliers and depended less on Britain, yet Britain's re-export trade continued to grow. Despite a challenge from France, Britain remained the world's most important securities market. Income from foreign investments rose steadily, as British investors poured capital into the United States, India, Japan, and South America.

It was apparent to some people that trade wars provoked hostility and could lead to violence. In *The Great Illusion,* first published in 1909, British businessman Norman Angell denounced economic nationalism whose "method is to secure the advantage for one country by killing the prosperity of some other through the exclusion of that other's products; to cure unemployment on one side of the frontier by increasing it on the other. . . . According to that doctrine, it is economic wickedness to buy of the foreigner, but virtue to sell to him. But the foreigner cannot buy from us unless he sells to us. We want to be sure that he does not sell more than he buys. To ensure the result there must be regulated quotas, state barter: Socialism in the field of international trade."[42]

Austrian economist Ludwig von Mises reflected, "The outstanding method of modern nationalism is discrimination against foreigners in the economic sphere. Foreign goods are excluded from the domestic market or admitted only after payment of an import duty. Foreign labor is barred from competition in the domestic labor market. Foreign capital is liable to confiscation. This economic nationalism must result in war whenever those injured believe that they are strong enough to brush away by armed violent action the measures detrimental to their own welfare."[43]

ARMS RACE

Following the defeat of Napoleon, no country rivaled the dominance of the British navy. But it had become big, bloated, and tradition-bound—which is why dramatist William S. Gilbert satirized it in the hugely successful comic operas *H.M.S. Pinafore* (1878) and *The Pirates of Penzance* (1879), with music by Arthur Sullivan.

"The British had coasted on their laurels for a century and had grown complacent and careless in their dominance," observed historian James L. Stokesbury. "The late nineteenth-century Royal Navy was a comfortable club ruled over by a group of old fuddy-duddies who thought God had ordained what their grandfathers had fought to achieve. There were on record captains who threw overboard their annual allotment of practice shells rather than have the powder smoke dull their paint-and-brass work."[44]

Economic rivalries provoked fears that led European powers to expand their navies—a policy, incidentally, urged by Friedrich List. In 1888 three British admirals recommended a "two-power standard," according to which their navy should be expanded until it was as

strong as the combined forces of its two principal European rivals—
at that time, France and Russia. The following year, Parliament
passed the Naval Defense Act, appropriating funds for naval budgets.

Germany's Kaiser Wilhelm II, who came to power in 1888, decided his country should have a great navy, and he launched an armaments program. The German Reichstag—its legislature—enacted a
succession of Navy Laws. Why did Germany, a land power, need a
navy? Probably for prestige more than anything else. Since Germany
didn't have a vast overseas colonial empire, it didn't need ships capable of going long distances. Germany's fleet would be concentrated in the North Sea.[45]

This spurred the British to expand and modernize their navy. In
1892, John Arbuthnot Fisher was appointed Third Sea Lord, and he
soon became the most dynamic personality pushing to reform the
British navy. He was named First Sea Lord a dozen years later.

"In appearance," wrote Robert K. Massie, "this naval titan was
short and stocky; an average Englishman, perhaps, until one looked
at his face. It was round, smooth, and curiously boyish. His mouth
was full-lipped and sensual and could be merry, but as he aged it
tightened and the corners turned down with bitterness and fatigue.
The extraordinary feature was his eyes. Set far apart, almost at the
edges of his face, they were very large, and light gray. Heavy eyelids,
which tended to droop, gave them an almond shape. When he looked
at a person, Fisher's gaze was fixed and compelling and gave no clue
to the patterns of thought or emotion behind the façade."[46]

Massie added that, compared with the aristocrats who had
dominated the ranks of naval officers for decades, Fisher was "barely
a gentleman by birth and not truly one in behavior. He owed nothing
to family, wealth, or social position and everything to merit, force of
character, and sheer persistence. . . . He brought to the fight an exceptional inventory of qualities: Herculean energy, burning ambition, towering ego and self-confidence, and fervent patriotism. He
was bold, quick-witted, and original, and in everything he did he was
passionately involved."[47]

In 1907, Britain introduced the HMS *Dreadnought,* the most
powerful ship on the seas. The name meant "dread nought but God."
Powered by quiet turbine engines, it had ten turreted twelve-inch

guns, all the same caliber, compared with four twelve-inch guns on
conventional battleships. Each of these guns fired an 850-pound explosive shell more than 6,000 yards.[48] The *Dreadnought* was also designed with a top speed of twenty-one knots (about twenty-four
miles per hour), fast for a big ship. The ship that could fire the heavi-
est shells the longest distances was bound to prevail, particularly
when such a ship was faster than its adversary.

The British didn't actually originate the idea of an all-big-gun
ship—credit belongs to an Italian designer named Vittorio Cuniberti.
But it was the British who started a race to see who could build the
largest number of these ships, and they became known as dreadnoughts
after the first of their class. Rather than attempt a sophisticated analysis of comparative naval strength, newspapers simply counted the number of dreadnoughts. London crowds chanted, "We want eight, and we
won't wait!" By 1914, Britain had twenty dreadnoughts, Germany had
thirteen, and other nations had smaller numbers.[49]

Although the race for a bigger navy was a sign of the trend away
from laissez-faire, it wasn't a reason for war between Britain and
Germany, because Britain had decisively won the race. As military
historian J. F. C. Fuller explained, "The Triple Entente [Britain,
France, Russia] was spending on new construction two and a half
times the amount spent by the Triple Alliance [Germany, Austria-
Hungary, Italy], and France and Russia spent approximately two and
a half times as much as Germany. How anyone could say that German naval expansion threatened England is difficult to understand;
yet from 1909 on it was said again and again."[50]

Fuller pointed out that Germany had concerns other than
Britain: "Her naval situation in a war against France and Russia was
overlooked, yet it was this situation which was, and had been, the
governing factor in her naval policy since 1900." Germany's Admiral
Alfred von Tirpitz remarked, "We should be in a position to blockade the Russian fleet in the Baltic ports, and to prevent at the same
time the entrance to the sea of the French fleet."[s51]

Influenced partially by Captain Alfred Mahan's book *Influence
of Sea Power Upon History* (1890), a United States naval committee
urged building a fleet of 100 ships, including twenty first-class battleships. Japan followed with its own naval development. A succession

	Britain	*France*	*Russia*	*Germany*
1909	£11,076,551	£4,517,766	£1,758,487	£10,177,062
1910	14,755,289	4,977,682	1,424,013	11,392,856
1911	15,148,171	5,876,659	3,215,396	11,701,859
1912	16,132,558	7,114,876	6,897,580	11,491,187
1913	16,883,875	8,093,064	12,082,516	11,010,883
1914	18,676,080	11,772,862	13,098,613	10,316,264

Source: J. F. C. Fuller, A Military History of the Western World, from the Seven Days Battle, 1862, to the Battle of Leyte Gulf, 1944 *(New York: Funk & Wagnalls, 1956), 177.*

of books and advocacy groups encouraged a steady military buildup during the next two decades.

By the late nineteenth century, with the Napoleonic Wars a distant memory, many people viewed Napoleon as a hero and found it easier to imagine that war might be a good thing. For example, the "progressive" American journalist Ida M. Tarbell—who wrote a famous muckraking biography of John D. Rockefeller and became a passionate admirer of Woodrow Wilson and Benito Mussolini[52]— wrote a worshipful biography of Napoleon, first published in 1894.

American "progressives," it seemed, had a blind spot for the perils of political power. "No man ever comprehended more clearly the splendid science of war," Tarbell gushed about Napoleon. "We cannot fail to bow to the genius which conceived and executed the Italian campaign, which fought the classic battles of Austerlitz, Jena, and Wagram. These deeds are great epics. They move in noble, measured lines, and stir us by their might and perfection. It is only a genius of the most magnificent order which could handle men and materials as Napoleon did. . . . It is only a mind of noble proportions which can grasp the needs of a people, and a hand of mighty force which can supply them. . . . He was the greatest genius of his time, perhaps of all time. . . ."[53] One of Tarbell's most ghastly lines dismissed those who, like Lafayette, courageously dissented from Napoleon's tyrannical rule: "It was only selfish, warped, abnormal natures, which had been stifled by etiquette and diplomacy and self-interest, who abandoned him."

ENTANGLING ALLIANCES

Although Europe continued to be at peace during the late nineteenth century, Bismarck anticipated the possibility of war and began negotiating alliances. In October 1879, he concluded a defensive treaty known as the Dual Alliance with Austria-Hungary. Two years later, France sent troops into Tunisia, aggravating the Italians, who were late to the game of acquiring colonies and coveted African territory. The following year, Italy secretly joined Germany and Austria-Hungary, forming the Triple Alliance.[54] Then, in 1887, came the Reinsurance Treaty with Russia—a juggling act, since Russia and Austria-Hungary were adversaries.

The German emperor Frederick III died in June 1888 and was succeeded by Wilhelm II of Hohenzollern, who was the grandson of Britain's Queen Victoria. "He was an excitable, impulsive, and headstrong man, industrious, pious and patriotic," observed historian J. F. C. Fuller. Wilhelm II, the new German Kaiser, proclaimed: "There is only one master in the country, and I am he." He fired Bismarck in 1890, and the alliances Bismarck had developed began to fall apart.

The alliance with Russia expired, and in 1894 French officials—heirs of the French Revolution—swallowed their supposedly radical principles and formed the Dual Alliance, a defensive alliance with czarist Russia against Germany and Austria-Hungary. That French republicans and Russian autocrats could come together had been considered a political impossibility. The Napoleonic Wars had climaxed with the French invasion of Russia.

In 1895, Kaiser Wilhelm II celebrated a quarter-century of the German Empire by describing a realm that extended beyond Europe, around the world—a rather inflammatory topic. Three years later he bragged about his navy: "Even for the greatest sea power [Britain], a war with it would involve such risks as to jeopardize its own supremacy."[55]

Britain began to reconsider its policy of going it alone, not allied with anybody, protected by its mighty navy. Britain had fought France in many wars, and France was still widely viewed as a potential threat. In 1894, British naval guru John Fisher wrote: "The French, no doubt, sincerely desire peace with England, provided they can replace England in Egypt and the Nile Basin and elsewhere. To obtain peace on these terms they would not shrink from trying a fall with England, if they thought there was a fair chance of success. The deadlock that ends in war can only be avoided by one of two means. Either the French may abandon their claims, or the English may strengthen their sea power to such an extent that the probable chances of an international struggle would leave France worse off than she is today."[56]

The French, who had been humiliated by Germany in the brief war of 1870 (started by the French ruler Napoleon III), were anxious for British help if they ever again found themselves fighting Germany. Concerned about the German navy, Britain agreed to forget past hostilities with France and reach a general understanding known variously as the *Entente Cordiale,* or the Franco-British Declaration, or the Declaration between the United Kingdom and France Respecting Egypt and Morocco, Together with the Secret Articles Signed at the Same Time, April 8, 1904. According to historian Niall Ferguson, the British were interested in reducing colonial conflicts, and there were more possible trade-offs with a country like France, which already had a lot of colonies, than with Germany, which aspired to have colonial possessions.[57] Because of French ties to Russia, the agreement suggested the possibility that Britain might improve relations with Russia. The agreement was signed by French foreign minister Paul Cambon and British foreign secretary Henry Lansdowne.

Although the *Entente Cordiale* specified that Britain would provide diplomatic support for French control of ports in Morocco, French and British military staffs had secretly met to discuss joint operations in the event of a war. French foreign minister Théophile Delcassé reported that Britain had agreed to deploy its navy against Germany in the event of war between France and Germany, but Lansdowne denied it.[58]

It was Edward Grey, British foreign secretary from 1893 to 1895 in Prime Minister William Ewart Gladstone's last government, and from 1905 to 1916 in the governments of Henry Campbell-Bannerman and Henry Asquith, who secretly transformed Britain's general understanding into an alliance with France and thereby played a critical role in the outbreak of World War I.

Grey approved continued secret meetings between British and French military staffs, who discussed joint action in a possible war with Germany. The only other members of Parliament who knew about these meetings were Campbell-Bannerman, Asquith, and Richard Burdon Haldane, who was the minister of war.[59]

Grey believed goodwill with France was so important that Britain couldn't risk it by trying to improve relations with Germany. He seemed to adopt an anti-German view to placate the French. "The danger of speaking civil words in Berlin," Grey wrote in October 1905, "is that they may be . . . interpreted in France as implying that we shall be lukewarm in our support of the entente [with France]."[60]

Meanwhile, the British had mixed feelings about Russia. Some influential Englishmen, including member of Parliament Joseph Chamberlain, talked about a possible alliance with Germany. This idea was abandoned when Germany began to expand its navy in the name of achieving "greatness" and protecting its overseas colonies.

In 1907, two years after the Russian navy had been destroyed by the Japanese in a brief war—and after French lenders had helped to rebuild the Russian navy—the Anglo-Russian Convention was signed, through which Britain and Russia resolved their colonial differences, recognizing each other's spheres of influence in Afghanistan, Persia, the Balkans, and elsewhere. The agreement wasn't intended as a balance against German power, but it blossomed into the Triple Entente, an alliance facing the Triple Alliance of Germany, Austria-Hungary, and Italy. Meanwhile, Russia received French funds to modernize its military and make possible a faster mobilization in the event of war.[61]

In 1911, British prime minister Asquith became uncomfortable about continued meetings between British and French military staffs, and he wrote Grey on September 5: "Conversations such as that between [French] General Joffre and [British] Colonel Fairholme seem to me rather dangerous; especially the part which refers to possible British assistance. The French ought not to be encouraged, in present circumstances, to make their plans on any assumptions of this kind."[62]

On September 8, Grey replied, defending secret support for the French: "It would create consternation if we forbade our military experts to converse with the French. No doubt these conversations and our speeches have given an expectation of support. I do not see how that can be helped."

In Britain there was growing suspicion that Grey was scheming to involve Britain in a continental war. F. W. Hirst, editor of *The Economist*, denounced the idea of "asking millions of his innocent countrymen to give up their lives for a continental squabble about which they know nothing and care less."[63]

Winston Churchill, who had become First Lord of the Admiralty, was among the few members of Parliament aware of Grey's secret dealings, and he defended them: "We were morally committed to France. . . . No bargain had been entered into. All arrangements were specifically preluded with a declaration that neither party was committed to anything further than consultation together if danger threatened. . . . [If in 1912] the Foreign Secretary had, in cold blood, proposed a formal alliance with France and Russia . . . the Cabinet of the day would never have agreed to it. I doubt if four Ministers would have agreed to it. But if the Cabinet had been united upon it, the House of Commons would not have accepted their guidance. Therefore the Foreign Minister would have had to resign. The policy which he had advocated would have stood condemned and perhaps violently repudiated; and upon that repudiation would have come an absolute veto upon all those informal preparations and non-committal discussions on which the defense power of the Triple Entente was erected."[64] In other words, Churchill believed that if Grey had operated openly, Britain might not have been able to get into the war!

The alliance had the potential to draw Britain into a war with which France became involved, yet didn't have the value of deterring aggression by other nations—in particular Germany—because it was secret. Churchill acknowledged as much: "An open alliance, if it could have been peacefully brought about at an earlier date, would have exercised a deterring effect upon the German mind, or at the least would have altered their military calculations."

Later, one of the ministers, the Earl of Loreburn—who had served from 1905 to 1912—complained: "We were brought into the war because Mr. Asquith and Sir Edward Grey and their confidants, by steps some of which are known while others may be unknown, had placed us in such a position toward France, and therefore also toward Russia, that they found they could not refuse to take up arms on her behalf when it came to the issue, though till the end they denied it to Parliament, and probably even to themselves. . . . We went to war unprepared in a Russian quarrel because we were tied to France in the dark. . . . In effect [Grey's secret dealings] left the peace of Great Britain at the mercy of the Russian Court."[65]

Although Grey operated in a parliamentary system, he had arrogated to himself supreme power over Britain's foreign policy. He wrote, "I did not regard anything except my own letters and official papers as deciding policy."[66]

Niall Ferguson pointed out that by 1912 there was a greater risk of war with Germany than with France or Russia, and therefore it would have made more sense to seek some kind of accommodation with Germany. Instead, Ferguson explained, "In his determination to preserve the Entente with France, Grey was willing to make military commitments which made war with Germany more rather than less likely, sooner rather than later. By a completely circular process of reasoning, he wished to commit Britain to a possible war with Germany—because otherwise there might be war with Germany. Appeasement of France and Russia had once made sense; but Grey prolonged the life of the policy well after its rationale had faded."[67]

All these alliances increased the risks of war two ways. First, they reduced the incentives for government officials to be cautious. Backed by allies, the participants were more likely to figure they might prevail and therefore to believe that the risks of war were worth taking. Government officials were less likely to risk war if they knew they would have to fight on their own and bear the costs themselves. In a 1911 speech to Parliament, Grey acknowledged the danger by emphasizing that Britain's "friendship" with France and Russia didn't involve alliances.[68]

Second, alliances increased the number of nations likely to become involved in a war. As historian Sidney B. Fay explained, "The members of each group felt bound to support each other, even in matters where they had no direct interest, because failure to give support would have weakened the solidarity of the group. Thus, Germany often felt bound to back up Austria-Hungary in her Balkan policies, because otherwise Germany feared to lose her only thoroughly dependable ally. Similarly, France had no direct political (only financial) interests in the Balkans, but felt bound to back up Russia, because otherwise the existence of the Dual Alliance would have been threatened, the balance of power destroyed, and the best guarantee to French safety from a German attack would have been lost. Likewise, the officials of the British Foreign Office became increasingly convinced that England must support France and Russia in order to preserve the solidarity of the Triple Entente as a check to the Triple Alliance."[69]

NATIONAL HATREDS

Government intervention in domestic policy inflamed national hatreds that eventually spread across European borders, increasing the likelihood that local conflicts might activate alliances and spread across Europe.

In the multinational Ottoman Empire, the Sultan's repressive policies sparked rebellion. Serbs and Romanians gained their independence in 1878. Albanians and Bulgarians became independent in 1912. Though all opposed the Turks, they also fought one another and manipulated political power to terrorize their own subject nationalities. They agitated against adjacent powers—Russia and Austria-Hungary—in the name of helping their compatriots across the borders. Meanwhile, Turks slaughtered Armenians and waged war with Greeks.

Russians used their power to suppress dozens of nationalities within their borders. The most restive were Poles, Lithuanians, Latvians, Finns, Ukrainians, Georgians, and Armenians. Revolts were brutally put down by Czar Alexander III, and he used government control of schools to suppress unofficial languages. He seized the funds of dissident churches. Not all anger was directed at Russians, though; Polish nationalists, for instance, clashed with Lithuanian and Ukrainian nationalists. Many nationalities persecuted Jews. The more government interfered with various nationalities, the worse became the conflicts that disrupted the economy and undermined the government itself.

Austria-Hungary was a cauldron of nationalities. Austria had Germans and Poles. Hungary had Magyars, Slovaks, Serbs, Croats, and Romanians. Galicia had Poles and Ukrainians. Silesia had Germans, Poles, and Czechs. Czechs dominated Bohemia and Moravia, but many Germans lived in those provinces, too. Italians were in South Tyrol. There were Serbs in Bosnia and Herzegovina, Serbs and Croats in Dalmatia, Slavs in Styria and Carinthia, Carniola and Istria. If permitted to go about their business without interference, the various nationalities would have been more likely to get along peacefully, as different nationalities have generally done in Switzerland and the United States.

But governments increasingly dominated their respective economies, and as a result whichever nationality controlled government could inflict its will on everyone else, thereby escalating potential conflicts. As historian A. J. P. Taylor wrote: "The Austrian state suffered from its strength: it had never had its range of activity cut down during a successful period of *laissez-faire,* and therefore the openings for national conflict were far greater. There were no private schools or hospitals, no independent universities; and the state, in its infinite paternalism, performed a variety of services from veterinary surgery to the inspecting of buildings. The appointment of every school teacher, of every railway porter, of every hospital doctor, of every tax-collector, was a signal for national struggle. Besides, private industry looked to the state for aid from tariffs and subsidies; these, in every country, produce 'log-rolling,' and nationalism offered an added lever with which to shift the logs. German industries demanded state aid to preserve their privileged position; Czech industries demanded state aid to redress the inequalities of the past. The first generation of national rivals had been the products of universities and fought for appointments at the highest professional level: their disputes concerned only a few hundred state jobs. The generation which followed them was the result of universal elementary education and fought for the trivial state employment which existed in every village; hence the more popular national conflicts at the end of the century."[70]

Austria enacted schooling laws to extend the political power of the dominant German-speaking minority. "Schools were designed to send forth obedient subjects, not critically-minded citizens," according to historian Arthur J. May. "The object of Austrian elementary

education, above all other objects, was to contribute to the preservation of the state."[71] National minorities had less money available for
education, because they paid taxes that were distributed among the
politically powerful. More government money spent on German
schools meant less government money for Slovene schools, and less
after-tax money for Slovenes to spend on their priorities.

In Hungary, politically powerful Magyars—a minority—
expanded government control over schools in 1879, 1883, and 1907.
Their official mission was to produce Magyar patriots. They taught
Magyar history, culture, and language. Only people who spoke Magyar could serve on a school board. The government mandated low
teachers' salaries at non-government schools, so they'd have to apply
for subsidies, thereby extending government influence over these
schools as well.[72] Although Slovaks and other non-Magyars had to
pay taxes, the government didn't provide any financial support for
non-Magyar schools.

The Magyar monopoly of schools enabled Magyars to monopolize government jobs and the professions. According to A. J. P. Taylor, "At the beginning of the twentieth century, 95 per cent of the
state officials, 92 per cent of the county officials, 89 per cent of the
doctors, and 90 per cent of the judges were Magyar."[73]

Political power was all-important as Magyars used it to promote
their interests at the expense of other people. Hungary annexed
Transylvania in 1865 and rescinded the traditional rights of national
minorities there. Romanian deputies weren't permitted to speak
their own language in the legislature. Magyars harassed the Romanian press. They packed juries with non-Romanians. Magyars suppressed Slovak educational, literary, and scientific societies. They did
what they could to prevent Croats from pursuing their lives freely.

Historian Oszkár Jászi maintained that rolling back government power in Austria-Hungary would have reduced potential conflicts among the nationalities. "There can be no doubt," he wrote,
"that, if all the possibilities of free trade policy had been utilized in
the right way, the centrifugal and particularistic tendencies could
have been checked by the growing economic solidarity of the various
nations and countries."[74]

Since interventionist policies continued, nationality conflicts raged across borders. The flashpoint turned out to be Macedonia, a hilly land flanked by Albania, Greece, Bulgaria, and Serbia. All these nationalities and more were represented in Macedonia, and memories of past oppression confirmed their hatred for one another as well as for the nationalities ruling Austria-Hungary and Ottoman Turkey.

Germany, Britain, France, and Russia used economic means to maneuver for political influence in the Balkans and Ottoman Turkey. For instance, in the spring of 1914, Ottoman Turkey was broke, and both France and Germany were eager to give away their taxpayers' money, extending loans that might never be repaid. France won the deal. Germany wanted Bulgaria as an ally, so it gave away money there. Britain and Germany competed to influence construction of the Baghdad Railway, and the resulting arrangement favored Britain.

FATAL MISCALCULATIONS

Imperceptibly, over the course of five decades, the relentless attacks on laissez-faire, the expansion of government power, Bismarck's willingness to seize territory and his system of military alliances, the scramble for colonies, the trade wars, the arms race, and national hatreds had subverted the great peace of the nineteenth century and transformed Europe into a powder keg.

As European opinion had swung away from a generally laissez-faire, noninterventionist foreign policy, nobody seemed to consider that an interventionist foreign policy is more complicated to manage. One never knows how different people might react to interventions, so there are more likely to be unintended consequences. Such a policy requires people with considerable knowledge and the ability to anticipate developments and make sound judgments. Nobody has figured out a way to assure that an interventionist foreign policy will always be managed by such people.

By 1914, many Europeans expected war. There was a war spirit in France. Helmuth von Moltke, chief of the German General Staff, expressed fear that Britain, France, and Russia had left Germany "in a condition of hopeless isolation which was growing ever more hopeless," and there was support among German strategists for a preventative war. "The sooner it comes, the better for us," Moltke report-edly remarked.[75]

Britain's foreign secretary, Edward Grey, told Cabinet members that the British government, "concerned to maintain some balance between groups of Powers, could under no circumstances tolerate France being crushed."[76] But on June 11, in response to war fears, Grey told the House of Commons: "If war arose between the European Powers, there were no unpublished agreements which would restrict or hamper the freedom of the Government or of Parliament to decide whether or not Great Britain should participate in a war. No such negotiations are in progress, and none are likely to be entered into as far as I can judge."[77] So he lied about his commitments to France, and he eliminated any potential value they might have had in deterring Germany from going to war.

The war began with an assassination and a series of miscalculations. On June 28, 1914, Archduke Francis Ferdinand, heir to the Austro-Hungarian Empire, was shot while driving through Sarajevo. The assassin was Gavrilo Princep, a Serbian nationalist student. Princep was involved with the Black Hand, a terrorist group promoting Greater Serbia. The Black Hand was directed by Colonel Dragutin Dimitrijević, head of Serbian military intelligence.[78]

During the 1912–13 Balkan Wars, Serbia had doubled its territory.[79] Officials in Vienna believed that the Serbs coveted some of their territory, that Serbs had plotted the assassination, and that they must be stopped. But what was Austria-Hungary to do?

If Austria-Hungary attacked Serbia, Russia might back Serbia, because Slav nationalists were agitating for Russia to be the protector of fellow Slavs. The Russian army was about twice the size of the Austro-Hungarian army, so Russian intervention would spell trouble. Since Russia had an alliance with Britain and France, it was possible that Russian intervention might draw in those countries as well.

Moreover, Russia's Czar Nicholas II knew that war meant risks for his regime. He had been humiliated just a few years before, in the Russo-Japanese War (1904–5) that triggered the Revolution of 1905 and brought the regime close to collapse. Russia certainly wasn't prepared for a major war and seemed unlikely to go into a war alone.

On July 3, Woodrow Wilson's principal adviser, Edward House, reported that Foreign Secretary Grey had let the Kaiser know about his desire for peace, but "Sir Edward said he did not wish to send anything official or in writing, for fear of offending French and Russian sensibilities."[80] Apparently Grey's commitments to these nations were such that he couldn't function as a peacemaker.

Before deciding to take action against Serbia, Austria-Hungary needed help, and the most likely ally was Germany. On July 5, Germany's Kaiser Wilhelm II gave Austria-Hungary his famous "blank check"—supporting Austria-Hungary in its view that Serbia must be dealt with firmly. The conflict looked like another Balkan War— no big deal. Officials in Austria-Hungary expected that German backing would deter Russia from entering the conflict and help recruit Bulgaria as an ally. The Germans didn't appear to be planning a general war, because when the Kaiser issued his "blank check," Moltke, Wilhelm Groener (head of the army's railroad department), and Walther Nicolai (head of military intelligence) were all away on a summer vacation.[81]

How could Germany and Russia fight each other? Kaiser Wilhelm II was a cousin of Czar Nicholas II and—one might add—an uncle of Britain's King Edward VII. Surely, royals ought to be able to talk with one another and avoid a war.

On July 23, Austria-Hungary's ambassador to Serbia presented an ultimatum: Serbia must eliminate terrorists based in the country and suppress publications critical of Austria-Hungary. Furthermore, representatives of Austria-Hungary must participate in the investigation of the assassination of Archduke Ferdinand.

Serbia wasn't ready for war, because it was still rebuilding its military forces after the recent Balkan Wars, which had resulted in 91,000 Serbian casualties. In many Serbian infantry units, about one-third of the soldiers lacked rifles.[82] Accordingly, Serbia tried to defuse the situation, saying it would go along with Austria's demands as much as possible. Serbia promised to suppress terrorism and publications critical of Austria-Hungary. The only point it couldn't go along with was the idea of having foreigners involved with the investigation.

Austria ordered the mobilization of its army on July 23. Serbia ordered its army to mobilize two days later. Mobilizing an army didn't mean war was inevitable, because it had served as a tool of diplomacy, to step up the pressure in a negotiation. But Austrian officials felt it was crucial to stop nationality conflicts from escalating before they blew apart their multinational empire. On July 28, Austria-Hungary declared war against Serbia.

The following day, foreign secretary Edward Grey told the Austrian ambassador: "I did not wish to discuss the merits of the question between Austria and Serbia."[83] Grey later confirmed his lack of interest in the dispute: "The notion of being involved in war about a Balkan quarrel was repugnant. Serbia, to British people, was a country with which a few years ago we had severed diplomatic relations, because of a brutal murder of the King and Queen; and though that was over, and we were now on good terms, there was no sentiment urging us to go into a war on Serbia's behalf."[84]

Austrian ambassador Friedrich Szápáry asked Russian foreign minister Sergei Sazonov not to mobilize the army, but then came reports that Austrian forces were bombarding Belgrade, the Serbian capital.[85] On July 30, with the implicit support of Britain and France, Czar Nicholas II decided to order a mobilization of the Russian army against Austria-Hungary and Germany. Such a mobilization had long been viewed as an act of war.[86] Presumably Russia's ally France would soon join the war, and Germany would find itself fighting on two fronts. Germany's best bet, militarily, seemed to be a quick victory over France in the west so it could focus on the much larger Russian armies in the east. Historian S. L. A. Marshall declared, "The news of full mobilization by Russia fixed Europe's fate."[87]

On August 1, Kaiser Wilhelm II supported his ally Austria-Hungary by declaring war against Russia. French war minister Cambon recalled demanding that Grey commit Britain to the defense of France, if France should enter the war. When Grey replied that the British government hadn't decided what it would do, Cambon fumed: "After all that has passed between our two countries, after the agreement between your naval authorities and ours by which all our naval strength has been concentrated in the Mediterranean so as to release your fleet for concentration in the North Sea, so that if the German Fleet sweeps down the Channel and destroys Calais, Boulogne, and Cherbourg, there can be no resistance, you tell me that your Government cannot decide upon intervention? How am I to send such a message? It would fill France with rage and indignation. My people would say you betrayed us. It is not possible. It is true the agreements between your military and naval authorities have not been ratified by our Governments, but there is a moral obligation not to leave us unprotected."[88]

On August 3, Germany declared war against France. How could Britain enter the war, since there wasn't an official alliance with France? British officials had discussed a naval blockade of Germany, and chief of staff John French expressed the view that "to bring the greatest pressure to bear upon Germany, it is essential that the Netherlands and Belgium should either be entirely friendly to this country, or that they should be definitely hostile, in which case we should extend the blockade to their ports."[89] British officials contemplated violating the sovereignty of Belgium, yet the rationale for fighting Germany on behalf of France turned out to be the German invasion of Belgium on August 4. Britain cited it as an excuse to declare war against Germany.

All the belligerents expected that the war would be brief. None had plans for a long military campaign. Officials throughout Europe were shocked when, in the fall of 1914, it became apparent that the killing might go on for a long time.

NEEDLESS TRAGEDY

None of this was inevitable. If the horrors of the Napoleonic Wars had remained fresh in people's minds—rather than having conquests glorified by "progressives"—and if the laissez-faire policies of Richard Cobden and John Bright had been continued, there never would have been a world war. Maintaining a separation of the economy and the state would have prevented politicians from turning business competition into political and military conflicts. There wouldn't have been nasty trade wars and empire building, contributing to paranoia and the arms race. If governments had let people live their lives as freely on one side of a border as on the other, there wouldn't have been much political support for war. What would have been the point?

Much discussion about World War I origins has focused on immediate factors. Barbara Tuchman, for example, chronicled the incompetence of the personalities who headed the belligerent governments.[90]
Her points were well taken, but there have always been incompetents
in government. Nobody has devised a way to keep them out. Why did
incompetents do more harm in 1914 than, say, in 1860 or 1850 or 1840?
By minimizing the power of government, laissez-faire policies mini-
mized the harm that might be done by incompetent or evil rulers.

Then there has been the debate about the war guilt of the belligerents. The Allied Powers blamed everything on Germany, and it
was hit with monstrous reparations bills. Later, revisionist historians
like Sidney Fay and Harry Elmer Barnes insisted that there was plenty
of blame to go around. German historian Fritz Fischer, after examin-
ing German archives, renewed the debate by presenting his case that
after Archduke Ferdinand was assassinated, German officials urged
Austria to send Serbia an ultimatum that was so strong, the Serbian
government would have to defy it. German officials, Fischer reported,
pledged to back Austria for provoking war—the policy that became
known as "Germany's blank cheque."[91] Fischer documented how
German officials later expanded their war aims. As with Tuchman,
one might acknowledge points, but note that he's discussing one of
the last steps in a long sequence of developments. Why didn't any of
a number of nineteenth-century provocations result in a general war?
Other factors, such as trade wars, alliance systems, and national hatreds, weren't present during the mid-nineteenth century. Also war
horrors were a more recent memory, and nineteenth-century political
leaders were probably much more anxious to avoid war.

Although laissez-faire policies could have been continued, once
they were abandoned, and more governments pursued aggressive interventionist policies, it would have been hard to avoid a general war.

2

WHY WAS THE WAR STALEMATED FOR THREE YEARS?

FROM THE WAR'S OUTSET, it appeared unlikely that one side would be able to dominate the other. In 1914 the combined armies of Britain, France, and Russia had a peacetime strength of 2.5 million and a wartime strength of 5.3 million men.[1] Germany and Austria-Hungary had a peacetime strength of 1.2 million men, a wartime strength of 3.4 million. On the other hand, the Germans had better generals—less inclined to squander the lives of their men—and France and Russia were too far apart to coordinate operations.

The British navy dominated the seas and enforced a blockade preventing goods from coming to Germany. Britain maintained a far-flung colonial empire and assured that sea lanes would be secure for commerce. The Kaiser was proud of his fleet of surface ships, on which he had spent so much money, but they didn't do Germany much good during the war. Germany had better luck with submarines for a while, until the British developed the convoy system.

Of these countries, Russia had the largest estimated population, 171 million versus 65 million for Germany, 52 million for Austria-Hungary, 45 million for Britain, and 39 million for France. Germany, however, had the largest economy, with national income estimated at $12 billion versus $3 billion for Austria-Hungary, $11 billion for Britain, $6 billion for France, and $7 billion for Russia.[2] But the British Empire spent the most on its military, an estimated $23 billion; France spent an estimated $9.3 billion and Russia $5.4 billion; Germany spent $19.9 billion and Austria-Hungary $4.7 billion.[3] So, even without the United States, the Allied Powers had important advantages.

Fighting began on August 3, 1914, when Germany sent seventy-eight infantry divisions heading west. The Germans invaded Belgium, then advanced deep into France—within thirty miles of Paris. The French army retreated to the south of the Marne River, and Paris anticipated a siege. General Joseph Joffre, the French commander-in-chief, ordered a counterattack, and on September 6 the French Sixth Army moved against the German First Army. The French Fifth Army and the British Expeditionary Force soon joined the battle. The rapid German advance was stopped. By September 10, the Germans had retreated to the Aisne River and dug trenches from which they would fire at advancing French and British soldiers. The French and British, in turn, dug trenches to return fire, and a stalemate began.

Some historians, including John Terraine, weren't happy that because of German initiative and the French alliance, Britain played to its weakness (the army) rather than its strength (the navy). "Britain," he wrote, "had to do pretty well what the French decided, for naturally Joffre's plans included participation by the British in the West on the largest scale possible; and the French were dancing to the German tune in that year and the next."[4]

The British struggled to restrain Joffre, who was determined to throw more and more men into the killing fields. In July 1915 there was a conference at Calais, France, including General Joffre on the French side and prime minister Herbert Asquith, war minister Lord Kitchener, and First Lord of the Admiralty Arthur James Balfour representing the British. Winston Churchill expressed frustration that Joffre agreed there wouldn't be any more French-British offensives in 1915. "No sooner had General Joffre left the Conference," he fumed, "than notwithstanding these agreements, he had calmly resumed the development of his plans for his great attack in Champagne, in which he confidently expected to break the German lines and roll them back."[5] Joffre began the attack on Sepember 25, and after ten days, 145,000 French soldiers had been killed without gaining any strategic advantage.[6]

A German general, Erich von Falkenheyn, became convinced that Germany didn't have enough manpower to win the war, and there wasn't any way to defeat Britain because of its naval power. So he proposed a strategy of attrition, aiming to lose soldiers at a slower rate than England and France. The Germans concentrated six infantry divisions and heavy artillery around Verdun, a town of little military importance. It was about 135 miles east of Paris and wouldn't have made an assault on the capital any easier. Verdun was served by only two rail lines, but it had psychological importance. At Verdun was a Gallic fortress built before Roman times. It was at Verdun, in A.D. 843, that the empire of Charlemagne was divided by his three grandsons. Falkenheyn figured the French would defend Verdun at all costs, furthering his strategy of attrition. As Churchill explained, "Verdun was to become an anvil upon which French military manhood was to be hammered to death by German cannon."

The Germans attacked Verdun on February 21, 1916, and for several days gained territory. But under General Philippe Pétain, the French rallied and regained territory they had lost. For seven months, until December 15, 1916, the armies alternated advancing and retreating. The Germans ended up with little to show for their 330,000 fatalities, compared with 350,000 French fatalities. No wonder the battle was called a "mincing machine."[7]

Then came the Battle of the Somme. British forces were led by General Douglas Haig, who, though credited as a military technician, was an incompetent strategist. He stationed himself far away from battle and never visited the front. He authorized a week-long bombardment on German positions, after which they were presumed to have been knocked out. Then he ordered British soldiers, each carrying perhaps sixty pounds of equipment, to walk upright in big lines toward the Germans, rather than more cautiously keeping themselves low and seeking cover from possible machine-gun fire. It turned out there were enough surviving German machine gunners for a massacre. More than 25,000 British soldiers were seriously wounded, and almost 20,000 were killed *on the first day of fighting,* July 1, 1916. According to historian James L. Stokesbury, this was *three times more battlefield deaths than Britain had suffered during the twenty-two years it had fought France and Napoleon.*[8] Pitifully little was gained.

Haig, who maintained his command thanks to friendship with

King George V,[9] was egged on by General Joffre. When the first tanks became available, the impatient Haig ordered them into action. Although they seemed to scare German soldiers, they had limited capability, and there were only forty-two of them, not enough to affect the outcome of the battle. Fighting continued until Haig abandoned the Somme campaign on November 18. The Allied Powers wore down the Germans at horrific cost: the death toll included some 200,000 French soldiers, 400,000 British soldiers, and 500,000 German soldiers. Some 23 million artillery shells had been fired by both sides.[10] Historian John Keegan called the Somme the worst military tragedy in the history of Britain.

For all this, the Allied Powers had advanced only about six miles—three miles from the town of Bapaume, which they had hoped to reach on the very first day of the battle. They had gained nothing of consequence. The catastrophe at the Somme led to the December 1916 resignation of British prime minister Asquith, the man who had made Douglas Haig commander-in-chief of British forces in France.

What if soldiers refused to charge into the machine-gun fire? Well, the French Ministry of War ordered that its soldiers be executed—shot within twenty-four hours. No trial. General Joffre declared, "We must be pitiless with the fugitives." The British had the same policy of killing their own soldiers if the Germans didn't do it.[11]

The Germans had just about given up hope that they could achieve a decisive victory or wear down the Allied Powers. The Kaiser suggested recruiting Polish nationalists to their cause by establishing a German-sponsored kingdom of Poland. Back in 1772, Polish territory had been split up among Austria, Russia, and Prussia, and Polish nationalists dreamed of reasserting their national sovereignty again. The Kaiser figured that Polish soldiers would focus on regaining Polish territory held by Russia. So, on November 5, the idea was announced.

But snags appeared immediately. The Polish military leader Josef Pilsudski demanded recognition of an independent Polish government, and Germany refused. Further, German chancellor Theobald von Bethmann-Hollweg was in Sweden, secretly discussing possible peace terms with Russia, but the czar would never accept a Polish state established at his expense. The peace talks collapsed. Historian Martin Gilbert wrote, "One person who was relieved at this was

Vladimir Lenin, who, from his Swiss exile, had been worried that the
conclusion of peace between Russia and Germany would prevent the
outbreak of revolution in Russia."[12]

BRITAIN'S NAVAL BLOCKADE VS. GERMAN SUBMARINES

The British naval blockade involved ships patrolling German waters
and laying mines around German harbors. By November 1914, the
British declared that the entire North Sea was a war zone, and neutral ships sailed at their own risk.[13] According to the prevailing doctrine of international law, a naval blockade was supposed to stop
only shipments of war materials, viewed as contraband. In the name
of humanity, a naval blockade wasn't supposed to prevent people
from getting food and other essentials for life. But, of course, the
more goods that reached the target country, the longer it could fight.
So the British disregarded international law, which in any case had
been framed by Europeans to curb the power of the British navy.
Britain refused to recognize a distinction between contraband goods
and non-contraband goods. The British resolved to stop everything,
which meant interfering with the prerogatives of neutral nations like
the United States.

Moreover, the British gained important advantages by acquiring
all three German naval codes by the end of 1914—Australians had obtained the code used by German merchant ships, Russians had seized a
naval codebook from a German cruiser that had run aground in the
Baltic Sea, and the third codebook, from a sunken German destroyer,
had been picked up in a British trawler's nets. The British were discreet
enough about their use of the codes that the Germans didn't realize
their military communications had been compromised.[14]

Moreover, the British navy was more discreet about their use of
radio communications. They maintained long periods of radio si-
lence, preferring to have ships communicate with each other by using
signal flags, even when bad weather made this difficult. This made it
much harder for the Germans to determine where British ships were
located.

Historian C. Paul Vincent explained, "Neutral ships were appre-
hended at sea, escorted into British or French ports, and detained at

great cost to both consignors and consignees. By September 1916 the British fleet was singlehandedly intercepting an average of 135 merchant ships weekly. The number evading the blockade was modest. Germany's ships, meanwhile, remained paralyzed in her ports."[15]

The Germans countered with submarines. The British had submarines, too—Winston Churchill promoted their development—but apparently there was resistance from naval officers who believed that resources should be put into building other types of ships. Before the war, it had been thought that submarines couldn't go far from shore, so they might be used only to help defend harbors, coastlines, and bases from enemy ships.[16] One has to dismiss as British propaganda the view that German submarines were sinister and immoral. Far more people were killed by machine guns than by submarines.

The Germans were slow to develop submarines. In December 1914, when German admiral Alfred von Tirpitz announced plans to establish a blockade around Britain, Germany had only twenty-one U-boats—twelve of which were early petroleum-powered models that couldn't go far from their home ports.[17]

According to prevailing rules of engagement, submarines were supposed to approach an attack like surface ships—surfacing, so that people aboard a target ship wouldn't be taken by surprise. But submarines were most vulnerable on the surface, and early on, in August 1914, a German submarine was rammed and sunk by a British warship. No wonder the Germans concluded that traditional rules of engagement didn't make sense for submarines.

Because the British knew the German military codes, they had substantial knowledge about where German submarines were located. Submarines could be attacked by ramming, dropping depth charges, and laying minefields.

German submarine commanders couldn't easily identify ships in their sights, and they couldn't remove passengers or goods, so the Germans declared that the most practical policy was to provide fair warning: ships in a certain area would be at risk. In February 1915 they announced that the waters around the British Isles were a war zone—the Germans even paid for advertisements in New York newspapers, warning Americans to stay out of the war zone.

This policy became explosively controversial when, on May 7,

1915, a German submarine sank the *Lusitania,* a British ship carrying 118 American passengers. President Woodrow Wilson expressed outrage. Although it was absurd for Americans to believe they were entitled to safe passage in a war zone, particularly on ships sailing under belligerent flags, the Germans curtailed their use of submarine warfare for two years. Only later was it revealed that the *Lusitania* was carrying 173 tons of rifle cartridges and shrapnel destined for Britain.[18]

By 1916, German naval commanders had become intensely frustrated at being confined in their harbors. They began to venture out and look for British ships, hoping that by sinking British ships one at a time they could reduce the British naval advantage. In January, Reinhard Scheer, an advocate of a more aggressive policy, was appointed commander of the German High Seas Fleet. He ordered that German ships gather off Jutland, the northwestern coast of Denmark. Scheer thought the British Grand Fleet was far away, at its principal base at Scapa Flow, north of Scotland.

But the British knew what Scheer was doing, because they had the German naval codes. The British Grand Fleet headed toward the Germans. German dreadnoughts chased British battle cruisers. The Germans were shocked to find themselves facing the British Grand Fleet. In the ensuing Battle of Jutland, the Germans lost a battle cruiser, four light cruisers, five destroyers, and a battleship, and many other German ships were seriously damaged. The British lost three battle cruisers, four armored cruisers, and eight destroyers. Not much to show for the fleet that Kaiser Wilhelm was so proud of.

This was the greatest naval battle of World War I, and many people in Britain were disappointed. They had hoped for another decisive victory like the one that Nelson achieved over Napoleon. But Britain did retain its naval superiority. Among other things, this meant a continued ability to blockade the Germans and impede their ability to get war materials.

STARVING THE GERMANS

As a consequence of the British blockade, there were pervasive shortages in Germany. The military had a hard time acquiring enough saltpeter, needed to make gunpowder, because everybody had assumed the war would be brief.[19]

Historian Gustav Stolper reported, "The effects of the blockade on the quantity and quality of available goods were to prove fatal in the long run. As to quality, the blockade denied Germany access to selected metals, rubber, oil, and certain other raw materials that are indispensable for armament production but which were not found, at least in sufficient quantities, within German territory. As to quantity, the blockade restricted Germany to her own economic resources, from which she was forced to supplement by various economic and financial expedients the even scarcer resources of her allies."[20]

Before the war imports accounted for a third of Germany's food supplies. German farmers depended on imported nitrogenous and phosphatic fertilizers, too. By making it harder for farmers to get these fertilizers, the blockade made it harder for Germans to grow their own food.

Shortages led to higher prices, and the German government responded by imposing price controls that discouraged production. The government followed with production quotas. All this regulation made it harder for farmers and other producers to work. "By 1916," wrote Vincent, "the government's program had collapsed. Heightened resistance, an increase in tension between urban and agrarian communities, food riots, and strikes—these were the result of Germany's plunge into a war for which she was neither administratively nor materially prepared. In 1916 the number of strikes increased to 240, compared to 137 for 1915."

Vincent reported that the German diet "was initially reduced to bread and potatoes. Then, with the failure of the potato crop in 1916, turnips became the principal staple. The impact on the population was notable. Thought and effort were devoted to the location of food. Rather than seek the customary pleasures of life, men and women were forced increasingly to seek the absolute essentials of survival. The days were filled with the labor necessary for purchasing scraps of food; the nights were absorbed with schemes for making the struggle a bit easier.

"Particularly severe was the so-called *Kohlrubenwinter* (turnip winter) of 1916–1917, during which period the collective weight of

the German population plummeted sharply. . . . The bad situation
was accentuated by ration lines. People were forced to waste precious
hours standing in line in an effort to obtain meager food rations. It
was a picture of bureaucracy sunk to its most debased level: despon-
dent people, desperate for food and enfeebled by malnutrition, compelled to wait hours in severely cold weather for their weekly allotment
of an egg (each rationed item had its own line)."[21]

Price controls and shortages of animal fodder led farmers to
slaughter their dairy cows and breeding stock, which resulted in
shortages of milk as well as other dairy products. Cooking became
more difficult because vegetable fats were reserved for manufacturing
propellants and explosives.

Malnutrition meant more disease. Vincent reported, "The
record of the period is replete with cases of tuberculosis, rickets, influenza, dysentery, scurvy, keratomalacia (ulceration of the eye), and
hunger edema. In almost every instance the disease could have been
arrested, and possibly cured, by proper diet. It is also clear, of course,
that an adequate diet would have more frequently prevented such in-
fections in the first place."[22] Altogether, reported historian Martin
Gilbert, some 750,000 German civilians perished as a consequence of
Britain's naval blockade.[23]

By contrast, the Allied Powers didn't have serious food problems. France was mainly an agricultural country, and everybody who
didn't live in the war zone had enough food.[24] Britain, substantially
dependent on imported food, didn't experience shortages until mid-
1917, when Germany's U-boat campaign began to disrupt shipping
significantly.[25]

In Germany, all kinds of things were scarce because of the
blockade. Since the blockade cut off imported cotton, and most fab-
ric was needed for making explosives, there was a severe clothing
shortage. The number of manufactured shoes fell about 90 percent
in 1916 as the armed forces took almost everything that came off assembly lines.[26]

There were many more kinds of shortages. "Lighting became a
significant problem, especially in the winter," noted Vincent, "as
both petroleum and methyl alcohol were completely used up. It was

not unusual for people to stand in ration lines for several hours in total darkness."[27]

THREE-YEAR STALEMATE

By the beginning of 1917, Western Europe had been embroiled in war for three years, but it was deadlocked. The United States was still on the sidelines.

Both the Allied Powers (principally Great Britain, France, Russia, and Italy) and the Central Powers (principally Germany, Austria-Hungary, and Turkey) had substantial resources. Each had military advantages. All had suffered horrendous losses. Neither side was able to achieve decisive victory and dictate surrender terms to the other.

Numerical superiority was no assurance of victory, because both sides had incompetent generals who squandered their resources, especially millions of young men. Great Britain had Douglas Haig, France had Joseph Joffre and Robert-Georges Nivelle, Germany had Erich von Falkenhayn, and Russia had the czar himself, Nicholas II, who spent most of his time on the battlefield rather than governing his country.

Germany's ally Austria-Hungary—the Hapsburg Empire—turned out to be a burden rather than an asset. Austria-Hungary failed to suppress the Serbs, who had provoked the war in the first place. Then Austria-Hungary tried to stop the Russians from advancing and failed at that, too. Austria-Hungary was "saved" by Germany, which took command of subsequent military campaigns involving soldiers from Austria-Hungary. Austria-Hungary was reluctant to be dragged into a war with the Allied Powers, since it didn't have any issues with them.[28]

Moreover, the Central Powers were threatened from within by disgruntled, rebellious nationalities. Magyar nationalists gained the upper hand in Hungary, and Czechs agitated for independence.[29] Historian Martin Gilbert observed that "Germany's troubles with the Poles were mirrored by Turkey's troubles with the Arabs. In the southernmost extremity of the Ottoman Empire, Arab hostility to their Ottoman masters was having its effect. On July 6, T. E. Lawrence was

present when 2,500 Arabs overwhelmed the three hundred Turkish soldiers defending the port of Akaba, at the head of the Red Sea. This
brought Arab forces to within 130 miles of the British front line in
Sinai, where General [Edmund] Allenby was under instructions from
London to reach Jerusalem by the end of the year, despite his predecessor's repeated failure to capture Gaza."[30]

Russia was disintegrating, and more and more Russians wanted
to get out of the war. A settlement with Russia would enable Germany
to move soldiers from the Eastern Front to the west—though Germany would still have to keep about a million soldiers in the east as an
occupying force. This might help the Germans make gains on the
Western Front that had eluded them for three years. The Western Front
had moved back and forth, with neither side able to secure gains.

Military technology contributed to the stalemate. Aviation was
in its infancy. Tanks didn't make their appearance until 1916, and
they didn't become reliable enough to have an impact on the war
until 1917. Thus, for most of the war, a military offensive depended
on soldiers. But they were easily stopped by machine guns. The result
was that neither side was able to improve its position much.

As historian David M. Kennedy explained, "The machine gun
hugely amplified the firepower of stationary forces and thereby con-
ferred nearly insuperable advantages on the defense. Its withering fire
consumed attacking troops wholesale, forcing the fighting on the
Western Front into a grisly deadlock. In the face of such awesome
implements of slaughter, 10 million men perished; another 20 million were maimed."[31]

GERMAN WAR SOCIALISM

World War I was a shock to the German economy. Germany had prospered as a participant in global commerce and accounted for a larger
share of world trade than any other country except Britain. The Germans excelled at producing industrial goods. They imported one-third
of their food and raised funds in capital markets. Suddenly, with the
war and the British naval blockade, Germany was thrown entirely
upon its own resources and what it could draw from its allies—which
wasn't enough.

When the war broke out, the German government tried to raise funds in the United States. It printed Treasury certificates for $175 million, equivalent to about 15 percent of the first war-credit appropriations. The plans were canceled.

Wartime spending soared more than sevenfold from 1914 to 1918, and most of this ended up being financed by higher taxes, domestic borrowing, and money-printing. Currency in circulation was up sixfold.[32]

In desperation, the German government asserted total control over the economy. This was the "Hindenburg Program," otherwise known as war socialism. The government suppressed consumption of anything not considered essential for the war. Rationing began on January 15, 1915, with the introduction of the "bread card," fixing the maximum amount of bread an individual could buy. The wheat content of bread declined during the war, as wheat was replaced with potatoes, turnips, and less desirable substitutes. Meat, milk, butter, and everything else was rationed, too. The trend was toward smaller and smaller rations.

Under war socialism, the government told people what they must do, and this backfired as socialism always does, because it's impossible for bureaucrats to have enough information for running a complex economy. For example, bureaucrats rejected or never considered the deregulation of grain prices, since prices would have gone higher, which would have given farmers incentives to produce more. German grain production fell to about half the prewar level, so incentives were desperately needed. Similarly, bureaucrats decided that pigs competed with people for potatoes, so the number of pigs must be drastically reduced. The result was the "pig massacre." In 1915 it became apparent that bureaucrats had underestimated the potato crop, and there weren't enough pigs to eat the potatoes, so there was spoilage.[33]

On December 5, 1916, the German government issued the law for Patriotic Auxiliary Service—forced labor in the civilian sector. Every German male between seventeen and sixty who wasn't serving in the armed forces was subject to be drafted into the Auxiliary Service. People had to work where they were ordered, and they couldn't change jobs without government permission. People were forbidden to work for businesses not considered essential for the war effort, a reason why many enterprises went out of business.

By enforcing their priorities, bureaucrats disrupted everything else. As historian Paul Kennedy explained, "The announcement of quite fantastic production totals—doubling of explosives output, trebling machine-gun output—led to all sorts of bottlenecks as German industry struggled to meet these demands. It required not only many additional workers, but also a massive infrastructural investment, from new blast furnaces to bridges over the Rhine, which further used up labor and resources. Within a short while, therefore, it became clear that the program could be achieved only if skilled workers were returned from military duty; accordingly, 1.2 million were released in September 1916."[34] That month, too, some 700,000 Belgians were deported to work in German factories.[35] Even this wasn't enough, and in July 1917, an additional 1.7 million German soldiers were released for factory work. "Given the serious losses on the western front, and the still-considerable casualties in the east," Kennedy wrote, "such withdrawals meant that even Germany's large able-bodied male population was being stretched to its limits."[36]

By 1917 the combination of forced labor, worsening working conditions, and shortages led to waves of strikes. The strike movement reached a peak the following year. The government responded by declaring that affected industries were subject to martial law.[37] Nazis later claimed these crises showed that Germans had been "stabbed in the back," when the problem was the British naval blockade and German war socialism.

GERMANY'S BEST BET: UNRESTRICTED SUBMARINE WARFARE

The Germans came to the conclusion that they were doomed if they couldn't end Britain's naval blockade. They were having a harder and harder time maintaining an adequate flow of war materials. German people were starving to death. German diplomats had failed in their efforts to negotiate a peace treaty with France or Russia, which would have taken one of these adversaries out of the war.[38]

German submarines seemed the only hope. Officials realized

that resuming unrestricted submarine warfare would probably bring the United States into the war, but they figured that for all intents and purposes the United States was already against them.

On January 31, 1917, the Germans announced they would resume sinking ships in the war zone around the British Isles. Admiral Henning von Holtzendorff, the head of Germany's naval general staff, predicted that if German submarines could sink 600,000 tons of British shipping per month, in five months Britain would be brought to its knees and forced to surrender.[39] For a while Germany approached or exceeded this target. German submarines sank 540,000 tons of ships in February, 578,000 tons in March, and 874,000 tons in April.[40]

Britain, threatened with a food shortage, adopted a variety of tactics. The British mined areas around German submarine bases, but German minesweepers cleared away enough mines that submarines could continue moving about, sinking Allied shipping. The British had modest success with submarine patrols and submarine nets. Dropping depth charges sank some submarines, and in one case a British dreadnought rammed a German submarine until it sank.[41] The most successful Allied tactic was the convoy, in which merchant ships traveled in groups accompanied by warships, making it more likely that submarines would be detected and their attacks deterred.

Submarine warfare actually backfired on the Germans. Holtzendorff, observed historian Hew Strachan, "had assumed that neutral tonnage would be frightened off the seas. It was not. Freight rates and London's control of the insurance market saw to that. Instead, less was imported into border neutrals for re-export to the Central Powers. In this respect, Germans shot themselves in the foot: the U-boat campaign tightened the Allied blockade. Moreover, Britain's own food supplies were more elastic than Holtzendorff had imagined. Britain imported about 64 per cent of its food in 1914, but it had spare pasture which it could bring into cultivation. Output was promoted rather than retarded. . . . Wheat yields rose 40 per cent between 1914 and 1918, and those of most other foodstuffs were at least constant."[42]

Britain's persistent antisubmarine campaign gradually reduced the number of German submarines—sinking 199 submarines overall.[43] Apparently, too, the Germans were having difficulty maintaining an adequate number of trained submarine crews.

"Behind the scenes," noted historian Paul Kennedy, "the German economy was weakening ominously. Its industrial output was down to 57 percent of the 1913 level. Agriculture was more neglected than ever, and poor weather contributed to the decline in output; the further rise in food prices increased domestic discontents. The overworked rolling stock was by now unable to move anything like the amount of raw materials from the eastern territories that had been planned."[44]

MUTINY AND MASSACRES

By 1917, the Allied Powers had 3.9 million soldiers on the Western Front, compared with Germany's 2.5 million.[45] Recognizing that defenders had the advantages in trench warfare, Ludendorff avoided further attacks.

In February, David Lloyd George, who had become British prime minister following the horrific Battle of the Somme, which brought down the ministry of Herbert Asquith, embraced a scheme for breaking through German lines, hatched by the impetuous French general Nivelle. British soldiers were to be under his command. This was ironic, since Lloyd George distrusted French generals even more than British generals. "We will win it all within twenty-four hours!" Nivelle declared.[46] From his army commanders he demanded an offensive "of violence, of brutality and of rapidity." German field marshal Paul von Hindenburg ordered a tactical retreat to more-defensible terrain near the Aisne River. Nivelle refused to revise his plans and charged ahead on April 16. Within two weeks an estimated 187,000 French soldiers had been killed without securing any of the high ground they had been seeking. Disgusted French survivors mutinied, and French general Pétain made sure that many were shot. Americans were kept in the dark about these mutinies and executions.

In March, German forces withdrew behind the "Hindenburg Line"—trenches heavily protected with barbed wire and concrete "pillboxes" for machine gunners. As they retreated, German soldiers mined roads and poisoned water supplies.

No matter how clever the battle plan, it didn't seem to gain much. British general Herbert Plumer conceived a scheme for driving

Germans away from a ridge near Messines. Plumer had his men dig a system of tunnels underneath German positions—some five miles of tunnels altogether. These were loaded with explosives, and on June 6, 1917, they were detonated. A reported 20,000 German soldiers were killed or injured. "The Germans who still remained alive after the earth fallout were shocked to a gibbering stupor," reported historian S. L. A. Marshall. "The great craters were one hundred yards across and one hundred feet deep." The British had suffered 25,000 casualties, so although the operation was successful, in terms of casualties the British were worse off than before.[47]

On July 12, 1917, the Germans began firing shells with mustard gas at British soldiers, near Ypres, France. "In the next three weeks," Martin Gilbert reported, "the Germans fired a million gas shells, killing five hundred more soldiers and incapacitating several thousand, but they were unable to break through the British lines."[48] Meanwhile, on July 17, the British began firing shells with chloropicrin at the Germans, causing more death and disability.[49]

Although Douglas Haig was no longer in charge of British forces in France, he still had a command, and he persuaded prime minister Lloyd George to approve an attack aimed at dislodging Germans from the Passchendaele village, northeast of Ypres in Flanders. Lloyd George hoped for a victory so that, as Hew Strachan put it, "Britain would not have to defer to American wishes at the peace talks."[50]

The idea was to prepare the way for attacks on German naval bases at Blankenberghe and Ostend, although skeptics pointed out that even if the campaign were successful, it wouldn't hinder German submarines, which could be based elsewhere. Surprise had proven to be an essential part of the few military operations that were successful in this war, but there had been widespread discussion of the attack Haig proposed, so he ended up going against Germans who were well prepared for him.

The attack began on July 31, and soon the soldiers were plagued by rainstorms. Fresh supplies of shells were brought on mules, walking along planks, but when they slipped off, they just disappeared in the mud. Soldiers were often up to their hips in mud. Many drowned in the mud. They were easy targets for German machine gunners, but still Haig insisted that the offensive continue. He never visited the front, and his assistants apparently didn't dare tell him how bad the conditions were. He sent London rosy reports ("highly satisfactory and the losses slight").[51] Lloyd George, increasingly concerned about lives squandered for little or nothing, wanted to avoid further fighting whenever possible, but apparently he didn't have the strength to go against Haig, who insisted that his offensive continue. Finally, on November 6, Canadian soldiers captured what was left of Passchendaele village, and Haig ended the offensive. He had advanced about five miles. He never got near the German naval bases at Blankenberghe or Ostend. There were 70,000 dead British soldiers and 170,000 wounded.[52] German losses, too, were high. This was the last great battle of attrition of the war.

The belligerents remained in the war as long as they did, in part, because of their alliances. Paul Kennedy observed that "France could hardly have kept going after the disastrous Nivelle offensive and the 1917 mutinies, Italy could hardly have avoided collapse after its defeat at Caporetto in 1917, and the Austro-Hungarian Empire could hardly have continued after the dreadful losses of 1916 (or even the 1914 failures in Galicia and Serbia) had not each of them received timely support from its allies."[53]

PLEAS FOR PEACE

Until the end of 1916, in Europe only a few individuals and groups spoke out for peace. But the shocking casualties, hunger, and mutinies undermined support for the war, and it became safe for political leaders to talk about ending the carnage.

Franz Joseph, the Hapsburg emperor of Austria-Hungary, died on November 21, 1916, at eighty-six. His successor was the twenty-nine-year-old Karl I. Foreign minister Graf Ottokar Czernin warned, "If the Monarchs of the Central Powers are not able to conclude peace in the next few months, the people will do so over their heads."[54] Karl's brother-in-law, Prince Sixtus of Bourbon-Parma, secretly told the French they were interested in negotiating peace terms. But the Italians were adamantly against peace at this time, because they were betting on a decisive defeat of Austria-Hungary that would yield some juicy spoils. The French rejected the offer.[55]

On July 6, 1917, Matthias Erzberger, a leader of the Catholic Centre Party in the German Reichstag, urged that the belligerents give up whatever territory they gained, so that a settlement could be negotiated.

German chancellor Theobald von Bethmann-Hollweg advocated a negotiated settlement of the war. On July 19, after the Reichstag was asked to appropriate more money for the German war effort, it tried to impose conditions by passing a resolution for peace—the *Friedenresolution*—by a vote of 212 to 126. Drafted by Erzberger, it said, "The Reichstag strives for a peace of understanding and a lasting reconciliation of peoples. Any violations of territory, and political, economic, and financial persecutions are incompatible with such a peace. The Reichstag rejects any plan which proposes the imposition of economic barriers or the solidification of national hatreds after the war." But this resolution was opposed by Kaiser Wilhelm and the German High Command—Paul von Hindenburg and Erich von Ludendorff.

Pope Benedict XV issued a Peace Note on August 1, in which he called on Germany to withdraw from France, the Allied Powers to withdraw from German colonies, independence to be granted to Serbia and Montenegro, and for all parties to consider territorial issues in a conciliatory frame of mind. But in the 1915 Treaty of London, Italy had staked out rather ambitious territorial claims, so the pope's appeal was disregarded.

On November 29, 1917, the London *Daily Telegraph* published a letter titled "Coordination of Allies' War Aims" by Henry Fitzmaurice, the Fifth Marquess of Lansdowne, a moderate who declared that prolonging the war "would be a crime, differing only in degree from that of the criminals who provoked it." He urged that the Allied Powers declare war aims that would encourage moderate opinion in Germany: "We do not desire the annihilation of Germany as a great power . . . we do not seek to impose upon her people any form of government other than that of their choice . . . we have no desire to deny Germany her place among the great commercial communities of the world . . . we are prepared, when the war is over, to examine, in concert with other powers, the group of international problems, some of them of recent origin, which are connected with the question of 'the freedom of the seas' . . . we are prepared to enter into an international pact under which ample opportunities would be afforded for the settlement of international disputes by peaceful means." Lansdowne noted that Germany's Bethmann-Hollweg had expressed support for the idea in speeches he gave in May and September 1916, as did the Austrian government in its reply to the Papal Peace Note of August 1917, and Austria-Hungary's Czernin in an October 1917 speech, and Arthur James, Lord Balfour, in his January 10, 1917, reply to Wilson's December 1916 Peace Note.[56] But British prime minister David Lloyd George rejected the idea.

British historians have traditionally dismissed Lansdowne's letter as defeatism or appeasement, but the Australian scholar Douglas Newton made a case that it should be viewed as a principled response to the gross mismanagement of the war that led to mindless slaughter.

Serious peace negotiations were delayed because dominant factions on both sides held out hope for a victory. The collapse of the Russian czar gave the Germans reason to believe they could negotiate a separate peace with Russia, thereby weakening the Allied Powers and securing Germany's war aims. The British and French hoped that Wilson would intervene on their side, enabling them to win. The number of war casualties continued to mount, generating more pressure for a negotiated settlement.

3

WHY DID WILSON DECIDE HE MUST BREAK THE STALEMATE?

MUCH HAS BEEN WRITTEN about economic and social forces supposedly driving history, but World War I and its unexpected consequences illustrate the crucial role of individuals. What gave Woodrow Wilson the idea that he could do good by participating in a senseless bloodbath? How did he imagine that he could impose his will on millions of angry, bitter people who lived thousands of miles away? Why squander tens of thousands of American lives when nobody had attacked the United States? How much better might history have turned out if the president of the United States had been someone with more humility?

Wilson was a stubborn, self-righteous man. Historian Margaret MacMillan referred to "his ability, self-deception perhaps, to frame his decisions so that they became not merely necessary, but morally right. Just as American neutrality in the first years of the war had been right for Americans, and indeed for humanity, so the United States' eventual entry into the war became a crusade, against human greed and folly, against Germany and for justice, peace and civilization."[1]

Historians Alexander L. George and Juliette L. George observed, "Once Wilson had emerged with a decision on an issue . . . his mind snapped shut. In such cases, he felt that his decision was the only possible one morally as well as intellectually."[2] They added: "To justify his aggressive treatment of opponents, he needed to regard himself as the best interpreter of the people's true aspirations. His estimate of public opinion became distorted by his need for rationalizing the aggressive tactics through which he sought to impose his will."[3]

Wilson was a distinguished-looking man. John Maynard Keynes observed that "his head and features were finely cut and exactly like his photographs, and the muscles of his neck and the carriage of his head were distinguished."[4] He was tall, with a narrow face. The photographs from his presidential years often show him with pince-nez glasses, a tailcoat, and a black top hat.

Thomas Woodrow Wilson was born the son of an Ohio printer who became a Presbyterian minister, in Staunton, Virginia, December 28, 1856. He attended Davidson, a small Presbyterian college near Charlotte, North Carolina. Then he transferred to the College of New Jersey (later Princeton University), where he participated in the Liberal Debating Club and began to distinguish himself as a public speaker. Although he had thought he would become a minister, he became interested in politics and law. He went on to graduate from the University of Virginia Law School.

He joined classmate Edward Renick to establish a law firm in Atlanta. Apparently he didn't do much to get business, since there wasn't much, if any. After a year of this, he entered Johns Hopkins University to study politics, economics, and history. He earned a Ph.D. in political science.

Wilson began a college teaching career at Bryn Mawr, but he found he wasn't comfortable teaching women. He acknowledged he had a "chilled, scandalized feeling that always comes over me when I see and hear women speak in public."[5]

While at Bryn Mawr, he wrote *Congressional Government* (1885), bemoaning the power of Congress, which at that time dominated the federal government. He thought the British cabinet system held officials to greater accountability and was superior. He overlooked the fact that the most serious threat to liberty was a concentration of political power, and the U.S. Constitution achieved a vital separation of powers. By contrast, the British system combined executive and legislative powers in a single body—Parliament—whose statutes couldn't be overturned by a supreme court. An unpublished manuscript, *The Modern Democratic State*, further expanded his views that the British parliamentary system was ideal.

Wilson left Bryn Mawr after three years to accept a better-paying job teaching history and political science to men at Wesleyan University. In 1890 he accepted a teaching position at Princeton. Because of his lectures and books, he became such a popular figure that when the college needed a new president in 1902, he was selected.

For the first five years, it seemed Wilson could do no wrong. He adopted the tutorial system used at British universities, where young teachers lived in dormitories and provided guidance for undergraduates. Wilson upgraded academic standards.

But arrogance and intolerance doomed his academic career. In 1900—before he became president of Princeton—the board of trustees had authorized Andrew Fleming West to establish a graduate school. West had traveled throughout Europe, studying universities, and he submitted a report, *Proposed Graduate College of Princeton University*. Apparently viewing West as a rival, Wilson stalled development of a graduate school. When, in 1906, the Massachusetts Institute of Technology offered West its top job as president, the Princeton board urged West to stay and develop the graduate school. Without consulting the faculty, Wilson countered by proposing a plan to have undergraduates live in quadrangles, as at Oxford and Cambridge universities. This delayed consideration of West's plan for a graduate school. He was furious, and so was the faculty. Alumni were furious, too, since the quadrangle plan was intended as a blow against Princeton's traditional "eating clubs," which had developed when fraternities were banished. The more opposition there was, the more stubbornly Wilson defended his quadrangle plan. He went on a speaking tour in an effort to secure alumni support, but the quadrangle plan was defeated. Wilson took it badly, and he suffered a breakdown. In his view, those who opposed him were morally wrong, and he lost friends in the battle.

Defeat of the quadrangle plan meant there wasn't any excuse for further delaying the development of a graduate school. Wilson tried to force West out of Princeton, and had responsibility for the graduate school transferred to a faculty committee whose members he would appoint.

In May 1909, soap entrepreneur William Procter offered Princeton $500,000 to build a graduate school at a location some distance from the existing campus, where West would be in charge. Wilson insisted that any graduate school must be part of the existing campus where he was in charge. Wilson warned the board that specifying the location of the graduate school meant Procter was trying to undermine the authority of trustees and the faculty. Nonetheless, Princeton's board of trustees approved Procter's gift for an offsite graduate school.[6] Wilson threatened to quit as president of the college if the Procter gift weren't rejected. When Procter offered to compromise on the location of the graduate school, Wilson countered by citing a copy of West's report, *Proposed Graduate College of Princeton University,* purportedly showing that West's vision was "radically wrong."[7] Wilson claimed West wanted to make the graduate school an exclusive club for rich boys. Historian Arthur S. Link, among Wilson's most ardent defenders, acknowledged that "there was no basis in fact for Wilson's charges . . . the vagaries of his mind . . . are unfathomable."[8]

Wilson went on to deliver tirades against Procter and other generous benefactors: "We should cry out against the few who have raised themselves to dangerous power, who have thrust their cruel hands into the very heartstrings of the many, on whose blood and energy they are subsisting."[9]

Procter eventually withdrew his gift, and Princeton alumni were furious that such a gift had been lost. Princeton's board was split into factions, the bigger of which concluded that Wilson was wrong. The board attempted a compromise in which the graduate school would be built offsite, as West wanted, but he would be relieved of responsibility for the graduate school and given another position at the college. Wilson rejected the idea because West would still be around. Wilson's stubbornness alienated more board members.

Then, on May 18, 1910, Princeton alumnus Isaac Chauncey Wyman died, leaving the college a reported $8 million. The actual amount turned out to be less, but it was still a substantial sum. Wilson was quoted as saying bitterly, "We have beaten the living, but we cannot fight the dead."[10] He recognized that the gift was too big to turn away, and there would be an offsite graduate school. An embittered board asked for his resignation. "A generation later," wrote

Wilson's biographer August Heckscher, "men and women still took sides and raked over with passion the embers of long-dead issues."[11]

Meanwhile, many Democrats were looking for a candidate to get control of the party away from William Jennings Bryan, who had been a presidential candidate three times. The Nebraska-born "Great Commoner" was known for his emotional speeches appealing to small-town folks. *Harper's Weekly* editor George Harvey thought Wilson might be their man, humiliated though he was by the fiascoes at Princeton. As early as 1906, Harvey had suggested that Wilson might someday be president of the United States. Wilson had urged that Bryan be "utterly and once for all thrust out of Democratic counsels."[12] Wilson wrote a railroad executive: "Would that we could do something at once dignified and effective to knock Mr. Bryan once for all into a cocked hat."[13]

New Jersey Democratic party boss James Smith Jr. thought Wilson could begin his political career by running for governor, and he was nominated in September. Wilson claimed he wasn't driven by political ambition. "I have all my life been preaching the duty of educated men to undertake just such service as this, and I did not see how I could avoid it."[14]

Wilson told a group of New Jersey political bosses that if he became governor, he wouldn't have obligations to anybody. Then he indicated he would play the patronage game: "I have always been a believer in party organizations. I should be very glad to consult with the leaders of the Democratic Organization."[15]

Wilson won the election by almost a two-to-one margin. Smith wanted to become a U.S. senator—at that time senators were elected by state legislatures—and he came calling on Wilson for political support. Smith, according to biographer Heckscher, was "worldly wise and genial, moving comfortably in journalistic and financial circles."[16] When Smith had been a U.S. senator from 1893 to 1899, he had been exposed for using insider knowledge for personal gain. Although Wilson owed Smith his nomination to the governorship, Wilson turned on him and posed as an anti-boss reformer. Wilson supported an admittedly unqualified "progressive" named James Martine, so that Smith could be defeated.[17]

"Wilson had no serious objections to the boss system," reported Alexander L. George and Juliette L. George. "His denunciation of it after his nomination can only be construed as an attempt to secure votes by pretending to believe what he knew would enhance his popularity. In either case, he was behaving expediently. He was also behaving expediently when he expressed conservative views at a time he needed conservative support and liberal views when he needed liberal support."[18]

During his first year as governor, Wilson pushed many laws and regulations through the legislature. But during his second year it became apparent that he didn't have any cures for New Jersey's problems. He was a new political personality without new ideas, and his popularity began to fade.

Soon Wilson focused on higher office. His disavowal of political bosses made him seem quite the reformer, and some leading Democrats hoped he would help regain the White House, which Republicans had controlled most of the time since the Civil War. He gave speeches around the country. When William Jennings Bryan gave a lecture at Princeton, the two men became acquainted.

In the fall of 1911, Wilson campaigned with "progressive" Democratic candidates for the state legislature, and they did well in the primaries. Republicans accused Wilson of neglecting state business while he traveled around promoting his presidential prospects, and he snapped that the charges were "absolutely untrue" and "grossly discourteous."[19] Democrats were hammered in the November general elections. Republicans actually regained control of the New Jersey legislature.

That fall Wilson met Edward Mandell House, a Texas businessman who had made money in sugar, cotton, and banking before becoming a backroom operator in state politics. House had gained practical political experience back in 1892 when, at age thirty-four, he'd helped manage the reelection campaign of Texas governor James W. Hogg, who wanted government control of private businesses, especially railroads. Considered the underdog, Hogg was reelected, and he dubbed House "Colonel." He liked to exert influence behind the scenes and served as informal adviser to Hogg and the next three Texas governors.

As House became an influential man in Texas politics, he hoped for an opportunity to play on the national scene, by finding a candidate to replace William Jennings Bryan as Democratic leader. House didn't believe Bryan would ever be elected president. Nor did House seem to expect that Bryan would take his advice. House began writing letters to Woodrow Wilson.

The two men met at Manhattan's Hotel Gotham on November 24, 1911. House convinced Wilson that they agreed on the most important issues, and that House had important political connections. "We found ourselves in agreement upon practically every one of the issues of the day," Wilson exulted. "I never met a man whose thought ran so identically with mine."[20]

House, reported Alexander L. George and Juliette L. George, "was a physically frail man. He was plagued by malaria. Hot weather prostrated him. When summer came, he quite literally fled north, or to Europe, as a matter of physical necessity. He was constitutionally unable to withstand the grueling routine to which the chief executive of this country is subjected. Furthermore, he lacked the physical attractiveness which figures so importantly in the success of popular political leaders. He was a short man. His chin receded. His voice lacked resonance—it was not the voice of a public speaker."[21]

Wilson won the Democratic presidential nomination, and he won the 1912 presidential election, since Republican votes were split between Republican incumbent William Howard Taft and former Republican president Theodore Roosevelt, who ran as a Progressive. House declined Wilson's offer of a cabinet post, so that he could retain his influence over Wilson by serving as an informal adviser. Wilson remarked, "What I like about House is that he is the most self-effacing man that ever lived. All he wants to do is serve the common cause and help me and others."[22]

When trying to persuade Wilson, House appealed to his vanity and sometimes to his place in history. If Wilson didn't like an idea, House dropped it. House indicated his disagreement by saying nothing. He never scolded Wilson when he was wrong. His general strategy: "I nearly always praise at first in order to strengthen the President's confidence in himself which, strangely enough, is often lacking."[23]

House didn't have much, if anything, to do with Wilson's domestic program of new laws and regulations, but he did play a role in
Wilson's foreign policy during World War I. From the beginning,
Wilson was sympathetic with Britain, whose parliamentary government he thought superior to the American constitutional system of
checks and balances. House, too, was pro-Britain.

Wilson named William Jennings Bryan as his secretary of state,
because of Bryan's efforts to win the Democratic presidential nomination for Wilson. Bryan certainly didn't look the part of a statesman.
"With his bald dome, portly build and baggy trousers," observed biographer Robert W. Cherny, "Bryan looked more like a small-town editor than an international diplomat. . . . Even though he served grape
juice and mineral water [instead of wine] at state banquets, his favorite drink was water. Radishes were his favorite snack."[24]

Bryan was a pacifist and a champion of Christian fundamental-
ism. "The Gospel of the Prince of Peace," he declared, "gives us the
only hope that the world has of the substitution of reason for the ar-
bitrament of force in the settlement of international disputes. And
our nation ought not to wait for other nations—it ought to take the
lead and prove its faith in the omnipotence of truth."[25] For years,
Bryan had spoken out against the arms race, and he insisted that
peace would best be preserved through negotiations and treaties.

As secretary of state, Bryan urged the principle that when nations are embroiled in a dispute, they ought to have a one-year "cool-
ing off" period—no war—during which there would be efforts to
resolve the disputes. Some thirty treaties resulted from Bryan's initiatives. Treaties were signed by all the Latin American nations except
Colombia and Mexico, and by most of the European nations. Germany, Austria-Hungary, Japan, and Ottoman Turkey declined.

WILSON'S FIASCO IN MEXICO

While promoting high-minded treaties, Wilson couldn't resist interfering in the affairs of other nations. In 1914 he had U.S forces occupy Nicaragua after a bungled effort to end a civil war. Wilson
gained exclusive canal-building privileges for the United States. The
following year he ordered U.S. forces to establish order in Haiti, and

they were stuck there nineteen years. In 1916 Wilson ordered thousands of U.S. marines to the Dominican Republic in what turned out to be an eight-year occupation. Marines established a centralized military force later used by Dominican politicians to secure their dictatorships. On the upside, U.S. forces enriched Dominican culture by introducing chewing gum and baseball.

Wilson's worst intervention was in Mexico, before he entered World War I. He imagined that with his good intentions he could succeed where local people had failed. By 1910, General José de la Cruz Porfiro Díaz had ruled the country for almost thirty-three years. He ruled in an increasingly arbitrary and corrupt manner, making many enemies.

One man dared to oppose him: thirty-seven-year-old Francisco I. Madero Jr., a big landowner. Historian John Eisenhower described him as "small of stature (five foot two, about a hundred pounds), gentle in personality, and colorless in manner. . . . Balding, with a weak, faltering voice, he had no power over a crowd."[26] Madero did, however, display courage in speaking out against Díaz, for which he had been imprisoned. He escaped, fled to San Antonio, and rallied Mexican dissidents and soldiers, among whom were Venustiano Carranza, Francisco "Pancho" Villa, and Emiliano Zapata. Madero returned to Mexico on November 20, 1910.

In May 1911, after rebels captured the town of Juárez, support for Díaz collapsed, and he fled to Spain. Enthusiastic crowds welcomed Madero to Mexico City in June 1911, and that fall he was elected president. But the goodwill didn't last long. Madero was a weak leader who put his relatives on the government payroll, didn't do much to cultivate his friends, and left many of his political enemies in positions of power. Since he didn't have a following in the military, he relied on associates of Díaz, including general Victoriano Huerta. So Madero's power was undermined. On February 22, 1913, Madero was overthrown in a military coup, then taken to the Lecumberri prison and shot. His vice president, José María Pino Suárez, was shot, too.

A key player behind the scenes was Huerta, who won some victories subduing the country after Díaz was overthrown. Huerta was a crafty, brutal man, and like Díaz he relied on his cronies to run the

government. Although he lived in a modest house, he lavished rewards on his top military commanders, to help maintain their loyalty. He didn't hesitate to have his opponents murdered—among them,
senator Belisario Domínguez, who had publicly criticized Huerta.
When the Mexican Congress began investigating Domínguez's murder, Huerta had his soldiers surround the building, and they arrested
and imprisoned about 100 members of Congress.

Huerta's coming to power provoked more rebellions. A principal
adversary was Venustiano Carranza, a fifty-four-year-old landowner.
He had a big white mustache, a big white beard, and a big potbelly,
and wore blue-tinted sunglasses because of eye problems. Appealing
to Americans, who might be a source of military supplies, he called
himself the "First Chief" of the so-called Constitutionalist movement. Reporting to him were three military leaders: Francisco "Pancho" Villa, Alvaro Obregón, and Pablo González, each of whom had
an army.

Woodrow Wilson, outraged at Huerta for murdering Madero,
believed Carranza should be president of Mexico. Wilson believed
that with Carranza's good intentions and some American soldiers,
Mexico could be fixed. But Carranza was furious that Wilson would
seriously consider sending American soldiers into Mexico.

Carranza, moreover, wasn't the only contender for power. Any
of his military leaders could challenge Carranza as well as Huerta,
since they controlled armies. Foremost among these was Villa, a virtually illiterate military leader who had spent years as a bandit. He
built an army in Chihuahua, the Mexican province bordering New
Mexico and Texas. In one of his more audacious raids, he robbed a
train that was carrying 122 silver bars belonging to the Mexican government. By 1913 he reportedly commanded 700 men. He bought
rifles from an arms merchant in New Mexico, and he captured rifles,
cannon, and ammunition in fights with Mexican government soldiers. One fight netted him some 600 rifles, 150,000 cartridges, and
360 hand grenades.

"Villa never forgot his days as a bandit," John Eisenhower reported, "when a price was affixed to his head. As a result, he never
trusted anyone. He never ate a bit of food unless someone else had
sampled it first. To guard against being shot or stabbed in the middle

of the night, he always slept away from camp. In his comings and goings, he invariably left in one direction and returned from another. A bandit Villa had been, and a bandit he would remain, no matter how accomplished his military exploits and no matter how impressive his titles."[27]

Villa was portrayed as a romantic hero by American journalists, especially the communist John Reed, who was later to romanticize mass murderers in the Soviet Union. Villa caused a firestorm of controversy when he seized the Mexican property of Scottish expatriate William Benton, then had him murdered. Woodrow Wilson called Villa a "high minded and noble citizen of Mexico."[28]

Wilson turned a minor incident in Tampico into a confrontation between the United States and Mexico, resulting in American intervention. On April 9, 1914, eight sailors from the USS *Dolphin,* led by assistant paymaster Charles Copp, took a whaleboat into Tampico for some gasoline. Tampico is a port on the Gulf of Mexico, in the northeastern Mexican state of Tamaulipas. Mexican colonel Ramón Hinojosa believed American sailors had no business being there and ordered their arrest. He soon realized the political complications and released them.

General Morelos Zaragoza arrested Hinojosa and sent an apology to admiral Henry Thomas Mayo, commander of the *Dolphin.* This ought to be have been enough, but Mayo dispatched an officer to see Zaragoza, demanding a formal apology, assurance that those involved (starting with Hinojosa) would be punished, and a twenty-one-gun salute to the *Dolphin.*

Word of the situation was passed all the way up to the heads of each government. Huerta agreed to apologize but balked at the demand for a twenty-one-gun salute. On April 14, Wilson ordered the U.S. Atlantic Fleet to Tampico. Four days later Wilson announced that Huerta must comply with Mayo's request for a twenty-one-gun salute. Then Wilson ordered that U.S. warships stop the *Ypiranga,* a German freighter bound for Veracruz, Mexico, with 500 rapid-fire guns and 15 million rounds of ammunition.

On April 21, American marines landed and began occupying facilities along the half-mile-long Veracruz port area. Wilson had been told there wouldn't be any resistance, but Mexican general Gustavo

Maas was outraged at the American landing and organized resistance. There were twenty-four American casualties the first day. Since Mexican snipers continued to fire at American positions, it was decided that American forces had to move throughout Veracruz to suppress resistance and establish order. This involved searching every house! When marines were finished searching one house, they blasted holes in the wall abutting the next house, then went right in, avoiding Mexican sniper fire on the streets. General Maas was reported to be gathering 16,000 soldiers twenty miles west of Veracruz.

Wilson was shocked when he heard there had been casualties and the conflict had escalated, but he ordered that 5,200 soldiers be sent to occupy Veracruz. An American civilian, Robert J. Kerr, was appointed mayor of Veracruz.

Somewhere along the way, Wilson realized he had approved of an act of war against Mexico. Rather than deal with Mexican president Huerta, Wilson had Secretary of State Bryan contact George C. Carothers, American consul in Chihuahua, where Carranza was based. Carothers managed to see Carranza, but Carranza refused to discuss the situation. He issued a written statement denouncing the American invasion that would "drag Mexico into an unequal war."[29]

Huerta tried to make the most of the situation. He protested Wilson's outrages against the national honor of Mexico, and he leaked to the press stories suggesting that Mexico might be going to war. Huerta broke off diplomatic relations with the United States. U.S. interests in Mexico were to be handled by Brazil. Huerta's official statements didn't indicate what else he planned to do.

Wilson ordered an embargo on arms shipments to Mexico. Apparently he didn't realize the embargo would affect only Carranza and Villa, since there was already an embargo against Huerta.

Throughout Latin America, there was anger at Wilson's interventionism. Anti-American demonstrations were reported in Chile, Costa Rica, Guatemala, Uruguay, and other countries. There was rioting in Baja California, prompting the government to dispatch the USS *Cheyenne* to protect American interests there.

Ambassadors from Argentina, Brazil, and Chile—the "ABC representatives"—proposed to help mediate a settlement between the United States and Mexico, and Wilson agreed. A conference began at Niagara Falls, Canada, May 20. But Wilson insisted no settlement would be acceptable if it failed to provide for the ouster of Huerta. Wilson demanded "an orderly and righteous government in Mexico."[30]

Wilson assumed that Huerta's departure would bring peace to Mexico, probably because he was unaware that Carranza and Villa were rivals. Villa's succession of military victories made him a power to reckon with, and Carranza referred disparagingly to the "hypocritical bandit Villa."[31] Villa resigned as a general in the Constitutionalist movement, and his officers decided to follow him rather than go with Carranza.

Yet another rival was Emiliano Zapata, an illiterate but highly skilled military commander from the state of Morelos. Newspapers referred to him as "the modern Attila."[32] His father had lost his small farm because of Porfirio Díaz, and Zapata was determined to avenge small farmers. He blamed Francisco Madero for failing to help them. He didn't think Carranza was much good, either. Zapata was a daring military commander who dominated his region of Mexico.

In any case, Carranza continued to denounce Wilson's relentless meddling in Mexican affairs. Thwarted by Wilson, the ABC negotiations failed to produce a settlement. U.S. congressmen, American journalists, Americans living in Mexico, British interests, and others were urging that Wilson expand the war.

Although Carranza's rivals were gaining power, it was one of his loyal commanders, Alvaro Obregón, who finally brought about Huerta's downfall. At the Battle of Orendáin, on July 8, 1914, Obregón crushed Huerta's forces—they suffered some 2,000 casualties. Obregón captured eighteen military trains and thirty locomotives, crucial for moving military forces around the country. He was in position to strike Mexico City. Huerta resigned July 15, secretly got on a train for Puerto México, then boarded the German cruiser *Dresden,* bound for exile in Spain.

The presidency was offered to Carranza, but there wasn't any stability. He struggled to hang on, while Villa, Obregón, and Zapata maneuvered to seize power. Villa and Zapata met in Mexico City and discussed how they might split power in Mexico if and when

Carranza was overthrown. They participated in a joint parade through Mexico City—about 50,000 men altogether.

Meanwhile, U.S. Army brigadier general Frederick Funston became military governor of Veracruz, and he adopted measures to improve the public health situation, which was a threat to American soldiers as well as Mexicans. He regulated prostitution and reduced the incidence of venereal disease, instituted a program for the prevention of yellow fever, and cleaned up the New Market, where contaminated food was a huge problem. "The urinals were used as repositories for cigarette butts and other trash," wrote John Eisenhower. "Animals wandered through the open markets at will. Food on display often attracted a thick black coat of flies." He cited a report that the floors were covered with "dried blood, fish scales, chicken feathers, entrails, putrid produce, and excrement."[33] The death rate from disease among Mexicans dropped an estimated 25 percent in three months. Carranza wanted to make Veracruz his base, so he declared an amnesty for Mexicans who had worked with Funston's occupation force there. The Americans left on November 13, 1914, and Mexico's public health situation soon was as bad as it had been before.

Zapata occupied Mexico City, Villa occupied the surrounding area, and together they launched a reign of terror against political opponents. Villa subsequently left to subdue the northern region of Mexico, while Zapata occupied the south. General Obregón moved into Mexico City and stripped it of factory machinery, cars, horses, hospital beds, and anything else that might be of value, all of which was shipped to Carranza in Veracruz.

In the largest North American land battle since the U.S. Civil War, Villa and Obregón fought the Battle of Celaya. Villa lost some 9,000 men, mostly in suicidal charges against Obregón's defensive positions, which, modeled after those on the Western Front, were fortified with barbed wire and machine guns.

Wilson announced that if Mexicans couldn't end the bloodshed, he would have to "decide what means should be employed by the United States in order to help Mexico save itself."[34] Wilson extended diplomatic recognition to Carranza's regime and declared an arms embargo against everyone in Mexico except Carranza.

Villa was outraged at Wilson for helping Carranza, and he contributed to escalating violence along the border between the United
States and Mexico. After Villa raided Columbus, New Mexico, in
March 1916, Wilson demanded that Carranza capture Villa. Wilson
decided he had to intervene, and much of the U.S. Army was assembled for an expedition aimed at capturing him.

The force, dubbed the "Punitive Expedition," was headed by
fifty-five-year-old brigadier general John J. Pershing, who had gradu-
ated from West Point (1886) and fought at the Battle of Wounded
Knee (1890, the last battle of the Indian wars) and in the Spanish-
American War (1898). His wife and three daughters died in a 1915
house fire, and he focused all his energies on his mission in Mexico.

Wilson's assumptions about Mexico were wrong. He assumed
Carranza would cooperate and approve having U.S. men and war
materials moved on Mexico's Northwestern Railway—at a time of
strong anti-American feeling. He assumed the Mexican people
would assist efforts to capture Villa, their folk hero.

On March 6, 1916, Pershing led some 10,000 men into Mexico
without any idea where Villa might be. He began looking in the region west of Chihuahua City, rugged terrain about 100 miles wide
and 500 miles long. Communication was difficult. Transporting
men, food, and weapons was difficult. The U.S. Army didn't have
many trucks. Roads were rough, and sometimes what appeared on a
map to be roads were little more than trails. One train had a wood
burner that didn't work, and the boxcars had holes in the floors
where hoboes had built fires. Another train loaded with soldiers ran
out of wood, then ran out of water in the middle of nowhere, and
when eventually replenished it turned out that the engine couldn't
pull the train up a grade.

Carranza demanded that American forces leave Mexico, and
Pershing countered that Wilson hadn't put any restrictions on how
far he might go into the country. On June 18, Wilson ordered a mobilization of the national guard—eventually, some 100,000 men. Three
days later American forces were humiliated at Carrizal. It was a very
small battle compared to what was happening in Europe, but it was
enough to make clear that the quest for Villa was a futile crusade,

and the more serious concern was to prevent Pershing's men from being massacred. Pershing acknowledged he was unable to deal with the bandits in a single Mexican state, Chihuahua.

Yet Pershing's forces remained in Mexico for another seven months. It wasn't until February 5, 1917, that Pershing's men crossed the border back into New Mexico. The Punitive Expedition was a fiasco from start to finish. It failed at its announced purpose, to find Villa. It did nothing to fulfill Wilson's goal of giving Mexico a responsible and just government. No surprise that Carranza did little to fulfill the reforms he promised. In 1920, when Carranza tried to force the election of his preferred successor, Ignacio Bonillas, Obregón led a successful rebellion, and Carranza was murdered. Three years later Villa was assassinated. None of this did the United States any good, since Wilson had poisoned relations between the two countries.

WILSON'S PHONY NEUTRALITY

Although Wilson's intervention in Mexico brought nothing but trouble, he had the arrogance to insist he could do good by intervening in the vastly more complicated and deadly European war. With some humility, Wilson might have realized that if the U.S. Army couldn't catch a Mexican bandit, it was probably going to have difficulty trying to "make the world safe for democracy."

Wilson, spurred on by his rapidly pro-British ambassador Walter Hines Page and by Colonel House, went along with Britain's naval blockade—a blatant disregard for international law.

"Simultaneously," reported historian Thomas Fleming, "the United States did little while the British navy slowly but steadily expanded the meaning of the word contraband (of war) until the definition included almost every imaginable article produced by farmers or industrialists. Cotton shipped to Germany had to be unloaded in New York and x-rayed, bale by bale, at the shipper's expense to make sure it did not carry concealed contraband. A few months later, cotton itself became contraband. American exporters and companies that did business with the English were ordered to form trade associations that solemnly promised to sell nothing to Germany or Austria. Finally, in July 1916, the British published a blacklist of 87 American and 350 South American companies that were trading with Berlin and Vienna."[35] Wilson had no public comment about the British blacklist.

Germany announced that after February 18, 1915, it would counter Britain's naval blockade by having submarines sink ships in a war zone around Britain. Germany followed this with a warning that after March 1915, its submarines would sink armed merchant ships on sight. The sinking of the *Sussex,* a French steamer that went back and forth across the English Channel, involved the deaths of two Americans. Secretary of State William Jennings Bryan urged that Americans be prohibited from traveling in a war zone, since more loss of life might convince more Americans that they should enter the war to avenge the deaths—and end up with far more people killed. Wilson could have taken a similar position, since he had told some 50,000 Americans in Mexico that because of the civil war they stayed at their own risk.[36] Instead, Wilson criticized Germany, while remaining silent about Britain's hunger blockade.

"I cannot understand his attitude," Bryan fumed.[37] In an April 6, 1915, note, Bryan told Wilson the key issue was "whether an American citizen can, by putting his business above his regard for his country, assume for his advantage unnecessary risks and thus involve his country in international complications. Are the rights and obligations of citizenship so one-sided that the Government which represents all the people must bring the whole population into difficulty because a citizen, instead of regarding his country's interests, thinks only of himself?" Wilson didn't respond.

Bryan wrote Wilson again on April 7: "I cannot help feeling that it would be a sacrifice of the interests of all the people to allow one man acting purely for himself and his own interests, and without consulting his government, to involve the entire nation in difficulty when he has ample warning of the risks which he has assumed." Bryan advised Wilson of State Department reports that Britain had started arming its merchant ships, making them ships of war. Still no response from Wilson.

On April 8, Bryan sent yet another note, asking, "What claim can this Government rightfully make for unintended loss which ordinary diligence would have avoided?" The United States Neutrality Board reported that according to international law, if new methods of warfare didn't threaten the United States, it wasn't obliged to do anything about them.

Bryan followed up to Wilson on April 19: "Why be shocked at the drowning of a few people if there is to be no objection to starving a nation [by Britain's naval blockade]?" This note, like Bryan's previous notes, went unanswered.

Finally, on April 22, Wilson sent Bryan a note he intended to send to Germany. Wilson insisted that Americans had the right to travel anywhere including a war zone, and submarines must observe traditional rules applying to surface ships—they must surface to notify ships that they were targets. But, as had already become clear, such practices made the submarines themselves easy targets for ramming or depth charges, which is why the rules had been abandoned. Wilson told Bryan that he took the position he did "in the interests of mankind."

Bryan replied, "If we admit the right of the submarine to attack merchantmen but condemn their particular act or class of acts as inhuman we will be embarrassed by the fact that we have not protested against Great Britain's defense of the right to prevent foods reaching non-combatant enemies. . . . Our people will, I believe, be slow to admit the right of a citizen to involve his country in war when by exercising ordinary care he could have avoided danger."

On May 9, appearing more openly as a British ally, Colonel House urged Wilson to step up his demands for Germany to abandon submarine warfare. "America has come to the parting of the ways," he wrote, "when she must determine whether she stands for civilized or uncivilized warfare. We can no longer remain neutral spectators."

After the *Lusitania* was sunk by a German submarine on May 15, Wilson issued a protest affirming his belief that Americans were right to travel on a belligerent ship in a war zone.

William Jennings Bryan's valiant efforts to keep America out of the war marked the high point of his political career. Under increasing pressure to march into war with Wilson, Bryan resigned as secretary of state on June 9. He was savaged in the press. *New York Evening Post* editor Oswald Garrison Villard observed that "never did a greater storm of abuse and vituperation burst upon a public man."

Bryan was succeeded by Robert Lansing, whom Wilson had appointed as a State Department lawyer. Lansing told Wilson what he wanted to hear, that a "state of war" with Germany would increase "our usefulness in the restoration of peace."

WILSON POSES AS PEACEMAKER

In the fall of 1915, Britain's foreign secretary, Edward Grey, contacted House, saying Britain would welcome American efforts to help secure peace. House specified two conditions: Belgium must regain its independence, and France must regain its prewar territory. House didn't say anything about Britain's naval blockade of Germany. If one of the belligerents rejected these terms, then the United States would ally with the other belligerent. Since the conditions House specified would have been acceptable to Britain and unacceptable to Germany, this was a crude way of establishing an open alliance with Britain. House had already assured British and French officials that the United States wouldn't permit their countries to be defeated.

In 1916, Jules Jusserand, the French ambassador to the United States, was opposed to peace initiatives. He was quoted as saying, "France wanted a real peace and not a breathing-spell for Germany."[38]

According to Heckscher, "Wilson was puzzled by so strong a stand by the leaders of countries that were paying an agonizing price in men and national wealth for each day's continuance of the conflict. Inevitably the ugly question arose of what the Allies were really fighting for, beyond the restoration of Belgium and arrangements to assure the future safety of France. What unspoken war aims justified the slaughter of trench warfare, the mowing down of a whole generation of the nations' youth?"[39]

On May 27, 1916, Wilson delivered a speech before the League to Enforce Peace. He made a general appeal for peace. Apparently the British and French didn't like it. They hoped to win the war.

Meanwhile, the British had been provocative. They seized mail from neutral ships. They pursued their blacklist. Much more serious, the British were suppressing the revolts in Ireland. A number of rebels, including Roger Casement, were executed. Wilson, to his credit, dispatched a protest note to the British.

Despite everything, American public opinion still favored staying out of the European war. In the 1916 presidential campaign, Wilson found it necessary to run on the slogan "He kept us out of war."
Had it not been for prevailing antiwar views, supported by Bryan
and many others, Wilson probably would have been able to maneuver the United States into the war as early as 1915.

After Wilson was reelected, Germany proposed a peace conference. The British and French were against the idea, since it would
probably mean accepting German occupation of Belgium and northeastern France.

Wilson drafted a peace note, hoping he could persuade the belligerents to rise above their desire for vengeance and offer generous
settlement terms. The German foreign secretary offered to discuss
peace at a neutral location. Britain's Minister of Blockade, Lord
Robert Cecil, declared that failing to defeat Germany "would leave
the world at the mercy of the most arrogant and the bloodiest
tyranny that had ever been organized."[40]

On January 22, 1917, Wilson addressed the U.S. Senate. He reported the responses to his peace note as encouraging news, and he
urged a "peace without victory." This was the last thing the British,
French, or Germans wanted, since their respective politicians were
under intense pressure to show that millions of their countrymen
hadn't died in vain.

Wilson talked about freedom of the seas, which the British certainly wouldn't accept. The British based their national security on
the superiority of their navy, and they wouldn't accept any limits on
the prerogatives of their naval forces.

British and French officials rejected peace negotiations before
they had won the war. Yet they were under increasing pressure from
their people who suffered from food shortages and lost loved ones.
The British were virtually broke.

Austrian foreign minister Czernin contacted Wilson and expressed his desire for peace negotiations—provided the Austro-
Hungarian Empire remained intact.

No Moral Case for Intervention

It was curious how Wilson could imagine himself making the world safe for democracy by allying with Britain and France, since both nations were determined to hold on to their colonial empires. France had rapidly expanded its colonial holdings since 1870, in Africa and East Asia. The French had a reputation for brutal colonial rule.[41] In terms of global extent, the British Empire was unmatched in human history, with a presence in Africa, Asia, and the Middle East. During World War I, Britain was trying to suppress the Irish struggle for independence.

The most brutal colonial rulers were the Belgians—British and French allies—who murdered perhaps 8 million people in the Congo,[42] a colony personally owned by Belgium's King Leopold II. The death toll has been estimated as high as 10 million.[43] Most of the murders occurred between 1890 and 1910. Leopold ordered that officials continuously conduct ivory raids, shooting elephants, seizing or buying (for a few trinkets) ivory to be shipped back to Europe. Ivory was carried by slave porters from the interior to the seaports, and very few of these people survived for long. They walked barefoot, with chains around their necks. The porters were often guarded by black men who themselves were slaves, and these guards, in turn, were controlled by Belgian soldiers.

Belgian murders in the Congo accelerated with the growing demand for rubber, used to make bicycle and car tires. African rubber was made from the sap of a vine that flourished in the Congo. By the late 1890s, Leopold was collecting more revenue from rubber than from ivory. He had soldiers go from village to village seizing hostages who might be returned when local people gathered enough rubber. Sometimes the Belgians paid for rubber by giving village chiefs captives who could be eaten or used as slaves.[44] When the Belgians encountered resistance, they shot everyone they could find in a village and cut off the victims' right hands as a signature. Occasionally ears and noses were cut off, but right hands were favored. They were smoked, gathered in baskets, and delivered to Belgian inspectors.[45] Leopold spent much of his blood money building palaces, parks, and monuments around Belgium.

During the two world wars, particularly World War II, Germany gained a reputation as a dangerous aggressor, yet before World War I it didn't have an empire like those of Britain or France, or a murder record like Belgium's. To be sure, during the late nineteenth century, the insidious trends toward socialism, nationalism, and collectivism gathered momentum in Germany as well as other countries. The major European countries were all in a race for more armaments and bigger navies. Germany's braggart-king, Kaiser Wilhelm II, dreamed of building a colonial empire.

For perspective, it's worth remembering that Germany, like Britain and France, had nurtured ideas on liberty. Germany had been the land of Wolfgang von Goethe and Friedrich Schiller, authors who had been great champions of liberty. Schiller's plays—the most famous of which was *Wilhelm Tell,* about the assassination of a tyrant—were banned by Napoleon and later would be banned by Hitler.

Germans had made many important contributions to civilization. They achieved advances in science, technology, and medicine. Germans gave us kindergartens, universities, language schools, beer, hamburgers, frankfurters, German chocolate cake, and Christmas trees.[46] Life in the United States has been immensely enriched by German immigrants who challenged the puritanical suspicion of having fun. "One of the most important social changes wrought by German immigrants was their promotion of numerous forms of innocent public family entertainment," explained Thomas Sowell. "Music, picnics, dancing, card playing, swimming, bowling, and other physical activities were among the American pastimes, now taken for granted, but introduced or promoted by Germans in the nineteenth century. The Germans organized marching bands, symphony orchestras, and singing groups of all sorts."[47] Americans of German ancestry included food entrepreneur Henry Heinz, petroleum entrepreneur John D. Rockefeller, and department store pioneer John Wanamaker, all of whom had humble beginnings. Among other notable German-Americans: baseball legends Babe Ruth and Lou Gehrig, engineer John Augustus Roebling, who helped build the Brooklyn Bridge, and Henry Engelhard Steinway, who became famous for his pianos. Woodrow Wilson disparaged such individuals as "hyphenated Americans."[48]

Historian Walter Laqueur offered this perspective: "Germany was certainly not a free country by West European or American standards, but it is useful to recall from time to time that there are degrees of oppression. It was no cruel dictatorship; there was a constitution and there were laws which had to be observed by rulers as well as ruled. In comparison with the dictatorships that were to emerge in Europe after the war, Wilhelmian Germany was a permissive country to an almost bewildering degree. Political murders were unknown, as was arrest and trial without due process of law. The Emperor himself was openly criticized in the press . . . and if an officer assaulted a civilian, as had happened in the little Alsatian town of Zabern, this became a *cause célèbre* all over Germany. Workers on strike were not shot, censorship was applied only in extreme cases of *lèse-majesté* and blasphemy, and it is doubtful whether justice could have been flagrantly perverted as in the Dreyfus case [in France]."[49]

None of the belligerents had clean hands, so it just wasn't possible to make a credible moral case for American intervention. If Wilson backed the British, French, and Belgians, he would have enabled them to seek vengeance against the Germans and protect their empires in Africa, Asia, and the Middle East. If Wilson backed the Germans, he would have enabled them to build an empire and seek vengeance against their adversaries.

Europeans had been fighting one another for thousands of years, and they were determined to continue fighting. There was much wisdom in the traditional American policy that Wilson ignored: namely, stay out of other people's wars.

WILSON GOES TO WAR AGAIN

Peace initiatives collapsed after the Germans announced that they would be resuming unrestricted submarine warfare. They anticipated that the United States would soon be entering the war, and unrestricted submarine warfare seemed to be their best hope for defeating Britain and France before American soldiers arrived in Europe.

On February 28, 1917, Wilson went public with the "Zimmermann telegram," in which Germany's foreign minister, Arthur Zimmermann, suggested to the German ambassador in Mexico City that in the event the United States entered the war against Germany, Mexico and Japan ought to consider allying with Germany. The American public was outraged, and many people declared that it was time for the United States to fight Germany. Wilson broke diplomatic relations with Germany.

Although Zimmermann made a diplomatic blunder, Germany didn't have the means to attack the United States. The British naval blockade generally kept German naval ships confined to their ports. As historian Hew Strachan observed, "If its High Seas Fleet responded to the challenge to break the blockade by taking on Britain's Grand Fleet in a major battle, it would lose."[50]

Mexico, of course, was going through a revolution, and its president, Venustiano Carranza, was struggling to retain his power against rebels. Mexico certainly wasn't in any position to threaten the United States.

It isn't known what Wilson was thinking between March 4 and April 2, 1917. "It may be," Heckscher wrote, "he came to the conclusion that the United States had to enter the war. . . . He maintained up to March 21 an impenetrable façade."[51]

Wilson called a cabinet meeting for March 20. "After some preliminaries," wrote Heckscher, "the President put two questions to his official family. Should he summon the Congress in extraordinary session? If so, what precisely should he put before it? Treasury Secretary William Gibbs, McAdoo and Houston were in favor of a declaration of war at the earliest possible moment. Redfield had always been strongly pro-Ally and was now for immediate engagement. Baker 'with wonderful clearness' argued for a declaration of war accompanied by rapid buildup of the armed forces. Lansing recorded his own comments, solemnly and at length; no one was surprised that he believed the United States should range itself on the Allied side."

According to Heckscher, Wilson continued to poll his advisers. " 'Well, Daniels?' the President inquired at last. Pacifist by disposition, a friend of Bryan's, no one believed Daniels could bring himself to agree with the majority. He 'hesitated a moment,' Lansing records, 'then spoke with a voice which was low and trembled with emotion. His eyes were filled with tears.' He saw no other course, Daniels declared, than to enter the war. Did he speak with conviction or from lack of strength of mind? Lansing wondered in an aside: 'I prefer to believe the former reason, though I am not sure.' (It is a rather typical Lansing remark, exhibiting his own virtue while casting subtle doubt upon that of another.) In his record of these events Daniels admits the challenge to have been 'a supreme moment' in his life. He had hoped and prayed 'this cup would pass'—'But there was no other course opened.'

"'Everybody has spoken but you, Lane,' the President continued, as calmly as if here conducting a Socratic dialogue. Lane favored war, expressing great indignation against the Germans. Thus the opinion of the cabinet was unanimous both in regard to calling an extraordinary session of the Congress and declaring war. 'Well, gentlemen,' said the President in a cool, unemotional way, 'I think that there is no doubt as to what your advice is. I thank you.' The meeting was over. The cabinet members passed silent and expressionless through the phalanx of waiting reporters. As to what was the President's decision, no one of his advisors knew."

Heckscher described the calm before the storm: "Early the next morning Wilson dictated a statement that he was calling the Congress into extraordinary session on April 2 for the purpose of receiving 'a communication concerning grave matters of national policy.' Then he and Grayson left the White House for a game of golf. The weather was bad and they did not play, but a long motor ride provided a substitute form of relaxation. The days that followed had an air of suspended reality. The president's desk, noted Thomas W. Brahany of the White House staff, was piled high with letters and papers. 'Apparently he is not in a working mood these days. He spends nearly all his time with Mrs. Wilson, reading, playing pool or visiting.' Brahany's description fits a man who is coming to a grave decision or who, having made one, invites his soul while the details of life take care of themselves."[52]

By March 28, Wilson had begun outlining and drafting the address he would give to Congress. He was still at work a week later. He didn't share his thoughts with cabinet members, even in the last cabinet meeting before the extraordinary session of Congress.

On April 2, around 8:30 P.M., Wilson left the White House for

Capitol Hill. "Having mounted the rostrum," Heckscher wrote, "with one arm resting upon it, Wilson began to read without ostensible emotion, but as he progressed the vibrancy of his voice increased and the marshaled sentences sounded out across the expectant hall, beautifully cadenced, complex and subtly rounded."[53]

His speech was loaded with glittering generalities. "The world must be made safe for democracy," he declared. He didn't explain how this was to be done by allying with the British Empire, which had colonies around the world; with France, which had colonies in Africa and Asia; and with Russia, which was ruled by a czar.

Wilson returned to the White House by nine-thirty. He spent time in the Oval Office with his wife, Edith, his daughter, Margaret, and Colonel House. Congress declared war on April 8, 1917.

A month later, on May 28, Wilson issued a proclamation accompanying his bill to establish military conscription. All young men between twenty-one and thirty years old had to register for conscription, and anyone who refused to appear when summoned was subject to imprisonment. Wilson tried to downplay the fact that military conscription was a form of involuntary servitude—slavery—by offering a fatuous claim that "it is in no sense a conscription of the unwilling; it is, rather, selection from a nation which has volunteered in mass."

WHY DID WILSON DO IT?

Clearly, Wilson didn't enter the war to defend the United States, because it wasn't under attack. Nor was it about to be attacked.

The Americans who were most at risk were those venturing into the war zone, with full knowledge of what they were doing. If the United States had maintained a truly neutral position, rather than providing covert support for the British and French, it's quite possible German submarines would have been careful to leave American ships alone. Blockaded by the British, starving Germans needed all the help they could get. In any case, the number of Americans lost because of German submarines would have been far less than the 116,516 young men with the American Expeditionary Force who died on French battlefields, where millions of European soldiers had already died.

If peace was what Wilson wanted, he should have stayed out of the war. But he would have needed humility to recognize that he could only try to control what the United States did. He couldn't possibly control what other people did, especially considering the deep hatreds that had intensified during the war.

Consumed by ambition to be a world statesman, Wilson was simply pursuing his self-interest as a politician. He had dreams of glory, telling other people what to do at the peace settlement. What other people actually did at the peace settlement, of course, would be another matter, but Wilson doesn't seem to have thought much about that. For him to participate in the settlement, the United States had to join the war. Wilson seems to have made his decision, probably the most fateful decision of the twentieth century, without seriously considering the possible consequences.

4

WHY DID WILSON PRESSURE AND BRIBE THE RUSSIAN PROVISIONAL GOVERNMENT TO STAY IN THE WAR?

THE BRITISH AND FRENCH were anxious to keep Russia in the war, and Wilson added his voice to theirs, so that German soldiers would be engaged on the Eastern Front. If the Russians ever negotiated peace with the Germans, German divisions would be transferred to the Western Front, making things tougher for the Allies.

In January 1917, Allied representatives gathered in Petrograd to discuss war strategy. French minister of colonies Gaston Doumergue, together with the British representatives, Alfred Milner and Henry Wilson, urged the Russians to expand their role in the war and to better coordinate their efforts.

In Washington, President Wilson was oblivious of the Russian situation. Diplomat and historian George F. Kennan noted that Wilson "was a man who had never had any particular interest in, or knowledge of, Russian affairs. He had never been in Russia. There is no indication that the dark and violent history of that country had ever occupied his attention."[1]

Apparently Wilson, who fancied himself a champion of democracy, didn't ask how the Russian people were affected by the war. Kennan explained: "It is difficult to see what stake the common people of Russia ever did have in the outcome of the war. A Russian victory would presumably have meant the establishment of Russia on the Dardanelles. For this, the Russian peasant could not have cared less. A German victory would obviously have affected the prestige of the Tsar's government. It might have led to limited territorial changes, and to some German commercial penetration. That any of this would have affected adversely the situation of the Russian peasant is not at all clear."[2]

When Wilson delivered his April 2, 1917, "War Message" to Congress, a few weeks after the Russian Revolution, he exulted that "the great, generous Russian people have been added in all their naïve majesty and might to the forces that are fighting for freedom in the world, for justice, and for peace." Wilson was referring to millions of conscripted Russian peasants who would rather go home.

By this time, Kennan reported, "not only had Russia become involved in a great internal political crisis, but she had lost in the process her real ability to make war. The internal crisis was of such gravity that there was no chance for a healthy and constructive solution to it unless the war effort could be terminated at once and the attention and resources of the country concentrated on domestic issues. The army was tired. The country was tired. People had no further stomach for war. To try to drive them to it was to provide grist to the mill of the agitator and the fanatic: the last people one would have wished to encourage at such a dangerous moment."[3]

WILSON'S IGNORANCE ABOUT RUSSIA

What gave Wilson the idea that Russia could continue enduring the stresses of war? Russia's wartime experiences revealed the weaknesses, not the strengths, of the regime.

Historian Richard Pipes cited "the loss of prestige of the tsarist government due to a series of military and diplomatic humiliations which Russia has suffered since the Crimean War. . . . This very negatively affected popular attitudes towards the regime. Because it maintained itself essentially by force, if tsarism was unable to defeat foreign powers, then there surely was something wrong with it."[4]

The Crimean War was the most important European war between the end of the Napoleonic Wars (1815) and the outbreak of World War I (1914). Five European powers were involved directly or indirectly. There was fighting in the Baltic Sea and Wallachia/Moldavia (modern-day Romania), but the most decisive battles were around the Black Sea.

The Crimean War began in 1853 as a dispute between France and Russia about the privileges of Roman Catholic versus Russian Orthodox churches in Palestine (then controlled by the Ottoman Turks). Czar Nicholas I demanded to be the protector of Russian Orthodox churches throughout the Ottoman Empire, an idea opposed by both the French and the British. Moreover, the czar disputed the Ottoman Empire's control of the Bosporus and Dardanelles, narrow waterways through which ships had to pass if they were to enter or leave the Black Sea. The czar wanted his ships to pass freely through these waterways. The Ottoman Empire declared war against Russia in October.

As has happened so often, the participants underestimated the horrors of war. Historian Trevor Royle described Russian lines: "Rudimentary landmines exploded beneath their feet while shrapnel and grapeshot thinned their ranks. Still they stumbled on; some managed to engage the enemy with the bayonet; others fell like ninepins before the weight of the artillery fire. Smoke enveloped the battlefield, adding to the confusion, and wounded men screamed for mercy from God or help from their mothers, anything to gain release from the hell in which they found themselves."[5]

The Russians had some success, destroying the Ottoman fleet at Sinop (on the southern coast of the Black Sea) on November 30. But when Britain and France came to the defense of the Ottomans, the Russians were routed. British and French soldiers landed on the Crimean peninsula, along the northern shore of the Black Sea, and in 1855 they seized Sevastopol, where the Russian fleet was based. The Russians had to sink their ships so they wouldn't fall into enemy hands. The czar's forces occupied the Ottoman city of Kars. Nicholas I, blamed for his meddling and incompetence, died on March 2, during the final phase of the war. In the peace negotiations, his successor, Alexander II, agreed to withdraw Russian forces from Kars so he could regain Sevastopol.

While both sides displayed plenty of incompetence, the Crimean War certainly highlighted Russia's weaknesses. Historian W. Bruce Lincoln cited "Russia's continuing financial crisis, her economic backwardness and underdeveloped industry, her inefficient bureaucracy, and underlying all of these problems, the antiquated institution of serfdom."[6] More than 250,000 Russians died during the war, from wounds or disease.

The Crimean War made a pacifist of author Leo Tolstoy, who served as a second lieutenant in the Russian army besieged at Sevastopol. Drawing on his observations, he wrote three pieces, gathered together as *The Sevastopol Sketches*. The first ("Sevastopol in December") expressed patriotism. By the time he began writing his third piece ("Sevastopol in August 1855"), he had become thoroughly disillusioned with the stupidity of the war. Sevastopol was "entirely saturated in blood; the place which for eleven months [Russian soldiers] had held against an enemy twice as powerful, and which [they] had now been instructed to abandon without a struggle. The first reaction of every Russian soldier on hearing this order was one of bitterness and incomprehension."[7]

A half-century later, another czar, Nicholas II, became embroiled in a disastrous war. He didn't cut an impressive figure. Of average height and solidly built, he always dressed in a khaki uniform. He had gray eyes and a reddish mustache.[8] Nicholas doesn't seem to have been a reflective man—he kept a diary for thirty-six years, but all it recorded were daily events, no thoughts or opinions.[9] Historian Barbara Tuchman described him as "a narrow, dull-witted man of no vision and only one idea: to govern with no diminution of the autocratic power bequeathed by his ancestors . . . the Czar found world affairs rather mentally taxing."[10]

Nicholas II, born May 18, 1868, had neither the temperament nor the training to manage a vast, multinational empire. He was given a military education and enjoyed the trappings of military life—exercises, parades, uniforms, and decorations. Having little interest in intellectual pursuits, he was pleased to descend from a long line of autocrats, and he succeeded to the throne following the death of his father, Alexander III, on November 1, 1894. He believed he ruled by divine right, with power from God, and that he was responsible only to God—not to any constitution or elected assembly. An indecisive character who was a poor judge of other men, he couldn't tolerate people with views different from his own.

Russia and Japan both wanted to grab territory in Manchuria and Korea. The czar rejected Japanese proposals to negotiate separate spheres of influence. Everybody seemed to expect that if there was a war, the Russians would win easily.

On February 8, 1904, Japanese ships launched a surprise attack on Russian-controlled Port Arthur. Lincoln reported that "the Russians against whom guns and torpedoes would be directed were scandalously unprepared. Not one gun on the battleships was manned or loaded, and only one ship's searchlights were in use. Port Arthur's shore batteries stood immobile, still heavily coated with grease to help them withstand the fierce winter storms. The great ten-inch guns on Electric Hill could not be fired because they had no fluid in their recoil cylinders. Nicholas's Far Eastern Commander in Chief, Admiral Evgenii Alekseev . . . allowed his great battleships to lie at anchor with all their lights blazing. He had not even taken the elementary textbook precaution of installing torpedo nets around them."[11]

The Japanese began a siege of Port Arthur, sank Russia's fleet, and gained undisputed control of the seas in that region. This meant the Japanese could land soldiers wherever they wished. The Japanese soon occupied Korea and Manchuria.[12]

Russia's Baltic Fleet was dispatched to help support the czar's ambitions in the Far East. All kinds of aged steamers were enlisted for the effort. When they were in the North Sea, they sank several British fishing boats that had been misidentified as Japanese torpedo boats. It isn't apparent how Japanese fishing boats would have reached the North Sea. In any case, Nicholas II stubbornly refused to apologize for the tragedy, and the British responded by denying the Russians access to the Suez Canal, a shortcut to Japan. Consequently, Russia's "Mad Dog" Admiral Zinovy Petrovich Rozhestvensky had to lead his fleet on an 18,000-mile, nine-month voyage around Africa to the Sea of Japan. This was daunting because of a lack of friendly ports where the Russians could replenish their supplies.

On May 14 and 15, 1905, the Russian fleet engaged Japanese admiral Togo Heihachiro in the Tsushima Straits. Born in 1848 to an aristocratic family in the small town of Kajiya, Togo was a master of calligraphy and a student of the writings of Confucius. As a child he displayed a flair for swordsmanship. Soon after his twelfth birthday, he started work copying manuscripts in the office of his Satsuma clan, for which he was paid a bushel of unhulled rice each month. He yearned for a more active life and began learning about guns.

After British warships sailed into Kagoshima Bay and displayed their formidable naval power by bombarding Japanese forts, Togo resolved to get naval training. The best place to learn was in Britain, and arrangements were made for him to travel to Plymouth and board the training ship *Worcester*. He struggled with the English language and with naval gear, procedure, and strategy, but he persisted.[13] Togo was with the new Japanese navy when it fought effectively against the Chinese in 1894 and 1895. He became an admiral by assessing battle risks cautiously and showing patience to wait for favorable opportunities.[14]

The Russians didn't seem to have anybody who could match the capabilities of Togo or other Japanese naval commanders. Russian gunners had had little training, because they couldn't spare the ammunition, but the Japanese were well trained, so they were able to hit their targets. Moreover, Rozhestvensky turned out to be a terrible strategist, ordering maneuvers that exposed his best ships to deadly shelling. Altogether, the Japanese lost three torpedo boats and 110 men, while Russia lost thirty-four ships and 4,830 men, with another 5,917 (including Rozhestvensky) captured. This, the first major war of the twentieth century, was the first in which a European power was defeated by an Asian power.

The loss was humiliating for Nicholas II, who, by this time, faced a revolution triggered by the mounting military disasters. On Sunday, January 22, 1905, Orthodox Church priest Georgi Gapon had led a march of well-dressed protesters to the czar's Winter Palace in St. Petersburg, where they intended to present a petition demanding civil liberties. As they approached the Winter Palace, soldiers guarding it panicked and fired on the crowd. An estimated 1,000 people were killed or injured. "Bloody Sunday" was followed by months of riots and strikes involving perhaps 400,000 people. There were mutinies in Kronstadt, Sevastopol, and Vladivostok. Perhaps the best-known mutiny occurred on the battleship *Potemkin*, when sailors refused to eat rotten meat they had been served. The captain ordered that the rebels be shot, but the firing squad refused.

Nicholas II countered by announcing the establishment of the Duma, an elected assembly that he agreed to consult—it wouldn't have the power to enact laws. The czar reserved the right to determine when the Duma would meet. It was not a Western-style legislature, but a hopeful beginning for Russia. When it was reported that few people would be eligible to vote, there were more protests.

The czar's authority seemed to crumble. Workers formed illegal labor unions. Uncensored publications appeared. Poles and Georgians acted independently of the czar's officials. Underground political parties operated openly. In St. Petersburg, Leon Trotsky and other Mensheviks established a "soviet"—a committee made up of intellectuals and factory workers, which assumed some powers of local government. This inspired people in some fifty other towns and cities to establish soviets.

TROTSKY, LENIN, AND STALIN

Leon Trotsky was born Lev Davidovich Bronshtein in Yanovka, Russia, on November 7, 1879. His biographer Dmitri Volkogonov described him as "of medium height, with a neat beard, and above a high forehead he had a full head of hair streaked with grey. His noble Roman nose was surmounted with an elegant pince-nez. He had lively, bright blue eyes."[15]

Trotsky's parents were Jewish farmers in the Ukraine. He encountered the ideas of Karl Marx while at school in Nikolayev (southern Ukraine) and helped organize the South Russian Workers' Union. In 1897 he was imprisoned in Siberia, but escaped after four years and made his way to London. There he met a number of exiled Russian Marxists. He made a strong impression with his boldness, eloquence, and enthusiasm for Marxist dogma.

The 1905 revolution was electrifying news for Vladimir Ilich Ulyanov, who later adopted the revolutionary name "Lenin." He was a short, neat, bald man with a beard. An associate, Gleb Krzhizhanovsky, stressed Ulyanov's proletarian appearance: "Wearing his usual cloth cap, he could easily have passed unnoticed in any factory district. All one could say of his appearance was that he had a pleasant, swarthy face with a touch of the Asiatic. In a rough country coat, he could

just as easily have passed in a crowd of Volga peasants."[16] Like many
observers, Krzhizhanovsky commented on Ulyanov's eyes, which
were "piercing, full of inner strength and energy, dark, dark brown."

Ulyanov was intolerant and fanatical about the pursuit of political power—by any reckoning, a difficult character. Biographer
Robert Service noted that "he cheated on his wife, he exploited his
mother and sisters, he was maudlin about his health, he had no great
opinion of Russians or even of most Bolsheviks. He relished terror. . . . He was still cruder in his letters and telegrams than in his
books. Much of his correspondence was so cynical. . . . He was
punctilious in his daily regime, being downright obsessive about si-
lence in his office. . . . He was an intruder on the privacy of his comrades. . . . Without his entourage of women, he would not have risen
to his historical eminence. There was something of the spoilt child
about him."[17]

Born in Simbirsk on April 10, 1870, Ulyanov grew up the third
of six children in a middle-class family—his mother was the daughter of a physician, and his father was an inspector of government
schools. His older brother Alexander had been hanged at age
twenty-three for his revolutionary activities back in 1887, and this
was believed to have concentrated his hatred at the czarist regime.
When Ulyanov was seventeen, his father died. He applied to Kazan
University where he intended to study law, but he was expelled in just
three months for his political activities. In 1895 he was arrested for
printing illegal literature and exiled to Siberia. He lived with his
wife, Nadezhda Konstantinova, in a remote village but wasn't imprisoned or forced to perform hard labor, as became standard practice under the Soviet regime. He enjoyed his books.

Five years later Ulyanov applied for permission to go abroad, and
government officials decided he would pose less of a political risk if
he was out of the country. He went to live in Zurich so he could see
Georgi Valentinovich Plekhanov, an exile who was among the earliest
Russian intellectuals to embrace Marxism. Plekhanov had a high-
domed forehead and a full, neatly trimmed mustache and beard. He
wrote books about Marx, dominated the first Russian Marxist organization, the *Gruppa Osvobozhdenie Truda* (Emancipation of Labor
Group), and was primarily responsible for the program that the

Social Democratic Labor Party adopted in 1903. "Almost all the leading personalities in the movement, including Ulyanov, began as his
disciples," observed biographer Samuel H. Baron.[18]

When the Social Democratic Labor Party was banned, the prin-
cipals lived in exile communities. Ulyanov and Plekhanov, however,
were uneasy rivals for influence among exiled Russian Marxists.
Ulyanov wanted to publish a Marxist journal, *Iskra (The Spark)*,
with financial backing from Alexandra Potresov—the St. Petersburg
bookseller who had supplied him with books when he was in Siberia.
But the arrogant Plekhanov was anxious to dominate the journal.

In August 1900, weary of Plekhanov's hysterics, Ulyanov moved
to Munich so he could publish much closer to the Russian Empire,
where he wanted the journal distributed. He also wrote a long pamphlet, *What Is To Be Done?* (1902), telling how to organize an underground revolutionary political party. To throw off the Okhrana
(Russian secret police) who would want to arrest the author of such
a pamphlet, he signed it "N. Lenin," a pseudonym he had used in recent letters to Plekhanov. He had used other pseudonyms, but this
pamphlet achieved substantial influence among Russian Marxists, so
he became famous as "Lenin."

While a substantial number of socialists tried to gain power
through labor unions, Lenin, in *What Is To Be Done?*, made a case
that a revolution had to be led by professional revolutionaries—an
elite leadership. He belittled the idea of a spontaneous revolution by
ordinary people. He rejected the view that the primary mission of
socialists was to issue propaganda, and sooner or later people would
act on it. Lenin insisted that a revolution must be planned. Professional revolutionaries like himself were needed to make things happen. There must be a secret, disciplined organization whose members
obeyed orders.

Although Lenin flourished in the comparatively free societies of
Western Europe, he denounced freedom of contract, freedom of
trade, and freedom of thought. He maintained that because a revolutionary organization must be secret, leaders couldn't be elected, and
in any case having free elections would "divert the thoughts of the
practical workers from the serious and imperative task of training
themselves to become professional revolutionaries."[19] Lenin de-

scribed a vision even more authoritarian than what had developed under the czars.

What Is To Be Done? had a huge impact because Karl Marx insisted that a revolution was impossible until a country had developed free markets (which were presumed to impoverish people). Russia abolished medieval serfdom a few decades earlier, but the country still had a feudal aristocracy and was just beginning to industrialize, so it seemed a long way from having revolutionary potential. Lenin declared that a revolution could be made to happen.

Soon Lenin became worried about possible arrest by the Bavarian police. He was off to London, where police weren't especially concerned about radicals, the government didn't routinely open people's mail, publications weren't censored, and there were great libraries.

In London, Lenin attended the second Congress of the Social Democratic Workers' Party, and he had a bitter debate with Julius Martov, one of his associates on *Iskra*. Martov, a thin, stoop-shouldered, bespectacled man with a stutter, was a skilled debater. Lenin affirmed his view that the key thing was developing a small, skilled, secret revolutionary cadre, whereas Martov insisted on the need for large numbers of party members. This debate split the party. Martov's allies included Plekhanov and Trotsky, and Lenin called them "Mensheviks" ("Minority Men"). He called his followers, who included Josef Dzhugashvili, the "Bolsheviks" ("Majority Men").

Dzhugashvili, then known to his comrades as "Koba" and later as "Stalin," was born December 21, 1879, in Gori—a small town near Tiflis, Georgia, in the Caucasus mountains. His father, Vissarion, was a drunken shoemaker. His mother, Ekaterina, a washerwoman, beat him frequently. Biographer Edvard Radzinsky described him as a "small, pockmarked Georgian with a shock of black hair . . . [and] angry yellow eyes."[20]

He attended a nearby church school, then won a scholarship at Tiflis Theological Seminary. He seems to have been impressed by the Jesuits' rigorous indoctrination of church dogma and their spying on one another. But he rebelled against the religious beliefs and became an atheist, which led to his expulsion from the seminary. Looking for a secular creed, he embraced Marxism and joined the Social Democratic Workers' Party in 1899. He adopted the revolutionary name

"Koba" after the hero of Georgian author Alexander Kazbegi's novel *The Parricide*.

"The paranoid secrecy of the intolerant and idiosyncratic Bolshevik culture dovetailed with Koba's own self-contained confidence and talent for intrigue," wrote biographer Simon Sebag Montefiore. "Koba plunged into the underworld of revolutionary politics that was a seething, stimulating mixture of conspiratorial intrigue, ideological nitpicking, scholarly education, factional games, love affairs with other revolutionaries, police infiltration, and organizational chaos."[21] He was first arrested and exiled to Siberia in 1902. He met Lenin at a Bolshevik conference in Tammerfors (Tampere), Finland.

Lenin and his wife moved back to Switzerland, perhaps because he had some kind of reconciliation with Plekhanov and wanted him more involved with the journal. Lenin was in Geneva when he heard the news that the 1905 revolution had started without him. He brooded in his apartment, and he argued endlessly with fellow exiles in a nearby Marxist-owned coffee shop. The man who would later demand death for millions was afraid to return to Russia, where he might get arrested. Friends told him he couldn't expect to direct events in Russia by writing letters from afar. He refused to return unless guaranteed freedom from arrest.

On October 30, 1905, a desperate Nicholas II issued his October Manifesto, granting some civil liberties including the right to establish political parties. Those satisfied with the czar's proposals formed the Octobrist party. Others, forming the Constitutional Democratic Party, wanted substantial limitations on the czar's power. Mensheviks and Bolsheviks were skeptical about the manifesto.

In a speech given at St. Petersburg University on November 12, Trotsky warned: "Citizens! Now that we have our foot on the neck of the ruling clique, they promise you freedom. Don't be in a hurry to celebrate the victory, it is not yet complete. Is paper money worth as much as gold? Is the promise of freedom the same as freedom itself? What has changed since yesterday? Have the gates of our prisons been flung open? Have our brothers come home from savage Siberia? . . . The Tsar's Manifesto is nothing but a piece of paper. Today they give it to you, tomorrow they will tear it into bits, as I do now!" He tore it up and tossed it into the wind.[22]

Despite Trotsky's dramatic speech, the October Manifesto convinced Lenin that it would be safe to return to Russia. In November
he boarded a train, crossed Germany, and took a boat to Stockholm,
where Bolsheviks had false ID papers for him. Then he took a ferry
to Helsinki and from there a train to St. Petersburg. Lenin had imagined he could operate in the open, but he soon realized that would be
risky. He spent his time behind the scenes, trying to find ways Bolsheviks and Mensheviks could work together.

But before much could be done, the Okhrana cracked down on
revolutionaries, and Lenin and his wife fled to Kuokkala, a Finnish
town near the Russian border. Although Russia had controlled Finland and always loomed as a fearful neighbor, there was much hatred
for Russia, and many Finns extended assistance to Russian revolutionaries. From his hideaway, Lenin began denouncing Mensheviks
whose cooperation he had courted. He worked to establish a secret
Bolshevik Center, a base of operations in Finland. Lenin was to remain an exile for another decade.

The first election for the Duma was held in March 1906. It was
boycotted by the Socialist Revolutionaries and Bolsheviks. The
Duma energized opposition to the czar, and he dismissed it and
called for new elections. Liberals, known as Kadets, fled to Finland
and urged that Russians refuse to pay taxes or submit to military
conscription until the czar agreed to deal reasonably with elected
representatives. The second Duma, too, expressed opposition to the
czar's policies, and he relied increasingly on repression.

Although the 1905 revolution failed to topple the czar, the experience showed how the stresses of war could unleash dynamic forces
threatening the regime. If the czar had been smart, he would have
avoided future wars. Lenin and other Bolshevik leaders bided their
time in exile, awaiting another opportunity for revolution. No one
could have expected Woodrow Wilson to have heard of any of these
people who, after all, missed most of the action during the 1905 revolution. But he might have appreciated that the country had potential for serious trouble.

CZAR UNDERESTIMATES STRESSES OF WAR

Czar Nicholas II made the worst decision of his life when, on July 26, 1914, he offered to help defend Serbia if it was attacked by Austria-Hungary, making it likely that Russia would be drawn into a war. Like so many rulers before and since, the czar grossly underestimated the consequences of war.

Although Russia was a big country, its capacity to fight a war was more limited than most people realized. The economy had only recently begun to emerge from centuries of inefficient government monopolies, suffocating taxes, and regulations. Russia was quite backward compared to the West. Russian government-owned arms factories couldn't match the efficiency of privately owned arms factories in the West. After the Russians mobilized, they had 4.6 million rifles for 6.5 million soldiers. They were frequently sent to the front without guns and told to grab guns from their comrades who had been shot. There were shortages of ammunition, too. A major reason why Russian soldiers didn't respond to German bombardment was that they lacked ammunition.

Historian Richard Pipes added, "Transport, too, was cause for concern. In relation to her territory, Russia fell far behind the other major belligerents: she had a mere 1.1 kilometers of railway track for each 100 square kilometers, compared with Germany's 10.6, France's 8.8, and Austria-Hungary's 6.4. Three-quarters of Russia's railways, including the Trans-Siberian, had only a single track. Improvidently, St. Petersburg did not consider the likelihood that in the event of war her major ports would be rendered useless by enemy action—German in the Baltic, and Turkish in the Black Sea—leaving her effectively blockaded. . . . Aside from Vladivostok, thousands of miles away, Russia was left with only two seaports to the outside world. One, Archangel, was frozen for six months of the year. The other, Murmansk, was ice-free but in 1914 had no railroad."[23]

Quite apart from the number of tracks, historian Peter Gatrell noted, the Russian railroad system was in poor shape: "Most operations, such as switching track and changing signals, were performed manually and unsystematically. Locomotives and wagons did not conform to any common standard. The majority of wagons lacked a roof. Locomotives were treated in a haphazard, laborious and dangerous fashion. Expert opinion commented on the lack of attention given to the maintenance of rolling stock."[24]

According to Gatrell, "What counted at the moment of mobilization and during the heat of a campaign, particularly when it was accompanied by an incessant flow of refugees and prisoners, was that the system should be well-administered. Unfortunately, the complex demands imposed by war exposed the deficient administration of the Russian railway network. Military authorities vied with each other and with civilian agencies for control over lines at the front."[25]

The demands of the transportation system might best be appreciated by considering what was required just to feed the Russian army. Historian Norman Stone reported that each day it needed "about 16,000 tons of flour, grits, fat, salt, sugar, preserved meat, and this took 1,095 wagons daily. Supplies for horses took 1,850 wagons daily, for 32,000 tons of barley, oats, hay and straw. Before an offensive, with a gathering of cavalry, demand for fodder rose even higher."[26]

Russian forces were hampered by primitive communications. This was critical, because ever since the Russo-Japanese War, there was less fighting in which adversaries were close to one another. The longer range of modern guns meant that military operations took place over a larger area—beyond the horizon. Officers could no longer issue orders based on what they could see.

"Only the Russians failed to profit from their own experience and entered the Great War with almost no modern communications systems," historian W. Bruce Lincoln observed.[27] Russia had little communications wire, and less than a quarter of the men assigned to string it had wire cutters. One Russian general, Aleksandr Samsonov, had just twenty-five telephones with which to relay battlefield information and coordinate thousands of men. Russia had an estimated 250 airplanes that might have been used for battlefield reconnaissance, but few could fly, owing to a shortage of spare parts.

DEBACLES ON THE EASTERN FRONT

Russian military leadership was as bad as the supply situation. Nicholas II insisted on giving his uncle supreme command of the

Russian armies. General Nikolai Nikolaevich could be a charming man, but otherwise there was little to recommend him. According to W. Bruce Lincoln, "A dashing cavalryman with a precisely-trimmed graying beard, six-foot-six-inch Grand Duke Nikolai Nikolaevich cut an imposing figure. Still straight as a ramrod at fifty-seven, he radiated all the aura of command that his nephew so sadly lacked. . . . Although charm and tact could win the hearts of men, strategic brilliance and logistical genius were needed to win battles, and these were the very elements of military command in which Nikolai Nikolaevich had the least expertise. . . . Utterly inexperienced in wartime command, the grand duke now took command of armies whose numbers soon rose beyond five million."[28]

Nicholas II insisted that General Nikolai Ianushkevich, forty-four, be appointed as army chief of staff, despite his lack of combat experience. Probably his greatest strength was as a courtier with a pleasing personality. In the field, he distinguished himself by persecuting Jews.

There was bitter disagreement about what Russia's military strategy should be. General Nikolai Nikolaevich defended traditional reliance on cavalry and fortresses. War minister Vladimir Sukhomlinov tried to overhaul the military, but he proved hopelessly out of touch with it. In July 1914, he advised the czar that the military was combat-ready, but it soon proved itself to be poorly trained and poorly equipped. He was charged with corruption contributing to the supply problems. He recommended that Russia conduct campaigns against Germany and Austria-Hungary simultaneously, which reduced Russia's ability to win against Germany, the stronger of the two adversaries.

In the opening weeks of the war, German forces invaded Poland. Desperate, General Ianushkevich promised Poles substantial independence if they would help fight the Germans, and Poles rallied. The Russians scored some gains with brilliant maneuvers, but ammunition shortages led to horrifying casualties. When forced out of Russian Poland, Russian armies lost access to Polish industry that had supplied many spare parts.

The most humiliating defeat occurred at the Battle of Tannenberg, in August 1914. General Yakov Zhilinski was Russia's North-west Army Group commander, with responsibility for military operations in East Prussia. An incompetent, he issued orders without knowing where his armies or enemy armies were. General Paul von Rennenkampf commanded Russia's First Army, and General Alexander Samsonov headed its Second Army. They hated each other and weren't cooperative. At decisive moments, neither knew what the other was doing. They lacked adequate weapons. They sent uncoded messages easily intercepted by the Germans, enabling German general Paul von Hindenburg's Eighth Army to win a decisive victory. The Russians lost an estimated 30,000 soldiers, and another 95,000 surrendered after they ran out of ammunition. The Germans needed some sixty trains to haul away all the captured Russian equipment. Having lost his entire army in five days, Samsonov committed suicide in the Tannenberg forest.

Following his indecisive and ineffectual maneuvers, Rennenkampf ordered his First Army in a frantic retreat. He ceased trying to communicate with Zhilinski and hid in a fortress at Kovno. Thanks to high-placed friends in the czar's court, though, Rennenkampf escaped punishment and went on to fight the First Battle of Masurian Lakes. This became Hindenburg's second big victory on the Eastern Front. The fighting, which took place from September 9 to September 14, led Rennenkampf to retreat again, as Russian forces pulled entirely out of East Prussia. He failed again in November, at the Battle of Lodz, after which he was finally dismissed.

Things got worse in 1915. Russian soldiers continued to be no match for the Germans, who were well armed and well trained. Russian commanders didn't bother to build entrenchments for fall-back positions. In a few April days, reported W. Bruce Lincoln, "the III and V Caucasus Corps lost seventy-five out of every hundred, while the X Corps lost eighty-five, and the IX Corps was destroyed. To fill the gap, the Russians threw reserve divisions against the Germans without artillery support, proper weapons, or even maps, only to see them melt away in a matter of hours."[29] Lincoln wrote that Russian soldiers "did not even have the wherewithal to build entrenchments because corrupt staff officers had sold the spades, barbed wire and entrenching timbers they had seized from the Austrians a scant two months before."[30]

In May 1915, conflicts along the Carpathian Mountains, which extended from Slovakia to Romania, left some 150,000 Russian soldiers dead. The Russians had little artillery support and sometimes no ammunition, so they had a chance only when fighting with bayonets. According to historian Nicholas V. Riasanovsky, as much as a quarter of the Russian solders were sent into action unarmed, hoping to get guns from the dead.

The Allies weren't much help, because the German Navy controlled the Baltic Sea, blocking possible arms shipments there. After Turkey joined the Central Powers in the fall of 1914, arms couldn't be shipped to Russia's ports on the Black Sea, either. Britain launched the Gallipoli campaign in an effort to access the Black Sea, but it was a flop.

During the first year of the war, Russia had suffered 4 million casualties. These included a substantial number of loyal army officers. As the war dragged on, Russia necessarily turned to officers who were less loyal and less competent. By degrading the officer corps, the war made Russia less able to resist revolution.

By the fall of 1915, Russia had lost fourteen provinces, with a population estimated at 35 million. "The debacle in Poland," observed Richard Pipes, "was for many Russians the last straw. It proved to them conclusively that tsarism, or, at any rate, the reigning tsar, was incompetent to carry out its supreme mission, which was to expand Russia's territory and defend it from foreign enemies."[31]

MASSIVE DEPORTATIONS

Contributing to the chaos were massive deportations ordered by General Ianushkevich. As Russian soldiers retreated, they forced everybody to move east—Poles, Latvians, Lithuanians, Ukrainians, Russians, Gypsies, and Jews.[32] Many Russian soldiers thought Polish Jews—who spoke Yiddish—were German and treated them as enemies. Historian Bernard Pares reported, "These measures were ruthlessly applied in the case of the Jews. Whole communities were driven from their villages, losing all regular means of livelihood and parting company for many years with all their settled habits; many victims were swept off by epidemics."[33] Historian Edmond Taylor added that these deportations tied up the railroads and dumped "several million demoralized refugees upon the overburdened towns of the interior with as little regard for the social and economic problems as for the human misery thereby created."[34]

Millions of other people were displaced by the war. Several hundred thousand Ottoman Armenians fled into Russia. German-speaking and Hungarian-speaking people in Russian territory had their land expropriated and given to Russian soldiers. Forced out of their homes with little more than the clothes on their backs and maybe a few small tools, refugees spread chaos as they fled east. They cleared woods and stole fuel to keep warm, and took food wherever they could find it. There were clashes with authorities trying to protect the property of local people.

On the run, often with little food, living in unsanitary conditions, the refugees were susceptible to epidemics—cholera, typhus, dysentery, smallpox, and tuberculosis. Refugee children died from diphtheria, measles, and scarlet fever. Few doctors were available, since they were overwhelmed by the needs of war.

While large numbers of Russians responded generously to the needs of refugees, there was also increasing alarm as more and more refugees poured into communities. They had been welcomed as guests, but it became apparent they might be there a long time. Most were unemployed. There were reports of thievery. When the government began distributing some relief funds, it offended people by paying refugees more than it paid the wives of Russian soldiers. Moreover, refugees of some nationalities were paid more than refugees of other nationalities, provoking resentment. It was an explosive situation.

Many Russians were outraged at the deportations, because of the wrongs inflicted on the refugees and the disruption of communities where refugees settled. "The events of summer 1915," observed historian Peter Gatrell, "demonstrated to critics of the old regime that Russia's rulers exercised no control over the Russian high command. The truth of the matter was that the government tried and failed to curb the arbitrary behavior of the generals."[35]

CASUALTIES, SHORTAGES, INFLATION

The government conscripted some 11 million peasants into the war, and horses were seized. This made it much harder for the remaining peasants to work the fields and produce and distribute grain. Thanks to conscription, noted historian Norman Stone, areas hit by grain shortages "were often deficient, not in grain, but in farmers willing and able to market it."[36]

Russian government spending soared from 3.5 billion rubles in 1914 to 15.3 billion by 1916, of which 11.4 billion was spent by the War Ministry.[37] The government didn't have a bureaucracy capable of collecting income taxes, and it didn't increase excise taxes nearly fast enough to pay for the war.

The government forfeited alcohol tax revenue by introducing alcohol prohibition in 1914, intended as a measure against alcoholism. As one might expect, prohibition didn't stop people from drinking alcohol. Instead of buying it from lawful, taxpaying businesses, people bought it from unlawful businesses that didn't pay taxes, or they made it at home. So the government lost alcohol taxes that had accounted for a quarter of its revenues.[38]

In any case, it would have been hard for taxes to cover Russia's war spending—which was comparable to Britain's and exceeded only by Germany's. Russia was a poorer country. Its prewar (1913) per-capita gross national product was estimated to be $44, compared with $146 for Germany, $185 for France, and $243 for Britain.[39]

Borrowing provided some funds, mainly by selling bonds to Britain, the proceeds used to buy war materials from Britain and the United States. But mainly what the government did was print money—inflation. The government abandoned the gold standard that obliged it to pay a ruble's worth of gold when presented with a ruble's worth of paper. Since gold was rare, the supply of gold was much more difficult to increase than the supply of paper money, so the gold standard limited the amount of paper money that could be issued. Going off the gold standard eliminated this constraint. Historians estimate that the Russian money supply soared between 400 and 600 percent by January 1917.[40]

As a consequence, prices soared. "In Simbirsk [now Ulyanovsk], for instance," Stone explained, "a pair of boots that cost seven rubles before the war cost thirty in 1916; in Ivanovo-Voznesensk, calico products rose to 319 per cent of their pre-war price in September 1916; horse-shoe nails, which cost three rubles and forty kopecks in 1914 rose, early in 1916, to forty rubles."[41]

With the value of the currency depreciating rapidly, people scrambled to get rid of it as quickly as possible and convert it into useful things or a store of value like gold. For example, even though grain prices were rising fast, by the time peasants were able to sell their grain and get someplace where they could buy manufactured goods, the prices of manufactured goods had risen, too, and often peasants couldn't afford to buy as much as they did before.

The government established price controls in an effort to limit price rises, but controls prevented suppliers from recovering their costs, which meant fewer supplies—shortages. Peasants hid their grain. There were critical food shortages in Russian cities, where an estimated 28 million people lived in 1916.[42] The government responded by sending goons into the countryside to seize grain.

People continued bidding for things, though, because the government was printing all that currency for its purchases, and the currency was circulating. It led to black markets where things were available for those willing to pay competitive prices. "In the end," wrote Stone, "the only part of the economic mechanism that functioned with efficiency was the Black Market."[43]

In a further effort to limit soaring prices, the government established wage controls. These just made it harder for working people to maintain their purchasing power. Stone reported that "railwaymen's wages were directly controlled by the government, and fell behind in the inflation. At one stage in the summer of 1917, there were complaints that railwaymen were not turning up to work because they had no shoes; and in any event there was a closing of the gap between skilled and unskilled railwaymen that demoralized the skilled, and drove them toward revolutionary courses."[44]

The government didn't pay what would have been required to attract the desired number of soldiers. Apparently recruits received limited training, and military leadership didn't provide compelling reasons for fighting. There were food shortages at the front as everywhere else in Russia. According to Stone, "Living from rotten herring, sometimes even given paper money in place of rations—paper money, moreover, that was almost useless in the stores of the rear area, where only black marketeering would succeed—the soldiers drank from illegal stills, mutinied, attacked and sometimes killed their officers." Contributing to poor morale were letters from home, about their cold, hungry, and perhaps sick families. Consequently, desertion was a serious problem.

NO POLITICAL LEADERSHIP FROM THE CZAR

As Russians became aware that the government was ordering soldiers into battle without enough ammunition, there was much resentment of the incompetent officials. Nicholas II fired some. In September 1915 he fired his uncle Grand Duke Nicholas as commander of the Russian armies. The firing didn't directly affect military operations, since General Mikhail Alexeyev remained chief of staff.[45] But the czar left the capital and traveled with the armies, a fateful move that directly linked his political standing with the performance of his armies, which had been losing.

The czar left the government without a responsible individual in charge. In his absence, his wife, Alexandra, took over much of the government, consulting with the semiliterate Siberian peasant, mystic, lover, and racketeer Grigory Rasputin. Biographer Alex DeJonge reported that "The mature Rasputin was a man of medium height, bony, tense, with a thin face, which was pale and yellowish, and a straggling, slightly curly beard. He could make a most powerful impression upon his listeners, staring at them with bright steady eyes that seemed to read their very souls. Everybody who described him in later years agrees that it was the eyes that made the greatest impression, and it was claimed by some that he was able to make his pupils expand and contract at will. The voice was strange too. He talked in a thick, almost incomprehensible Siberian accent, but without the booming sonority that its rounded vowel sounds usually impart to it. His conversation was desperately hard to follow, for he often spoke in riddles, accompanied by strings of spiritual adages and half-remembered passages from the Scriptures. As he talked and stared at his listeners, his face would frequently cloud over with an air of mistrust, a combination of hesitancy and arrogance: was he making a fool of himself or was it perhaps that his listener was un-worthy of him?[46]

"He had already developed the extraordinary sexual dominance which was one of his most remarkable characteristics, effortlessly taking over a woman's will and persuading her that she would find salvation in her submission to his authority," De Jonge continued.[47]

The czarina consulted him in a desperate effort to save her son and only heir, Aleksay Nikolayevich, who suffered from hemophilia. When his life was in jeopardy, and doctors feared the worst, Rasputin predicted recovery, and he was right—for a while, anyway—and the czarina gave him the run of the government. He found prostitutes for government ministers. He humiliated his adversaries. Rasputin be-came increasingly reckless—on one occasion he became drunk in a Moscow nightclub and suggested that he was the czarina's lover.

Alexandra plotted to dismiss some of the best ministers in the government. She harangued her husband about General A. A. Poli-vanov, the administrator who maintained shipments of munitions to the front. Alexandra also set her sights on dismissing Serge Sazonov, the foreign minister who had dealt effectively with Russia's allies.

Without the czar, Rasputin took over much of the government. He got involved with government loans. He made decisions about the food supply and transportation. He issued orders about military campaigns and sent messages to the kings of Serbia and Greece.[48] Rasputin was also reported to have sold Russian military secrets to German agents.[49]

Meanwhile, Russia's position in the war deteriorated. Russia had originally declared war to save Serbia, yet Serbia was in enemy hands. Russia had liberated Bulgaria, but Bulgaria joined Germany and Austria-Hungary. Poland, as noted, was in German hands. And Russian casualties mounted.

The lack of ammunition had become a major scandal. The Duma—the elected body that, along with the State Council, served as a national legislature—convened on November 27, 1916, and a succession of speakers attacked the czar's government. Liberal leader Paul Milyukov asked, "Is this folly or treason?"[50]

In an effort to save Russia from further disasters, Prince Feliks Yusparov and Grand Duke Dmitry Pavlovich plotted to kill Rasputin. On December 30 they lured Rasputin to Yusparov's house. Rasputin was given poisoned wine and tea cakes, but he survived. So he was shot once, but he survived that, too, and he was shot again. Still he wouldn't die. Finally he was tied up and dumped through a hole in the ice of the Neva River, where he drowned.

Nicholas II attended Rasputin's funeral and afterwards remained at his palace, apparently paralyzed by the chaos around him. There was open talk of a revolution as the war continued to grind the country down.

According to historian Nicholas V. Riasanovsky, "the Russian army mobilized 15.5 million men and suffered greater casualties than did the armed forces of any other country involved in the titanic struggle: 1.6 million killed, 3.8 million wounded, and 2.4 million taken prisoner. The destruction of property and other civilian losses escaped count."[51]

FEBRUARY REVOLUTION

Soaring war casualties meant the Russian government had to conscript men in their thirties and forties who neither expected nor wanted to fight. In Petrograd, 160,000 soldiers had to live in barracks built for 20,000.[52] They received little training before being shipped to the front. In November 1916, the Petrograd military censor reported, "One cannot but notice that in letters from the army as well as letters to the army, discontent arising from [the] internal political situation of the country is beginning to grow."[53]

Florence Farmborough, a thirty-year-old English nurse who volunteered to work with the Red Cross in Russia, kept a diary that revealed a dramatic ground-level view of war and revolution. In January 1917, she wrote: "Disparaging statements concerning the Government are being voiced—at first, they were surreptitious, and now, more bold and brazen, at meetings and street-corners. We feel sorry for the Imperial Family and especially for the Tsar. He, it is said, wishes to please everybody and succeeds in pleasing nobody. As time goes on, rumors of disorder become more persistent. Sabotage has become the order of the day. Railroads are damaged; industrial plants destroyed; large factories and mills burnt down; workshops and laboratories looted. Now, rancor is turning toward the military chiefs. Why are the armies at a standstill? Why are the soldiers allowed to rot in the snow-filled trenches? Why continue the stalemate war? 'Bring the men home!' 'Conclude peace!' 'Finish this interminable war once and for all!' Cries such as these penetrate to the cold and hungry soldiers in their bleak earthworks, and begin to echo among them. Now that food has grown more scarce in Petrograd and Moscow, disorder takes the shape of riots and insurrections."[54]

Czar Nicholas II, at military headquarters in Mogilev—in western Russia near Minsk—was warned about the worsening crisis in many telegrams, but he discounted those warnings, figuring that the Duma was just maneuvering for more power. Established to discuss laws and advise the czar, as part of the political settlement following the 1905 revolution, it still didn't have power independent of the czar. Duma members were mainly supporters of the monarchy, and they met at Tauride Palace, Petrograd, which had belonged to Count Grigory Potemkin, one of Catherine the Great's lovers. Nicholas II ordered the Duma to stop meeting, but members defied his orders. On March 8, Nicholas II ordered that riots be suppressed, but soldiers refused. It became clear that he had no control over events. A revolution was under way without him.

It's known as the February Revolution because, until 1918, Russia used the Julian (or Old Style) calendar, according to which the revolution started in February. During the twentieth century, the Julian calendar was thirteen days behind the Gregorian calendar used elsewhere.

The Constitutional Democratic Party had a majority in the Duma, and it formed a Provisional Committee to assume governmental functions, headed by Duma chairman Mikhail Rodzianko. A principal member was Paul Miliukov, fifty-eight, a historian and journalist. These were comparatively liberal intellectuals with little in the way of practical political experience.

The Provisional Committee became the Provisional Government, and Prince Georgii Lvov headed that. He envisioned a liberal democracy based on tolerance and universal suffrage. There was a promise to hold elections for representatives to a Constituent Assembly that would assume power from the Provisional Government. Lvov favored granting Poles and Finns their independence. Lvov's hope was that such measures would inspire patriotism to help achieve victory in the war.

Socialist Revolutionaries supported the Petrograd Soviet of Workers and Soldiers, established on March 13. It was an impromptu political action group that harked back to the Soviets formed during the 1905 revolution and subsequently crushed by the czar's police. Despite the name, the Petrograd Soviet consisted mainly of socialist intellectuals rather than workers and soldiers—not elected by the general population. "There were no formal agendas, minutes or procedures for decision-making in the Soviet," reported historian Orlando Figes. "Every decision was arrived at through open debate, with speakers in different parts of the hall all talking at once, and the resolutions passed by general acclamation, much as at a village assembly. Because such a body was incapable of any constructive work it soon took on a purely symbolic role."[55]

If anything was going to happen, somebody had to be in charge, and so an executive committee (Ispolkom) was formed. Members weren't elected by the Soviet. Rather, they were nominated by socialist parties participating in the Soviet—each socialist party was given three representatives. "This fact, little noticed at the time," Richard Pipes explained, "had three grave consequences. It expanded artificially the representation of the Bolshevik Party, which had a small following among the workers and virtually none among the soldiers. It also strengthened the moderate socialists, who, though popular at the time, would soon lose favor with the population. And, most important, it bureaucratized the Ispolkom, making it a self-appointed executive body that acted independently of the Soviet plenum, whose decisions were predetermined by caucuses of socialist intellectuals."[56]

Although the Petrograd Soviet didn't have any official authority, it had the closest thing there was to popular support, a force that must be reckoned with. The Duma had the closest thing to official authority, but it didn't have much popular support. Leaders of the

Petrograd Soviet wanted to extend the revolution, whereas leaders of the Duma wanted to limit the revolution. The Duma and the Petrograd Soviet functioned uneasily at the same time.

Alexander Kerensky served as vice-chairman of the Petrograd Soviet, and he appeared unannounced at a meeting of the Provisional Government, making a pitch to be named minister of justice. He got the job, because he was well known as a speaker who could stir crowds. Florence Farmborough described Kerensky's impact on a crowd: "His main theme was freedom, that great, mystical Freedom which had come to Russia. His words were often interrupted by wild applause. . . . When he left, they carried him on their shoulders to his car. They kissed him, his uniform, his car, the ground on which he walked. Many of them were on their knees praying; others were weeping."[57]

The Petrograd Soviet was scandalized at Kerensky's ambition to participate in both bodies and, in effect, be an intermediary. With an offputting burst of hyperbole, he vowed: "I cannot live without the people, and the moment you come to doubt me, kill me!"[58] Kerensky subsequently resigned as vice-chairman of the Petrograd Soviet, but remained a member of the executive committee.

Kerensky, born May 2, 1881, had grown up in Simbirsk, where his family knew Lenin's—both fathers were school administrators.[59] Kerensky seems to have been radicalized when Lenin's older brother Alexander was executed in 1887 for conspiring to kill Czar Alexander III.

Kerensky had studied law at the University of St. Petersburg. Following graduation (1904), he joined the Socialist Revolutionary Party and married the daughter of a Russian general—straddling the divide between radicalism and respectability. He wanted his children to be brought up in the Russian Orthodox Christian faith. As a lawyer, he represented socialist dissidents such as a leader of the All-Russian Peasant Union. In 1912, Kerensky was elected to the Duma. He supported Russia's entry in the war, although he criticized the czar's leadership. He plotted to overthrow the government and install stronger leadership, in the hopes of improving prospects for victory.

On March 14 the Petrograd Soviet issued Order No. 1, requiring military units to form soviets whose members were elected from lower ranks. They, in turn, would select officers. Many disciplinary rules for soldiers were eliminated. The intention was to focus on cruel excesses, but the process didn't stop there. Soon soldiers were electing officers and planning military strategy. The army became less responsive to anybody's commands, in particular commands by the Provisional Government. Soldiers began deserting the Russian army by the thousands.[60]

Czar Nicholas II abdicated on March 15, 1917, handing power over to Prince G. E. Lvov, whom Pipes described as "an innocuous and indolent civil activist chosen because, as head of the Union of Zemstva and City Councils he could be said to represent society at large. Lvov understood democracy to mean that all policy decisions were made by the citizens directly affected by them and that government served essentially as a registry office. Convinced of the infinite wisdom of the Russian people, he refused to give any guidance to provincial delegations that came to Petrograd in quest of instructions."[61]

Obviously, if the czar's regime collapsed after only five days of workers' demonstrations and a mutiny, it was much weaker than most people seem to have realized. The czar hadn't anticipated the collapse, and neither had anybody else. Historian Nicholas Werth noted, "At no time did the political forces of the opposition shape or guide this spontaneous popular revolution."[62]

WILSON AND ALLIES: RUSSIA, STAY IN WAR

After the czar abdicated, British, French, and U.S. ambassadors rushed to embrace the new regime as an ally in the democratic crusade against Germany. When the French ambassador to Petrograd, Maurice Paleogue, visited Tauride Palace, where both the Duma and the Petrograd Soviet held their meetings, he reportedly told the enthusiastic revolutionaries: "Forget about your Revolution. Think of the war."[63]

Wilson expressed satisfaction that Russia had overthrown its czar.[64] U.S. ambassador David R. Francis urged him to extend diplomatic recognition, and he agreed. In his April 2 address seeking a declaration of war, Wilson hailed "the wonderful and heartening things that have been happening within the last few weeks in Russia." Soon came pressure for Russia to stay in the war. Secretary of state Robert Lansing, who had succeeded William Jennings Bryan, cabled Francis in Moscow. The message: Tell Russian officials that the United States expects "a Russia inspired by these great ideals will realize more than ever the duty which it owes to humanity and the necessity for preserving internal harmony in order that as a united and patriotic nation it may overcome the autocratic power [Germany] which by force and intrigue menaces the democracy which the Russian people have proclaimed."[65]

A succession of American advisers descended on the Provisional Government, hoping to influence its decisions. The most important was the Root Mission, named for Elihu Root, former secretary of state for President Theodore Roosevelt. Root traveled from Vladivostok to Petrograd with a number of officials and attended many Russian banquets and ceremonies. Secretary of state Lansing described the Root mission as studying "the best ways and means to bring about effective cooperation between the two governments in the prosecution of the war." Root's slogan was "no fight, no loans." His principal recommendations included a propaganda campaign to drum up support for the war and a program to help boost Russian military morale by having soldiers participate in YMCA recreational activities.

Other missions to Russia included the Red Cross Commission and the Stevens Railway Mission. The Russians don't seem to have wanted any of these missions, but they held out hopes of some kind of assistance (such as railway equipment). Wilson did agree to extend $325 million of credits (worth about $4 billion in today's money).[66] This might not seem like much, but the Russians were broke and had been blockaded by German forces in the Baltic Sea and Turkish forces in the Black Sea. Shortages of guns, ammunition, and other war materials had plagued them ever since the war began.

European socialists appealed to Russian socialists, encouraging them to help Russia stay in the war. Belgian socialists urged Russia to stay in the war. British Labour Party socialists weren't in any hurry to end the war. French socialist leader Albert Thomas went to Russia. "His main assignment was to encourage the Russians to take a more active role in the war, hopefully in the form of an offensive," reported historian Rex A. Wade.[67]

The Provisional Government and the Petrograd Soviet debated what Russia's war aims should be. Some, like foreign minister Miliukov, thought people had lost confidence in the czar because he had done a poor job handling the war, which was half right. Miliukov concluded that a liberal government could do a much better job managing the war, and this would make people enthusiastic for more fighting. He wrote: "We expected that an outbreak of patriotic enthusiasm on the part of the liberated population would give new courage for the sacrifices still to be made."[68]

Miliukov declared that the February Revolution had established democracy, and Russia could fight alongside Western democracies. He didn't exactly mean Woodrow Wilson's high-minded principles. He meant scrambling for more territory along with Britain, France, and Italy. He affirmed Russia's aim to annex enemy territory if Russia won the war. In particular, he wanted to secure for Russia the Bosporus, the Sea of Marmara, and the Dardanelles, thereby making it possible for Russia's Black Sea fleet to sail into the Mediterranean. He asserted Russia's prerogative to determine its western borders, acquiring territories controlled by Germany and Austria-Hungary.

Many Russians were alarmed that Miliukov's view, if pursued, would prolong the war. Demonstrators demanded Miliukov's resignation. Newspapers warned about the perils of continuing territorial ambitions. More and more Russians came to believe that Allied war aims should be revised, so that it might be possible to end the war. The British ambassador to the United States, George Buchanan, acknowledged that Miliukov had "little influence with his colleagues."[69] The executive committee demanded and got his resignation as foreign minister.[70]

There was an emerging Russian consensus for "peace without annexations or indemnities"—meaning Germany and Russia would give up any territory they occupied and not demand indemnities of the other. The problem, of course, was that Germany occupied Russian territory. Germany, not Russia, was in a position to demand indemnities. By undermining military discipline, the Petrograd Soviet reduced the likelihood that Russia's fortunes would change on the battlefield. Indeed, socialist talk about redistributing land made conscripted Russian peasants eager to quit the army and go home so they could get land. "For the government to attempt, in these circumstances, to spur the semi-demoralized and land-hungry troops into a new war effort could only tend to force it into opposition to the rank and file," Kennan observed.[71]

Although there was mounting Russian opposition to Allied territorial claims—as evidenced by Miliukov's fall from favor—it was precisely such claims that the Allies defended. Since Russians had embraced Woodrow Wilson's formula "peace without annexations or indemnities," proposed in his December 4, 1917, message to Congress, they figured that surely Wilson would understand the Russian view. But as historian Wade pointed out, "There was a difference in both the purpose and the use of the slogan. The Soviet viewed it as the basis of an *immediate, negotiated peace*; Wilson saw it as the basis of a *future* peace *imposed* by *victory*." Russian leaders, Wade added, weren't aware that "after the United States entered the war, Wilson had decided nothing more should be done about the peace terms, and that all such statements should wait until the war had been won. The British, however, had been informed of the American position by Wilson's intimate adviser, Colonel House."[72]

And so, when Kerensky became minister of war in the Provisional Government, he helped plan yet another military offensive against the Germans. Apparently he was convinced that Germany, if it won the war, would suppress the Russian Revolution. In the name of keeping the revolution alive, Kerensky did everything he could to prevent a German victory. His view, however, disregarded the overwhelming evidence of Russian collapse, a consequence of the war.

As the United States, Britain, and France maintained pressure on the Provisional Government to stay in the war, and as Russia's military, economic, and political situation deteriorated, some observers noted the ominous connections. Consular and military officials tended to be more observant of political realities than did ambassadors who spent their time cultivating relationships with Provisional Government politicians. For example, Ferdinand Grenard, a French diplomat in Russia during the Revolution, wrote: "Russia's allies were blinded by their desire to keep Russia in the war at all costs. They were unable to see what was possible and what was impossible at the moment. Thus they only furthered Lenin's game by isolating the Prime Minister of the Provisional Government from the people to an even greater extent. They could not understand that in keeping Russia in the war, they had to accept the inevitable concomitant of internal strife."[73]

Kennan explained, "The demand of the Allies, including the United States, that Russia should renew and reinvigorate her war effort (bluntly expressed by Root in the formula 'no fight, no loans') was actually in conflict with the other major aim of American policy toward the Provisional Government—namely, that the experiment in constitutional democratic government should proceed successfully."[74]

LENIN ON THE MOVE

News of the February Revolution, the czar's abdication, and the Provisional Government had an electrifying effect on Lenin, who was living in Zurich with his wife, Nadya. He had been wandering around Europe for a decade, hunted by the czar's police, since having participated in the unsuccessful Revolution of 1905.

Lenin, a prolific author of Marxist newspaper articles and pamphlets, had been thrilled at the coming of the European war. He was convinced that it would bring chaos, the downfall of old empires— and opportunities for socialist revolution. Although socialist parties in Britain, France, Germany, Austria, and Russia rallied to support their respective national governments in the war, Lenin hoped his country would be defeated.[75] He wrote novelist and dramatist Maxim Gorky: "War between Austria and Russia would be a very useful thing for the revolution."[76] Arguing against his own country cost Lenin many of his Russian friends.

Lenin's influence was dwindling, particularly since Bolsheviks in Russia had been arrested, their newspapers shut down, and their surviving units heavily infiltrated by police. "To those few persons who followed Lenin's professional activities," wrote Robert Service, "he seemed a cantankerous, somewhat unhinged utopian."[77]

Lenin reinforced this perception by cabling Bolsheviks in Petrograd, a week after the Provisional Government came to power: "no support for the new government . . . no rapprochement with the other parties."[78] Not knowing what else they could do in the circumstances, the Bolsheviks in Petrograd had already expressed limited support for the Provisional Government, so they must have had quite a discussion about what to do after receiving Lenin's cable—documents relating to such discussions were apparently destroyed.[79]

With revolution in Russia, Lenin was desperate to go home, but the European war made this difficult. The most likely way back was through Sweden, but how to get there? The Allies weren't likely to grant him permission to travel through France and the North Sea. He figured it was too dangerous to travel through Ottoman Turkey. He didn't seriously consider traveling through Germany, Russia's enemy.

A friend of Lenin's, Robert Grimm, approached the German consul in Bern, Switzerland, and the government was interested in the idea of giving Lenin safe passage through Germany. The war had been stalemated for three years on the Western Front, and Germany's best hope was to disrupt the British-French-Russian alliance by knocking Russia out of the war. Germany had tried and failed to defeat Russia on the Eastern Front. Germany's Kaiser Wilhelm reflected, "From the strictly military point of view, it is important to detach one or another of the Entente belligerents by means of a separate peace, in order to hurl our full might against the rest."[80] The Germans recognized that Lenin had the ambition and ability to promote chaos in Russia, and he could very well succeed in his objective of getting Russia to withdraw from the war. So arrangements were made for Lenin, his wife, and seventeen other Bolsheviks to travel on a sealed train, to prevent their revolutionary contagion from reaching Germans.

On April 9, 1917, Lenin left the room he and Nadya occupied at No. 14 Spiegelgasse, Zurich. The German train headed to Frankfurt, then Sassnitz—a port on the Baltic Sea. The party took a ferry to Trelleborg, Sweden, then a train to Stockholm. There they switched trains for Helsinki, Finland. Finally, they boarded the Finland Railway to Petrograd. They arrived April 16.

5

WHY DID WILSON ASSUME HIS ALLIES WOULD NOT DEMAND VINDICTIVE SURRENDER TERMS FROM GERMANY?

IF WOODROW WILSON KNEW little about the political situation in Germany and Russia, he seems to have known even less about his allies. Apparently he didn't realize how determined British prime minister David Lloyd George and French premier Georges Clemenceau were to avenge their grievances against Germany, and this gross misjudgment doomed his hopes for peace. He was unprepared, outmaneuvered, decisively beaten by his own arrogance.

GERMAN COLLAPSE

After the March 3, 1918, signing of the Treaty of Brest-Litovsk, which marked Russia's exit from the war, fifty-two German divisions were transferred to the Western Front, increasing by one-quarter the force strength there.[1] But because of potential rebellion in the Ukraine and Baltic regions, Germany still had to leave about 1.5 million soldiers in the east—some forty divisions.[2]

With American soldiers expected in a few months, the Germans were anxious to launch one more offensive—their last chance for a knockout blow. To fill their depleted ranks, the Germans had to draft older men and young boys.[3] General Erich von Ludendorff decided to advance toward the Somme River, because British troops were located there, and they tended to be less effective than the French at defensive operations. Ludendorff might not have known that the British were at a minimum force level, because the commander was Douglas Haig, who had squandered hundreds of thousands of lives in futile battles, and British prime minister Lloyd George didn't want him to have more troops than absolutely necessary. On March 21, Ludendorff's men began to move. They broke through British lines and advanced faster than they had since the beginning of the war.

The advance slowed down, however, when the Germans reached the Somme battlefields. They were full of obstacles, including barbed wire, trenches, shell craters, and badly damaged roads. Moreover, German soldiers stopped to feast on provisions that the retreating British had been forced to leave behind. "The Germans, when they got into British rear areas, were astounded and appalled by the wealth of materiel, rations, clothes, and general sense of well-being they found," reported historian James L. Stokesbury. "They knew Germany was close to starvation. They had been told by their leaders that the Allies were in even worse shape, but now they found out that they had been deceived. The British took as a matter of course items that had not been seen by a German soldier for two or three years."[4]

By June 3 the Germans advanced to within forty-five miles of Paris, but that was about as far as they could go. They were ahead of their supply lines and communications lines. They were exhausted, and Ludendorff didn't have enough reserves to keep up the pressure.[5] Both British and French soldiers were building defensive positions. After the German advance had halted, they began encountering American soldiers. Approximately 200 British and 600 French airplanes joined the battle.[6] On July 14 the Germans fired 17,500 rounds of gas shells on lines of trenches near Château-Thierry, but when German soldiers advanced, they found the trenches were a decoy. Some thirty-five tons of shells had been wasted, and by the time the soldiers reached the real trenches beyond, they were exhausted and under heavy fire.[7] By July 18 the Germans were retreating. They had suffered some 600,000 casualties. German soldiers began deserting their units in droves.

During the preceding six months, the German army had declined from 5.1 million soldiers to 4.2 million. In desperation, the Germans turned to hospitals that released some 70,000 convalescent soldiers per month, though their capabilities couldn't be counted on.[8]

The German Empire was larger than it had ever been before,

extending from near Paris in the west to the Ukraine in the east, but the Germans were in big trouble. They had thought their submarines could win the war, and they were wrong. They had scored huge territorial gains with the Treaty of Brest-Litovsk, but that wasn't enough to win. Then they failed with their last offensive on the Western Front, and American forces weren't yet at full strength. During the summer of 1918, the Allied Powers captured some 6,400 German guns and 363,000 German prisoners—half of the German guns in the field, and one-quarter of the soldiers.[9]

Then came influenza. An ordinary variety had appeared in many parts of the world, and it disrupted operations on the Western Front. The flu hit the Germans harder than the British or French, probably because the Germans were poorly nourished as a consequence of the British naval blockade.[10] Some weeks later came an unusual, deadly variety of influenza, and it became the worst epidemic in history— killing between 20 million and 100 million people around the world, including tens of thousands of soldiers.[11] "Doctors and nurses learned to spot the signs," explained author Gina Kolata. "Your face turns a dark brownish purple. You start to cough up blood. Your feet turn black. Finally, as the end nears, you frantically gasp for breath. A blood-tinged saliva bubbles out of your mouth. You die—by drowning, actually—as your lungs fill with a reddish fluid."[12] More American soldiers died from this influenza than from enemy bullets.[13]

Germany's allies were all trying to quit the war. Bulgarian officials were negotiating with the Allied Powers. Turks were negotiating their surrender. The Austrians were looking for a way out—they had appealed to Wilson, but he didn't want to deal with them. The German government suppressed as much bad news as possible.

WILSON DISCREDITS GERMAN DEMOCRACY

On September 30, Ludendorff and Hindenburg told the Kaiser that they were going to lose. Germany hadn't lost a war in more than a century, since Napoleon had marched through Central Europe, and it wasn't clear how they should proceed. Ministers were told they had no choice but to seek an armistice. The bad news was disclosed to the Reichstag on October 2, and the members were shocked. Everybody had anticipated victory.

Chancellor Georg von Hertling resigned two days later, and Kaiser Wilhelm II asked Prince Maximilian of Baden to form a new government. Maximilian was known as a humanitarian; he had served in the Red Cross and helped prisoners of war on both sides. He assembled a coalition of the Center, Progressive, and Socialist parties, and helped a genuine parliamentary system begin to develop in Germany. Since 1848, German liberals had been struggling to rein in the power of Prussian autocrats, and suddenly the dream was coming true, but in treacherous circumstances.

On October 7 the German government informed Wilson that they wanted peace negotiations and embraced the Fourteen Points outlined in his January 8, 1918, speech to a joint session of Congress. Back then, Wilson had generous words that gave German leaders hope: "We have no jealousy of German greatness, and there is nothing in this program that impairs it. We grudge her no achievement or distinction of learning or of pacific enterprise such as have made her record very bright and very enviable. We do not wish to injure her or to block in any way her legitimate influence or power. We do not wish to fight her either with arms or with hostile arrangements of trade if she is willing to associate herself with us and the other peace-loving nations of the world in covenants of justice and law and fair dealing."

Much has been made of this speech, which outlined high-minded terms of a just peace. The key points included (1) "open covenants of peace, openly arrived at"—no more secret diplomacy; (2) "absolute freedom of navigation upon the seas"—in other words, no naval blockades such as Britain was imposing on Germany; (3) "the removal, so far as possible, of all economic barriers and the establishment of an equality of trade conditions among all the nations"—though this ambiguous language didn't promise free trade, at least it suggested a critique of trade restrictions; (4) "a free, open-minded, and absolutely impartial adjustment of all colonial claims"; (5) Wilson suggested that the vague principle of "self-determination" should be a major consideration when adjusting borders between countries. And (6) Wilson plugged his abstract vision of the League of Nations: "A general association of nations must be formed under specific covenants for the purpose of affording mutual guarantees of political independence and territorial integrity to great and small states alike."

Historian Richard Watt pointed out that "there were certain ambiguities in the Fourteen Points which went largely unobserved at the time. Several of the Points were mutually contradictory. For example, the one relating to Poland called for the new nation to be 'inhabited by indisputably Polish populations, which should be assured a free and secure access to the sea.' It was little noted that access to the sea had to be made across territory which was indisputably populated by Germans."[14]

Wilson replied to the Germans on October 8, asking for confirmation that their government would accept his Fourteen Points. Wilson said that the "object of entering into discussion would be only to agree upon the practical details of their application."[15] On October 12 the German government confirmed their agreement.[16] Wilson conveyed additional points to the Germans: Allied military advisers would work out details of an armistice agreement; German submarine warfare must stop; Germany must confirm that they have a representative government. The Germans accepted the first two points and reported that they had a Constitution, and policies were determined by the Reichstag. Wilson secured these concessions on his own, without consulting Britain or France.

On October 16, Prince Max received a note from Wilson demanding that Kaiser Wilhelm abdicate.[17] Wilson wouldn't approve an armistice if the Kaiser remained in power. This note underscored a point Wilson had made in a Mount Vernon, Virginia, speech the previous July 4, when he demanded "the destruction of every arbitrary power anywhere that can separately, secretly and of its single choice disturb the peace of the world."[18] Wilson's demand proved to be a catastrophic blunder, because it meant that the government officials who had brought Germany into the war wouldn't have to acknowledge responsibility for defeat. Wilson let the Kaiser and his cohorts off the hook. Since Wilson demanded that democratically elected German representatives sign the armistice, they would be the ones discredited in the eyes of the German people. Wilson helped assure that German democracy would be doomed soon after it was born.

On October 17, Wilson dispatched Colonel House to Paris. French premier Georges Clemenceau and British prime minister David Lloyd George were pleased that the Germans had made many concessions, but they objected to Wilson's Fourteen Points. Wilson had never asked either man how he felt about the Fourteen Points. Lloyd George objected to Point Two, about "freedom of the seas," since it would limit the prerogatives of the British navy. Clemenceau objected to Point One, for "open covenants, openly arrived at," since he believed British foreign secretary Edward Grey's secret alliance had served French interests. Clemenceau and Lloyd George drafted amendments to undermine the Fourteen Points.

Wilson countered by threatening to announce that Britain and France opposed the Fourteen Points. They realized immediately that they would be perceived as cynical and greedy for opposing freedom of the seas and insisting on secret diplomacy. They agreed to accept peace terms based on Wilson's Fourteen Points. This was Wilson's high point as a negotiator.

"November Criminals"

Clearly, the most unpopular job in Germany was to sign the armistice. Ludendorff and Hindenburg could see this coming, so they quit the government to avoid being blamed by the public.

The Reichstag became a sovereign body, to whom ministers were responsible. Reichstag representatives were elected on universal suffrage by secret ballot. The German Social Democrats came to power at what turned out to be the worst possible time, for they faced the humiliating task of surrender.

German morale collapsed, starting with the navy that had made the Kaiser proud. On October 29, 1918, German sailors in Kiel defied orders to engage the British navy in what appeared to be a pointless, suicidal mission. Some 600 sailors were imprisoned, and demands to free them led to an uprising. Naval officials caved in, and soon Kiel was controlled by sailors who elected a governing council.[19] Mutinies spread to all the German naval bases.[20] Apparently the sailors were mainly determined to comply with the government's peace policy.

In early November, Austrian forces disintegrated, and Munich residents feared an Italian invasion. People lost confidence in city authorities, and there was an uprising of Munich workers. "The desire for peace rather than radical social change was the prevailing mood," observed historian Hajo Holborn.[21] Upheaval spread to Berlin, where socialists saw their big chance to seize power. They called a general strike.

On November 8, German representatives met Allied representatives and were told what the armistice terms would be. Germany must withdraw from France, Belgium, Alsace-Lorraine, and other territory west of the Rhine River. Germany had to repatriate all prisoners of war. The Allies would take possession of German military equipment including six dreadnoughts, eight light cruisers, 160 U-boats, 5,000 artillery pieces, 25,000 machine guns, 1,700 aircraft, 5,000 locomotives, and 150,000 railroad cars. German soldiers had to leave East Africa. German forces in Eastern Europe had to move back within Germany's prewar boundary—thereby nullifying the harsh terms that the Germans had imposed on Russia in the Treaty of Brest-Litovsk.

Article 26 was a shocker: "The existing blockade conditions set up by the Allied and Associated Powers are to remain unchanged, German merchant ships found at sea remaining liable to capture."[22] The German delegation responded: "The effect of Article XXVI would be a one-sided continuation of warfare by the Allies and the United States during the armistice, which openly contradicts the purpose of an armistice."

Events, in particular Wilson's demands and the Reichstag elections, were passing the Kaiser by, and Prince Max of Baden repeatedly urged that the Kaiser abdicate. He delayed, hoping to think of some way out of his mess. Finally, on November 9, Prince Max simply announced the abdication, and it was done. The Kaiser sought political asylum in the Netherlands. Then the Prince of Baden himself resigned, to be succeeded as chancellor by Friedrich Ebert, leader of the Majority Social Democratic Party.

Ebert authorized State Secretary Matthias Erzberger, a Centre Party politician who had criticized the government's war policies, to

accept the armistice demands.[23] Field marshal Paul von Hinden-
berg—who didn't want his fingerprints on the armistice agreement—cabled Erzberger, suggesting that he make one more attempt
to have Article 26 dropped, but if the Allied Powers refused, the
armistice should be signed. Hindenburg was well aware that the German army was disintegrating.

On November 11, armistice negotiators met in a railroad car at
Compiègne, perhaps twenty miles northeast of Paris. Erzberger
protested Article 26, pointing out that it continued the Allied Powers' wartime policy of starving the Germans. British general Wemyss
dismissed this, saying that the Germans had sunk British ships—although that point had been addressed by the armistice term specify-
ing that the Germans would hand over their U-boats.[24] The hapless
Matthias Erzberger was hated for his "crime" of signing the armistice
agreement. He would be assassinated on August 26, 1921.[25]

Supposedly the hunger blockade was being maintained to force
German compliance with armistice terms—withdrawing from territories and surrendering guns, ships, railroads, and so on. But a shortage of German locomotives and rail cars slowed down the process of
delivering assets to the Allied Powers, and the armistice agreement
and blockade were extended. The British navy continued to block the
flow of food to hungry Germans. British journalist H. N. Brailsford
visited Germany in January 1919 and observed many signs of dis-
couragement. One woman was quoted as saying, "During the war
we had hope. We knew it must end one day. Now there is no hope."[26]

Historian C. Paul Vincent reported, "The motivation to work
had all but disappeared. . . . Wages provided no incentive as there
was so little to buy. The goods that were available were prohibitively
expensive. Since the unemployment allowance only just sufficed for
the purchase of the inadequate rations, there seemed little logic in
working for money that could not buy anything. . . . Amidst conditions of anarchy, smuggling had become common and overt. The demoralized state of the returning troops only intensified the chaotic
situation. Unguarded stores of the Military Food Office, including
supplies on forgotten army trains, were frequently plundered. Civilian food offices were also robbed, resulting in the additional loss of
already limited provisions."[27]

WILSON, WEAKEST OF THE MAJOR PLAYERS AT VERSAILLES

The armistice provided that there would be a conference to negotiate a final settlement, and everybody would meet in Paris. The location all by itself had a dynamic impact on the proceedings, since almost 1.4 million Frenchmen had died in the war, and most of the fighting had taken place on French soil. When the French demanded that harsh terms be imposed on the Germans, who, ultimately, could say no? Apparently British prime minister David Lloyd George had favored a neutral site like Geneva,[28] Switzerland, but French premier Georges Clemenceau insisted on Paris, and Woodrow Wilson went along.

Both Colonel House and secretary of state Robert Lansing advised Wilson not to attend the conference. Since he had already secured British and French agreement on the Fourteen Points, he could only lose by attending. He would inevitably be drawn into negotiations resulting in concessions. If he sent a representative who was not authorized to depart from the Fourteen Points, it would have been easier for the United States to maintain a strong negotiating position with Britain and France. When pressured for concessions, the representative could always say that he was obliged to follow Wilson's instructions. Delays communicating between Paris and Washington would provide time to determine the best moves. But Wilson insisted on going to the conference, because his dream was to play on a world stage.

Despite that tactical blunder, a skilled American negotiator still might have performed adequately. After all, the French wouldn't have been on the winning side without American taxpayers and soldiers. Unfortunately, Wilson wasn't a skilled negotiator.

He compounded his blunders by refusing to take any Republican senators along to Paris. The result of the November 1918 elections was that the Democrats lost control of the U.S. Senate. There would be forty-eight Republicans, forty-seven Democrats, and a Progressive. Apparently voters had already become disillusioned with Wilson's war. If Wilson had reached out and brought along even one Republican senator, he might have encountered less opposition when the treaty came before the Senate for a vote. But he was an arrogant and bitter man.

Wilson and his entourage arrived in Paris on December 14, assuming that the conference would begin right away. In fact there had been hardly any discussion about how it would be set up. During the month that was required to get the conference under way, Wilson was welcomed by adoring Paris crowds. He visited Italy and alienated Premier Vittorio Orlando. He visited Britain and insulted the British. Most important, Clemenceau and Lloyd George sized Wilson up, and they concluded he could be rolled when the peace negotiations began.

"I have an impression that Mr. Wilson had the idea he would be asked to preside over the Conference and act as chairman of the committee, commission, or council which would direct the proceedings," recalled Lansing.[29] Clemenceau, a shrewd operator, maneuvered Wilson into a subordinate position. Clemenceau, not Wilson, presided at the conference, and Clemenceau persuaded Wilson to be a delegate sitting around a table with other delegates, one among equals. Wilson's voice counted for no more than any of the Allied Powers who had been recipients of American largesse.[30]

Clemenceau had quite a presence with his weathered face, big mustache, and bulky figure. "At the Council of Four," wrote John Maynard Keynes, "he wore a square-tailed coat of very good, thick black broadcloth, and on his hands, which were never uncovered, gray suede gloves; his boots were of thick black leather, very good, but of a country style, and sometimes fastened in front, curiously, by a buckle instead of laces. . . . His walk, his hand, and his voice were not lacking in vigor, but he bore nevertheless, especially after the attempt upon him, the aspect of a very old man conserving his strength for important occasions. He spoke seldom, leaving the initial statement of the French case to his ministers or officials; he closed his eyes often and sat back in his chair with an impassive face of parchment, his gray gloved hands clasped in front of him."[31]

Georges Clemenceau was born September 28, 1841, in Vendée, on the west coast of France. He came of age under Emperor Napoleon III, and through his father he met many people, including historian Jules Michelet, who talked about overthrowing the government. Clemenceau helped establish a journal, *Le Travail (Work)*, that published dissident views, for which he was imprisoned for seventy-three days in 1862. He helped launch another publication, *Le Matin (Morning)*, that was shut down by the police. When he visited the

United States, he noted the comparatively greater freedom of the press and freedom of speech. For a while he taught at a girl's school in Stamford, Connecticut, and he married one of his students.

He returned to France and got involved with politics. He was in Paris when, in July 1870, Napoleon III started a war with Germany, and within two months Germany won and secured some humiliating territorial concessions—in particular, Alsace-Lorraine, which was a center for coal and steel production. The government of Napoleon III collapsed, and Clemenceau supported Léon Gambetta, who was seeking to establish a republic. After participating in the brief rebellion known as the Paris Commune, Clemenceau was chosen administrator of the Montmartre district of Paris, then elected to represent the Seine district in the National Assembly. In 1880 he launched the newspaper *La Justice (Justice)* to express radical views, and established himself as an influential political commentator who could help bring down ministries but who apparently wasn't interested in national political office himself. When he decided to pursue national office, he was attacked by all the enemies he had made. He burnished his reputation by spending eight years defending the Jewish army officer Alfred Dreyfus, who had been wrongfully accused of selling military secrets to Germany.

Clemenceau was elected to the National Assembly as a senator from Var. He joined the cabinet in 1906 as interior minister and premier. In November 1917, President Raymond Poincaré, Clemenceau's political enemy, asked him to head the war government. At seventy-six, Clemenceau proved to be a relentless fighter. He was utterly devoted to the destruction of Germany, and he pushed for larger production of munitions. He appealed to Woodrow Wilson for help. Despite horrifying casualties, in May 1918 Clemenceau insisted that war be waged "to the last quarter hour, for the last quarter hour will be ours." He told a reporter, "My life hatred has been for Germany because of what she has done to France."[32]

Of all the participants at the treaty negotiations, Clemenceau went with the clearest idea of what he wanted to do. He was convinced that Germany might again threaten France, and his aim was to put off that day of reckoning as far as possible into the future. The only way he thought he could do that was by eliminating Germany's military establishment and crushing the country economically. Clemenceau believed that being generous to Germany would only bring the world closer to the time when Germany would wage war again.

The blue-eyed, white-haired British prime minister, David Lloyd George, was an exceptionally skilled politician because of his tactical and people skills. Keynes observed that Lloyd George had "six or seven senses not available to ordinary men, judging character, motive, and subconscious impulse, perceiving what each was thinking and even what each one was going to say next, and compounding with telepathic instinct the argument or appeal best suited to the vanity, weakness, or self-interest [of the person he was dealing with]."[33]

U. S. secretary of state Lansing portrayed Lloyd George as a political chameleon who could be counted on to change his views on practically everything except insisting on German reparations, defending the prerogatives of the British navy, and maintaining the British Empire. "Ready as Mr. Lloyd George was to declare a position on any subject," Lansing wrote, "he seemed to be equally ready to change that position on obtaining further information or on the advice of his expert counselors. He did this with an avowal that he had not previously been in possession of facts or else with an explanation intended to show that his new attitude was not contradictory of the former one. His explanations were always clever and well presented, but they were not always convincing. . . . [He] put aside that which had gone before and proceeded to handle the question under discussion as if nothing had occurred to change the course of the debate. Inconsistency never seemed to disturb him or cause him to hesitate."[34]

Lloyd George was a Welshman whose father had served as headmaster of a Manchester elementary school. He died in 1864, when David was just one year old. His mother, daughter of a Baptist minister, had no money. Mother and son went to live with her brother, a Baptist minister and shoemaker. David studied law and began work for a law firm. He championed the rights of Welsh people, who, like the Irish, had long been dominated by English Tories. Also, as might be expected, he championed the independence of Non-Conformists—those whose religion was other than the (Anglican) Church of England.

Lloyd George was a charming man who did well with the ladies, making him a natural politician. He won election to Parliament in 1890, as a Liberal representing Caernarvon Boroughs. He opposed the Boer War of 1899–1902, where British soldiers fought to subdue rebellious Boers (South Africans of Dutch descent) in South Africa. A Liberal government, formed in December 1905, included Lloyd George as president of the Board of Trade. Three years later he was named chancellor of the exchequer (equivalent to the U.S. secretary of the treasury). He promoted higher real estate taxes, higher income taxes, and higher death taxes. He admired Germany's compulsory government-run pension system, introduced by the autocratic chancellor Otto von Bismarck. When the House of Lords blocked proposed welfare spending, Lloyd George supported the Parliament Act of 1911, limiting the power of Britain's upper house. He denounced "the rich" when this was politically fashionable, although in 1913 it was revealed that he had bought shares in the Marconi Wireless Telegraph Company for much less than other investors had to pay, hoping to get rich himself.

As minister of munitions during World War I, Lloyd George recruited business executives who knew how to manage large organizations efficiently, and production of munitions enabled Britain to keep fighting the war of attrition on the Western Front. He was, however, skeptical that the war could be won there.

On December 7, 1916, Lloyd George became prime minister, heading a coalition government with Liberals and Conservatives. To accelerate the decision-making process, he reduced the number of ministers in the war cabinet from twenty-three to five. In early 1917 his major challenge was breaking the German submarine blockade of Britain, which sank a substantial amount of shipping and led to food shortages. He supported the idea of having British soldiers join Robert-Georges Nivelle, commander-in-chief of the French armies, in the April 1917 Aisne offensive, over the objections of British generals Douglas Haig and William Robertson. Nivelle's offensive was a flop, with 120,000 French casualties. Next time around—on July 31, 1917—Lloyd George went along with his generals, who recommended the Passchendaele offensive (July–November 1917), another flop with a horrendous loss of life. Such flops convinced Lloyd George that British generals were incompetent. Robertson resigned, but Haig stayed on, and Lloyd George prevented Haig from having enough soldiers to launch a new attack.

Wilson was by far the weakest of the major players in Paris. Keynes observed that Wilson "was in many respects, perhaps inevitably, ill-informed as to European conditions. And not only was he ill-informed—but his mind was slow and unadaptable. The president's slowness among the Europeans was noteworthy. He could not, all in a minute, take in what the rest were saying, size up the situation with a glance, frame a reply, and meet the case by a slight change of ground; and he was prone, therefore, to defeat by the mere swiftness, apprehension, and agility of a Lloyd George. There can seldom have been a statesman of the first rank more incompetent than the president in the agilities of the council chamber. A moment often arrives when a substantial victory is yours if by some slight appearance of a concession you can save the face of the opposition or conciliate them by a restatement of your proposal helpful to them and not injurious to anything essential to yourself. The president was not equipped with this simple and usual artfulness."[35]

Though Wilson's weakness was as a debater and negotiator with a small group, and his strength was as a speaker with a large group, he was maneuvered into playing to his weakness in Paris. "Never could a man have stepped into the parlor a more perfect and predestined victim," Keynes said. "The Old World was tough in wickedness; the Old World's heart of stone might blunt the sharpest blade of the bravest knight-errant. But this blind and deaf Don Quixote was entering a cavern where the swift and glittering blade was in the hands of the adversary."[36]

The junior partner in the Big Four was Vittorio Emanuele Orlando, prime minister of Italy during the last years of the war and the Paris Peace Conference. Lansing described him thus: "Short and rotund in person, with thick white hair worn pompadour and a white mustache partially covering his rather full lips, he was not in personal appearance typical of Italy. His shortness of stature, which was about that of Mr. Lloyd George, was emphasized by his usual custom of wearing a close-fitting sack coat, which he generally kept tightly buttoned. With a friendly eye and a smile which dimpled his cheeks, one knew at a glance that he was of a kindly nature."[37]

Orlando was born on May 19, 1860, in Palermo. In his thirties, he gained some attention by writing on politics, and he was elected to Italy's Chamber of Deputies. Italy had stayed out of the war for a year, but Orlando favored getting in. The government talked with Germany and Austria-Hungary about potential rewards of joining their side, and with Britain and France about how Italy could gain by joining them.

There was also a cast of supporting players, each of whom sought to resolve grievances and gain territory at the expense of somebody else: Ignace Paderewski, a famed pianist, who served as a representative of the Polish people; Eleutherios Venizelos, a Greek patriot; T. E. Lawrence (of Arabia), who spoke out for Muslims in the Middle East; and Queen Mary of Romania.

WILSON'S SECRET BLUNDERS

The Paris Peace Conference began on January 12, 1919. Initially there were representatives from ten nations, then the Big Four (France, Britain, Italy, and the United States).

Clemenceau and Lloyd George outmaneuvered Wilson throughout the negotiations. Although Wilson had denounced treaties negotiated in secret and called for "open covenants of peace, openly arrived at," these peace negotiations were negotiated in secret. The Council of Ten was abandoned in favor of the Big Four supposedly because a smaller committee could make decisions more quickly than a larger committee, but according to Lansing, a major consideration was that a smaller committee would be more likely to keep secrets. In any case, Big Four deliberations were kept secret from all the other delegates.[38] Wilson was blamed for the policy of secret negotiations, but Lansing said he thought it was more likely that Lloyd George originated the scheme. Most important, Germany was excluded from the proceedings and wouldn't be officially informed about evolving treaty terms until they were approved by the Allied Powers.

The French and British drafted treaty terms, putting Wilson in the position of objecting to terms he didn't like. It would have been politically difficult to raise a lot of objections, since he would have been perceived as an obstructionist. If he seemed to be objecting to everything, he would have been viewed as just a naysayer.

Wilson couldn't draft treaty terms, as Keynes pointed out, because he hadn't thought anything through. "It was commonly believed at the commencement of the Paris Conference," Keynes wrote, "that the President had thought out, with the aid of a large body of advisors, a comprehensive scheme not only for the League of Nations, but for the embodiment of the Fourteen Points in an actual Treaty of Peace. But in fact the President had thought out nothing; when it came to practice his ideas were nebulous and incomplete. He had no plan, no scheme, no constructive ideas whatever for clothing with the flesh of life the commandments which he had thundered from the White House."[39]

Lansing confirmed the shocking superficiality of Wilson's mind: "As to a complete project, or even an outline of terms which could be laid before the delegates for consideration, he apparently had none; in fact when this lack was felt by members of the American Commission they undertook to have their legal advisors prepare a skeleton treaty, but had to abandon the work after it was well under way because the President resented the idea, asserting emphatically that he did not intend to allow lawyers to draw the treaty, a declaration that discouraged those of the profession from volunteering suggestions as to the covenant and other articles of the treaty."[40]

Consequently, Lansing explained, "Clemenceau, and in a lesser degree Lloyd George, took the initiative on practically all subjects requiring settlement . . . even in the case of the Commission on the League of Nations, of which the President was the presiding officer, the initiative apparently passed from him. . . . Thus the United States was forced into the position of following instead of leading in the drafting of the terms formulated in the Council of Four, a position which was as unnecessary as it was unfortunate."

Lansing continued, "As a master of the fine art of flattery none could equal the French Premier [Clemenceau]. It was interesting to see how accurately he estimated the personal peculiarities of his colleagues and how tactfully he regulated his intercourse accordingly.

With President Wilson he was politely deferential but never sub-servient; with Mr. Lloyd George he showed his wit and sometimes his sarcasm; with the Italians he was cynical and caustic and not in-frequently vehement; and with the Japanese, indifferent or patiently tolerant. He had read with remarkable keenness the temperament and the characteristics of each, and seemed to understand the best way to deal with each one."

After having self-righteously opposed Britain and France when they sought exemptions from the Fourteen Points, Wilson had to plead that the Monroe Doctrine be exempted. He had been advised that such an exemption would improve prospects for Senate approval of the treaty. Clemenceau and Lloyd George undoubtedly enjoyed Wil-son's embarrassment, since it enabled them to push more aggressively for their exemptions. "Betrayed by his own political weakness, his rep-utation declining," reported historian Richard Watt, "Woodrow Wil-son found the daily meetings of the Council of Four becoming an ordeal. The Allies no longer troubled to pay much more than lip service to his Fourteen Points."[41]

There were other uneasy compromises with Wilsonian prin-ciples. The Japanese, seeing a draft of the Covenant with a clause supporting religious freedom, asked that the clause be amended to specifically include Japanese. But Australians, fearful of the "yellow peril," objected, which might have reminded Wilson that there were anti-Japanese voters on the West Coast of the United States. It was agreed that the whole clause about religious freedom would be dropped.

Proposals adopted by the Big Four were presented to delegates from all participating nations. "Free debate and actual voting by the delegates had no place in the proceedings with M. Clemenceau in the chair," wrote Lansing. "There was an occasional attempt at discus-sion, but the Clemenceau method discouraged it. After listening with a tolerant manner and with his half-closed eyes turned toward the ceiling, the old French autocrat would slowly rise from his chair, glare fiercely about the room as if to say, 'We have had enough of this,' and then ask whether any one else desired to speak; and then, before an-other delegate could collect his wits and get to his feet, he would snap out the inevitable *Adopté* [adopted]. That always ended it."[42]

The Allied Powers aimed to redraw the map of Europe, and they were well aware that they had a limited time to do it. Soldiers and civilians alike were weary. There was plenty of discontent at home, with general strikes in Brussels, Glasgow, Lyon, Paris, San Francisco, and Winnipeg.[43] Armies were being demobilized, which meant less and less ability to enforce whatever agreements were made.

Wilson liked to pose as a wise peacemaker, generous to all sides, but there are reasons to believe he might have been almost as eager for vengeance as Clemenceau. He had, indeed, acted vengefully toward his enemies while in Princeton and in Washington. Wilson was quoted as telling Lloyd George at a Council of Four meeting in June 1919: "I have always detested Germany. I have never gone there. But I have read many German books on law. They are so far from our views that they have inspired in me a feeling of aversion."[44]

Historians have debated whether these lines reflect long-held feelings or anger in the aftermath of the war. After reflecting on the evidence, Manfred F. Boemeke reported: "Analyses have convincingly shown that it is no longer tenable to claim that all Wilson desired at Paris was a moderate peace of reconciliation and understanding. However, none of them, it seems, has adequately explained the rationale behind Wilson's insistence on a harsh treatment of Germany, a treatment, moreover, that he continued to advocate even after the German people had heeded his implicit demand to overthrow their militaristic rulers and had apparently joined the family of democratic nations."[45]

Wilson, who had proclaimed the noble goal of "peace without victory," demanded victory. He expressed contempt for compromise and supported a policy of "disciplining Germany." He relished his role at Versailles, "sitting with judges . . . [and the] great task to establish justice and right."[46] So an alternative interpretation of events might be that Wilson wasn't such a terrible negotiator at Versailles; he continued posing as a generous peacemaker while letting Clemenceau do the dirty work for revenge they both wanted. In any case, it appears that, at Versailles, Wilson never thought much about the possible consequences of revenge.

WILSON'S BIGGEST DELUSION

Wilson's top priority was establishing the League of Nations, because he believed it had the potential to eliminate future wars. He insisted that the League of Nations be part of the treaty they were negotiating. Lloyd George and Clemenceau went along with Wilson as long as they eventually got what they wanted.

The League of Nations was a winner's club. The original members were to be nations on the winning side of World War I, and their friends—namely, the United States, Australia, Belgium, Bolivia, Brazil, the British Empire, Canada, China, Cuba, Czechoslovakia, Ecuador, France, Greece, Guatemala, Haiti, Honduras, India, Italy, Japan, Liberia, New Zealand, Nicaragua, Peru, Poland, Portugal, Siam [Thailand], Serb-Croat-Slovene State [Yugoslavia], South Africa, and Uruguay. Invited to join were the Argentine Republic, Chile, Colombia, Denmark, the Netherlands, Norway, Paraguay, Persia, Salvador, Spain, Sweden, Switzerland, and Venezuela.

Notably absent were the World War I losers: Germany, Austria, Hungary, Bulgaria, and Turkey. Russia, too, in the throes of the Bolshevik revolution and civil war, was absent.

The core provision of the Versailles Treaty was Article 10: "The Members of the League undertake to respect and preserve as against external aggression the territorial integrity and existing political independence of all Members of the League. In case of any such aggression or in case of any threat or danger of such aggression the Council shall advise upon the means by which this obligation shall be fulfilled." In other words, the countries that had not been fighting one another would agree to continue not fighting each one another.

What if a member were attacked? Article 11: "Any war or threat of war, whether immediately affecting any of the Members of the League or not, is hereby declared a matter of concern to the whole League, and the League shall take any action that may be deemed wise and effectual to safeguard the peace of nations."

So the League of Nations amounted to a traditional alliance, and an attack on one member would oblige other members to join the conflict, expanding it—which, of course, is how World War I happened in the first place: a Serbian nationalist assassinated Archduke Ferdinand; Austria threatened Serbia; Russia came to the defense of Serbia; Germany came to the defense of Austria; France came to the defense of Russia; and Britain came to the defense of France and Russia. By the time this process was done, Bulgaria, Italy, Japan, and Turkey were involved, too.

There was talk about the League of Nations having its own armed force, but it was easy to imagine power struggles for control of such a force—as has always happened when people disagreed about how force should be used. Aggrieved minorities within the League of Nations would have complained about abuses and injustices.

Negotiators agreed that the League of Nations wouldn't interfere in the affairs of member nations, specifically including trade restrictions, immigration restrictions, and civil wars. Yet trade restrictions and immigration restrictions provided incentives for war. Both types of restrictions meant it mattered where a national border happened to be. If mineral resources were within one's country, then they were available. If they were on the other side of the border, access was either limited or blocked. By contrast, with a laissez-faire policy, it didn't much matter where the borders were, because people on both sides were free to buy and sell as they wished. Similarly, since immigration restrictions limited freedom of movement, it mattered whether a border placed people of a particular ethnic group, religion, or language in one country rather than another; with free migration, nobody was trapped or excluded, so borders weren't a fighting issue.

To exclude civil wars from League of Nations intervention meant doing little if anything while tens of millions of people were murdered. During the twentieth century, more people were murdered by their own governments than by foreign governments—civil wars were more deadly than wars among nations. R. J. Rummel estimated that more than 160 million people were the victims of what he called "democide" by their own governments, in Nazi Germany, Soviet Russia, Communist China, and elsewhere.[47] Of course, intervening effectively in a civil war is nearly impossible. The point is that excluding civil war intervention drastically reduced the potential value of the League of Nations. One couldn't claim the League of Nations would have been a mighty instrument for peace while at the outset it was excluded from intervening in the worst episodes of violence.

Supposedly, it was essential for the United States to join the League. The subsequent failure of the League was blamed on the refusal of the U.S. Senate—dominated by what have been derided as "isolationist sentiments"—to ratify the treaty with the League of Nations provisions. This suggests the League was never much more than a scheme to drag the United States into other people's wars around the world. Indeed, as historian Margaret MacMillan observed, "Many French officials persisted in seeing the League as a continuation of the wartime alliance, still directed against Germany."[48] Americans would be taxed, and American soldiers would be sent to die, in an effort to resolve conflicts that had little if anything to do with American vital interests, never mind national defense. In some cases—as in the Balkans, Eastern Europe, and the Middle East—League of Nations membership would have drawn the United States into conflicts that began before a country existed.

Wilson was willing to make concessions on the territorial settlements in order to get his beloved League of Nations, but the League of Nations never had much potential for maintaining peace, and the territorial settlements—with trade restrictions, immigration restrictions, and socialism—had immense potential for war. Wilson gave up the most important settlement terms for the sake of the least important.

Wilson was so convinced about the overriding importance of the League of Nations that he left the Paris Peace Conference after he presented the draft provisions on February 14, 1919. MacMillan wrote that Wilson was "confident that he had accomplished the main purpose in attending the conference."[49] Until Wilson returned, he was leaving decisions up to others.

THE VERSAILLES TREATY TERMS THAT COUNTED MOST

Germany was demilitarized and left with an army not to exceed 100,000 men—more like a police force.[50] The German navy couldn't exceed 15,000 men.[51] The air force, 1,000 men.[52] The treaty specified the maximum number of guns and the maximum stock of ammunition the Germans could have.[53] German submarines and surface warships were handed over to the Allied Powers, and the Germans were forbidden to replace them.[54] The air force was limited to sea-

planes capable of searching for submarine mines. Imported munitions were banned.[55] Military conscription was abolished.[56] German
military forces were forbidden to leave the country.[57]

The most important single clause, the one for which Clemenceau
fought hardest, was number 231, the "war guilt" clause: "The Allied
and Associated Governments affirm and Germany accepts the responsibility of Germany and her allies for causing all the loss and
damage to which the Allied and Associated Governments and their
nationals have been subjected as a consequence of the war imposed
upon them by the aggression of Germany and her allies."

This was the most bitterly debated and preposterous clause in
the entire treaty—the idea that one nation was responsible for everybody's stupid decisions in the war! The Germans must bear responsibility for prodding the Austrians to provoke the Serbians in 1914, but
the Russians bear responsibility for mobilizing their army, the French
bear responsibility for backing the Russians, and the British bear responsibility for secretly agreeing to back both. Britain, France, and
Russia must also bear responsibility for staying in the war and spurn-
ing opportunities to cut their losses and get out. It wasn't the fault of
the Germans that the British had incompetent generals like Douglas
Haig, that the French had incompetent generals like Robert-Georges
Nivelle, or that the Russians had incompetent generals like Nikolai
Yanushkevich.

The Allied Powers considered the war guilt clause the rationale
for trying to collect damages and get back all the money they had
squandered on the war. During the 1920s, revisionist historians
countered that all participating countries had a hand in the catastrophe. Sidney B. Fay, for instance, pointed out that all the belligerents
were in an alliance system that drew one nation after the other into
the conflict. Fay further observed that none of the belligerents—
including Germany—expected or prepared for the war as it developed: a long, calamitous conflict. If Germany didn't prepare for the
conflict, how could it be claimed that Germany deliberately caused
it?[58] Fay concluded: "In each country political and military leaders
did certain things, which led to mobilizations and declarations of
war, or failed to do certain things which might have prevented them.
In this sense, all the European countries, in a greater or less degree,

were responsible. One must abandon the dictum of the Versailles Treaty that Germany and her allies were solely responsible."[59]

Fritz Fischer countered by citing documentary evidence from German archives, that German officials urged Austrian officials to take a hard line against Serbia, following the assassination of Archduke Francis Ferdinand. Fischer claimed German officials were well aware of the risks of a general war. He explained how German war aims expanded during the negotiations for the Treaty of Brest-Litovsk—and after it was signed.[60] Fischer, however, focused on only one among many factors contributing to the war. While the Treaty of Brest-Litovsk robbed Russia of substantial—non-Russian—territories it had previously conquered, the Allied Powers had their secret treaties about carving up their adversaries, too.

The war guilt clause was followed by number 232: "The Allied and Associated Governments require, and Germany undertakes, that she will make compensation for all damage done to the civilian population of the Allied and Associated Powers and to their property during the period of the belligerency of each as an Allied or Associated Power against Germany by such aggression by land, by sea and from the air, and in general all damage."

How much did Germany owe the Allies? Neither Clemenceau nor Lloyd George wanted to name a number during the Paris Peace Conference, because political adversaries might have charged that the number was too low and that Germany got off easy. So an Inter-Allied Commission was established to determine the reparations bill and report its findings after May 1, 1921. The commission wasn't told how to arrive at a number. Meanwhile, as a kind of down payment, Germany was supposed to pay the Allies a total of 20 billion gold marks during 1919, 1920, and the first quarter of 1921.[61] In the event Germany defaulted on its treaty obligations, the Allies could adopt "economic and financial prohibitions and reprisals and in general such other measures as the respective Governments may determine to be necessary in the circumstances."[62]

Apparently unmentioned during the proceedings was the American role in reparations. Private financiers (notably J.P. Morgan & Co.) loaned some $2 billion to Britain, France, and Italy, and those creditors expected to be repaid. But after the war, those countries were broke. The French faced financial collapse as early as 1916 and became dependent on British subsidies. The French had not only suffered huge losses on their own soil, but had also invested in Russia, which, following the revolution, had defaulted on its loans. After Wilson decided to enter the war, the U.S. government became the principal lender to the Allies: $4.2 billion to Britain, $3.4 billion to France, $1.6 billion to Italy, $379 million to Belgium, $159 million to Poland, $192 million to Russia, and tens of millions more to other countries in southern and eastern Europe. Their only hope of repaying American creditors was to squeeze the Germans.

The case for reparations, as historian Sally Marks explained, was that "the war had been fought on the soil of the victors; they were devastated, and Germany was not. Most European belligerents had large domestic war debts, the victors had vast foreign ones as well but Germany did not. In addition, the continental victors had immense reconstruction costs. Somebody would have to pay to clear the fields and provide new plows, rebuild factories, purchase new equipment and tools, reconstruct bridges and railroads, drain and restore coal mines flooded during the armistice negotiations, and revive the economies of thoroughly devastated and denuded territories. If the Allies, and especially France, had to assume reconstruction costs on top of domestic and foreign war debts, whereas Germany was left with only domestic debts, they would be the losers. Reparations would both deny Germany that victory and spread the pain of undoing the damage done."[63]

It's hard to be sympathetic with those, such as the French, who were eager to fight a war and stick somebody else with the costs. They didn't have to enter the war, and having entered, they had many opportunities to quit. Like the rest of the belligerents, they wanted to hang on for glory and loot. They could have negotiated a settlement, given up some territory, and spared the lives of hundreds of thousands of Frenchmen. It would probably be a wiser policy if nations entered wars only if they were willing to assume all the costs. Perhaps that would discourage some fighting.

As things turned out, the Treaty of Versailles provided a long list of assets Germany had to give the Allied Powers. This included over 20 percent of Germany's merchant fleet. Germany had to build

merchant ships for the Allied Powers.[64] Germany had to give the
French farm animals, including 500 stallions, 30,000 fillies and mares,
2,000 bulls, 90,000 milch cows, 1,000 rams, 100,000 sheep, 10,000
goats.[65] The French were scheduled to get 7 million tons of coal annually for ten years.[66] Also annual deliveries for three years: 35,000
tons of benzol, 50,000 tons of coal tar, 30,000 tons of ammonia.[67]
Half of Germany's dyestuffs and chemical drugs had to be delivered
to the Allied Powers.[68]

Moreover, France regained Alsace-Lorraine. France took possession of the Saar coal region, as compensation for French coal
mines that the Germans destroyed—even though people in the Saar
spoke German, thereby violating Wilson's general principle of self-
determination. Germany was stripped of its colonies and outposts in
Equatorial Africa, China, and Siam. Upper Silesia in eastern Germany—where the Germans obtained about a quarter of their coal—
went to Poland. Overall, the secretly negotiated treaty provided that
Germany would lose 13 percent of its prewar territory and 10 percent of its population.[69] Taking all these assets away from Germany
obviously made it harder to pay reparations. Especially obnoxious
were articles—such as number 122—providing that the Allies could
seize property without compensation to *private* owners.

In territorial terms, the British Empire was a big winner. It expanded by about a million square miles, to some 12 million square
miles.[70] Bigger than ever before, this was the largest empire in history.
So much for Woodrow Wilson's claim about making the world safe
for democracy!

Britain and France split what was left of the Ottoman Empire,
with Britain acquiring "mandates" for Iraq, Jordan, and Palestine—
colonies in all but name. Britain acquired the former German
colonies of Cameroon, Tanganyika, and Togoland, while the French
gained Syria and Lebanon.[71] The British gained influence in Persia.[72]
In the Middle East and East Africa, the British already controlled
Aden, Cyprus, Egypt, Kuwait, Muscat, Oman, Qatar, Somaliland,
Sudan, and the Trucial States (later merged to form the United Arab
Emirates).[73] Size wasn't everything, however. Britain spent more on
the war than any other power, and colonies generally cost more to

govern and protect than the revenue they generated.[74] The British were also drawn into myriad local disputes, revolts, and civil wars.

On April 28, German diplomats, support staff, and journalists—180 people altogether—left Berlin to receive the treaty. The French made sure that their special train slowed down when passing through the areas devastated by the war. In Paris they boarded buses for Versailles. When they arrived at their hotel—which was enclosed in a stockade—their baggage was dumped on the ground, and they were told to take care of it themselves. They were kept waiting at their hotel for a week.[75]

On May 7—the anniversary of the day in 1915 when a German submarine sank the *Lusitania*—the Germans were summoned to the palace of Versailles. The German representatives had anticipated some tough terms in the treaty, including financial payments, but Wilson's lofty rhetoric about the "Fourteen Points" led them to anticipate goodwill. They pinned their hopes for a reasonable treaty on the allegedly idealistic Woodrow Wilson. Germany had, after all, become a republic—the Germans at Versailles were not the Germans who had been in power back when the war started in 1914. The German representatives were shocked to see the treaty. They were stunned at the prospect of accepting total responsibility for the war, losing so many assets, losing all their colonies, making huge initial payments with total reparations liabilities unknown.

Germany's foreign minister, Ulrich von Brockdorff-Rantzau, an officious aristocrat, offered a belligerent response. Although he had criticized Germany's war policies, he was a tactless wonder when dealing with Clemenceau and Lloyd George. Historian MacMillan described him as "haughty, monocled, slim, immaculately turned out . . . as though he had just stepped out of the Kaiser's court."[76]

Brockdorff-Rantzau denounced Article 231, since the "war guilt" clause was the rationale for huge reparations. Clemenceau dismissed the objections. Lloyd George wrote that "I could not accept the German point of view without giving away our whole case for entering into the war."[77] Wilson snapped, "We don't believe a word of what the German government says."[78]

Of course, the Germans had no choice but to accept the treaty. It was signed June 28, 1919. Britain's hunger blockade continued until July 12, 1919.

Surely things wouldn't have turned out so badly if Wilson had demanded a peace conference in neutral Geneva instead of in battle-scarred France; if Wilson had understood that the settlement terms were more important than his illusory League of Nations; if Wilson had insisted on a magnanimous peace with toleration, free trade, and the free movement of people; and if Wilson had emerged from the fog of his glittering generalities and taken the initiative to draft specific proposals.

Most important, things wouldn't have developed as they did if Wilson had stayed out of the war. Britain and France wouldn't have won a decisive victory. They wouldn't have been in a position to dictate vindictive surrender terms. Since the German offensive of the spring of 1918 ran out of steam before American soldiers had much of an impact on the war, and the British naval blockade continued to be highly effective, the Germans wouldn't have been in a position to dictate surrender terms, either. A more likely outcome would have been eventual recognition of stalemate, then exhaustion and some kind of negotiated settlement.

Since the United States intervened, helped win a decisive victory, and put the British and French in a position to dictate harsh surrender terms, it seems unlikely any American president—even one who was well informed, clear-thinking, and politically astute as Wilson was not—could have prevented the Treaty of Versailles from becoming a treaty of revenge. As an outsider, the best American president wouldn't have had the intensity of motivation and singleness of purpose of the Europeans, particularly the French, who were convinced that protecting their national security required crushing their enemies.

In an evaluation of the Versailles Treaty after seventy-five years, Manfred F. Boemeke, Gerald D. Feldman, and Elizabeth Glaser offered this defense when they wrote: "The peace settlement and its subsequent revisions ... represented the most stable arrangement that could have emerged from the contentious peacemaking process in Paris."[79] But this view assumed a decisive victory by Britain and France, thanks to Wilson's intervention. A negotiated settlement wouldn't have resulted in the Treaty of Versailles as we know it.

The most serious blunder was made not at the 1919 Paris Conference but in Washington, when in 1917 Wilson decided to bring the
United States into the war, enabling the Allies to win a decisive victory and dictate the harsh surrender terms. Having done this, he unleashed forces that soon exploded around the world.

WILSON AND HITLER

The postwar German government—the Weimar Republic—lost criti-
cal public support by accepting the harsh terms of the Versailles
Treaty. Germans across the political spectrum felt that the Versailles
Treaty was unjust and that it prolonged the war by economic means.[80]

The first sign of trouble came from the Free Corps, groups of
Germans who volunteered to help protect their country after the
army was substantially dismantled under the terms of the Versailles
Treaty. There were reportedly sixty-eight of these groups, headed
variously by generals, lieutenants, captains, and others who had
fought in the war.[81] In March 1920, backed by Erich von Ludendorff,
Wolfgang Kapp, and others, the Free Corps attempted a *putsch*—
revolt. The Free Corps occupied briefly the section of Berlin where
government buildings were located, because what was left of the regular German army did nothing.[82] But some leading industrialists,
among others, were concerned about where such spontaneous military action would lead, so the *putsch* collapsed, and the Free Corps
fled to Dresden. Bavaria, in southern Germany, became a haven for
people impatient with the Weimar experiment in democracy.

Among those agitating against the Weimar government was the
Austrian-born war veteran Adolf Hitler. Born on April 20, 1889, the
son of a customs official in Braunau am Inn, he moved to Vienna
when he was a teenager. "In the summer of the same year, 1889,"
wrote biographer Alan Bullock, "Lenin, a student of nineteen in
trouble with the authorities, moved with his mother from Kazan to
Samara. Stalin was a poor cobbler's son in Tiflis, Mussolini the six-
year-old child of a blacksmith in the bleak Romagna."[83]

An aspiring artist, Hitler hoped to enroll at the Academy of
Fine Arts, but failed the entrance examination. He spent what little
spare money he had going to see Richard Wagner's heroic operas. He

had to move from one dismal rented room to another, until he ended up in a charitable hostel for men, at 27 Meldemannstrasse. There, apparently, he read authors who were lost souls like himself, obsessed with fears of being exploited by Jews and having German blood contaminated by Slavs—and he dreamed of reviving a pure Aryan race.[84] To earn money, Bullock reported, Hitler "beat carpets, carried bags outside the West Station, and did casual labouring jobs, on more than one occasion shoveling snow off the streets."[85] Then he got the idea of painting postcard views of Vienna.

According to Bullock, "Everyone who knew him was struck by the combination of ambition, energy, and indolence in Hitler. Hitler was not only desperately anxious to impress people but was full of clever ideas for making his fortune and fame—from water-divining to designing an aeroplane. . . . His enthusiasm would flag, he would relapse into moodiness and disappear until he began to hare off after some new trick or shortcut to success."[86]

Hitler discovered and thrived on anti-Semitic periodicals that abounded in Vienna. He came to believe there was a Jewish conspiracy to dominate what he imagined to be the Aryan race, and he had no patience with liberal, democratic institutions such as toleration, free speech, and elected representatives. When he visited the Reichstat, Austria's representative assembly, he was impressed by the mediocrity and corruption of the politicians.

He came to believe in a Greater Germany: Germany should run Austria, and German should be the only official language. As a nationalist, he didn't like the Social Democratic Party, which promoted class conflict. These views were the stock-in-trade of the Pan-German movement. He admired Georg von Schonerer, leader of the anti-Semitic Pan-German Nationalists, and Karl Lueger, leader of the anti-Semitic Christian Socialists, which was the strongest political party in the Austrian Reichstat. Hitler was intrigued by the Social Democratic Party's propaganda techniques to help develop a mass following. He envisioned a party embracing both nationalism and socialism.

By 1913, Hitler had inherited a little money following his mother's death from cancer, and he went to live in Munich. After the war broke out, he volunteered for the Bavarian army and served as a

runner carrying messages between company and regimental commanders. In October 1918 he was briefly blinded during a British
poison gas attack. He thrived on military discipline and war. He despised civilians who, back home, evaded military service and engaged in black-market dealings and endless political debates. He
thought representative assemblies should be suppressed.

Hitler got a job working for the army's Press and News Bureau
in Munich, and somebody suggested that he keep an eye on the
Workers' Party. It was one of fifteen groups in Munich and seventy-
three in Germany, almost all of which were started after the war, that
offered a devil's brew of anti-Semitism, anticapitalism, nationalism,
and socialism.[87] The Workers' Party was a tiny outfit that met in a
Munich bar and kept its money in a cigar box. The party attacked
conservatives as lacking concern for the poor, and it attacked leftists
as lacking patriotism. Hitler joined the party as its seventh member.
Apparently he saw an opportunity to play an important role that
would probably have been denied him at one of the larger, established political parties. In February 1920 the German Workers' Party
became the National Socialist German Workers' Party (NSDAP).

In his memoir, *Mein Kampf,* Hitler promoted the legend that he
was an immediate hit, an exaggeration according to historian Ian
Kershaw—newspapers didn't much notice his early speeches. But
there's no doubt Hitler was developing a reputation for fireworks,
with his bold denunciations of Jews, speculators, and other alleged
enemies, and his appeal to restore German greatness.

The vindictive Versailles Treaty played right into his hands. Hans
Frank, who later became Hitler's governor of Poland, recalled the ex-
citement at seeing Hitler speak in 1920: "He took the overwhelmingly
dominant topic of the day, the Versailles Diktat, and posed the question of questions: What now, German people? He spoke for two and
a half hours, often interrupted by frenetic torrents of applause—and
one could have listened to him for much, much longer. Everything
came from the heart, and he struck a chord with all of us."[88]

Hitler spoke to more and more mass meetings in Munich, where
his associates could effectively promote the events. In 1920 he gave
ten speeches outside Munich. Party membership rose from 190 in
January 1920 to 2,000 by December and 3,300 by August 1921.[89]

This was small compared with the socialist, Catholic, and older nationalist parties, and Hitler knew he had to reach out. He was introduced to army captain Ernst Röhm, who had organized the Iron Fist Club for radical nationalist officers. Born in 1887, Röhm was a career army man who cherished the World War I days when the army dominated Germany, and his personal mission was to help restore the army to its glory. Röhm had been wounded three times—a bullet had left a scar across his left cheek, and part of his nose had been blown away. He felt the humiliation of defeat and despised the civilian authorities who had signed the armistice and the Treaty of Versailles. He became an armaments officer, supplying weapons to several paramilitary organizations, including the Einwohnerwehr, which had a quarter of a million members and fought revolutionaries and armed gangs.[90]

Röhm seemed to see a fit with Hitler, whose top priority was propaganda—he viewed his role as a public speaker rousing the masses against their tormenters. Röhm supplied contacts. When, pressured by Britain and France, the German government disarmed and disbanded the Einwohnerwehr, Röhm persuaded many outraged army officers to join the NSDAP. The nationalist Thule Society's newspaper *Völkischer Beobachter* was going bankrupt, and Röhm persuaded General Ritter von Epp to provide the 60,000 marks needed to buy it and turn it into the NSDAP's newspaper. It became a principal outlet for Hitler's writings. Hitler resolved to make the NSDAP a force far beyond Munich. In July 1921 he won a bitter struggle for party leadership, and took over as chairman. Röhm provided bodyguards to help control his meetings. These bodyguards became the *Sturmabteilung* ("Storm Section"), also known as storm troopers, or SA for short—Hitler's personal army that would help propel him to power.

6

WHY DID WILSON IGNORE THE RISK OF VIOLENT SOCIALIST REVOLUTION IN RUSSIA?

IF RUSSIA'S PROVISIONAL GOVERNMENT had quit the war and negotiated a peace with Germany in early 1917, we might never have heard of Lenin. He would have returned home to find Russians celebrating the end of the war. Soldiers would have been returning home and the process of reviving the economy would have begun. To be sure, some Russians would have been shocked that the country had to give up so much territory, but it was territory occupied by non-Russian people. Finally, of course, the czar was gone, and the Russian army would have been there to defend the Provisional Government, virtually ruling out prospects for a Bolshevik coup.

Alexander Kerensky and some others in the Provisional Government wanted Russia to stay in the war, and maybe they would have prevailed if they had decided on their own. But relentless diplomatic pressure from Britain and France, and diplomatic pressure and bribes from Woodrow Wilson, helped assure that the virtually bankrupt Provisional Government would stay in the war. The British and French plotted a coup when it appeared the Provisional Government might drop out.

President Wilson utterly misunderstood what was going on in Russia. Socialist revolutionaries of various stripes were struggling for power, and all wanted government control of the economy. It never occurred to Wilson that government control of the economy would make possible government control of everything else. The result would probably be a totalitarian regime and reign of terror such as developed during the French Revolution. In his April 2, 1917, war message, Wilson hailed Russian socialist revolutionaries as "forces that are fighting for freedom in the world, for justice, and for peace." Wilson seemed to have no idea that by pressuring the Russian Provisional Government to stay in the war, he was playing with fire.

So when Lenin arrived in Petrograd, he didn't encounter celebrations of peace that would have doomed his revolutionary dreams; instead he found chaos. He began planning how he could exploit that chaos to overthrow the Provisional Government. It was an unintended gift from Woodrow Wilson and his allies.

Lenin's Bolshevik comrades had already accepted the Provisional Government for the time being, so they needed a little persuading. The most cautious Bolsheviks were Grigory Zinoviev and Lev Kamenev. Lenin wrote what came to be known as the "April Theses," which called for abolishing the army and establishing a people's militia, nationalizing land, and withdrawing from the war. While his aim was to grab power for himself and the Bolsheviks, he didn't dare call for that, since he didn't have any political support. Instead he urged that power be transferred to the soviets, the committees of urban workers, and of course he planned to gain control of those. The editors of *Pravda (Truth)*, the Bolshevik newspaper, refused to print his "April Theses," but Lenin persisted, and his piece appeared on April 20.

Lenin wrote more articles for *Pravda*. He blamed bankers, industrialists, and agricultural landlords for Russia's troubles. He attacked socialists who supported the Provisional Government, discreetly downplaying his belief in dictatorship, terror, and civil war.

Lenin gave talks wherever he could. "Ruin, catastrophe and destruction ran like a red threat through his vocabulary," wrote biographer Robert Service. "When he got up on a platform, the audience was transfixed. He paced up and down. He fixed the crowd with a piercing gaze. He pinned his thumbs in his waistcoat like a schoolteacher, which added to the impression he gave of purveying genuine knowledge. He was not a conventionally brilliant orator. His enunciation was imperfect, since he still failed to say his *r*s properly. He also took time to settle into a rhythm in the course of his speeches. But this did not matter to his audiences. The very opposite was the case:

the awkwardness of his stocky, unprepossessing figure on the platform conveyed the impression of passion and willpower. In any case,
it was often difficult to hear exactly what he was saying at the open
public meetings, and the audiences were attracted as much to what
they saw—an uncompromising militant leader speaking for the
people's cause—as by the precise verbal content of his oratory."[1]

Lenin organized street demonstrations against the Provisional
Government. He encouraged civil disobedience. He did what he
could to promote more chaos, undermine confidence in the Provisional Government, and convince people that change was coming.

On May 3, Russian newspapers published a statement from the
Provisional Government affirming its intention to stay in the war.
Most Russian socialists supported that, but they objected to what
they considered the government's ambition to gain territory. The
next day there were spontaneous protests in the streets of Petrograd.
Soldiers were encouraged to disobey orders because the government
was betraying the revolution by pursuing an imperialist war rather
than a war for supposedly democratic ideals. Bolshevik agitators
went to factories, urging that workers join the demonstrations. Banners proclaimed, "Down with the Provisional Government" and "All
power to the Soviets." Armed workers moved toward the center of
the city. Since the Bolsheviks had a highly centralized organization, it
was presumed that Lenin ordered these actions.

There were counterdemonstrations, and General Lavr Georgevich
Kornilov, who was responsible for maintaining security in Petrograd,
prepared to put down the disturbances, but city officials decided a
show of force might be inflammatory, and they canceled his orders.
Instead, officials denounced demonstrators as traitors. Perhaps
because big crowds supported the government, support for the
demonstrators faded away. It soon became apparent that the attempted coup was a failure, and the Bolsheviks denied any role in it.
Lenin maintained a low profile by staying at home, away from the
disturbances.

Kerensky responded to the disorders by forming a coalition government. This effort took on new urgency when, on May 13, minister of war Alexandr Ivanovich Guchkov resigned after concluding
that the country couldn't be governed. Kerensky wanted to recruit

ministers from the business community and the military, but socialist intellectuals were adamantly against this. Kerensky turned to the executive committee. It voted 44–19 that its members could accept positions in a coalition government. By joining the government, the socialists ceased to be part of the opposition, and they could be blamed for subsequent failures. By staying out, the Bolsheviks became the only effective opposition.

STAYING IN THE WAR: CATASTROPHE
FOR THE PROVISIONAL GOVERNMENT

The Allied Powers stepped up their pressure for the Russians to launch a new offensive against Germany on the Eastern Front. Russian officials couldn't delay much longer if they hoped to continue receiving military aid from the United States, Britain, and France. Kerensky, who had taken over as minister of war, named Alexei Brusilov as commander-in-chief of the Russian army. Brusilov was perhaps the only Russian general who had distinguished himself in the war. He planned a "Grand Offensive" for July, against Austrian forces. He warned: "If we fail to cooperate with our allies, we cannot expect them to come to our aid when we need it."[2]

The English Red Cross nurse Florence Farmborough, helping wounded Russians on the Eastern Front, wrote in her diary on June 7: "Our Allies were pressing the Provisional Government to start an offensive as soon as possible, and it was expected to be a successful one."[3]

Meanwhile the First All-Russian Congress of Soviets had gathered in June to deliberate on their situation. The Bolsheviks had 105 delegates, trailing the Social Revolutionaries (with 285) and the Mensheviks (with 248).[4] But the Bolsheviks were more single-minded in their pursuit of power, and they sought to destroy anything that was in the way. The other socialists had a less appealing message: maintain army discipline, maintain factory production, and delay reforms until after the war.

To achieve the coup that he envisioned, Lenin needed a military force at his command, so he promoted the arming of workers. The czar's arsenals had been looted, and thousands of guns were in private hands. Lenin referred to his army as a "Workers' Militia." Its mission was to oppose "reactionary" forces and protect the revolution.

Lenin had also launched a propaganda campaign by expanding the press run of *Pravda*. Some 85,000 copies were reportedly printed in June 1917. This jumped to 320,000 in July. They published an edition adapted for soldiers, *Soldatskaia Pravda*—some 350,000 copies. Such ventures seem to have been funded by the Germans, who provided subsidies through the German embassy in Stockholm. Total German subsidies to the Bolsheviks in 1917 and 1918 were reported to be 50 million deutsche marks' worth of gold—perhaps nine tons.[5]

Lenin conceived a plot to seize control of the government on June 23. The idea was to get 40,000 armed soldiers marching in the streets, denouncing the coalition government.[6] Then the soldiers would be led to take over government offices and other key facilities. Bolshevik agitators went to barracks and factories, looking for recruits. But when the Congress of Soviets heard about the plot, delegates emphatically denounced it. They sent people into barracks and factories, warning against participating in the demonstrations. The Bolsheviks, apparently not yet ready to take on the soviets, canceled the demonstrations.

Although the Congress of Soviets criticized the Bolsheviks, it didn't try to limit the amount of trouble they might cause in the future. Indeed, when one of the delegates, Irakli Georgievich Tsereteli, proposed that the Bolsheviks be disarmed because they were trying to overthrow the government, a majority voted no. *Pravda* published an editorial declaring that Bolsheviks would defy the Soviet if it tried to impose any restrictions on them.

Russian soldiers stationed in Petrograd—especially the 11,000-man Machine Gun Regiment—were sympathetic to the Bolsheviks, and in July the Provisional Government ordered them to the front. This was intended to get potential rebels out of the capital and prepare for an anticipated German offensive. The Bolsheviks responded with propaganda attacking the government and encouraging soldiers to resist their orders. Half the regiment decided to participate in an attempted coup planned for July 16. Then, late in the afternoon, came word that the Bolshevik Central Committee had called it off. Available records don't indicate the reasons why. Perhaps not enough regiments favored a coup; most remained loyal to the Provisional Government.

The following day, rebellious soldiers marched toward the building where the Soviet met and entered the offices of anti-Bolshevik newspapers and the government's intelligence office, with evidence documenting German funding of the Bolsheviks. A Bolshevik delegation, supposedly representing fifty-four factories, went to the Soviet and demanded that it assume power—the Soviet had only six guards to provide security.

The Bolsheviks seemed close to seizing power, yet they didn't finish the job. Richard Pipes explained, "It was due to a last-minute failure of nerve on the part of the commander-in-chief. Lenin simply could not make up his mind: according to Zinoviev, who spent these hours by his side, he kept wondering aloud whether this was or was not the time to 'try,' and in the end decided it was not."[7]

Provisional Government officials countered by releasing some of the information they had about Lenin's financial dealings with the Germans. This outraged Russian soldiers who, though weary of the war, didn't like the idea of a Russian seeming to serve as a German agent. About 800 pro-Bolshevik soldiers were captured, and *Pravda*'s offices and printing plant were destroyed. The Bolsheviks denied the accusations against Lenin. He fled to the countryside outside Petrograd. Again, the Socialist Revolutionaries and Mensheviks were reluctant to take action against the Bolsheviks.[8] Kerensky, who had become prime minister after the failed Grand Offensive, didn't do anything. Although Lenin had failed in three attempts to seize power, he demonstrated that he was determined to keep trying until he was successful.

The Grand Offensive turned into a debacle. Russian forces advanced toward Lwow, capital of Galicia (southern Poland). But then, because of uncertain command and low morale, the soldiers started to abandon their positions. By July 6, German reinforcements appeared on the scene, and demoralized, often unarmed Russian soldiers refused to fight. They fled. There were reports that the death penalty would be revived to punish deserters, but still Russian soldiers deserted.

Nurse Farmborough reported, "The traffic on the road was be-coming thicker and less controlled; wagon-wheel interlaced with wagon-wheel; frantic drivers shouted, frightened horses reared. . . . The spectacle of the many struggling vehicles on the road was a dreadful one. There was tremendous surging forward, no matter what the cost, no matter what the injury to man, horse, or cart. All was a hectic scramble, a headlong rush eastward."[9]

It had been estimated that the offensive might involve 6,000 Russian battle deaths. In fact, about 400,000 Russians died in battle, and hundreds of thousands of soldiers deserted.[10] Altogether, the Grand Offensive brought total World War I Russian casualties to an estimated 1.7 million killed and 4.9 million wounded, and there were approximately 3.9 million Russian prisoners of war.[11] How could Woodrow Wilson, in his wildest dreams, have imagined that the Provisional Government would remain in power by continuing the war and piling more horrors upon horrors?

The Grand Offensive, the last Russian military operation of the war, was a catastrophe for the Provisional Government. According to historian Orlando Figes, "There is no doubt that the launching—let alone the failure—of the offensive led directly to the summer crisis which culminated in the downfall of the Provisional Government and the Bolshevik seizure of power. More than anything else, the summer offensive swung the soldiers to the Bolsheviks, the only major party which stood uncompromisingly for an immediate end to the war. Had the Provisional Government adopted a similar policy and opened negotiations with the Germans, no doubt the Bolsheviks would never have come to power."[12]

BRITISH AND FRENCH ADVISERS: ONLY A COUP COULD KEEP RUSSIA IN THE WAR

The Russian situation had deteriorated so badly by the fall of 1917 that British and French military advisers supported the idea of a mil-itary coup to avert chaos and keep Russia in the war.[13] After all that had happened, the Allies could still think of nothing but to keep Rus-sia in the war!

They thought the most likely leader was General Kornilov, a courageous and patriotic man who had been asked to take over as commander-in-chief of Russian forces. Aware of dwindling morale and discipline, he demanded what amounted to dictatorial power as a condition for accepting the responsibility. He seems to have had an eye on General Erich von Ludendorff, who secured near-dictatorial power in Germany as that country faced multiple wartime crises. Kornilov's orders were to be law. Kornilov wanted the death penalty for deserters. He believed that those working in defense industries should be subject to military discipline. He was eager to suppress the Bolsheviks.

The British and French threatened to cut off military aid to Russia unless Kerensky—who by now had become prime minister—suppressed disorder.[14] The British and French felt politically vulnerable to complaints that they were squandering their taxpayers' money on Russia, which was going from bad to worse.[15]

Kerensky was furious that the Allies were so desperate to keep Russia in the war that they would conspire against the Provisional Government. He wrote, "There was one thing the Allies failed to take into account when they lent their support to Kornilov. It did not occur to them that, having seized power, the military dictator would not have had time for the imperialist war—all his efforts would have been directed toward civil war."[16]

Fearing a military coup, Kerensky had Kornilov imprisoned. Kerensky snapped, "It seems that the Allies learned nothing from the Kornilov affair, and the ignominious failure of the plot did not cause them to modify their disloyal attitude to the Provisional Government."[17]

Richard Pipes doubted that there was a Kornilov plot. "All the available evidence," he wrote, "points to a 'Kerensky plot' engineered to discredit the general as the ringleader of an imaginary but widely anticipated counterrevolution, the suppression of which would elevate the Prime Minister to a position of unrivaled popularity and power, enabling him to meet the growing threat from the Bolsheviks. It cannot be a coincidence that none of the elements present in a general coup d'etat ever came to light: lists of conspirators, organizational charts, code signals, programs."[18]

If Kornilov weren't conspiring to seize power, Kerensky's move certainly backfired. Imprisoning Kornilov destroyed what little confidence the military still had in Kerensky. Soldiers despised him. When he faced another challenge to his power, who would defend him?

LENIN'S FOURTH COUP ATTEMPT IS SUCCESSFUL

With Lenin in hiding, Trotsky assumed command of Bolshevik forces. "Trotsky was an ideal complement to Lenin," observed Pipes. "Brighter and more flamboyant, a much better speaker and writer, he could galvanize crowds: Lenin's charisma was limited to his followers. But Trotsky was unpopular with the Bolshevik cadres, in part because he had joined their party late, after years of acerbic attacks on it, and in part because he was unbearably arrogant. In any event, being Jewish, Trotsky could hardly aspire to national leadership in a country in which, Revolution or no, Jews were regarded as outsiders."[19]

A German military advance provided the next opportunity for a coup. Germans captured three islands in the Gulf of Riga, preparing to land behind Russian forces. This seemed like a prelude to an advance on Petrograd.

Kerensky advocated moving the government to Moscow, but Trotsky denounced this proposal as abandoning the place where the revolution began. He declared that if the Provisional Government wouldn't defend Petrograd, it should resign. Kerensky stayed in Petrograd.

On October 23, Lenin met with twelve of the twenty-one members of the Bolshevik Central Committee. They talked for ten hours before making their historic decision: to seize power by November 7. Committee members agreed with Lenin that the coup had to happen before the election of the Constituent Assembly, because the Bolsheviks weren't expected to gain more than a third of the seats there. If the Constituent Assembly gained legitimacy, the Bolsheviks would lose. The coup would be achieved by a military takeover. The Bolsheviks abandoned Lenin's earlier ideas about generating political pressure through crowds. Informers told Kerensky about these plans, but he imagined he could summon enough military force to crush the Bolsheviks.

Trotsky set up the Petrograd Military Revolutionary Committee (PMRC) to defend the city and, if necessary, protect against the Provisional Government. The PMRC consisted of some sixty officials, forty-eight of whom were Bolsheviks.[20] The PMRC operated in the name of the Petrograd Soviet, but it was Bolshevik-controlled. It functioned for fifty-three days and issued some 6,000 orders signed by some thirty different people as "chairman."[21]

On November 2, General Alexander Verkhovsky, the Provincial Government's minister of war, told his associates that the Russian army was hopeless. He warned that the only way of stopping a Bolshevik coup was to quit the war. Kerensky wouldn't hear of it. Vladimir Lvovich Burtsev, Russian nationalist newspaperman, blasted Verkovsky as unpatriotic, and he was forced out of the government.

On November 6, the battleship *Nova*, controlled by a pro-Bolshevik crew, went up the Neva River toward the Winter Palace, which the Provisional Government had been using for its headquarters. That night Bolshevik soldiers took positions controlling access to bridges, telephone centers, post offices, railroad stations, and banks. The next morning Kerensky realized what had happened, and he started calling his military commanders for help, but there weren't any around. He disguised himself as a Serbian officer and escaped from the Winter Palace in a car with an American flag.

There wasn't much of a fight for the Winter Palace itself. The cruiser *Aurora* fired one blank, because that's all it had—no live ammunition. Some Red Guards entered the palace and were captured, but defenders became discouraged by the lack of support and left. Bolshevik soldiers subsequently entered through unlocked gates and open windows.

On November 7 at 2:35 in the afternoon, there was an emergency meeting of the Petrograd Soviet. Trotsky announced, "Kerensky's power has been overthrown. Some of the ministers have been arrested."[22] Then Lenin declared: "Comrades! The workers' and peasants' revolution, which the Bolsheviks have all this time been talking about the need for, has been accomplished." This is called the October Revolution because events took place in October according to the Julian calendar Russia was still using.

As Pipes pointed out, nobody outside the Bolshevik Central

Committee had authorized the coup. "The Petrograd Soviet," he explained, "had formed the Milrevkom (Military Revolutionary Committee) to defend the city, not to topple the government. The Second Congress of Soviets, which was to legitimize the coup, had not even opened when the Bolsheviks had already acted in its name."[23]

A new Soviet government, the Sovnarkom, was proclaimed on November 8. Lenin was chairman, Trotsky was the People's Commissar for External Affairs, and Joseph Stalin was the People's Commissar for Nationalities Affairs. "Had it not been for the Great War," biographer Robert Service pointed out, "there would have been no October Revolution. Lenin had been given his chance because of the wartime economic dislocation, administrative breakdown and political disarray."[24]

Comparatively few people in Russia had any idea what was going on. Since power had been seized in the name of the soviets, which arose during the February Revolution, the Bolsheviks created the impression that not much was really new. Foreign observers seemed to have a better understanding of events. Between November 5 and November 17, the ruble plunged from 6.20 per U.S. dollar to 12/14—losing half its value.[25]

For the moment the Bolsheviks had the advantage of surprise. But there were plenty of rivals for power—socialist parties, labor unions, factory committees, neighborhood organizations, and especially the soviets. Lenin was determined to achieve dominance over all these.

In his office at the Smolny Institute, Lenin drafted decrees—the Bolshevik government was to rule like the czars, by decrees. The Decree on Peace excited people's hopes, but of course Russia was still at war, and Lenin was about to launch a terrible civil war. He called for negotiations with Germany to negotiate a peace settlement that would save Russia from having to give up territory or pay reparations.

The Decree on Land called for the confiscation of landed estates and "socialization" of other private land to peasant communes. This represented a tactical compromise for Lenin, whose aim was to have land nationalized, under government control. Peasant control of land was a priority of the Socialist Revolutionary Party, and peasants had been seizing land since the summer of 1917, so Lenin bowed to the inevitable rather than risking a confrontation between the minority Bolsheviks and the vast majority of Russian peasants.

During these early days of the revolution, Lenin's public utterances were surprisingly low-key. "He was keeping his political cards close to his chest," wrote Robert Service. "He was a party boss, and wanted Bolshevism to be attractive to those workers, soldiers, peasants and intellectuals who had not yet supported it. And so terms such as dictatorship, terror, civil war and revolutionary war were yet again quietly shelved. He also continued to leave aside his lifelong imprecations against priests, mullahs and rabbis, against industrialists, the landed gentry and kulaks, against liberal, conservative and reactionary intellectuals."[26]

At the same time, the Bolsheviks began suppressing their rivals. Lenin signed "Order Number One" abolishing all laws "in contradiction with the worker and peasant government." He signed a decree saying that "all leaders of the Constitutional Democratic Party, a party filled with enemies of the people, are hereby to be considered outlaws, and are to be arrested immediately and brought before a revolutionary court."[27] Since existing laws had been abolished, there were few if any constraints on the penalties the court could impose.

On November 30 the Bolsheviks established the Food Commission, and it promptly denounced "the rich classes who profit from the misery of others . . . the time has come to requisition the surpluses of the rich, and all their goods as well." This commission began to organize gangs to move through the countryside, seizing grain from peasants.

The Military Investigation Commission, established December 7, focused on arresting and punishing "counterrevolutionary" military officers. Novelist Maxim Gorky, writing in *Novaya Zbizn (New Life)*, November 1917: "Lenin, Trotsky, and their followers were already afflicted by the rotten poison of power, as shown by their disgraceful attitude toward freedom of speech and of the individual and the whole sum of those rights for which democracy had struggled."[28]

Mindful of his party's minority position, Lenin decided he had to distract people while he consolidated power. He promoted class envy and class warfare. According to historian Figes, "In the minds of ordinary people, who had never read their Marx, class divisions were based much more on emotion than objective social criteria. The popular term *burzhooi,* for example, had no intrinsic class connotations, despite its obvious derivation from the word 'bourgeois.' It was used as a general form of abuse against employers, officers, landowners, priests, merchants, Jews, students, professionals, or anyone else well dressed, foreign looking or seemingly well-to-do. Hungry workers condemned the peasants as *burzhooi* because they were thought to be hoarding foodstuffs; while peasants—who often confused the word with *barzhui* (the owners of a barge) and *birzhye* (from the word for stock exchange, *birzh*)—likewise condemned the workers and all townsmen in general, because they were thought to be hoarding manufactured goods."[29] Marxist newspapers denounced *burzhooi* as "enemies of the people."

Lenin imposed confiscatory taxes on *burzhooi,* even though most were small businessmen, teachers, doctors, and others impoverished by the war and inflation. Lenin encouraged people to *Grabi nagrablennoe* ("Loot the loot").[30] Bolshevik officials broke into homes and seized food, clothing, furniture, typewriters, anything. The Bolshevik regime took over church property. Factories were seized. Banks were nationalized, and depositors were effectively prevented from withdrawing their money. The contents of safe deposit boxes were confiscated—during the first half of 1918, Bolsheviks plundered some 35,000 of these.[31]

Lenin replaced the old ruling class with a new ruling class. According to Figes: "The flea-markets of Petrograd and Moscow were filled with the former belongings of fallen plutocrats: icons, paintings, carpets, pianos, gramophones, samovars, morning coats and ball dresses—all could be picked up for the price of a meal or two. The more precious items were snapped up by the *nouveaux riches* of the Soviet regime—commissars and officials, looting soldiers and sailors, petty traders and bandits—as they sought to acquire the status symbols of a ruling class. The new masters of Russia were easily distinguishable by the way they wore their long and dirty hair greased back, by their gold-toothed smiles and their eau-de-cologne smells."[32]

While people were busy looting, they lost interest in politics, and Lenin consolidated his power. He faced considerable pressure to share power with other socialist parties. The Union of Railroad

Employees threatened a nationwide strike if Bolsheviks continued to monopolize power—this was a serious threat since, back in October 1905, a railroad strike had forced the czar to grant his political opponents major concessions. Lenin's comrades were ready to share power, but he would have none of it. Trotsky weighed in with a vehement denunciation of power-sharing. When word came that Bolshevik forces had defeated Krasnov's pro-Kerensky forces, the idea of power-sharing was dropped. Lenin figured socialists had no other alternative but to support the Bolsheviks.

In January 1918 there was a Bolshevik decree authorizing the suppression of "counterrevolutionary" newspapers. Soon almost seventy newspapers were shut down in Petrograd and Moscow.[33] Later, more newspapers were closed, and editors were arrested.[34] Some of Russia's best-known writers protested, but the Bolsheviks had the upper hand. The following year, in August 1918, the Bolsheviks would ban all independent publications.

Still, large numbers of people opposed the Bolshevik coup. The Union of Government Employees ordered its members to stop work, and government ceased to function. In Petrograd, banks closed, telephone, telegraph, and post office workers walked off the job, and pharmacists and teachers went on strike, all demanding that the Bolsheviks share power. Printers threatened to go on strike if the Bolsheviks continued to ban the publication of dissident views. Similar strikes spread to provincial towns.

When the State Bank refused to cash Bolshevik checks, soldiers showed up, forced open the vaults, and took the money. To intimidate financial people and assure the flow of money into Bolshevik coffers, on January 2, 1918, Lenin started the *Vserossiiskaya Chrezvychainaya Komissiya po bor'be s kontr-revolyutsiei, spekulyatsiei i sabotazhem*—translated as the All-Russian Extraordinary Commission to Combat the Counterrevolution, Speculation, and Sabotage. This was abbreviated as VC*h*K, or Cheka. There was no legal basis for it.[35]

Lenin selected Felix Dzerzhinsky to run it, in part because Dzerzhinsky had spent more years in czarist prisons than any of the other Bolshevik leaders. A Pole, Dzerzhinsky probably wouldn't be reluctant to get tough on people of another nationality—namely,

Russians. Dzerzhinsky was born September 11, 1877, near Minsk, the son of a Polish aristocrat. "As a child he was obsessively religious," wrote historian George Leggett. "In adolescence his consuming Catholic faith was replaced by the crusading creed of revolutionary Marxism."[36] Dzerzhinsky rebelled against czarist authority, joining the Lithuanian Social Democratic Party, a Marxist organization, in 1895. Because of his political activities, he was arrested by the Russian Imperial Police five times. He participated in the Russian Revolution of 1905 and continued agitating against the czarist government. By the time the czar was overthrown, in March 1917, Dzerzhinsky had spent about a quarter of his life in czarist prisons or exile. He joined the Bolsheviks that year. He pushed himself relentlessly despite frail health, weakened by his years in prison. He suffered from tuberculosis and was spitting blood when named to head the Cheka.

Driven by resentment, bitterness, and hatred, he was utterly devoted to exterminating political opponents. Leggett observed that "Dzerzhinsky subordinated all accepted ethical principles to whatever cause he was serving. Lenin's word, the Party's command, these were his only laws. His revolutionary zeal was fanatical; he was prepared to sacrifice countless lives in the interests of the dictatorship of the proletariat."

Dzerzhinsky declared that "the task of the Commission [Cheka] is as follows: (1) to suppress and liquidate an act or attempted act of counterrevolutionary activity or sabotage, whatever its origin, anywhere on Russian soil; (2) to bring all saboteurs and counterrevolutionaries before a revolutionary court."[37] The Cheka started out by arresting about a hundred people, and within months its web had snared some 12,000.

Trotsky warned, "In less than a month, this terror is going to take extremely violent forms, just as it did during the great French Revolution." Lenin declared that "for as long as we fail to treat speculators the way they deserve—with a bullet in the head—we will not get anywhere at all." In practice, anybody could become a victim of the terror.

What of elections for the long-discussed Constituent Assembly? The Provincial Government had scheduled them for November 23— as it happened, about two weeks after the Provincial Government was overthrown. Since the Bolsheviks had demanded elections as a tactic against the Provisional Government, suddenly opposing them wouldn't have been credible. As expected, the Socialist-Revolutionaries got the most votes (40 percent). The Bolsheviks polled less than a quarter of the votes. In the Bolshevik strongholds of Petrograd and Moscow, the non-socialist Kadets did nearly as well as the Bolsheviks, and the Kadets actually did better in almost a third of the provincial capitals.

Lenin belittled the importance of the Constituent Assembly, concocting dubious reasons, such as the outbreak of counterrevolution, why the election results weren't valid. Bolsheviks delayed the opening of the Constituent Assembly as long as they could. When it finally opened, demonstrators turned out to show their support, but Bolshevik soldiers chased them away and destroyed their banners. Soldiers fired on demonstrators—for the first time since the February Revolution. When Lenin heard that the demonstrators were gone, he let the proceedings begin on January 18, 1918.

After the Constituent Assembly had endorsed previously adopted measures such as nationalizing land and banks, the Bolsheviks introduced a resolution that would renounce the Constituent Assembly's power to legislate. The resolution said the Constituent Assembly would be "confined to working out in general the fundamental bases of reorganizing society on a socialist basis."[38] The resolution was defeated, and the Bolsheviks walked out, claiming that the Constituent Assembly was dominated by counterrevolutionaries. The Bolshevik Central Committee ruled that the Assembly had completed its business, and it was shut down.

Few Russians seemed to care what had happened to the Constituent Assembly. A small number of demonstrators showed up to protest. The Bolsheviks killed about twenty of them.

LEAVE THE WAR—OR BE OVERTHROWN

Having eliminated the immediate threats to his power, Lenin faced the task of getting Russia out of the war. He realized that if he failed, he would be toppled like the czar. But because everybody knew he had been permitted to travel through Germany, and there had been reports about the Germans channeling funds to the Bolsheviks, there was widespread suspicion that Lenin was a German agent, so he had to handle things carefully.

Lenin was adamant that such a peace must be achieved, but most of his compatriots were opposed because they didn't want to sign a treaty with imperialist Germany and Austria. Lenin proposed that all the combatants stop fighting and negotiate an armistice. Britain and France rejected the proposal immediately. Then Lenin declared that he would negotiate peace terms with the Germans and Austrians, who had expressed interest.

He was, of course, in a weak bargaining position, since Russia had suffered terrible war losses, the economy was a mess, the government had collapsed, and the Bolsheviks were about to default on all of the country's debts to domestic and foreign lenders.[39] But the Central Powers were under pressure, too. "The economic situation of the Central Powers," Pipes explained, "had become so desperate that they were unlikely to stay in the war much longer. Austria-Hungary was in a particularly precarious condition: its Foreign Minister, Count Ottokar Czernin, told the Germans . . . that his country probably could not hold out until the next harvest. The Germans were only marginally better off: some German politicians believed that the country would run out of grain by mid-April 1918.

"Germany and Austria also had problems with civilian morale," Pipes continued, "for the Bolshevik peace appeals aroused great hopes among their peoples. The German Chancellor advised the Kaiser that if talks with the Russians broke down, Austria-Hungary would probably drop out of the war and Germany would experience domestic unrest. The leader of the German Majority Socialists (who supported the war), Philip Scheidemann, predicted that the failure of peace negotiations with the Russians would 'spell the demise of the German Empire.' For all these reasons—military, economic, and psychological—the Central Powers needed peace with Russia almost as much as Bolshevik Russia needed peace with them."[40]

Talks began on December 16. The Germans, concerned to establish a buffer zone between Germany and Russia, proposed turning Russia's western provinces—including Poland and Lithuania—into independent states that would be German protectorates, with German soldiers and German business interests. German soldiers already occupied these territories. The horrified Russian delegation, headed by Lev Borisovich Kamenev, proposed a peace "without annexations and indemnities" and "self-determination." This was an odd position since the Russian Empire included many conquered peoples who hoped to gain their independence.

While the Russians stalled for time to figure out what they might do, the German position hardened. German military advisers urged that in the name of national security, Germany should seek a bigger buffer zone. The Germans were also becoming more concerned about Russian soldiers who, during the cease-fire on the Eastern Front, were fraternizing with German soldiers, encouraging revolution.

Trotsky succeeded Kamenev at Brest-Litovsk, but he continued stalling. Kuhlmann reaffirmed Germany's intention to annex Russian territories and establish a buffer zone between the two countries. The Germans began negotiating a separate peace with representatives from the Ukraine who wanted to break away from Russia and become an independent state. Rather than respecting the right of Ukrainians to "self-determination," the Bolsheviks dispatched forces to regain control there. No wonder, since the Ukraine produced an estimated one-third of Russian grain and 70 percent of its iron and coal. But on December 30, Germany recognized the Ukraine as an independent state and soon afterwards signed a peace treaty with the Ukraine.

In February 1918, weary of Trotsky's stalling and posturing, German representatives told him Germany would invade Russia if their proposals weren't accepted soon. Trotsky replied that Russia was simply withdrawing from the war. The Germans concluded that Trotsky's aim was to promote revolution, not peace.

A majority of Bolsheviks still refused to sign a treaty with the Central Powers, and on February 17, German forces reached Divinsk. They continued on to Minsk and Pskov. Lenin reportedly believed the Germans were seriously considering trying to capture Petrograd and Moscow.

Lenin appealed to Britain and France, whose sole interest in Russia was to keep their ally in the war. Britain and France desperately wanted to avoid a separate peace between Germany and Russia, because it would enable the Germans to transfer divisions to the Western Front. Both the British and French representatives recommended financial assistance if the Bolsheviks resumed fighting on the Eastern Front—despite overwhelming evidence that staying in the war had been a catastrophe for Russia.

On February 22 the Germans demanded the Russian territories they had previously occupied and territories they entered after the armistice talks had broken down. Specifically, the Germans wanted Russian soldiers to withdraw from the Ukraine and Finland, and they would become buffer states along with the others previously sought. Russia was to pay some reparations to Germany. Russia had forty-eight hours to respond, and a treaty had to be signed within seventy-two hours after that.

Lenin told the Bolshevik Central Committee: "Undoubtedly the peace that we are currently compelled to conclude is an obscene peace; but if war begins, our government will be swept aside and peace will be concluded by another government."[41] He pointed out that at least the Germans would permit the Bolsheviks to remain in power. Lenin declared that if the Bolsheviks continued to resist negotiating with Germany and Austria, he would quit the Central Committee and somehow pursue peace on his own. Lenin issued another warning: "History will say that you gave away the Revolution."[42] By a vote of seven to four, with four members abstaining, the Bolshevik Central Committee agreed to accept terms offered by the Central Powers.

Meanwhile, German forces marched toward Petrograd. By February 24 they were some 250 kilometers from the city. On March 2, German airplanes bombed it. The Bolsheviks prepared to move their offices farther away, to Moscow.

Lenin biographer Robert Service observed, "If Lenin had not won the debate, there is little doubt that the Central Powers would have concluded that the Bolsheviks were no longer of any use to them. The result would have been the occupation of the Russian heartland and the collapse of the October Revolution."[43]

The Central Powers took possession of Poland, the Baltic provinces, Transcaucasia, and the Ukraine—altogether some 750,000 square kilometers. This cut back Russia to the approximate size it had been two hundred years earlier, and Germany tripled its territory. The Treaty of Brest-Litovsk was ready to be signed March 3, 1918. Who among the Bolsheviks would sign it? Lenin, who had advocated the peace, didn't want his name on the document, in case the treaty turned out to be a political liability. Neither Trotsky nor Bukharin was willing to sign the treaty, either. Grigori Sokolnikov, who had edited *Pravda,* was ordered to do the job.

This treaty has been viewed as evidence of how vindictive the Germans would have been if they had won the war. But Germany didn't demand any part of Greater Russia. Germany demanded territories that had been previously conquered by the Russians, territories with nationalities yearning to be independent. Russia didn't have legitimate claims to the territories. Though Germany undoubtedly would have tried to subdue these territories, too, it probably would have found itself drawn into endless fighting with rebellious nationalities. Historian Evan Mawdsley expressed the view that the treaty "gave the border territories a certain chance to develop, clear for the first time of Great Russian (if not foreign) influence."[44] Ironically, the Treaty of Brest-Litovsk—opposed by the Allied Powers—moved at least a step toward the principle of self-determination outlined by Woodrow Wilson.

7

HOW DID HITLER EXPLOIT WILSON'S BLUNDER TO RECRUIT 50,000 NAZIS?

Woodrow Wilson seemed never to seriously consider the possibility that amid all the bitterness of warfare, if he helped Britain and France win the war, they would demand huge reparations from Germany—and such reparations would plunge Germany into financial and political chaos. The consequences would reverberate throughout Europe. That Wilson would overlook such dangers seems incredible, since he knew all the belligerents were broke.

Like the other belligerents, Germany had spent money assuming it would win the war and be able to push war costs on its enemies. All the belligerents had financed the war mostly by borrowing. Britain and France pushed war costs onto their friends by borrowing billions of dollars from the U.S. government as well as from private American lenders, then reneging on many of the loans.

German war spending soared beyond what anybody had expected. In 1914–15, the government spent 6.9 billion marks on the war. War spending hit a high of 42.1 billion marks in 1917–18.[1]

The German government issued war bonds twice a year—nine times altogether. At the beginning of the war, the Germans printed treasury certificates in English, hoping to raise funds in the United States, perhaps because there were so many German-Americans, but the issue was canceled. The Reichsbank, apparently desperate, borrowed from foreign lenders some 2.5 billion gold marks that had to be repaid in the lenders' currencies, which meant the borrower—the

Reichsbank—assumed considerable risk. The last bond issue came just before Germans were shocked to hear the news that their government was seeking an armistice. Censorship had suppressed news that they were losing the war. Indeed, censorship prevented open discussion of inflation.

Borrowing wasn't enough to cover Germany's war costs, so the government resorted to inflation—a form of tax. The man who, more than anyone else, launched Germany's inflation was Rudolf von Havenstein (1857–1923), who had been named head of the Reichsbank in 1909, after having served as president of the Prussian State Bank. Economic historian Gerald D. Feldman described him as an "extraordinarily conscientious, hard-working, and tenacious administrator."[2]

Havenstein bragged about how much paper money his printers could turn out. At one point, a strike at a money-printing plant stopped the production of currency—and the inflation stopped! Unfortunately, Havenstein was able to arrange for other people to resume the operation of the printing presses, and inflation resumed.

He inflated both to finance current war costs and pay back loans with depreciated currency. The process started at the beginning of the war. Prior to it, coins accounted for between 52 percent and 65 percent of money in circulation.[3] Germany had become an industrial powerhouse by honoring the gold standard, which assured everybody that German paper money and its unit of account—the mark—was likely to retain its value in the future, because by law the amount of currency in circulation could not be more than three times the amount of gold in the government's vaults. The ultimate check on power of the Reichsbank was the ability of the people to redeem their paper money for gold.

During the last week of July 1914, more and more Germans realized that war was likely, and they were frantic to protect their savings as people have done for thousands of years—with gold and silver. These precious metals were scarce and costly to mine, so the supply couldn't be arbitrarily inflated like paper money. Gold and silver were cherished for their beauty, which was why they were fashioned into jewelry. They were durable—they didn't rot, break, or burn. And so thousands of Germans lined up around the Reichsbank building in Berlin, hoping to redeem their paper money for gold and silver. The Reichsbank paid out 163 million marks' worth of the precious metals.[4] On July 31, to prevent the further decline of its hoard, the Reichsbank broke the law, abandoned the gold standard, and refused to pay out any more gold.

This enabled the Reichsbank to finance the war by stepping up the printing of paper money—no obligation to exchange any of it for gold or silver. At the beginning of the war, a reported 7.4 billion marks' worth of currency were in circulation. This soared to 44 billion by the end of the war.[5]

Then the Reichsbank began a propaganda campaign, urging Germans to bring in their gold in exchange for paper money. A typical poster said, "Gold for the Fatherland! Increase our gold stock! Bring your jewelry to the gold purchasing bureaus. Full gold value will be given in return!"[6] There was a campaign urging children to hector their parents about surrendering their gold for paper money.

Germany's defeat meant it was stuck with its war debts. The Versailles Treaty further undermined Germany's financial condition in two ways: the loss of territories and business assets reduced the government's potential for tax revenue, while reparations added to expenditures.

In April 1921 the Allied Powers announced the reparations they wanted: 132 billion gold marks, then equivalent to about $30 billion. The Allied Powers considered this a generous compromise, since the French had demanded 269 billion gold marks.[7]

By itself, though, the Versailles Treaty needn't have posed a financial crisis. On an annual basis, reparations peaked in 1921 at 1.2 billion marks, only 11.8 percent of the national government's budget.[8] The German government conceivably could have cut some non-reparations spending and raised taxes to eliminate budget deficits, although such measures would have intensified an already volatile political situation.

The German government maintained a costly welfare state, and increasingly financed it by printing money rather than by taxation. The national government subsidized municipalities. It provided health "insurance" for increasing numbers of people. It supported 1.5 million disabled veterans and subsidized artists. There were government-run pensions. There were government theaters and government opera houses. The government owned many businesses, including those producing margarine and sausages, and they lost money. Government-owned railroads were bankrupt because, among other things, freight rates weren't increased fast enough. Financially disastrous though these programs were, they were aggressively defended by special interests, and essential budget cuts were delayed.

POSTWAR TRADE RESTRICTIONS MADE IT HARDER FOR GERMANS TO PAY REPARATIONS

The Allied Powers didn't give much thought to how the Germans would generate revenue for reparations. Trade restrictions made it harder for German companies to earn money through exports. European tariffs were more than tripled and in some cases soared as much as 800 percent compared with prewar levels.[9] In 1921 the British Parliament passed the Safeguarding the Industries Act—high tariffs on goods supposedly related to national security. Other countries embraced similar measures.

The destruction of the Austro-Hungarian Empire, which had been substantially a free-trade area, led to the creation of seven new states. All enacted trade restrictions. Political borders were extended by some 12,500 miles, and tariffs were collected every time goods crossed a border.

Tariffs were high enough to provoke incessant trade wars aggravating already severe nationalist conflicts. Germany and Poland retaliated against each other for nine years. To protect its farmers, Czechoslovakia banned agricultural imports from Romania and Yugoslavia; Czechoslovak manufacturers wanted minerals from those countries, but they refused to sell to Czechoslovakia because Romanian and Yugoslav peasants were angry. Although Czechoslovakia had better-developed manufacturing industries than did other Hapsburg successor states, it never realized its potential, since its neighbors closed their borders to manufactured goods.

The United States was no help. During January 1921, 416 lobbyists generated 4,466 pages of testimony before the House Ways and Means Committee, almost all of it demanding higher tariffs. They got protection first in a 1921 "emergency" tariff for major agricultural commodities, then in the 1922 Fordney-McCumber tariff, which raised tariffs as much as 400 percent.[10]

Not to be overlooked is the fact that war and revolution wiped out the Russian market for German goods. Imports as well as exports plunged more than 85 percent from prewar levels.[11] Lenin declared: "There are two ways to fight hunger, a capitalist one and a socialist one. The first consists of free trade. . . . Our path is that of the grain monopoly."[12] Bolsheviks banned private trade and declared that traders were *lishenets*—disenfranchised people without rights. The results were terror, famine, and cannibalism.[13]

INFLATION MORE DEVASTATING THAN WAR

Inflation devastated more Germans than the war itself.

German officials issued warnings about the risks of investing in private assets. This was forbidden for programs intended to help invalids and senior citizens, whose funds were channeled into supposedly safe government bonds. These assets became worthless during the inflation.[14]

Inflation devastated libraries and museums. They couldn't afford to maintain what they had, much less acquire new books and works of art. Scientists couldn't afford to do their work, and scholars couldn't do theirs. As Feldman observed, "It wasn't possible any longer successfully to separate a discussion of the maintenance of German science, scholarship, and artistic life from a discussion of the social condition of their practitioners."[15]

New housing wasn't being built because rent controls discouraged entrepreneurs from building it, but rather than abolish the rent controls, cities took out loans—repayable in foreign currencies like Swiss francs and Dutch gulden—to go into the housing business. As German marks depreciated, cities had a harder and harder time paying the interest on their debts, and they begged the national government to help. Government-run enterprises, too, had taken loans repayable in foreign currency, to import milk and cattle, and they were desperate. Retailers liked rent controls because their store space was a bargain, even though landlords couldn't afford to maintain it.

But retailers lost to inflation anyway, because price controls made it hard to recover their other costs.

In an effort to prevent the new issues of money from leading to higher prices, on July 7, 1921, the Reich Supreme Court ruled that when sellers priced their goods, they couldn't fully factor in the depreciation of the mark. To illustrate what such a policy led to, Feldman related the story about "a rope manufacturer who had become convinced he could do splendid business by selling his rope for ever increasing amounts of paper marks. He rapidly became a millionaire and then a billionaire, but each time he used his capital to buy hemp, he noted that he progressively received less hemp for more money and that his production steadily decreased. Finally, the day came when he could produce only one piece of rope, and he used it to hang himself at the gate of his desolated factory."[16]

Government regulations bankrupted most of Germany's insurance funds. They had been forced to invest in bonds issued to finance the government's failed venture in the housing business. The value of the bonds was wiped out by inflation. Inflation devastated German insurance companies that had business in other countries, because customers needed payments in their own currencies, not in marks. German regulations limited the ability of insurance companies to maintain accounts in other currencies sufficient to discharge their obligations.

By disrupting all kinds of contracts, inflation led to the collapse of the German economy. Nobody could count on anything. Many judges accepted the cancellation of contracts provided it could be established that inflation was unexpected, so courts were deluged with claims that nobody could have foreseen the inflation going on for years. According to historian Feldman, "German businessmen were sending their domestic and foreign customers learned summations of cases and opinions by company lawyers or printed compilations of German court decisions allegedly sanctifying the cancellation or revision of contracts."[17] Debtors were pitted against creditors, with hundreds of thousands of debtors rushing to pay off their mortgages and other loans with worthless currency, and creditors helplessly insisting that the value of money borrowed be repaid. One embittered banker remarked that "our real estate credit, to which Germany owes so much for its past reconstruction and which is also so indispensable for a solid reconstruction, must be buried in the grave."[18]

Judges monitoring trust funds traditionally were supposed to see that they were secure investments, meaning government bonds. But by 1921, well before the peak of the postwar inflation, the value of the bonds had depreciated sharply. When judges gave their permission to cash in some of the bonds, the proceeds were less than their nominal value. Dr. Rechtsanwalt Stiel, a Dulsburg judge, published an article titled "The Robbery of the Wards of the Court." He recommended that the government should compensate bondholders for losses suffered as a result of the inflation caused by the government's monetary policies, and that trust accounts should be invested in industrial stocks and other securities more likely to hold their value than government bonds.[19]

RUNAWAY INFLATION

During the fall of 1922 the Allied Powers and Germans were deadlocked in their negotiations about reparations. The Germans insisted they couldn't pay. In December 1922, Germany twice defaulted on reparations payments.[20]

On January 11, 1923, French prime minister Raymond Poincaré declared the Germans to be in default, citing their failure to deliver 135,000 meters of wooden telegraph poles to justify having French troops occupy Germany's Ruhr industrial area. This was where about 80 percent of German coal, steel, and pig iron was produced.[21] Shipments of goods to other regions were disrupted, and German unemployment soared from about 2 percent to 23 percent.[22] This had the unintended consequence of unifying the German people, and the government called for passive resistance. There were strikes, sabotage, and even guerrilla warfare. The French responded with arrests, deportations, and an economic blockade.

French soldiers plundered the Ruhr. Feldman reported that they "regularly seized money sent by the Reichsbank to cover wage costs, going so far as to blow up the safe of the Reichsbank branch in

Gelsenkirchen and to occupy the printing plants involved in the production of emergency money for some of the Ruhr municipalities."[23]

Wilhelm Cuno, a businessman who had served as a director of
the Hamburg-American Line shipping company, had become chancellor of the Weimar Republic in November 1922, and on January
13, 1923, he urged passive resistance to the French. Industries shut
down. The government committed itself to paying money to the
thousands of workers who became unemployed. As Feldman reported, "Passive resistance was a phenomenally expensive enterprise.
By the end of June [1923], the Reich had guaranteed about two and a
half trillion paper marks in credits. . . . In addition to heavy industry,
government-guaranteed credits had been granted to banks in the occupied areas, to wine growers to maintain operations, and to various
cooperatives for the purchase of food and clothing for the population of the occupied areas . . . a trillion marks a month, most to
cover social costs and to the railroads and post to cover the deficits
arising from the occupation."

With this collapse of the German economy, the value of the
mark plunged. On July 1, 1923, one U.S. dollar would buy 160,000
marks. By August it would buy a million marks.[24]

Taxes didn't begin to cover the costs of reparations, passive
resistance, and the welfare state, so the Weimar government accelerated the printing of paper money, but as the money circulated, and
people used it to bid up prices for goods and services, the paper
money didn't buy as much as it used to, and the government further
accelerated the money-printing.

The government blamed the depreciation of the mark on foreign
exchange speculation, and officials tried to make it more difficult for
Germans to exchange marks for stronger currencies. But when Austria, which also was experiencing a serious inflation, imposed foreign
exchange restrictions, the result was that traders left the organized
exchanges and conducted their business in cafés and other "underground" locations.

"Starving Billionaires"

Inflation made people desperate. Germans cut up leather chairs to get leather for their shoes. Draperies were cut up to make children's clothing. Thieves stripped railroad cars for copper wire.

Historian Konrad Heiden reported, "On Friday afternoons in 1923, long lines of manual and white-collar workers waited outside the pay-windows of the big German factories, department stores, banks, offices. . . . They all stood in lines outside the pay-windows staring impatiently at the electric wall clock, slowly advancing until at last they reached the window and received a bag full of paper notes. According to the figures inscribed on them, the paper notes amounted to seven hundred thousand or five hundred million, or three hundred and eighty billion, or eighteen trillion marks—the figures rose from month to month, then from week to week, finally from day to day. With their bags the people moved quickly to the doors, all in haste, the younger ones running. They dashed to the nearest food store, where a line had already formed. Again they moved slowly, oh, how slowly, forward. When you reached the store a pound of sugar might have been obtainable for two millions; but by the time you came to the counter all you could get for two millions was half a pound, and the saleswoman said the dollar had just gone up again. With the millions or billions you bought sardines, sausages, sugar, perhaps even a little butter, but as a rule the cheaper margarine—always things that would keep for a week, until the next pay-day, until the next stage in the fall of the mark."[25]

People employed in the private sector were enraged when unionized government employees—who carried out the government's disastrous economic policies—succeeded in having their salaries prepaid, so they could convert the currency to goods before the currency depreciated further. The publication *Soziale Praxis* reported: "It seems significant to us that public opinion is now gradually turning against the civil service to an extent that gives great concern. How much hostility is daily directed against that portion of the employed German people with civil service status is shown by the press and also even by those parties which previously supported the civil service through thick and thin and now press for a reduction of the civil service."[26]

Bank depositors were wiped out. "A man who thought he had a small fortune in the bank," Heiden wrote, "might receive a letter from the directors: 'The bank deeply regrets that it can no longer administer your deposit of sixty-eight thousand marks, since the costs are all out of proportion to the capital. We are therefore taking the liberty of returning your capital. Since we have no bank-notes in small enough denominations at our disposal, we have rounded out the sum to one million marks. Enclosure: 1,000,000-mark bill.' A cancelled stamp for five million marks adorned the envelope."[27]

Professional people were devastated. Independent lawyers weren't able to increase their fees fast enough to keep up with inflation, since they were regulated by the government. Many lawyers couldn't afford to attend a professional meeting in Hamburg about inflation in the law. Most doctors' fees were paid by health insurance funds, and the lags in receiving such payments meant big losses. Doctors went on strike in Berlin and elsewhere.

Farmers were squeezed by inflation. Farmers tried to keep the food they produced, rather than give it up for worthless paper money. Historian Feldman reported, "The harvest was satisfactory; there was sufficient oil in the country to make margarine; adequate supplies of other fats were on their way to Germany. The problem was prying the food from the farmers and getting the necessary foreign exchange [sound currencies]."[28] This led hungry city people and gangs of unemployed coal miners to plunder farms.

By this time, of course, not many foreigners were willing to accept marks, either. The government desperately sought to borrow dollars abroad, to buy food and avoid having people starve. The government pressured big businesses to loan it gold marks. Incredibly, the government—which caused the inflation—tried to put taxes on a gold basis, meaning that taxes would be indexed and go up exponentially along with everything else during the inflation.

Heiden described the impact of the inflation about as well as anybody ever has: "The State wiped out property, livelihood, personality, squeezed and pared down the individual, destroyed his faith in himself by destroying his property—or stores: his faith and hope in property. Minds were ripe for the great destruction."[29]

Hitler needed some kind of action to keep his Stormtroopers

fired up, and there appeared to be an opportunity with upcoming May Day festivities. Munich officials had given their approval to communists who wanted to hold a parade through the city. Hitler demanded the right to hold counterdemonstrations, for which he wanted guns from the army. General Otto von Lossow, commander of the German army in Bavaria, refused to hand over guns. The Stormtroopers were limited to gathering the next day north of Munich, surrounded by police. The result was a tame demonstration involving only about 1,000 Stormtroopers. The event was a setback for Hitler, and he recognized how much he needed the cooperation, if not the backing, of the army.

WHAT TO DO?

There was a public debate about the Reichsbank's inability to "support" the mark by going into foreign exchange markets and buying marks and selling other currencies. Such efforts were futile as long as the Reichsbank continued to churn out trillions of marks.

Austrian-born Marxist finance minister Rudolf Hilferding blamed bureaucratic bungling: "The Finance Ministry has no control over the financial administration. . . . While the Reichsbank was doing its mark support action, Herr [Wilhelm] Groener was conducting his coal policy that happened to ruin the currency policy, but since these are two separate ministries, it is not something that has anything to do with the Cabinet. We do not have economic policy in this government, because it is no economic policy if three or four different principles of economic policy are meshed with one another in the Cabinet."[30]

Chancellor Cuno's campaign of passive resistance bankrupted the government and intensified the inflation. He resigned as chancellor in August 1923. He was succeeded by Gustav Stresemann, a Prussian supporter of the monarchy and an enthusiastic booster of the German Empire who adapted to changing circumstances and embraced the Weimar Republic.

An economist by training (his doctorate was titled "The Growth of the Berlin Bottled-Beer Industry"), Stresemann started his career as an administrative assistant for the German Chocolate Makers'

Association. He worked for other manufacturers before being elected to the Reichstag in 1907—a National Liberal from a mining region in Saxony. He was mainly interested in economic policy and championed the interests of private businesses while advocating a welfare state. In the years leading up to the war, Stresemann displayed his colors as a nationalist. He supported Germany's plans to build a navy rivaling Britain's. He was exempted from military service because of his health, but as a member of the Reichstag he worked with the German Army Supreme Command—Field Marshal Paul von Hindenburg and General Erich von Ludendorff. Stresemann supported unrestricted submarine warfare. He opposed the idea of peace talks, advocated by chancellor Theobald von Bethmann-Hollweg. Indeed, Stresemann played a key role in the downfall of Bethmann-Hollweg's government.

Following the end of the war, Stresemann served in the German National Constituent Assembly, which drew up the constitution for the Weimar Republic—he didn't like it. He devoted the rest of his career to securing a revision of the Treaty of Versailles. So he was an able, well-connected man who shared the political sentiments of many of his countrymen, and he was comparatively tolerant—his wife was Jewish. After the June 1922 assassination of the Jewish industrialist Walter Rathenau, who had played a major role in German war production and negotiated the Treaty of Rapallo, which established economic relations with the Soviet Union, Stresemann was the leading figure in German politics.

As chancellor of what came to be known as the "Great Coalition" (People's Party, Social Democrats, German Democrats, Centre), Stresemann began quite a juggling act. He was convinced he had to end the policy of passive resistance and end the enormous drain on government finances, a major factor in the inflation. This meant going against the so-called right wing that, based in Bavaria, supported passive resistance. He pleased the right wing by getting tough with communist governments in the states of Saxony (central Germany) and Thuringia (where Weimar was located), which were harsh on employers, and declared an amnesty for all those convicted of crimes against property—sanctioning robbery by private individuals as well as the government. The most notable crimes occurred when gangs of so-called "workers" plundered farms. On the other hand, Stresemann had to restrain the politically powerful left-wing interest groups, such as unions that demanded more and more money from the government.

On August 23, Friedrich Ebert, the Social Democratic president of the Weimar Republic, issued a decree ordering companies to hand over a substantial portion of their holdings of strong foreign currencies. The Foreign Exchange Procurement Board was set up, with some 400 employees. On September 17 there were two decrees establishing pervasive restrictions on people trading currencies.

Passive resistance to the French officially ended on September 26. This enabled German workers to go back to their jobs, and the government began to phase out related subsidies that had overwhelmed the budget. In an effort to further reduce the pressure for money-printing, Stresemann raised taxes—in October, for instance, already steep auto taxes were raised fifty-fold compared with what they had been on September 1![31] He introduced an "Enterprise Tax" that doubled payroll tax withholding.

Hilferding reported that the situation was still so volatile he was unable to give the Reichstag Budget Committee any meaningful numbers. Officials wanted to demand that business pay taxes in strong foreign currencies rather than the worthless currency that they themselves printed! This led to a flood of petitions from people hoping to delay their tax payments. Hilferding eventually concluded that finances couldn't be reformed until the government achieved some kind of foreign-policy success.

Throughout all this, few in the government seemed to understand what was going on. As Austrian economist Ludwig von Mises noted, "Herr Havenstein, the governor of the Reichsbank, honestly believed that the continuous issue of new notes had nothing to do with the rise of commodity prices, wages, and foreign exchanges. This rise he attributed to the machinations of speculators and profiteers and to intrigues on the part of internal and external foes. Such indeed was the general belief. Nobody durst venture to oppose it without incurring the risk of being denounced both as a traitor to his country and as an abettor of profiteering."[32] Mises's first major work, *The Theory of Money and Credit* (1912), explained how increasing the quantity of money generated upward pressure on prices, regardless of where this was done.

The mark was so discredited that it became clear a reform had to involve a new currency. There was considerable maneuvering among interest groups that agitated for various reform plans. Ironically, the plan that was adopted came from finance minister Karl Helfferich, who had worked for Deutsch Bank, then joined the Finance Ministry during the war. He subsequently served as vice-chancellor and minister of the interior. An ardent supporter of the military, he was opposed to the Weimar Republic. He became active in the German National People's Party. As the inflation spiraled out of control, he proposed exchanging depreciated marks for an emergency currency to be backed by the "free forces of the economy," namely, industry, commerce, and agriculture. This emergency currency would be a transition to a new, stable currency.

On October 27 the government issued a decree establishing the Rentenmark as a transitional currency. The new currency would be the Reichsmark. Because the reform was close enough to what Helfferich had suggested, he became known as the "father of the Reichsmark." At the time, the French were trying to get people in the Ruhr to use French francs, as they were encouraging separatists seeking to make the Ruhr part of France. The Germans were concerned that the French might block the issuance of the Rentenmark in the Ruhr.

Government employees vehemently opposed putting currency reform into effect, because it required big cuts in government spending. The crisis itself, though, finally made it politically possible to overcome such opposition. Suddenly gone was the perk in which government employees had their salaries prepaid, enabling them to endure the ravages of inflation better than ordinary people. Government employees were to get weekly paychecks. They bitterly protested that such a scheme jeopardized the stability of the government. Nonetheless, reforms continued. President Ebert declared a hiring freeze.

Then came the Civil Service Reduction Decree. At the bloated nationalized railroads, payrolls were cut from 576,083 to 186,658.[33] Altogether, national government payrolls were cut almost 25 percent, by 396,838 employees.

Deficits at the government-run health-care system were reduced rather than eliminated. The Personnel Reduction Decree was applied to health regulatory boards, which were cut, and these boards were empowered to fire doctors who performed what were considered to be excessive services. Patients had to begin paying a health-care premium. Other efforts to cut deficits were less successful, as Feldman reported: "Bills presented by pharmacists were subject to review by a staff of one doctor, two pharmacists, and several inspectors, while doctors' bills were reviewed by a number of doctors and the statistical section of the fund. The review of each lower official was checked by a higher official, with the result that the expense and effort involved was in total disproportion to the money saved."[34]

It was impossible to save the government-run social security system. Individual contributions were made by purchasing insurance stamps at government post offices, but by the time the proceeds had been deposited in the social security funds, they had become worthless. Retired people who needed help had to accept poor relief. Feldman explained, "Widows, the disabled, social pensioners, and aged rentiers were now deliberately given lower levels of welfare support as part of a kind of social triage favoring the potentially productive over the unemployable or the less employed."[35]

Stresemann was worried about how the new currency, inevitable spending cutbacks, and higher unemployment would play out in Bavaria, a hotbed of paramilitary agitation. One-quarter of the Reichsbank's gold was stored in Bavaria, and there was talk that Bavaria might try to launch a currency of its own.

The prime minister of Bavaria was Gustav von Kahr, son of a Bavarian bureaucrat, who became a lawyer with ardent nationalist views. As head of the Bavarian People's Party after World War I, he led the provincial government in Upper Bavaria. He was known to favor the idea of reestablishing a monarchy and possibly making Bavaria an independent state. But he was overthrown in November 1918 and succeeded by the German communist Eugen Levine, who, inspired by the Bolsheviks in Russia, seized factories, buildings, and other private assets, distributing them among political favorites.

Back in May 1919, Chancellor Ebert had ordered the Free Corps into Bavaria, and it ousted the communists. Some 700 people were arrested, many of whom were subsequently executed—including

Levine. Kahr resumed his leadership role in the government. He forced farmers to deliver food and prosecuted alleged profiteers. He aggravated shortages by ordering that rents and beer prices be cut while inflation was still raging. Similarly, he ordered shopkeepers not to raise prices more than once a day. He banned strikes and political demonstrations, and he suppressed communist newspapers. Fear of Bolsheviks was a major factor spurring "right wing" groups. Few people at the time seemed to recognize this omen: Kahr ordered the expulsion of Polish Jews from Bavaria.

HITLER'S BEER HALL PUTSCH

According to historian Peter Padfield, "The Nazi Party, whose growth had been modest until then [1923], began to count its members and sympathizers in tens of thousands."[36] "Nazi" was a short version of the party's full name, *Nationalsozialistische Deutsche Arbeiter-Partei.*

Economist Constantino Bresciani-Turroni called Hitler "the foster child of the inflation."[37] He had gone beyond serving as chief speechmaker to become party chairman, viewed by many as a future leader for Germany. He had gathered some 5,000 of his Stormtroopers in Munich for a rally and declared, "the betrayers of the German Fatherland must be done away with. . . . Down with the perpetrators of the November crime [armistice] . . . there are two million dead."[38]

In his speeches, Hitler began denouncing the "November Criminals," as he called those Germans who had accepted the Armistice and the Treaty of Versailles. Historian Ian Kershaw observed that "without a lost war, revolution, and a pervasive sense of national humiliation, Hitler would have remained a nobody. . . . Hitler's message did capture exactly the uncontainable sense of anger, fear, frustration, resentment, and pent-up aggression of the raucous gatherings in the Munich beer halls. The compulsive manner of his speaking derived in turn much of its power of persuasion from the strength of conviction that combined with appealingly simple diagnoses of and recipes to Germany's rebirth. Above all, what came naturally to Hitler was to stoke up the hatred of others by pouring out to them the hatred that was so deeply embedded in himself."[39]

Success brought Hitler into contact with powerful people. "In his gangster hat and trenchcoat over his dinner jacket, toting a pistol and carrying as usual his dog-whip," Kershaw reported, "he cut a bizarre figure in the salons of Munich's upper-crust. But his very eccentricity of dress and exaggerated mannerisms—the affected excessive politeness of one aware of his social inferiority—saw him lionized by condescending hosts and fellow-guests."[40]

Inflation intensified during the summer and fall of 1923. The price of black bread hit 1 billion marks, businesses were losing money, and the government couldn't meet its own payrolls. "The crisis, without which Hitler would have been nothing," wrote Ian Kershaw, "was deepening by the day. In its wake, the Nazi movement was expanding rapidly. Some 35,000 were to join between February and November 1923, giving it a strength of around 55,000 on the eve of the *putsch* [revolt]."[41]

Hitler had little use for Gustav von Kahr and his idea of an independent Bavarian monarchy, since Hitler wanted all Germans to be ruled by a "dictatorship of the national will." He had worked up his followers to a fever pitch, and he had to attempt a *putsch*. He conceived a plot to kidnap several Bavarian government leaders, namely, Kahr, Lossow, and Colonel Hans Ritter von Seisser (head of the state police), and force them to accept Hitler as the leader. Hitler anticipated support from General Erich von Ludendorff, who had dictatorial powers in Germany between 1916 and 1918. Ludendorff was an ardent nationalist who denied the legitimacy of the Weimar Republic.

Hitler heard that Kahr and other Bavarian officials would be speaking at the Bürgerbräukeller, a Munich beer hall, on November 8. There were an estimated 3,000 people in the place, which meant it was the size of a big hotel ballroom. Hitler had the building surrounded with Stormtroopers. He went inside and stationed himself near the podium. After Kahr had been speaking for about twenty minutes, Hitler's henchman Hermann Göring entered the hall with an estimated twenty-five armed Nazis in their brown shirts. A machine gun was set up. To get everybody's attention, Hitler jumped on a chair and fired a pistol into the ceiling. He declared that 600 of his followers had surrounded the building. Ordering everyone to stay where they were, he told the crowd that the Bavarian and Reich governments had been overthrown, and new governments were being established. People remained in the hall, not sure whether Hitler was bluffing.

While Göring kept order in the hall, Hitler led Kahr and his associates into a backroom. Hitler sent his co-conspirator Max Erwin von Scheubner-Richter to Ludendorff's residence, informing the general that a coup had taken place and offering him command of the army. Hitler demanded that the captured officials join his new government, then returned to the crowd and announced that they were with him. Everybody cheered Ludendorff when he arrived. Ludendorff was angry that Hitler had made himself, rather than Ludendorff, the head of the new government, but he went along with the scheme. Kahr expressed his willingness to cooperate. Each of the officials made a speech to the assembled multitude.

Hitler reportedly declared, "I am going to fulfill the vow I made to myself five years ago when I was a blind cripple in the military hospital: to know neither rest nor peace until the November criminals have been overthrown, until on the ruins of the wretched Germany of today there should have arisen once more a Germany of power and greatness, of freedom and splendour."[42] Everybody sang Germany's national anthem, "Deutschland über Alles" ("Germany over All").

Meanwhile, Stormtroopers had taken over army headquarters and police headquarters, but word got out, and soldiers loyal to the government were dispatched. Informed that there was fighting between Stormtroopers and soldiers at an army barracks, Hitler left the Bürgerbräukeller to see what was happening. Once he had left, the crowd headed for the door, and Kahr, Lossow, and Seisser disappeared. Hitler returned to find his hostages gone. German radio stations broadcast news that they had repudiated the statements they had made at gunpoint. Lossow ordered army units to shut down Nazi operations.

Thousands of weary Stormtroopers wandered around Munich, awaiting orders. Hitler ordered some of them to break into a government printing plant and seize bundles of 50-billion-mark notes, making it possible to pay his men.

On November 9, in a desperate bid to enlist the army in their revolt, Hitler led between 2,000 and 3,000 Stormtroopers from the

Bürgerbräukeller, along the River Isar, across the Ludwig Bridge toward the War Memorial on the Odeonplatz and toward the War Ministry. Police blocked the way. Hitler demanded that they surrender, and they opened fire. Ludendorff kept marching forward, and apparently the police didn't shoot at him. Göring was hit. Hitler ducked into a car and escaped, leaving those he had led into battle to fend for themselves.

Historian Feldman observed that "Hitler and his followers never could have developed that measure of strength which they did have or risked a *putsch* had they not enjoyed a considerable amount of sympathy as a result of the desperate conditions of the hyperinflation."[43]

Göring escaped across the Austrian border. Röhm was arrested. Ludendorff was arrested, brought to trial, and acquitted. Hitler was trailed to a house in Uffing, where he was arrested and charged with high treason. The February 1924 trial became a circus when Hitler was permitted to speak for four hours. He snapped, "There is no such thing as high treason against the traitors of 1918."[44] He was sentenced to five years in Landsberg prison, about fifty miles west of Munich. "Conditions were more akin to those of a hotel than a penitentiary," Kershaw reported. "The windows of his large, comfortably furnished room on the first floor afforded an expansive view over the attractive countryside . . . he could relax with a newspaper in an easy wicker chair, his back to a laurel wreath provided by admirers, or sit at a large desk sifting through the mounds of correspondence he received."[45]

Hitler had plenty of time for reflection. He had shown himself to be a bumbling amateur. Nothing was thought through. He had counted on intimidating people with a show of force. He never planned an organized campaign. He assumed he could win over the army. He didn't even remember to secure his hostages. But he had displayed his formidable skills as a public speaker, his capacity for bold if reckless ideas, and his ability to exploit the bitterness resulting from the war and inflation.

Hitler vowed that next time—and he was sure there would be a next time—he would be better organized, and he would triumph. He never forgot the beer hall where his quest for power began. Historian Alan Bullock wrote that Hitler "built up the failure of 8 and 9 November into one of the great propaganda legends of the movement.

Year after year, even after the outbreak of war, he went back to the
Bürgerbräukeller in Munich on 8 November, and to the Feldherrn-
halle, the War Memorial on the Odeonplatz, to renew the memory
of what had happened there on that grey November morning in
1923. Regularly each year he spoke to the Nazi Old Guard in the
Bürgerbräukeller, and the next morning on the Odeonplatz solemnly
recalled the martyrs of the movement who died for their faith."[46]

8

HOW DID LENIN TAKE
ADVANTAGE OF WILSON'S
BLUNDER AND SECURE POWER?

B Y THE TIME Woodrow Wilson began to have concerns about Lenin, it was too late. Having pressured and bribed the Provisional Government to stay in the war, thereby accelerating the collapse of the Russian army, Wilson helped make it possible for Lenin to seize power. Lenin was extraordinarily single-minded and ruthless, and it proved impossible to overthrow him.

Lenin understood, as Wilson did not, why Russia must quit the war. In his "Fourteen Points" speech of January 8, 1918, Wilson denounced the harsh terms Germany was demanding from Russia during the Brest-Litovsk negotiations. Of course, he opposed this treaty because he still wanted Russia to stay in the war and tie up German divisions that might otherwise be transferred to the Western Front.

Once the Brest-Litovsk Treaty was signed and Russia was out of the war, the Bolsheviks could focus on crushing their enemies. They controlled a region including Petrograd, Moscow, and a few other cities, where some 140 revolts occurred. Peasants, who accounted for about 80 percent of the population, were against them. In the south, anti-Bolshevik forces were gathering—Cossacks under Ataman Krasnov and a "White" army under General Anton Denikin.

During May and June 1918, the Bolsheviks launched a campaign to suppress political opposition. Non-Bolshevik newspapers—205 altogether—were shut down. Historian Nicolas Werth reported that "the mostly Menshevik or Socialist Revolutionary soviets of Kaluga, Tver, Yaroslavl, Ryazan, Kostroma, Kazan, Saratov, Penza, Tambov,

Voronezh, Orel, and Vologda were broken up by force."[1] Mensheviks and Socialist Revolutionaries were expelled from the All-Russian Central Committee of Soviets. In Petrograd, Cheka soldiers fired on hunger marchers, killing ten. In Ekaterinburg, Red Guards killed fifteen people who were protesting Bolshevik property seizures. Protesters were also shot in Uralsk, Nizhni-Tagil, Beloretsk, and Zlatoust.

BOLSHEVIK HOSTAGE-TAKING AND CONCENTRATION CAMPS

From the very beginning, the Bolshevik regime was based on hostage-taking, concentration camps, and mass murder. In June, Lenin wrote Gregory Zinoviev, chairman of the Council of Commissars: "It is of supreme importance that we encourage and make use of the energy of mass terror directed against the counterrevolutionaries, especially those of Petrograd, whose example is decisive."[2] Lenin told People's Commissar of Food Aleksandr Tsyurupa: "In all grain-producing areas, twenty-five designated hostages drawn from the best-off of the local inhabitants will answer with their lives for any failure in the requisitioning plan." In August, Cheka chief Felix Dzerzhinsky declared, "Most effective are the taking of hostages among the bourgeoisie, on the basis of the lists drawn up for exceptional taxes levied on the bourgeoisie . . . the arrest and incarceration of all hostages and suspects in concentration camps." In his August 30 "Appeal to the Working Classes," he announced that "anyone caught in illegal possession of a firearm will be immediately executed, and that anyone who dares to spread the slightest rumor against the Soviet regime will be arrested immediately and sent to a concentration camp!" On September 3, People's Commissar for Internal Affairs N. Petrovsky wrote a notice published in *Izvestiya*: "Hostages must be taken among the officers and the bourgeoisie. The slightest resistance must be greeted with widespread executions. . . . No weakness or indecision can be tolerated during this period of mass terror." As a bid to murder not individuals but members of a class, this notice and decree marked the official beginning of the Red Terror. It was to be a prelude to Stalin's mass murders and Hitler's Holocaust.

The Cheka arrested and executed people on a larger scale. There were an estimated 1,300 executions in Petrograd during September

1918.[3] One night in Kronstadt, some 400 people were shot. Dzerzhinsky established *Ezhenedelnik VChK (Cheka Weekly)*, which wasn't
for the faint of heart. Historian Nicolas Werth cited a typical report,
from the city of Nizhni Novgorod, in which the Cheka "executed 141
hostages after 31 August, and once more took more than 700 hostages
in a mere three days. Other publications," Werth noted, "bragged
about the Cheka's exploits—for instance, *Izvestiya Tsaritsynskoi
Gubcheka (News of the Tsaritsyn Province Cheka)*, which ran a story
about 103 people executed between September 3 and September 10.
Cheka's internal reports, known as *svodki*, provide additional documentation for mass murders. Altogether, during the fall of 1918,
probably between 10,000 and 15,000 people were executed."[4]

As a reward for this handiwork, Dzerzhinsky was named
People's Commissar of Internal Affairs, responsible for putting all
the militias, city soldiers, and other armed forces under a single unified military command. Within three years these forces were to grow
to some 200,000—strictly for suppressing domestic opposition to
the Bolshevik regime.

Dzerzhinsky turned his forces against workers, who, though a
base for Bolshevik support, had become as disgusted as everybody
else at the suffering. Cheka was increasingly busy suppressing
strikes. Particularly worrisome to the Bolsheviks were strikes at munitions factories supplying the Red Army. Explosive violence occurred in Tula, Astrakhan, and other cities. In Astrakhan, according
to Werth, "When the prisons were full, the soldiers and strikers were
loaded onto barges and then thrown by the hundreds into the Volga
with stones around their necks. From 12 to 14 March between 2,000
and 4,000 strikers were shot or drowned. After 15 March the repres-
sions were concentrated on the bourgeoisie of the town, on the pretext that they had been behind this 'White Guard' conspiracy for
which the workers and soldiers were merely cannon fodder. For two
days all the merchants' houses were systematically looted and their
owners arrested and shot. Estimates of the number of bourgeois victims of the massacres in Astrakhan range from 600 to 1,000. In one
week between 3,000 and 5,000 people were either shot or drowned."[5]

Lenin was adamant that his commissars set an example by treat-
ing strikers harshly. On January 29, 1920, he wrote Vladimir Smirov,

who headed the Revolutionary Military Council of the Fifth Army: "I am surprised that you are taking the matter so lightly, and are not immediately executing large numbers of strikers for the crime of sabotage."[6]

Lenin was equally determined to punish deserters. People thought that withdrawing from World War I would enable them to return home and live in peace, but of course they were wrong. Millions of people were conscripted for the war to achieve Bolshevik supremacy within Russia, and increasing numbers of people wanted to stay out of that war, too. Werth reported, "It is now believed that in 1919 and 1920 there were more than 3 million deserters. In 1919 around 500,000 deserters were arrested by various departments of the Cheka and the special divisions created to combat desertion; in the following year the figure rose to between 700,000 and 800,000. Even so, somewhere between 1.5 and 2 million deserters, most of them peasants who knew the territory extremely well, managed to elude the authorities."[7]

This situation led Lenin, on May 12, 1920, to issue an order: "After the expiration of the seven-day deadline for deserters to turn themselves in, punishments must be increased for these incorrigible traitors to the cause of the people. Families and anyone found to be assisting them in any way whatsoever are to be considered as hostages and treated accordingly."[8]

Peasant rebellions became perhaps the biggest threat, because Bolsheviks were seizing peasants' grain—often leaving them without any food. During March 1919, in the provinces of Samara and Simbirsk, a 30,000-man peasant army gained control of the region. The peasants demanded free trade, free elections, and an end to the seizures. The Bolsheviks, of course, would have none of this and dispatched tens of thousands of soldiers to suppress the rebellion. Thousands of rebels were killed in the fighting, and thousands more were shot. The death toll exceeded 10,000.[9]

Following the Treaty of Versailles, German and Austrian soldiers withdrew from the Ukraine, and Bolshevik soldiers reconquered it and began seizing the peasants' grain. There were, according to Cheka internal documents, 210 peasant revolts in July 1919 alone. The Cheka dispatched some 100,000 soldiers to fight several hundred thousand peasants.[10]

As these peasant revolts were put down, other revolts erupted where people faced seizures that meant starvation, for example in Tambov, Penza, Saratov, Tsaritsn, and elsewhere in the mid-Volga region. In May 1920 the situation was so serious in the Ukraine, where some 15,000 rebels resisted Soviet authority, that Felix Dzerzhinsky himself was asked to take charge of a campaign to exterminate peasant guerrillas. This took two years, with a death toll in the thousands.

Bolsheviks murdered an estimated 8,000 Cossacks in February and March 1919, and this led to a rebellion involving about 30,000 Cossacks. Bolsheviks fought back in early 1920, the Cossacks were put down, and perhaps 6,000 more Cossacks were executed. Thousands more were sent to concentration camps, where they perished in the bitter cold. This was followed by a "de-Cossackization" of the region, in which all males between eighteen and fifty years old were sent north for heavy labor, women and children were driven from their homes, cattle and portable property were seized, and entire towns were burned.[11] Altogether, between 300,000 and 500,000 Cossacks were believed to have been killed, out of a total Cossack population of around 3 million.

Much of this slaughter had been reported by "White" Russians when they gained territory abandoned by "Reds" and discovered large numbers of recently executed victims. The Socialist Revolutionary Sergei Melgunov provided much documentation in his 1916 book *Red Terror in Russia*. The findings were confirmed after Soviet archives, including Cheka records, were opened in the early 1990s.

Having used terror to establish control over a region, the Bolsheviks proceeded to rob as much as they could. They banned private trade, seized businesses, and imposed huge taxes. For instance, Werth reported, "600 million rubles in Kharkiv in February 1919, 500 million in Odessa in April 1919. To ensure that this contribution was paid, hundreds of bourgeois would be taken as hostages and locked up in the concentration camps. In fact this contribution meant a sort of institutionalized pillaging, expropriation, and intimidation, the first step in the destruction of the 'bourgeois as a social class.'"

Humiliation was a deliberate Bolshevik strategy. Werth cited an April 26, 1919, report in an Odessa newspaper: "We must treat them the way they deserve: the bourgeois respect only authority that punishes and kills. If we execute a few dozen of these bloodsucking idiots, if we reduce them to the status of street sweepers and force their women to clean the Red Army barracks (and that would be an honor for them), they will understand that our power is here to stay, and that no one, neither the English nor the Hottentots, is going to come and help them."[12] Apparently such reports grossly understated the humiliation, which included large-scale rape of bourgeois women.

PLANNED CHAOS

As professional revolutionaries, the Bolsheviks knew virtually nothing about how an economy worked, but they didn't let their ignorance stop them.

Lenin, as his decrees made clear, thought the government should seize everybody's assets. About the only economist Lenin was familiar with, other than Karl Marx, was the Austrian Rudolf Hilferding. In his book *Finance Capital* (1910), Hilferding claimed the banks were the key to capitalism, from which Lenin concluded that by nationalizing banks, he would have the economy by the throat.

Nicolai Ivanovich Bukharin was the leader of the Left Communists, and their chief theoretician was Iurii Larin, who relentlessly promoted more government control over the economy. They wanted the government to monopolize everything and run the economy by having bureaucrats issue orders. These theoreticians even wanted to abolish money, a huge improvement over barter, which had made it possible to expand markets and give people more choices.

The Bolshevik regime, however, needed money. The factories it had seized were losing money, and factory commissars were begging for a bailout.[13] The banks that had been seized were shut down because they didn't have cash. Military spending was up. In 1917 the Bolsheviks' budget deficit was equal to about 80 percent of total spending.

The regime began printing massive amounts of paper money, hoping to fool people into believing that the currency was worth something. "At the time the Bolsheviks took power in Petrograd," explained Richard Pipes, "paper money circulating in Russia totaled 19.6 billion rubles. The bulk of it consisted of Imperial rubles, popularly known as 'Nikolaevki.' There were also paper rubles issued by the Provisional Government, called either 'Kerenki' or 'Dumki.' The latter were simple talons, printed on one side, without serial number, signature, or name of issuer, displaying only the ruble value and a warning of punishment for counterfeiting. In 1917 and early 1918, 'Kerenkis' circulated at a slight discount Imperial rubles. After taking over the State Bank and the Treasury, the Bolsheviks continued to issue 'Kerenkis' without altering their appearance."[14] During the first six months of 1918, Pipes reported, "the Bolsheviks printed between 2 million and 3 million rubles a month. By January 1919 there were reportedly 61.3 billion rubles in circulation, and at the end of the year this had soared to 225 billion rubles. Currency in circulation exploded fivefold to 1.2 trillion rubles in 1920, and 2.3 trillion rubles in 1921. As a consequence of this paper money inflation, prices of goods skyrocketed 10 million times! In free markets, a pint of milk reportedly cost 500 rubles, a pound of meat 3,000 and a pound of butter 5,000."

In an effort to suppress general price increases that were an inevitable consequence of inflating the money supply, Bolshevik bureaucrats issued decrees fixing maximum prices, particularly for grain. As a result, in real terms peasants received less and less for their labor, so naturally they cultivated less land. Pipes reported that cultivated acreage declined 12.5 percent between 1913 and 1920.[15] More important, yields per acre plummeted. In 1920 they were reportedly 30 percent less than before the war.

In their arrogance, Bolshevik officials believed they were smart enough to run an entire economy. They didn't care about what people wanted. Their concern was to provide what they thought people ought to have (and what they ought not to have). Naturally, they believed politically correct classes like themselves deserved more than did politically incorrect classes such as the "bourgeoisie" and "kulaks."

The Bolsheviks thought that an economy was best run by bureaucrats sitting on committees, drafting decrees telling other people what to do. The Bolsheviks were adamantly opposed to the idea that an economy should be driven by consumers freely voting with their money, deciding which quantities, qualities, brands, styles, colors, prices, and so on that they preferred.

Accordingly, the Bolsheviks established the Supreme Council of the National Economy (VSNKh). It was, Silvana Malle explained, "in charge of the coordination of economic life, the coordination and unification of the activity of central and local regulating institutions (the fuel committee, the metal, transport and central foodstuffs committees and other relevant people's commissariats, for trade and industry, foodstuffs, agriculture, finances, war and the fleet, and so on)."[16]

The Bolsheviks failed to understand that prices were extraordinarily efficient signals, enabling producers to determine what they could produce and what consumers wanted. Market participants don't need to know one another, they might not like one another, and they might be thousands of miles apart, but they can interpret prices to determine the current market situation, even if they don't know what's causing it. When, for instance, Bolshevik officials interfered in market processes and set prices too low, they didn't seem to realize they were simultaneously signaling producers to produce less and consumers to demand more. By paying workers less than they were worth, the Bolsheviks discouraged work, and to get what they considered essential work done, they reintroduced serfdom and slavery, which had disappeared in the Western world.

Suppressing market prices made it impossible to arrive at rational economic decisions in the Soviet Union. It wasn't possible to compare the costs of doing something one way versus another. "Suppose, for instance," explained Austrian economist Ludwig von Mises, "that the socialist commonwealth was contemplating a new railway line. Would a new railway line be a good thing? If so, which of many possible routes should it cover? Under a system of private ownership we could use money calculations to decide these questions. The new line would cheapen the transportation of certain articles, and, on this basis, we could estimate whether the reduction in transport charges would be great enough to counterweigh the expenditure which the building and running of the line would involve. Such a calculation could be made only in money. . . . We can make systematic economic plans only when all the commodities which we have to take into account can be assimilated to money. True, money calculations are incomplete. True, they have profound deficiencies. But we have nothing better to put in their place."[17] Thus did Bolshevik economic planners squander Russia's rich endowment of natural resources and produce chaos.

Despite all of Lenin's decrees asserting government control of land, banks, and wholesale and retail trade, free markets flourished. They just went underground. Indeed, according to Pipes, Russians bought an estimated two-thirds of their food from black market dealers.[18] People peddled their meager possessions in the streets. Soldiers offered their uniforms. Ladies, their dresses.[19]

BOLSHEVIK WAR AGAINST PEASANTS

Since the Bolsheviks' main political support came from big cities, especially Petrograd and Moscow, they were desperate to assure adequate food supplies there. On May 13, 1920, the Bolsheviks issued a decree empowering the People's Commissariat of Food to seize food from peasants. Soon there was a 12,000-man force for seizures. When they came back with less food than needed, they escalated violence against peasants. For many months after the Cheka was established in December 1917, its principal business was extracting grain from peasants.[20]

Peasants were outraged not only that the fruits of their labor would be seized, but that the Bolsheviks planned to force them into government-controlled communes. Moreover, peasant savings were wiped out by runaway inflation. All this triggered a reported 110 peasant rebellions against the Bolsheviks.

In February 1918 the Bolsheviks began imposing the death penalty on peasants accused of withholding food. Lenin heartily approved of shooting peasants. Such policies didn't appeal to the peasants who accounted for about 80 percent of the population. Lenin tried to provoke class hatred, but there weren't significant differences among peasants. One peasant might be better off than another because he had a cow. Lenin claimed that what distinguished kulaks was hired labor, but the Russian agrarian census of 1917 suggested that an estimated 103,000 of 5 million rural households hired some

129,000 farm workers—a little more than one farm worker per household, so obviously these were small operations. Desperate to exploit class hatred, Lenin concocted the myth of the "kulak," variously meaning rich peasants or agricultural middlemen. "The trouble was," Pipes reported, "that whereas Hitler would be able to produce genealogical ('racial') criteria for determining who was a Jew, Lenin had no standards to define a kulak. This term never had a precise social or economic content: in fact, one observer, who spent the Revolution in the countryside, found that the peasants themselves did not use it."[21]

Nonetheless, the mythical "kulak" became a staple of Lenin's propaganda. For example, in August 1918 Lenin told Bolshevik soldiers: "The kulaks are the most beastly, the coarsest, the most savage exploiters. . . . These bloodsuckers have waxed rich. . . . These spiders have grown fat. . . . These leeches have drunk the blood of toilers. . . . These vampires have gathered and continued to gather in their hands the lands. . . . Death to them."[22]

Some 125,000 Bolshevik soldiers were dispatched to oppress peasants. Pipes reported one case, for instance, where "the chairman of the village Executive Committee regularly beat peasant petitioners, sometimes with canes. Some of his victims were stripped of their shoes and forced to sit in the snow. So-called food requisitions were really ordinary robberies."[23] In August 1918, Bolshevik soldiers began taking hostages to terrorize the peasant population. According to Pipes, "All who resisted seizures of surplus grain, including 'bagmen,' were to be turned over to Revolutionary Tribunals, and if caught armed, to be shot on the spot."[24] Lenin ordered that all the peasants' grain be seized, including grain needed to sow the next year's crop.

Historian Alexander N. Yakovlev reported how the Bolsheviks promoted famine among the peasants. For instance, "According to reports from Tambov province, the populace in the Usmansk, Lipetsk, Kozlovsk, and Borisoglebsk districts 'fed not only on husks and wild grass but on bark and nettles.' In other provinces, too, the condition of the peasants was catastrophic. A report submitted by Chief Commissar Sergei Kamenev in October 1920 speaks of crowds of hungry peasants in Voronezh and Saratov provinces pleading with the local authorities to give them at least some of the grain taken at the collection centers. Often, Kamenev writes, 'these crowds were mowed down by machine guns.' "[25]

Bolshevik savagery triggered more peasant rebellions. Yakovlev wrote, "Driven to despair, they began to sack the premises of the food agencies and to beat up Communists and food workers. . . . In 1918, according to incomplete data, there were 245 such uprisings in the country as a whole, and close to 100 during the first seven months of 1919. At the beginning of 1921, when the peasant war reached its apogee, 118 of Russia's districts were caught up in these rebellions . . . these attacks became increasingly large-scale, and the clashes with military forces increasingly fierce."[26]

On Lenin's order, Yakovlev reported, "Cossack villages and settlements were subject to destruction and their adult populations to wholesale execution. Relatives of insurgents were declared hostages, and they, too, were subject to being shot when the 'bands' went on the offensive; children were exiled to the central provinces. In case of mass demonstrations in the villages or cities, wrote this emissary of Lenin's, 'we will subject such places to mass terror: for every murdered Soviet activist, hundreds of inhabitants will pay with their lives.' "[27]

According to Yakovlev, a June 11, 1921, order "provided for the execution of hostages in districts caught up in the insurgency. Under the same order, persons refusing to give their names were to be shot without trial. The next day, General Mikhail Tukhachevsky, acting for the Politburo, ordered that 'forests where the bandits are hiding be cleared by poison gas.' Elaborating, the army commander demanded that the 'cloud of toxic gases be made to spread throughout the forest, killing anyone hiding there.'

"As late as June 1921, when the rebellion was already subsiding, the authorities 'removed' 16,000 'bandit-deserters,' confiscated the property of 500 peasant households, and burned down 250 peasant homes. The province acquired a network of mobile concentration camps containing not only insurgents but hostages, including women and infants. A report on a 'big influx' of children is found in the minutes of a meeting of the Commission on Child Hostages in Concentration Field Camps in Tambov Province. Even after an operation in

July 1921 to 'unload' the concentration camps, they still contained more than 450 child hostages between ages one and ten."[28]

Despite all this, the amount of grain coming from peasants increased only about 1 percent—the yield had been about 49 million tons, and terror brought an additional 580,000 tons. But clearly future production was imperiled, which meant worsening food crises.

Though the campaign against peasants was a disaster as far as food supplies were concerned, genocidal terror was the basis of the Bolshevik state—long before Stalin came to power. Indeed, as Pipes pointed out, during Lenin's very first day as head of state, there was a discussion about possibly abolishing the death penalty for soldiers who deserted the front lines, and Trotsky reported Lenin as saying, "How can you make a revolution without executions? Do you expect to dispose of your enemies by disarming yourself? What other means of repression are there?"[29]

Peasants yearned for independence, which posed a serious political problem for the Bolsheviks. Karl Radek, a member of the Bolshevik Central Committee, reflected, "The peasants had just received the land from the state, they had just returned home from the front, they had kept their guns, and their attitude to the state could be summed up as 'Who needs it?' They couldn't have cared less about it. If we had decided to come up with some sort of food tax, it wouldn't have worked, for none of the state apparatus remained. The old order had disappeared, and the peasants wouldn't have handed over anything without actually being forced. Our task at the beginning of 1918 was quite simple: we had to make the peasants understand two quite simple things: that the state had some claim on what they produced, and that it had the means to exercise those rights."[30]

TERRORIZING THE ENTIRE POPULATION

Lenin was constantly hectoring his comrades to terrorize the population, but he didn't want his great name spattered with blood. He insisted that underlings sign decrees ordering mass murder.

Lenin understood that the most reliable way to terrorize a population was to have somebody from another nationality do it. His ace was Felix Dzerzhinsky, who established the Cheka. From a Polish family near Vilna, he had joined the Lithuanian Social-Democratic Party. Agitating for socialism landed him in Russian prisons for eleven years. He was a tough, cruel man.

The Cheka didn't have any official legal standing. It wasn't mentioned in the Collection of Laws and Ordinances. Information about the Cheka had to be cleared by Cheka officials before anything was published.

Early on, the Cheka was empowered to both conduct police investigations and render guilty verdicts. It had the power to execute people without having to bother with legal proceedings. Like Dzerzhinsky himself, a substantial number of people with the Cheka were non-Russians unlikely to hesitate about suppressing Russians.

"The first step in the introduction of mass terror to Soviet Russia," Pipes wrote, "was the elimination of all legal restraint—indeed of law itself—and its replacement by something labeled 'revolutionary conscience.' Nothing like this had ever happened anywhere. Soviet Russia was the first state in history formally to outlaw law. This measure freed the authorities to dispose of anyone they disliked and legitimized pogroms against their opponents."[31]

On November 22, 1917, Lenin issued a decree declaring that judges shouldn't be bound by legal precedents established under the czarist regime. On the same day he introduced Revolutionary Tribunals for proceedings against individuals who challenged his authority and were accused of "counterrevolutionary crimes." There weren't any legal constraints on the prerogative of these tribunals to issue death sentences.

When, on December 15, 1917, Commissar of Justice Isaac Nachman Steinberg ordered that prisoners held by the Cheka be released, Dzerzhinsky refused. Steinberg tried to overrule Dzerzhinsky, but the Sovnarkom—the Council of People's Commissars, an administrative branch of the Bolshevik regime—sided with the Cheka. Steinberg persisted, demanding that his approval be required before the Cheka could make arrests for political crimes. Lenin agreed that the Cheka was for conducting police investigations, but he warned Steinberg or anybody else from interfering with its arrests of political criminals.

Meanwhile, the Cheka maintained armed forces. By April 1918, Pipes reported, the Cheka had "six companies of infantry, fifty cavalrymen, eighty bicyclists, sixty machine gunners, forty artillery-men, and three armored cars."[32] The Cheka kept firing squads busy with executions around the clock. Principal victims were ex–army officers, "capitalists," and priests. Cheka actually issued a weekly publication bragging about all their executions.

Executions were carried out by the Red Army and the Red Guards as well as the Cheka. During the first six months of 1918, 882 executions were reported in Soviet publications. Lenin wasn't satisfied. As Pipes wrote, "He kept on badgering Communist offi-cials and the citizenry to act more resolutely and rid themselves of all inhibitions against killings."[33] Not to be outdone, the bloodthirsty Trotsky declared that if Red Army officers didn't follow orders, "nothing will remain of them but a wet spot." Grigorii Evseevich Zi-noviev suggested that as many as 10 million people should be mur-dered. No Bolshevik officials objected to such talk.

On June 16, 1918, the Cheka went to Ipatiev House in Yekaterin-burg, where former czar Nicholas II, his wife, Aleksandra, and their children Olga, Tatiana, Maria, Anastasia, and Aleksei had been transferred by the Kerensky government. They were all murdered, supposedly to prevent anti-Bolsheviks from rallying behind Nicholas.

During the summer of 1918, as a consequence of the Brest-Litovsk Treaty and peace on the Eastern Front, some 2 million pris-oners of war were released from camps that the czar's government had set up. Lenin had the Cheka take over the empty camps as places for imprisoning "class enemies" of his regime. Historian Ann Apple-baum explained, "The Red Terror was crucial to Lenin's struggle for power. Concentration camps, the so-called 'special camps,' were cru-cial to the Red Terror. They were mentioned in the very first decree on Red Terror, which called not only for the arrest and incarceration of 'important representatives of the bourgeoisies, landowners, in-dustrialists, merchants, counter-revolutionary priests, anti-Soviet of-ficers' but also for their 'isolation in concentration camps.'"[34]

Children were frequent victims of Bolshevik violence. Yakovlev reported "mass terror, concentration camps, hostages, with mothers, wives, and children shot because their sons, husbands, and fathers refused to cooperate with the adventurers in power. The number of hostages runs into the thousands. As early as 1918, on orders from the Petrograd Cheka, 500 hostages were shot. Shot the following year, also in Petrograd, were the relatives (including the children) of officers of the Eighty-sixth Infantry Regiment who had gone over to the Whites. In May 1920 the newspapers told of the execution in Elizavetgrad of the elderly mother and four daughters, ages three to seven, of an officer who had refused to serve the proletarian regime, Arkhangelsk, where the Cheka shot children of twelve to sixteen, was known in 1920 as the 'city of the dead.' Between 1918 and 1922 the Bolsheviks frequently held children hostage in their struggle against peasants attempting to resist the regime's agrarian policy. The fall of 1918 saw the creation of concentration camps whose prisoners at first were largely hostages, including women with infants, taken as relatives of the 'rebels.'"[35]

On September 5, 1918, the Sovnarkom approved a resolution for intensifying the Red Terror. As usual, Lenin's name wasn't on the resolution, but it's inconceivable that such a resolution would have been adopted without his approval. As the Nazis were to do later, large numbers of people were executed because they happened to be of a particular nationality, occupation, or some other category condemned by the state.

According to one account, "For executions there was set up a special garden by the house at 40 Institute Street . . . where the Provincial Cheka had moved. . . . [T]he executioner—the commandant, or his deputy, sometimes one of his assistants, and occasionally a Cheka 'amateur'—led the naked victim into this garden and ordered him to lie flat on the ground. Then with a shot in the nape of the neck dispatched him. The executions were carried out with revolvers, usually Colts. Because each shot was fired at such close range, the skull of the victim usually burst into pieces. Then the next victim was brought in a like manner, laid by the side of the previous one. When the number of victims became too large for the garden to hold, fresh victims were placed on top of the previous ones. . . ."[36]

Dzerzhinsky acknowledged imprisoning and executing large numbers of people despite lack of evidence: "The law gives the Cheka the option of isolating by administrative measures those violators of labor laws, those parasites and persons suspected of counterrevolution, against whom we do not have enough evidence for punishment by trial and whom any court, even the strictest, will always or usually find not guilty."[37] Dzerzhinsky's associate I. S. Unshlikht made a similar admission: "There is a whole range of cases where the tribunals, for lack of factual evidence, will hand down decisions of not guilty even though we have quite enough information from our agents to justify the severest sentences, up to and including capital punishment. In certain conditions in the republic as a whole or in certain localities, it is necessary to take repressive measures of various kinds against those active in the anti-Soviet parties, even when we have no concrete evidence against them."[38]

The Cheka infiltrated every area of life. It suppressed "speculation," meaning common trading. The Cheka asserted substantial control over the flow of passengers and freight through waterways and on highways and railroads. And when officials debated how to get foresters to chop more wood, the suggestion was made that production quotas should be set, and foresters failing to fulfill their quotas should be shot by Cheka forces.

The Cheka introduced concentration camps, which were to become a major feature of later Soviet regimes as well as of Nazi Germany. These weren't a wartime phenomenon, disbanded when peace came. The concentration camps were a standard Bolshevik method for suppressing political dissidents, and they expanded dramatically in peacetime. The Soviet Union's political prisoners performed slave labor. In 1920 the Soviet Union had eighty-four concentration camps holding an estimated 50,000 prisoners. Three years later, there were reported to be 315 concentration camps holding 70,000 prisoners.[39]

Terror kept the Bolsheviks in power, because they were so unpopular. They never received more than a quarter of votes, before the Constituent Assembly was suppressed in January 1918. Peasants hated the Bolsheviks, and the worsening economic situation undermined their political support in the cities.

Reports of Bolshevik horrors came out in letters, newspaper stories, and the accounts of refugees, but most people in the West, certainly in Woodrow Wilson's administration, preferred their illusions. Wilson's friend William Bullitt downplayed the terrible conditions in Russia, as did such "progressive" visitors to the Soviet Union as the muckraker Lincoln Steffens, socialist author Upton Sinclair, and British philosopher Bertrand Russell.

Bolshevik forces continued to arrest peasants and seize food. The Bolsheviks demanded more wheat in 1920 than they did in 1919, but peasants had sowed less, since they would be penalized rather than rewarded for additional production. Seizures became ever more brutal. Werth cited a report acknowledging that "the detachments committed a series of abuses. They looted everything in their path, even pillows and kitchen utensils, shared out the booty, and beat up old men of seventy in full view of the public."[40]

These brutal seizures sparked more rebellions. The biggest rebellion occurred in Tambov Province, the most important wheat-producing region near Moscow. In August 1920, Aleksandr Stepanovich Antonov led an estimated 14,000 men, armed with little more than pitchforks and rifles, and they overwhelmed Bolshevik soldiers stationed in the province. Antonov was a Socialist Revolutionary who had been an activist against the czar since 1906, then had sided with the Bolsheviks before becoming a deserter and a rebel leader.

Antonov's success drew more and more peasants and deserters, and the force swelled to some 50,000. Initially, the Bolsheviks could muster only about 5,000 soldiers, but after they had defeated White general Pyotr Wrangel in the Crimera, the Bolsheviks amassed 100,000 soldiers against Antonov. Meanwhile, revolts had developed along the lower Volga region in the provinces of Samara, Saratov, Tsaritsyn, and Astrakhan.

Reflecting on the origins of Soviet violence, historian Alexander N. Yakovlev observed, "The responsibility for the genocide—or, rather, democide—that took place in Russia and the entire Soviet Union rests on the ideology of Bolshevism, in the form it took within various Communist organizations under different names. With the close participation of Bronstein (Trotsky), Rosenfeld (Kamenev), Alfelbaum (Zinoviev), and Dzerzhinsky, these crimes were committed under the direct supervision of Ulianov (Lenin) and Dzhugashvili (Stalin). Vladimir Ilyich Ulianov (Lenin) . . . exponent of mass terror, violence, the dictatorship of the proletariat, class struggle, and other inhuman concepts. Oganizer of the fratricidal Russian civil war and the concentration camps, including camps for children. Personally responsible for the deaths of millions of Russian citizens. By every norm of international law, posthumously indictable for crimes against humanity."[41]

FORCED LABOR

Between 1917 and 1920—*after* World War I—the number of industrial workers in Russia plunged about 50 percent.[42] This reflected revolutionary chaos, famine, and the determination of the Bolsheviks to pay people less than they were worth in a free market.

Bolsheviks figured that since they controlled the government, a monopoly on coercion and violence, they might as well use it to serve their interests as the new ruling class. They began nationalizing industries and forcing people to work for starvation wages—and frequently without compensation. Trotsky declared, "The principle of compulsory labor is absolutely beyond dispute for a Communist."[43] The Bolshevik newspaper *Pravda* published a series of points inspired by Trotsky, including: "Socialist reconstruction repudiates the liberal capitalist principle of 'freedom of labor.'"[44]

The Bolsheviks began imposing forced labor on "bourgeois" people, and Lenin claimed this would "bring the state machinery into motion." But there weren't enough bourgeois people to make this happen, so increasingly the Bolsheviks began conscripting "working" people.

The Bolsheviks increasingly tied people to particular places, such as a factory or a farm, so they could be more easily controlled. Thus, Bolshevism evolved into a modern form of serfdom, backward and barbaric in every way.

Forced labor backfired. "Forcing the bourgeois to dig trenches or clean snow from the streets did not contribute much to the effectiveness of the administrative machinery of the Soviet Union," explained historian James Bunyan. "It did produce, however, a situation that forced large numbers of the formerly well-to-do classes to flee from the areas under Bolshevik control and to join forces with those who had taken arms against the Bolshevik dictatorship. This gave an added impetus to the civil war, deepened the political and military crises of the country, and called for greater sacrifices by the population under Bolshevik control."[45]

A June 25, 1919, decree ordered registration for forced labor, as for military conscription: "All citizens who have reached the age of sixteen are under obligation to have labor books as evidence that their holders are engaged in productive activity. These books are to be used as personal identity documents throughout the R.S.F.S.R. and also as documents entitling the owners to receive food-ration cards as well as social security benefits in case of loss of working capacity or unemployment."[46] Despite such measures, fewer people seemed to be showing up for work, owing in part to the flight from industrial centers as people searched for food during the famine.

A contributing factor to declining production was the communist method of paying people. They were paid partially with currency and partially with food. Since the Soviet government was broke, it tried to buy what it needed by printing huge quantities of paper money whose value depreciated daily, so this part of a worker's pay was worthless. The food people received had nothing to do with how productive they were. Rather, they were paid based on whether they did heavy physical work, light work, or office work. There were no incentives for people to be productive.

Trotsky promoted the idea of forming "labor armies." Lenin gave his approval on January 12, 1920, and Trotsky drafted a decree for the First Labor Army. Joseph Stalin was made head of the Ukrainian Labor Army, whose top priority was "to increase as much as possible the procurement of food supplies"—which meant seizing crops from peasants. There was a succession of mobilization decrees for Former Railway Workers (January 20, 1920), Workers in the Sugar Industries (March 24, 1920), Mining Workers (April 16, 1920), Construction Workers (May 5, 1920), Statistical Workers (June 25, 1920), Medical Personnel (July 14, 1920), Workers Formerly Employed in Fishing Industries (August 6, 1920), Workers in Wool Industries (August 13, 1920), Domestic Servants (August 31, 1920), Women for Sewing Underwear for Red Army Men (October 30, 1920), and Tailors and Shoemakers Who Worked in Great Britain and the United States (October 1920), among others.

Forced labor, along with terror, became such an essential

Bolshevik policy that on January 29, 1920, there was a proclamation of universal forced labor. It authorized the establishment of the Central Committee on Compulsory Labor. This, in turn, started bureaucracies such as the Central Extraordinary Commission on Firewood and Cartage Duty, or *Tsechrezkomtopguzh.*

The Bolsheviks viewed those who refused to follow orders as "deserters from the labor front."[47] Missing work more than three days a month was declared to be sabotage. Those who persisted in passing up their Labor Army opportunities were subject to imprisonment and possibly the death penalty.

Despite all the orders, threats, and punishment that the Bolsheviks could dream up, the number of industrial workers continued to decline. For example, Bunyan reported, "During the first nine months of 1920, 38,574 workers were mobilized and delivered to thirty-five armaments plants. During the same period, 34,939 workers deserted from these plants. In the transport machinery and locomotive repair plants, conditions were even worse. The data for the first six months of 1920 show that, of the 16,223 workers mobilized, 15,201 deserted."[48] Further, Bunyan noted in a study of heavy industry: "In 1917 there were 3,024,000 workers; in 1918 the number fell to 2,486,000; by 1920 and 1921, the industrial labor force had declined to 1,480,000; and it reached the lowest point—1,243,000—in 1922."

BOLSHEVIK ECONOMIC COLLAPSE

By 1921 the Bolsheviks had come close to destroying the Russian economy. Industrial production was estimated to be only about 10 percent of what it had been in 1913.[49] Agricultural production ground to a halt amid continued Bolshevik seizures, executions, and riots.

In March 1921, with peasant revolts very much on their minds, the Bolsheviks met for their Tenth Party Congress and discussed what to do about the mess they had made. Lenin, who feared his regime could be toppled, became convinced that crop seizures had to be suspended for a while. He favored collecting taxes rather than crops, but many of his comrades adamantly opposed any compromise. Lenin, ever the cautious operator, worked in the background and relied on others to speak out, lest his views fail to attract enough

support. News of revolt at the Kronstadt Island naval garrison persuaded Bolsheviks that they must compromise, and Lenin prevailed.[50] There would be peasant taxes rather than crop seizures.

This was hardly liberalization, but it was a step. The government would continue to be a centralized, one-party, one-ideology
dictatorship with secret police, executioners, and concentration
camps. Bolsheviks would still monopolize banking, industry, transportation, communications, and international trade.

It soon became apparent more had to be done, because peasants
wanted to buy things—consumer goods—that the government-
owned factories couldn't produce. So private entrepreneurs were permitted to engage in small-scale manufacturing. The goods had to be
distributed, and the government couldn't do that, either, so private
middlemen and shops were permitted to do business again. Suddenly
goods became available, and rationing ended in November 1921.[51]
Lenin and his comrades accepted these policies as a tactical retreat, but
their goal remained a 100-percent government-controlled economy.

Meanwhile, the Politboro appointed General Mikhail Tukhachevsky to suppress peasant rebels who were hiding in forests. On
June 12, 1921, he issued an order that the forests be gassed, killing
everyone there.[52] Another tactic was to destroy the places where
rebels lived, as this July 10 report indicates: "Regarding the village of
Kareevbka, which was a bandit stronghold because of its geographi-
cal situation, the commission decided to strike it from the map. The
whole population was deported and their possessions confiscated,
with the exception of the families of soldiers serving in the Red Army,
who were transferred to the town of Kurdyuki and relocated in
houses previously occupied by the families of bandits. After objects
of value had been removed—window frames, glass, wooden objects,
and other such items—all the houses in the village were set on fire."

Then came another mutiny at Kronstadt. When the Cheka arrived, they shot hundreds, and some 8,000 escaped across ice to Finland. The Bolsheviks promised amnesty if they returned, and those
who did were taken to concentration camps. "The Kholmogory
camp, on the great river Divina," reported Werth, "was sadly famous
for the swift manner in which it dispatched a great number of its
prisoners. They were often loaded onto barges, stones were tied

around their necks, their arms and legs were tied, and they were thrown overboard into the river."[53]

In official reports about the famine, the Bolsheviks cited inadequate tools, poor agricultural practices, drought, and other factors—everything except the murder of peasants and seizure of their crops. Lenin wanted to seize more property—including seed for next year's crops—and bombarded peasants with more Bolshevik propaganda about the importance of paying taxes.

Risking reprisals from the Bolsheviks, Nikolai Kondratyev, Sergei Prokopovich, and other members of the Moscow Agricultural Society formed the Social Committee for the Fight Against Famine. Somehow they persuaded the Bolsheviks to tolerate their existence, and some members were able to seek help from friends overseas.

Finally, in July 1921, acknowledging the horrors that could no longer be denied—including some cannibalism—the Bolsheviks gave the committee some legal sanction, renaming it the All-Russian Committee for Aid to the Starving. Western relief organizations were permitted to ship food intended for Russian peasants. The Red Cross, Quakers, and the American Relief Association (ARA) participated in the relief efforts.[54] They provided food for some 11 million people.

Soon, though, Lenin had had enough. On August 27, 1921, he announced: "I propose to dissolve the Committee immediately. . . . Prokopovich is to be arrested for seditious behavior and kept in prison for three months. . . . The other Committee members are to be exiled from Moscow immediately, sent to the chief cities of different regions, cut off if possible from all means of communication, including railways, and kept under close surveillance."[55]

In place of the committee, the government set up the Central Commission for Help for the Hungry, consisting of a bunch of Bolshevik corrupt bureaucrats and thugs. This operation managed to feed only about 3 million people, less than one-third as many as those fed by the private organizations from the West.

As a consequence of Lenin's fanatical quest to achieve totalitarian power over the Russian Empire, an estimated 5 million Russians starved to death in 1921 and 1922. By comparison, the previous famine that had hit the region, back in 1891, had resulted in 400,000 to 500,000 deaths.

Total human cost? "This," explained historian Evan Mawdsley, "is bound up less with Red Troops fighting White troops or Cheka executions; what killed most were the dreadful epidemics. The official statistics show 890,000 deaths from typhus and typhoid in 1919, and 1,044,000 in 1920 (compared with 63,000 in 1917). In addition to that there was dysentery, cholera, and the *Ispanka,* the Spanish influenza pandemic of 1918–19. The effects of hunger were tremendous. One source estimated that 3 million or more deaths could have come from higher child mortality."[56] One must also take into account the estimated 2 million people who fled the chaos of the Russian Revolution and Civil War.

As if all this weren't bad enough, the worst period of Bolshevik inflation began in December 1921 and finally ended in January 1924. During that time, according to economist Phillip Cagan, prices rose an average of 57 percent per month, and toward the end prices were rising over 200 percent per month. Altogether, prices skyrocketed 124,000-fold during the twenty-six-month period![57]

Mawdsley concluded, "The Civil War unleashed by Lenin's revolution was the greatest national catastrophe Europe had yet seen."[58]

9

HOW DID WILSON'S FATEFUL DECISIONS PAVE THE WAY FOR THE NAZI REGIME?

A DOLF HITLER SKILLFULLY exploited bitterness about Germany's humiliating defeat, the discredited Weimar Republic, the vindictive Versailles Treaty, the reparations and runaway inflation—all of which were consequences of Woodrow Wilson's decision to have the United States enter World War I. These crises enabled Hitler to launch his political career, but he needed another crisis to gain power.

While he was in Landsberg Prison following his conviction for the Beer Hall Putsch, the German runaway inflation was ended, and a sound currency was introduced.

The economy began to recover. Reparations had been renegotiated, and the Dawes Plan—named after the American banker Charles Dawes, who produced a report for the Allied Reparations Committee—reduced the annual burden on the German economy. German officials accepted the Dawes Plan in August 1924.

French prime minister Raymond Poincaré, who had ordered French troops to occupy the Ruhr, was defeated in the May 1924 elections as voters repudiated his occupation policy, which had provoked alarming political turmoil. The French withdrew their forces from the Ruhr following the December 1925 Locarno Pact, negotiated in Locarno, Switzerland, by representatives of Britain, France, Belgium, Poland, Czechoslovakia, and Germany. The pact was intended to maintain borders specified in the Versailles Treaty. The Treaty of Berlin, signed in April 1926, provided that Germany and Russia would remain neutral if one of them was attacked by another nation—this treaty resulted from concern by Russia that the Locarno Pact might signal an alliance of France and Germany, possibly aimed against Russia. In September 1926, Germany was admitted into the League of Nations. Such developments meant that Germany didn't need Hitler to gain acceptance as an equal partner in the international community.

MEIN KAMPF

Meanwhile, the Nazi party splintered. Hitler's associates quarreled when he was in Landsberg prison, and he did nothing since he didn't want them to thrive without him. Julius Streicher and Hermann Esser accused Alfred Rosenberg, Gregor Strasser, Ernst Pöhner, and Erich von Ludendorff of undermining the Nazi party, and they, in turn, demanded that Streicher and Esser be expelled. Rosenberg, Strasser, and Ludendorff wanted to participate in the 1924 elections, but Hitler was still an Austrian citizen and couldn't participate, and he had denounced elections. When Ernst Röhm was released from prison (he had been jailed for his role in the Beer Hall Putsch), he began to rebuild his private army—the *Frontbann*, as it was called, succeeding the Stormtroopers. Hitler's enforced absence from leadership made clear that he was the only one capable of unifying the movement. He seems to have concluded that he wasn't just a propagandist preparing the way for a political leader; *he* was the political leader.

He worked on his book *Mein Kampf (My Struggle)*, which he had begun dictating to fellow inmate Rudolf Hess. The man who agreed to publish the book, Max Amann, wanted this to be a memoir, but Hitler mainly embellished the legendary beginning of his career and vented his hatred for Marxists and Jews. Hitler hoped *Mein Kampf* would give him an intellectual credential, since other Nazis had written books or pamphlets.

It was evidently during his time reading and writing at Landsberg that Hitler developed the last of his bad ideas, to complement nationalism, socialism, and anti-Semitism: Germany needed more *Lebensraum* (living space), and a war should be fought to get it from Russia. The idea that a nation might run out of living space was nonsense, of course, since nations don't need more territory to prosper. What they need is economic liberty and free movement of people, goods, and capital. Many small, comparatively free places like Hong Kong, Switzerland, and the Netherlands have been far more prosperous than large, unfree nations like Russia and China. Hitler didn't care about prosperity. He sought glory for himself as a warrior.

Hitler's political supporters agitated for his release from prison. Presiding judge Georg Neithardt was sympathetic with Hitler and approved parole, despite the state prosecutor's objections.[1] Hitler was out after only nine months, on October 1, 1924.[2] Bavarian officials tried to have Hitler immediately deported, but Austrian officials didn't want him—their excuse was that he'd served in the German army. So he was paroled in Munich.[3]

The 400-page first volume of *Mein Kampf* was edited by the anti-Semitic priest Bernhard Stempfle to make it a more readable tirade, and it was published in 1925. It sold 9,473 copies that year. Sales fell to 6,913 in 1926, when the second volume was published. Sales continued to fall, hitting 3,015 in 1928. Yet the book seems to have been a principal source of Hitler's income—an indication of how far he had fallen.[4]

RECRUITING NAZIS

Hitler called a meeting at the Bürgerbräukeller on February 27, 1925. He explained, "I must have a crowd when I speak. In a small intimate circle, I never know what to say. I should only disappoint you, and that is a thing I should hate to do. As a speaker at either a family gathering or a funeral, I'm no use at all."[5]

He proved to be as big a drawing card as ever. Although many of his former associates like Röhm, Strasser, and Rosenberg stayed away, an estimated 3,000 filled the Bürgerbräukeller, and another 2,000 were gathered outside. He spoke for about two hours with his standard attacks on Jews, the November criminals, and the Treaty of Versailles, demonstrating that he had lost none of his ability to manipulate a crowd. The meeting climaxed as former enemies, including Julius Streicher, Hermann Esser, and Wilhelm Frick, shook hands and vowed their loyal support for Hitler.

Government officials were so concerned about Hitler's strong showing that he was subsequently banned from speaking at public meetings in Bavaria and most other German states. Hitler spent his time traveling around Germany, speaking at party meetings.

Hitler, however, had no interest in the details of party-building or administration. He left that to others, especially Gregor Strasser, a tough, burly, balding man. Born to a middle-class family in 1892, he trained to be a pharmacist, served in the army during the war, fought with the Free Corps afterwards, joined the Nazis in 1920, and participated in the Beer Hall Putsch. He was a fanatical socialist devoted to enlisting urban factory workers, though he embraced Hitler's nationalist and anti-Semitic views. Strasser proved himself to be a good speaker and a tireless organizer.

Hitler, who had few followers outside Bavaria, asked Strasser to organize the Nazi party in north Germany. Strasser recruited people, organized meetings, got publications out, handled promotion, raised money, and developed useful contacts throughout the country. During the late 1920s, Strasser did more than anyone else to build the party organization. "His contribution to the growth of the NSDAP," observed Ian Kershaw, "had been second only to that of Hitler himself."[6]

Hitler recruited more and more people with unquestioning loyalty. According to Heiden, "He purposely sought men of small stature with whom he could easily deal; men whom he could impress even when he was in the humblest circumstances, who would take anything from him; who were literally willing to be beaten, and remained loyal because they could not find easier or more abundant bread anywhere else. He consciously gathered little men around him—and this quite literally; for it is noteworthy that the intimate circle of Hitler's old guard, the Streichers, Amanns, Hoffmanns, Webers, Berchtolds, were physically puny, some of them dwarf-like."[7]

Among the recruits was Joseph Goebbels, who began producing Nazi propaganda. Born in 1897, Goebbels was exempted from military service because he had a clubfoot, and he earned a Ph.D. in linguistics at Heidelberg University. Evidently his years of graduate education didn't save him from bad ideas. He became a passionate public speaker, and during the occupation of the Ruhr, he helped organize sabotage against French forces.[8]

Heinrich Himmler, born in 1900, the son of a Catholic school-teacher, joined *Reichskriegsflagge* ("Imperial War Flag"), a paramilitary group started by Ernst Röhm, and participated in the Beer Hall Putsch. Himmler, wrote biographer Peter Padfield, had "a militarily stiff posture, sloping shoulders, short arms, wide hips and a pinched, pale face dominated by round spectacles giving him a prim, clerkish look. A neat moustache, tight, pursed lips . . . his short-sighted, steel-blue eyes glittered behind thick lenses."[9] This was the man who would establish Hitler's first concentration camp at Dachau (1934) and run Hitler's black-shirted *Schutzstaffel* (SS)—this was much more disciplined than Röhm's army, which Hitler spurned as a bunch of brawlers "playing at soldiers."

He relentlessly attacked Gustav Stresemann, who, as foreign minister of the Weimar Republic, had scored these diplomatic successes. Hitler rejected the very idea of reconciliation with the nations that had humiliated Germany at Versailles. He warned that prosperity couldn't last. He predicted that bad times were around the corner—though he expected another runaway inflation rather than depression.

While prospects for the Nazi party were beginning to improve, extreme nationalist parties fared poorly at the polls. Hitler apparently helped persuade Ludendorff to run for Reich president in 1925, with the idea of eliminating him as a rival. Nearly 27 million people voted, but Ludendorff received only 286,000 votes because he didn't have much of a following outside Bavaria.[10] Politically, this election was the end of him, and Hitler became the dominant leader among extreme nationalists.

The Nazi party increasingly became a Hitler cult. Worshipful propaganda, the outstretched-arm salute, and the "Heil Hitler" greeting all promoted his personality. There were Nazi organizers in the thirty-four Reichstag electoral districts. To promote Hitler's views, special organizations were set up, including the Hitler Youth, the Nazi Schoolchildren's League, the Nazi Students' League, the Order of German Women, the Nazi Teachers' Association, Nazi Lawyers, and Nazi Physicians.

There's conflicting evidence about how successful all this was during the late 1920s. According to Alan Bullock, the number of dues-paying Nazis rose from 27,000 in 1925 to 49,000 in 1926, 72,000 in 1927, 108,000 in 1928, and 178,000 in 1929[11]—numbers still below the peak reached during the 1923 inflation. By contrast, Ian Kershaw reported that Hitler was no longer playing to full houses. For example, when he spoke at Munich's Circus Krone in 1927, it was reportedly half to three-quarters full. Another Munich appearance drew some 1,500 in a hall that had seats for about 7,000. Outside Munich, Hitler's crowds were much smaller.[12] Kershaw cited smaller Nazi crowds as a reason why German states lifted their bans against Hitler speaking at public meetings.

Nazi candidates did poorly in the 1928 Reichstag elections, winning just 2.6 percent of the vote. Nazi support was a mere 1.57 percent in Berlin, and Nazis didn't do much better in other cities. Nazi candidates did best in rural Upper Bavaria, where prices of agricultural commodities were depressed.

The reparations issue was revived when the Allied Reparations Committee asked the American banker Owen D. Young to investigate the situation and make recommendations. He issued his report on June 7, 1929. The result was that the total reparations bill was set at $26.2 billion, to be paid over the next fifty-eight and a half years. Germany was to pay $473 million annually. France agreed to withdraw their forces in Occupied Rhineland, five years earlier than provided in the Treaty of Versailles. The Young Plan was the last diplomatic coup of Gustav Stresemann, who died on October 3, 1929. Hitler denounced the idea that Germany should have to pay any reparations at all.

FINANCIAL CONNECTIONS

During the late 1920s, Hitler spent a lot of time fundraising, but he had little luck with big businessmen. Among other things, this was because the Nazi party didn't appear to be going anywhere.[13] The bulk of Nazi revenues continued to come from membership dues and admissions fees and collections at public meetings.

But a few big businessmen helped Hitler. In September 1929 he joined forces with German Nationalist Party co-founder Alfred Hugenberg, formerly the chairman of Krupp Armaments Company and a well-connected businessman who owned major newspapers and news agencies. Hugenberg, like Hitler, wanted to renounce the Versailles Treaty and destroy the Weimar Republic. Both opposed the Young Plan, since it meant that Germany would continue paying reparations. Hugenberg thought that Hitler's effectiveness as a public speaker would help his cause. Hitler believed that working with Hugenberg would bring him in contact with wealthy industrialists who might help finance the Nazi party.

Hugenberg and Hitler proposed a "Law Against the Enslavement of the German People," renouncing reparations and calling for the firing of the chancellor, the cabinet, and other officials if they agreed to any further reparations. The Reichstag rejected the draft. It still could have become law if at least 21 million voters supported it in a plebiscite. Fewer than 6 million people voted yes.

Defeat of the proposed law tarnished Hugenberg's credibility, but Hitler emerged in a much stronger position. His speeches had been widely reported in Hugenberg's newspapers. He had met many industrialists and financiers, including Emil Kirdorf, largest shareholder of the Gelsenkirchen Mine Company and founder of the Ruhr Coal Syndicate. These people seemed to view Hitler as an impressive talent who could serve their interests in the future. Nazi coffers were soon overflowing, and Hitler moved his headquarters to a Munich mansion on Briennerstrasse, which became known as "Brown House." Hitler's office featured a portrait of Frederick the Great, the eighteenth-century king of Prussia.

Other industrialists backing Hitler included Fritz Thyssen and Albert Voegler (United Steel Works), Friedrich Springorum and Ernst Tengelmann (Gelsenkirchen Mine Company), E. G. von Stauss (Deutsche Bank), and Eduard Hilgard (Allianz Insurance Corporation). Apparently these businessmen thought they were buying favors from Hitler the way they bought favors from other politicians.

Support from big business brought criticism within his ranks. Otto Strasser, younger brother of Gregor Strasser and also a fanatical socialist, told Hitler, "You want to strangle the social revolution for the sake of legality and your new collaboration with the bourgeois parties of the Right." Apparently, many of Hitler's contemporaries wouldn't agree with the common characterization that he was "on the right."

Hitler replied to Strasser, saying "I am a Socialist. . . . What you understand by Socialism is nothing but Marxism. Now look: the great mass of working-men want only bread and circuses. They have no understanding for ideals of any sort whatever, and we can never hope to win the workers to any large extent by an appeal to ideals. We want to make a revolution for the new dominating caste which is not moved, as you are, by the ethic of pity, but is quite clear in its own mind that it has the right to dominate others because it represents a better race."[14]

HITLER COURTS THE ARMY

Mindful of how he had been crushed by German army forces in November 1923, Hitler courted the army. He gave a speech in Munich, expressing support for the army, which he felt had been betrayed by the politicians in 1918. He suggested that opposition to a nationalist movement such as he headed would be contrary to the army's traditions. The speech was widely published in publications seen by army officers.

The Weimar government was reluctant to do much about Hitler. President Hindenburg was eighty-four and didn't have the political judgment that he used to. Major-General Kurt von Schleicher, the dominant voice on army policy about political issues, hoped to bring Hitler into a coalition government and share the blame for any unpopular antidepression policies that might have to be adopted. Minister of defense Wilhelm Groener despised the Nazis and believed that they should be suppressed, but he wasn't sure he'd have the backing of the army.

In 1930, three army officers, lieutenant Wilhelm Scheringer and two associates, were put on trial for promoting Nazi propaganda within the ranks. Hitler was called as a witness in September, and his testimony was aimed to reassure the generals who were concerned about his SA Stormtroopers. Hitler said, "They were set up exclusively for the purpose of protecting the Party in its propaganda, not to fight against the State. I have been a soldier long enough to know that it is impossible for a Party Organization to fight against the disciplined forces of the Army. . . . I have always expressed the opinion that any attempt to replace the Army would be senseless. . . . My only wish is that the German State and the German people should be imbued with a new spirit. . . . I have always held the view that every attempt to disintegrate the Army was madness."[15] Hitler vowed that when he came to power, "there will be a Nazi Court of Justice, the November 1918 revolution will be avenged, and heads will roll."

In 1931, Hitler criticized the government for not doing enough with the army: "For us the Army is the expression of the strength of the nation for the defense of its national interests abroad. . . . The triumph of our ideas will give the entire nation a political and philosophical outlook which will bring the Army in spirit into a truly close relationship to the whole people and will thus free it from the painful circumstances of being an alien body within its own people."[16]

HITLER EXPLOITS THE DEPRESSION

In 1929 the German economy began to stumble. Falling agricultural prices led to higher farm debt, more bankruptcies, and forced sales of land. Industries were beginning to order layoffs. Some 1.3 million Germans were unemployed in September 1929, and unemployment was heading up sharply.

In an effort to deal with the Great Depression, President Hindenburg had named Heinrich Brüning as Reich Chancellor on March 30, 1930. A member of the Catholic Centre Party, he had a Ph.D. in economics and served in the Machine Gun Corps during World War I. He emerged as a leader of the Reichstag. His immediate concern was to stop the government's budget deficits. Since Germany had a disastrous experience with inflation, they weren't going to try that again, so he proposed raising taxes, even though this meant there would be less money available for businesses to invest and less money for consumers to spend.[17] Especially in bad times, interest groups demanded barriers to competition, and Brüning didn't have the political support to resist, even if he had understood that such barriers promoted contraction, and it was inconceivable that employment could be expanded while the economy was contracting. Among other things, Brüning approved higher tariffs for imported food, making it more expensive for millions of Germans to buy food.

In other ways, the German government prolonged the depression by preventing markets from functioning. As economist Gustav Stolper explained, "Prices and wages were largely determined by the government or by agencies under direct or indirect state influence. Prices were largely political or [government-enforced] cartelized prices, wages were political wages. Closely tied as the price system was to government decisions, it had lost much of the flexibility that prices display in a free capitalist economy."[18]

On July 16 the Reichstag rejected Brüning's efforts to balance the budget, and he began issuing emergency decrees. When some members of the Reichstag objected to the decrees, he asked President Hindenburg to dissolve the session of the Reichstag, which he did two days later. New elections were scheduled for September 14.[19]

Hitler's depression-era speeches didn't talk about how to revive the economy. He never discussed how the government could make it easier for private employers to hire people. He didn't talk about how people needed tax relief. He had no interest in economics even though his country faced a severe economic crisis. He viewed the depression not as a problem to be solved, but as an opportunity for power.

Again and again, Hitler appealed to the resentment of Germans betrayed by leaders who had accepted the humiliating surrender terms in the Armistice and in the Treaty of Versailles. He declared that their tormenters were envious of Germany's greatness. He said it was time to trash the treaty and reestablish Germany's position in the world.

The Reichstag elections resulted in a deadlock. Ten parties each received over a million votes, which meant none of them had a majority. There had to be some sort of coalition, and because all the politicians would be maneuvering for power, the coalition probably wouldn't last long. Notably weakened were the parties that had supported the Weimar Republic: Social Democrats, the Catholic Centre, and the Democrats.

The Nazis were the biggest winners. They won a total of 6.4 million votes versus 810,000 in 1928. They won 18.3 percent of the vote and 107 seats in the Reichstag, compared with twelve in 1928.[20] Hitler offered a warning in a Munich speech ten days after the election: "We are not on principle a parliamentary party—that would be a contradiction of our whole outlook—we are a parliamentary party by compulsion, under constraint, and that compulsion is the Constitution. The Constitution compels us to use this means. And so this victory that we have just won is nothing else than the winning of a new weapon for our fight."[21] Some 3 million Germans were unemployed by September 1930.

Nazi gains undermined confidence in the German banking system. A substantial portion of bank capital had been wiped out during the inflation, and banks had taken in substantial short-term foreign deposits—some 40 percent or 50 percent of the capital of major Berlin banks consisted of such deposits that could be quickly withdrawn.[22] Many foreign creditors became alarmed and pulled their funds out of Germany.

While still reeling from these blows, German banks were further hit by the May 1931 failure of Austria's Kreditanstalt, among the oldest and largest banks in Central Europe. Much like Germany's, the postwar Austrian economy was a welfare state with soaring entitlement costs, high taxes, and above-market wages that led to chronic high unemployment. It was no wonder so many Austrian banks were in trouble. Kreditanstalt acquired many of these. Then, on May 11, it was disclosed that one of its acquisitions, Bodenkreditanstalt, had lost 140 million Austrian schillings—all but 45 million schillings of Kreditanstalt's capital.[23] Naturally, depositors withdrew their funds.[24]

On June 6 the German government announced its intention to suspend reparation payments, and foreign creditors interpreted this to mean the economy was in big trouble. The run on German banks accelerated on June 30 with reports about the extent of foreign withdrawals. German banks were closed July 13, and when they reopened July 16, foreign deposits were blocked.[25]

This led to ever more complicated foreign exchange controls that throttled capital markets, hamstrung the economy, and made recovery more difficult. "German exporters, in the autumn of 1931," explained historian Margaret S. Gordon, "were not only leaving the proceeds of their exports abroad, but were repaying their foreign debts with foreign balances acquired from sales of exports. As regulations were progressively tightened and penalties made more severe, new means of evasion were discovered. Exporters were found to be accepting, in payment for their goods, German securities held by foreigners who wanted to evade the regulations stipulating that the yield from sale of such securities must remain in Germany. . . . Prices at which goods were invoiced were carefully checked by the authorities, to make certain that exporters were not under-valuing their shipments, in order to leave part of the proceeds abroad. Frequently, prior permits or licenses had to be obtained before goods could be shipped.[26]

"A further explanation of the failure of exporters to turn over foreign drafts to the authorities," Gordon continued, "was to be found in the fact that exchange restrictions abroad made it difficult for exporters to collect payment from their foreign debtors. Frozen commercial debts were piling up at an alarming rate during the latter half of 1931 and all through 1932 in the central banks of many countries in Central Europe."[27]

All this made it harder for German businesses to produce things and collect revenue, prolonging the depression. In effect, the German government blockaded the German economy with taxes, import restrictions, and exchange controls much as Britain had blockaded the German economy with its navy in World War I.[28] German industrial production plunged almost 50 percent from 1929 to 1932. The gross national product sank to about 38 percent during this period.[29] German unemployment hit 5.1 million in September 1932.

POLITICAL VIOLENCE

Although Hitler was anxious to convince officials that he would seek power by legal means, he realized that illegality was a fundamental appeal for Nazi recruits. Lieutenant William Scheringer, who had been convicted and imprisoned, felt betrayed by Hitler and became a Communist.

As the depression worsened, the SA fought with the armies of other political parties, especially the Communists. An SA slogan was "Possession of the streets is the key to power in the State." Nazis killed in battle, such as Berlin leader Horst Wessel, were subsequently portrayed as great martyrs.

Describing SA rampages, Bullock wrote, "Night after night, they and the Communists marched in formation singing down the streets, broke up rival political meetings, beat up opponents, and raided each other's 'territory.' As the unemployment figures rose, the number of recruits mounted. Anything was better than loafing on the street corners, and the SA offered a meal and a uniform, companionship and something exciting to do."[30] The point was to maintain agitation year-round until Nazis were in power.

The 107 Nazi members of the Reichstag, elected in 1930, did their part. Wearing brown uniforms, they seized every opportunity to shout down speakers and otherwise disrupt proceedings.

The Depression Drives 13 Million to the Nazis

Germany's presidential election was scheduled for March 13, 1932, and Hitler decided to challenge Hindenburg.[31] At a Berlin rally that attracted some 25,000 people, Hitler declared, "Old man, you must step aside."[32]

In an effort to bolster his prospects, Hitler reached out to the business community, giving a talk to Dusseldorf's Industry Club on January 27, 1932. As with so many other speeches, Hitler began by denouncing the Treaty of Versailles and the Germans who accepted it. He insisted that a political leader doing anything other than rejecting should be considered a traitor. Posing as a savior of the nation, he appealed to widespread fears of communism. The businessmen responded enthusiastically, and there were major financial contributions to the Nazi cause.

Hitler traveled all around Germany. Nazi organizers were in every district. Goebbels organized dramatic mass meetings—Hitler delivered nineteen speeches in Berlin alone. Biographer Joachim C. Fest reported, "Fifty thousand copies of a phonograph record were distributed. Sound movies were made, and pressure was exerted on cinema owners to have these shown before the main film. A special illustrated magazine, devoted to the election, was launched and what Goebbels called a 'war of posters and banners' unleashed, which overnight would paint whole cities or districts of cities bloody red [with swastikas]."[33] Hitler ended up winning 30 percent of the vote. Since Hindenburg fell short of a majority, with 49 percent, there would have to be a runoff election.[34]

Three days after the first election, Chancellor Brüning and defense minister Wilhelm Groener persuaded Hindenburg to outlaw
Nazi paramilitary organizations, namely the SA and SS.[35] The ban on
the SA led to escalating violence. Bullock reported, "In the weeks
which followed, murder and violence became everyday occurrences in
the streets of the big German cities. According to [Albert] Grzesinski,
the Police President of Berlin at the time, there were 461 political riots
in Prussia alone between June 1 and July 20, 1932, in which eighty-
two people were killed and four hundred seriously wounded. The
fiercest fighting was between Nazis and the Communists."[36]

General Kurt von Schleicher opposed the decree because he was
negotiating with SA head Röhm about the possibility of the SA becoming part of the German army. They agreed that if there was a
war, the SA would be subject to the army's command. Schleicher
hoped to bring Hitler into the government. To proceed with these
schemes, he had to undermine the decree, and he talked President
Hindenburg into protesting the decree with Defense Minister Groener.
Nazi members of the Reichstag criticized Groener. He soon concluded there was enough opposition to the decree that the army no
longer had confidence in him, and he resigned. Hitler's most important adversary in the government was gone. The decree banning the
SA and SS was lifted June 16, 1932.[37]

By this time there was widespread dissatisfaction with Chancellor Brüning, since he had been in office for two years, and his emergency decrees had failed to bring Germany out of the depression.
Schleicher announced that the army no longer had confidence in
Brüning. Hindenburg asked for Brüning's resignation, and on May
30 he was out.

Schleicher recommended Franz von Papen to replace Brüning.
Papen was a charming man who had married the daughter of a
wealthy industrialist. He hadn't distinguished himself in politics, so
there didn't appear to be much chance that he would be able to get
any measures passed by the Reichstag. Communists, Social Democrats, and the Centre Party were against him. Hitler offered to support him for a while if the ban on the SA was lifted, the Reichstag
session was ended, and new elections were scheduled. Papen declared
that the Prussian government—which had been supportive of the

Weimar Republic—was incapable of stopping the violence, and he used his emergency powers to fire Prussia's ministers and replace them with people loyal to him.

For the presidential runoff election, Goebbels organized a "Hitler over Germany" election campaign in which Hitler chartered an airplane to attend many more mass meetings than would be possible if he traveled by train. In one day, for instance, he attended four mass meetings and spoke to an estimated 250,000 people.[38] He reportedly visited twenty-one cities in a week.[39] The April 10 runoff election gave Hitler 13.4 million votes (37 percent). Hindenburg, with 19.2 million, won his majority (53 percent).[40]

The runoff election was followed fourteen days later by elections for the Prussian Diet (legislature). Prussia was the largest German state, accounting for two-thirds of Germany's territory and 40 million out of 65 million people. Although Prussia had a reputation for militarism and war, it had been the most steadfast defender of the Weimar Republic and opponent of the Nazis. So Nazi success at the polls would have a dynamic impact on what happened in Germany. Hitler gave speeches in twenty-six Prussian towns. The Nazis received 8 million votes. Though not enough for a majority, the Nazis had become the largest single party in Prussia, with 36.3 percent of the vote,[41] displacing the Social Democrats. Still, they lacked a majority and couldn't form a government.

There were also state elections in Bavaria, Württemberg, and Anhalt. About three-quarters of Germany would be voting.[42] Again, the Nazis did well, polling 32.5 percent in Bavaria, 26.4 percent in Württemberg, and 40.9 percent in Anhalt.[43]

Hindenburg dissolved the Reichstag and called elections for July 31, 1932. The Nazis increased their number of seats to 230 out of 608.[44] Although this was short of a majority, the Nazis were the leading party in Germany, having polled 13.7 million votes—not much of an improvement over the second presidential election.[45] This was 37.3 percent of the votes cast, the best Hitler would ever do in a free election. By contrast, the Social Democrats received less than 8 million votes.[46] The Nazis had a million members, and the SA had 400,000 men, so Hitler was clearly the country's most powerful political leader. Hitler demanded full power, but the most that Hinden-

burg would offer him was vice-chancellor, which Hitler viewed as
a snub.

The German government was as deadlocked as ever. As biographer Fest described the situation, "Three sharply divided groups now
faced one another: the nationalist-authoritarian group around
[Chancellor] Papen, who in parliamentary terms represented barely
10 per cent of the voters but who had the backing of Hindenburg
and the army; the exhausted democratic groups, which however could
still count on considerable support by the public; and the totalitarian
opposition consisting of both Nazis and Communists. Together
these last held a negative majority of 53 per cent. But just as the Nazis
and Communists could not work together, all the groups blocked and
paralyzed one another."[47]

On August 13, Hitler met Schleicher and Papen. They proposed
that Hitler serve as vice-chancellor, and one of his associates as Prussian minister of the interior. Hitler, outraged, demanded total power.
He shouted and threatened to order the SA to go on a killing spree
against Marxists.[48] Hitler rejected the idea of serving as foreign minister or minister of defense. Schleicher and Papen concluded this meant
Hitler wanted to rule without constraint from any cabinet officers.

Hitler stormed out of the meeting and met at Goebbels's apartment to review their options. Hindenburg called to ask if Hitler would
discuss the situation in his office. Hitler said that he wanted to comply
with the law, but he was determined to gain power. According to Otto
Meissner, the state secretary who was at the meeting, Hindenburg expressed concern about Nazi violence and urged Hitler to cooperate
with other parties. Hindenburg said that if Hitler could do something
constructive, he would gain influence in a coalition government.

Hitler had had enough of constitutional legalities. When, on
August 22, five Nazis were sentenced to death for killing a Communist, Hitler denounced the "bloodthirsty sentence" and vowed his
"boundless loyalty" for the Nazi murderers.

There were rumors that the Nazis would attempt a *putsch*.
Hitler's SA had four times as many members as did the German
army, whose numbers had been limited by the Versailles Treaty. Although Hitler had publicly called for compliance with the decree ordering that the SA and SS be disbanded, and the uniforms were no

longer worn in public, and the fighting stopped, both armies were maintained.

The recently elected Reichstag met for its first session on September 12. Nazi Hermann Göring was elected president of the Reichstag, and he used his power to arrange a no-confidence vote—513 to 32—in Papen's government. Papen, in turn, used his emergency power to dissolve the Reichstag, after this single session that lasted only about an hour. Papen called for new elections to be held November 6.

The fifth election campaign of the year drained Nazi finances. Hitler gave some fifty speeches—as many as four a day.[49] Contributions dwindled as more businesspeople became concerned about SA violence, Hitler's quest for total power, and his refusal to accept a post in the government. Nazi vote totals declined to about 11 million. They won 196 seats in the Reichstag, compared with the 230 that they had from the previous election. This might have meant the Nazis were losing their appeal. Communists won a hundred seats. Reportedly a substantial percentage of Communist voters were people who used to support the Nazis and wanted revolutionary action rather than Hitler's pursuit of power by legal means. The government was still deadlocked.

DEADLOCK DEAL

Papen began to negotiate with Hitler, but Hitler demanded a high price for his cooperation, and the negotiations stalled. Schleicher beame impatient with Papen, because of Communist gains in the Reichstag. Moreover, following wage cuts that Papen had demanded, Berlin transportation workers went on strike, and both Communists and Nazis supported the strikers. Schleicher, worried about an alliance between Communists and Nazis to topple the government, became more anxious to do a deal with Hitler. Schleicher pressured Papen to resign, and he did. Papen figured events would go his way, and he would be asked back into the government.

On November 18, Hitler met with Hindenburg at the Palace. Hindenburg told Hitler he might become chancellor if he could get the backing of a majority in the Reichstag for a specific legislative program. Hitler's problem was that he couldn't command a majority, and Hindenburg knew it.[50] Hindenburg was calling Hitler's bluff that he could be successful participating lawfully in a parliamentary government. On November 24, Hindenburg told Hitler, "A presidential cabinet led by you would develop necessarily into a party dictatorship with all its consequences for an extraordinary accentuation of the conflicts in the German people."[51]

Hindenburg named Schleicher as chancellor on December 4. Schleicher sounded out Hitler about possible ways of participating in his cabinet, but Hitler declined.[52] Schleicher asked Gregor Strasser if he would consider serving as vice-chancellor and as minister-president of the Prussian state government. Whereas Hitler was mainly interested in the tactics of seizing power, Strasser was more interested in enforcing a socialist program. He believed Nazis should be true to their anticapitalist faith. Schleicher's idea was to have Strasser pursue a socialist program for reducing unemployment. Scheicher hoped that his proposal would split the Nazi movement, with Strasser drawing critical support away from Hitler.

Hitler was outraged that Strasser would even consider accepting positions in the government. Over the years, Strasser had criticized Hitler's inconsistencies, particularly his willingness to consort with industrialists, but Strasser had always capitulated to Hitler's demands. This time Strasser expressed his disgust for Hitler and went into hiding. Hitler summoned a meeting of party leaders and insisted that they sign a statement condemning Strasser. Schleicher wasn't able to get any prominent Nazis to join his cabinet.

Furious at how Schleicher had forced him to resign as chancellor, Papen schemed to bring him down. On January 4, Papen met with Hitler at the home of banker Kurt von Schröder. Papen offered conciliatory words about their past disputes. Hitler declared that if he were chancellor, he would have to have supreme power in the government. Hitler suggested that Papen's associates might serve as ministers.

Meanwhile, Hindenburg's son Oskar became embroiled in illegal dealings. Some 5,000 acres had been added to the Hindenburg estate tax-free, and he got a big promotion in the army, from colonel to major-general. Hitler apparently used his knowledge of the dealings to blackmail Oskar Hindenburg into supporting the view that Nazis must be in the government.

By January 23, Schleicher conceded to President Hindenburg that he had been unable to recruit any Nazis in the government. He couldn't command a majority in the Reichstag. Schleicher asked for authority to end the Reichstag's session and rule by issuing decrees. He found himself in the same situation as Papen a month before.

At his wits' end for a way to end deadlock in the Reichstag, and no doubt weary of resisting Hitler's relentless pressure, the eighty-five-year-old Hindenburg was willing to name Hitler as chancellor— provided that field marshal Werner von Blomberg was willing to serve as minister of defense. Hindenburg hoped Blomberg's presence would ensure that the government had the backing of the army. Blomberg agreed. On Monday morning, January 30, Hindenburg summoned Hitler and made him Chancellor of Germany. The Nazis were awarded three of eleven cabinet posts, and they were minor posts. The Foreign Ministry and Defense Ministry were in the hands of individuals loyal to Hindenburg.

Not many Germans spoke out against Hitler, but there were some. On February 8, for example, Wilhelm Röpke, a thirty-two-year-old economics professor at the University of Marburg, denounced Nazism as a "revolt against reason, freedom and humanity." Röpke declared that freedom required "truthfulness instead of obscurantism, clarity instead of hysteria, the advancement of knowledge instead of sensationalism for the masses, logic instead of wallowing in moods and emotion. . . . It is only the liberal ideal of the use of Reason in the service of truth that has engendered science . . . that alone has liberated Europe from the stupor and wretchedness of barbarism."[53] Röpke also denounced the expulsion of Jewish professors. For speaking out, Nazis condemned him as "an enemy of the people," he was fired, and he left the country, ending up with a teaching position at the Institute for International Studies in Geneva.

That Hitler finally became chancellor was the result of many bad breaks. If Woodrow Wilson had kept the United States out of World War I, and neither side were able to dictate surrender terms to the other, there probably would have been some kind of negotiated settlement, the Treaty of Versailles never would have developed as it did, and there surely wouldn't have been the bitter nationalist reaction that generated political support for Hitler. Without the reparations bills and the French occupation of the Ruhr, both of which were a consequence of the decisive defeat of Germany, made possible by American entry in the war, there might not have been the ruinous runaway inflation that enabled Hitler to recruit thousands of Nazis.

After Hitler's conviction for treason, he wouldn't have been treated leniently if the presiding judge hadn't shared Hitler's resentment at how Germany had been humiliated and impoverished. Hitler would have been more likely to serve his full term, in which case he would have been unavailable to help rebuild the Nazi party in time to take advantage of the depression crisis.

If the prosperity of the Weimar Republic had continued, there wouldn't have been much interest in Hitler's tirades—recall the Nazi party's dismal showing in the 1928 Reichstag elections. Hitler needed the widely shared bitterness of depression as well as the bitterness of war and the bitterness of inflation to give him a large audience.

If, in December 1932, Gregor Strasser had the fortitude to go against Hitler and participate in the government, this might have split the party, undermining Hitler's position and making it harder for him to become chancellor.

Since the preceding (November 6) Reichstag election suggested that Nazi popularity was starting to decline, it seems quite possible that if Hindenburg had been able to avoid naming Hitler the chancellor for several more months, Hitler's restless SA and SS men might have rebelled, splitting the party.

It was extremely difficult for Hitler to become chancellor. There wasn't anything inevitable about it. Hitler needed a lot, if not everything, to break in his favor. If one or more things had gone differently, he probably never would have made it.

Having become chancellor, his obsession with achieving totalitarian power, an obsession he shared with Lenin and Stalin, gave him crucial advantages over rivals who were unwilling to commit murder.

ESTABLISHING A NAZI DICTATORSHIP

Hitler immediately began to consolidate his power. He met with Monsignor Kaas, leader of the Centre Party, about a possible alliance with the Nazis that might help achieve a majority in the Reichstag. He gave

Hitler a list of questions intended as starting points for discussion. Hitler announced that negotiations were impossible, and it wasn't possible to form a majority. He demanded that Hindenburg sign a decree dissolving the Reichstag and calling for yet another election.

Hitler made a lot of campaign speeches, but he refused to spell out a specific program for fighting the depression. In Munich, for instance, he declared, "If, today, we are asked for the program of this movement, then we can summarize this in a few quite general sentences: programs are of no avail, it is the human purpose which is decisive. . . . Therefore the first point in our program is: Away with illusions!"[54]

Hitler campaigned against the Weimar Republic itself and the Social Democrats who had dominated it. Nazi goons assaulted members of other parties, suppressed their newspapers, and destroyed their campaign materials.

Hermann Göring, president of the Reichstag, acquired control of the Prussian police force and government administration, whose jurisdiction covered two-thirds of Germany. Göring made sure that his supporters occupied all important positions. On February 22, Göring announced that the police couldn't do everything that needed to be done, and he recruited 25,000 men from the SA and 15,000 from the SS. This meant it was impossible for anybody in trouble to call the police for help, because the trouble was probably caused by the police or their Nazi recruits themselves.

On February 27, 1933, the Reichstag was set afire. A young communist, Marianus van der Lubbe, was arrested at the Reichstag, convicted of having set the fire, and executed. Hitler, Göring, and other Nazis claimed that the fire proved a Communist conspiracy to overthrow the government, and they launched a ruthless campaign to exterminate Communists. There has been considerable debate about who actually started the fire, with many believing that the Nazis themselves did it.

The day after the fire, Hitler issued a decree, signed by Hindenburg, that suspended Weimar Republic guarantees of civil liberties. It said, in part: "Restrictions on personal liberty, on the right of free expression of opinion, including freedom of the Press; on the rights of assembly and association; violations of the privacy of postal, telegraphic and telephonic communications; warrants for house searches; orders for confiscation as well as restrictions on property, are permissible beyond the legal limits otherwise prescribed."[55]

Hitler's campaign climaxed with a succession of mass demonstrations, torchlit parades, and violence against political opponents. Göring vowed to "destroy and exterminate" Communists. Hitler secured the blessing of the establishment in a March 1 ceremony at Garrison Church, Potsdam. This was the church of the Hohenzollern monarchs, and it still had a throne where Kaiser Wilhelm II used to sit. In attendance were generals and admirals wearing splendid uniforms from the prewar days of the German Empire. Hitler, in a cutaway coat, walked down the aisle with Hindenburg. After Hindenburg spoke, Hitler said, "The revolution of November 1918 ended a conflict into which the German nation had been drawn in the most sacred conviction that it was but protecting its liberty and its right to live. Neither the Kaiser nor the Government nor the Nation wanted the war. It was only the collapse of our nation which compelled a weakened race to take upon itself, against its most sacred convictions, the guilt for this war. . . . By a unique upheaval, in the last few weeks our national honor has been restored, and, thanks to your understanding, Field-Marshal, the union between the symbols of the old greatness and the new strength has been celebrated."[56] This ceremony was followed by a parade involving the German army and the SA. Then, at night, there was a torchlit parade of some 10,000 SS troops.

Despite all the pageantry and the intimidation of voters and political opponents, Hitler still couldn't gain a majority in the March 5 election. The Nazis polled 17.2 million votes—43.9 percent—out of 39.3 million cast. The Centre Party, rebuked by Hitler, actually increased their total, to 4.4 million votes. So almost 56 percent of voters preferred somebody other than Hitler.

On March 23, Hitler announced the Enabling Law ("Law for Removing the Distress of People and Reich"), which empowered him to enact laws without the approval of the Reichstag for four years. Hitler's laws could violate the constitution and take effect the day after he issued them. Passage required a two-thirds majority in the Reichstag. To secure this, Hitler outlawed the Communist Party, thereby reducing the total number of Reichstag members and the number of votes needed to secure the majority he needed.

Hitler proceeded to assert central government power over the states. He began by arranging the overthrow of the Bavarian government, and Nazis were appointed to all the important positions. He appointed a Nazi governor to carry out Nazi policy in every state. Nazis took over as police commissioners in Baden, Saxony, and Württemberg, and they installed Nazi ministers there. His January 1934 Law for the Reconstruction of the Reich abolished state legislatures and transferred all power from the states to the central government. The Weimar Republic was history.

Rival political parties were suppressed, starting with the Social Democrats, who had been the principal party during the Weimar era. Göring, on May 10, had troops occupy Social Democratic offices, shut down their newspapers, and seize their money. The party was banned as an enemy of the state. Leaders of the Catholic Centre Party were arrested. On July 14 the Nazi regime announced a law saying that "the National Socialist German Workers' Party constitutes the only political party in Germany."[57]

Labor unions remained as a possible source of opposition, and Hitler went after them. He began by praising workers. Then he issued a decree that abolished collective bargaining and asserted the government's power to determine working conditions.

This succession of measures gave Hitler undisputed power over the government. He was unconstrained by the Reichstag, President Hindenburg, the states, the constitution, or anything else. Whereas Papen and many other Germans had thought that power consisted of parliamentary maneuvering, Hitler understood that power consisted of coercion and violence. He was determined to monopolize it.

HITLER'S AUTARKY

Hitler sanctioned a government-run economy, not because he thought it would cure the depression, but because it would give him more power. Effective resistance to a regime was difficult if government controlled an individual's ability to make a living. Hitler's scheme involved nominal private ownership but government control of property.

While Hitler denounced Marxism, he also denounced capitalism, which he associated with Jews. He was opposed to free markets. Nazis had embraced such anticapitalist slogans as "break the bond of interest slavery."[58]

The government seized control of cartels whose existence had already depended on government enforcement. For example, historian Gordon explained, "Germany had centralized control in the hands of the Reich Food Estate, a public corporation or national cartel, embracing agriculture, forestry, horticulture, fisheries, and game resources. Within these branches of the national economy, all producers, laborers, processors, importers and wholesale or retail dealers, have been required to belong to the cartel. Under the general supervision of the Minister of Agriculture, an attempt has been made to fix prices, and, in many cases, sales quotas, throughout the national cartel from the first producer to the final purchaser."[59]

The German economy moved toward autarky—self-sufficiency even when it meant producing goods that people elsewhere could produce better and for less money. The government embraced regulations that made it more difficult for Germans to buy or sell with foreigners. The plan, Gordon wrote, was "for foreign trade control, whereby foreign exchange to pay for imports was to be released only on presentation of official exchange certificates which were to be procured by importers for each individual transaction before goods were brought into the country. The power to issue these certificates was given to twenty-seven Import Control Boards, each responsible for certain groups of goods, and each rendering its decisions in accordance with a comprehensive governmental scheme designed to discourage all imports except those considered essential for the German economy."[60]

PERSECUTING JEWS

Hitler didn't waste any time launching his crusade against Jews. In February 1933, *Der Stürmer*, the Nazi party's weekly publication issued since 1923, became an official government organ. Its slogan: "The Jews are our misfortune."

On April 1 Nazis ordered a boycott of Jewish stores, doctors, and lawyers. SA troops provided pickets to enforce the boycott. At the same time, all sorts of places in Germany began excluding Jews. Signed appeared saying "Jews not admitted." The government began firing Jewish employees on April 7.

Heinrich Himmler established the first Nazi concentration camp at Dachau on March 20, 1934. It had a capacity of 3,000 prisoners. Initially, Dachau was for Social Democrats, Communists, conservatives, labor union leaders, and other political opponents of the regime. Homosexuals, Gypsies, and other unpopular minorities were dispatched to Dachau. Initially, Jews were sent to Dachau because of their political views, but increasingly Jews ended up at Dachau because they were Jews. Some 10,000 Jews arrived after "Crystal Night," in October 1938.

Hermann Göring separated the political and espionage units from the Prussian police—that is, police who pursued people because of their political views. He staffed these units with Nazis, and this new force became the *Geheime Staatspolizei* (State Secret Police), abbreviated as Gestapo. Göring became commander on April 26. Later, one of the principal jobs of the Gestapo was to round up Jews for the concentration camps.

THE NIGHT OF THE LONG KNIVES

Meanwhile, Ernst Röhm and his more than 2 million[61] SA troops were becoming increasingly disgruntled. These were mainly street toughs who had anticipated that when Hitler came to power, they would gain booty and prestige, only to find that Hitler didn't seem to need them anymore. He was anxious to avoid a conflict with the army, even though it was still small because of the Versailles Treaty. Opposition from the army had thwarted his November 1923 *putsch*, and the lack of opposition from the army had enabled him to become chancellor in January 1933.

The generals were concerned with maintaining their privileged status in Germany, and Hitler pledged his loyalty to them. He affirmed his goal of rearming Germany, which would improve the position of the army. On April 11, 1933, Hitler observed naval maneuvers, which afforded an opportunity to meet with the minister of defense, General Werner von Blomberg, a key figure in maintaining the army's support for Hitler; Colonel General Freiherr von Fritsch, commander-in-chief of the German army; and Admiral Erich Raeder, commander-in-chief of the German navy. Among other things, Hitler aimed to win enough support to secure his position after the death of Hindenburg.

Although Hitler announced that SA members would be eligible for government disability and pension benefits, and Röhm was made a member of Hitler's cabinet, Röhm was outraged to learn that Hitler favored cutting down the size of the SA. His idea was to incorporate the SA into the army and remodel it. Röhm and Hitler were at odds, but Hitler was allied with Hermann Göring, whom Hindenburg had made a general. Göring won over Heinrich Himmler, head of the black-shirted SS, as an ally by naming him head of the Prussian Gestapo. At that time the SS was part of the SA, and Himmler was a bitter rival of Röhm. Göring and Himmler urged Hitler to take action against Röhm.

Hitler met with Röhm on June 4, 1934, and reportedly urged him to abandon his idea of continuing a revolution with the SA. Röhm urged Hitler to lead a Second Revolution, with the SA against the generals and the rest of the German establishment. Hitler scolded Röhm for his luxurious, homosexual lifestyle.

With each passing day there seemed to be more tension in the air, more speculation about a possible coup or civil war. On June 20, Papen met with Hitler, protested Hitler's ban on free speech, and reported that conservative government ministers were threatening to resign. The following day Hitler saw Blomberg and Hindenburg. Blomberg warned Hitler that if he didn't take action against the SA, Hindenburg would order martial law, and the army would take charge of the government. Hindenburg affirmed that the army, having supported Hitler as chancellor, expected Hitler to uphold the army's position in the state.

Hitler agreed to take action. Göring and Himmler issued the actual orders for the purge. On June 29, local SA leaders were arrested. They were told, "You have been condemned to death by the Führer!

Heil Hitler!"[62] At Wiessee, Edmund Heines was dragged out of bed and shot. Röhm, also at Wiessee, was taken to Munich's Stadelheim Prison and shot. General Schleicher and his wife were shot at their villa. Gregor Strasser was seized and shot in the prison below the Gestapo offices on Prinz-Albrecht-Strasse 8, Berlin. Several dozen SA officials were reportedly shot in Breslau, and dozens more in Silesia. The murders continued through June 30. It isn't known how many people were killed during this purge, because Göring had many documents burned.[63] Surviving lists include the names of eighty-five people who had been shot. During the next year, the purge—including dismissals as well as murders—cut the size of the SS by a reported 40 percent.[64]

Hitler was praised for taking decisive action to save the nation from the lawless SA. Minister of Defense Blomberg praised Hitler's "soldierly determination and exemplary courage." Hindenburg praised Hitler for his "determined action and gallant personal intervention." Just in case people changed their minds, Hitler secured passage of the Law for the Emergency Defense of the State, which said, in part, "The measures taken on 30 June and 1 and 2 July for the suppression of high treasonable and state treasonable attacks are, as emergency defense of the state, legal."[65]

News of the murders was suppressed—newspapers were forbidden to run obituaries of the victims. On July 13, Hitler gave a speech at the Reichstag in which he blamed Röhm for what had happened, citing his corruption and homosexuality. Hitler referred to the purge as "the night of the long knives," after a phrase from a Nazi song.

"If I am reproached with not turning to the law-courts for sentence," he declared, "I can only say: In this hour, I was responsible for the fate of the German nation and thereby the supreme judge of the German people. . . . I gave the order to shoot those most guilty of this treason, and I further gave the order to burn down to the raw flesh the ulcers of our internal well-poisoning and the poisoning from abroad." Thirteen members of the Reichstag were among those shot, yet those who heard the speech applauded!

The murders ended the SA as a serious threat to Hitler's power. For its role in the purge and its demonstrated loyalty to him, Hitler granted Himmler's SS quite a bit of independence, and in a few years it was to displace the authority of the German army.

Biographer Joachim C. Fest observed, "Hitler, with his intuition for power relationships, had realized that if the Army would stand for the murder of army men [like Schleicher], he had achieved the breakthrough to unlimited control. An institution that accepted such a blow could never again effectively oppose him."[66]

Hindenburg died on August 2, 1934. About an hour later the government announced that the offices of president (Hindenburg's) and chancellor (Hitler's) would be merged, essentially promoting Hitler to the supreme civilian position that had been Hindenburg's. Hitler was also named Supreme Commander of the Armed Forces.

Army officers swore their loyalty to Hitler personally, rather than to a constitution or the nation: "I swear by God this holy oath. I will render unconditional obedience to the Führer of the German Reich and People, Adolf Hitler, the Supreme Commander of the Armed Forces, and will be ready, as a brave soldier, to stake my life at any time for this oath."[67]

This completed Hitler's dictatorship. He had shut down the legislature and discarded the constitution. He had secured the support of the army, tamed the rogue SA, and confirmed the loyalty of the SS and Gestapo. He held the highest political and military offices. All this was remarkable considering that he had never been in government before. His only previous experience in politics was as an agitator.

Evidently it wasn't enough to possess the power. Hitler felt it was necessary to have the appearance of public approval, which led to a rigged plebiscite giving him 89 percent of the votes cast. Proud of how he had outsmarted all those who had dismissed and humiliated him over the years, Hitler boasted that his Third Reich would last a thousand years.

He had come a long way since he started out as a young World War I veteran, bitter at the way his country had been humiliated by the British, the French, and Woodrow Wilson's United States.

1 0

HOW DID WILSON MAKE
POSSIBLE STALIN'S TERROR?

I F I T H A D N ' T B E E N for Woodrow Wilson, Joseph Stalin
might have ended his days as a petty bandit in his native province
of Georgia. Instead, Wilson pressured Russia's Provisional Government to stay in World War I, accelerating the collapse of the Russian
army until there was hardly anybody left to defend the government.
Lenin seized power in November 1917, and Stalin, once he gained
control of the regime Lenin had established, murdered millions.

Stalin's ascendancy seems to have taken everybody by surprise.
For years he didn't do much to distinguish himself. He wasn't a theoretician like Lenin or a public speaker like Trotsky. He didn't do
much during the 1905 revolution, when he met Lenin.

He certainly wasn't much to look at. "Stalin," according to historian Robert Conquest, "grew to a height of five feet four inches. In addition to his smallpox-pitted face and his crippled arm, the second
and third toes of his left foot were joined (as a police record tells us).
The height, at least, always seems to have been a regret. . . . In the
1930s, Stalin got the head of his NKVD guards, K. V. Pauker, to find
him 'platform' shoes, and at parades he usually stood on a slightly
raised wooden slab. . . . His eyes seem to have been among his most
striking characteristics. The Bolshevik leader Krestinsky was to speak
of his 'tigerish eyes,' and the writer Sholokhov, too, was to comment,
'He smiles, but his eyes are like a tiger's—the supreme beast of prey,
which yet has the capacity to lie patiently in wait for its victim.' "[1]

According to historian Walter Laqueur, Stalin "had a quick intelligence and a phenomenal memory but little education and few interests outside Russian working-class politics. His command of the Russian language was perfect, but he spoke with a strong Georgian accent."[2]

From the collapse of the 1905 revolution until 1917, he lived mainly in Baku, an industrial city in the Caucasus. He was arrested and imprisoned four times. He attended Bolshevik party meetings in Finland (1906), Sweden (1906), and England (1907). He raised funds for the Bolsheviks by robbing banks, mail coaches, and steamships.[3] In St. Petersburg, 1912, Koba, as Stalin was then known, met twenty-two-year-old Vyacheslav Skryabin, who assumed the revolutionary last name "Molotov" and was to become one of his closest surviving associates. Koba and Molotov were working at *Pravda* at the time. The following year he signed an article with an alias, "Stalin"— sounding like the name of his hero, Lenin.[4]

Stalin did work exceedingly hard at mundane administrative tasks, and he learned to assess people shrewdly. He mastered the tactics of bureaucratic infighting. The Bolsheviks didn't have many capable administrators, but he proved himself to be one, and he gradually earned the confidence of Lenin. A supporting player during the 1917 upheavals, he was named the commissar of nationalities.[5]

After the czar's decision to enter World War I led to inflation, food shortages, military disasters, and the collapse of his regime in February 1917, Lenin, Stalin, and other Bolsheviks went to St. Petersburg and agitated against the new Provisional Government, which, given its continued involvement in the war promoted by Woodrow Wilson, was easy prey for the Bolsheviks in October 1917. Stalin took over Molotov's job editing *Pravda*, the Bolshevik newspaper.[6] When, in 1918, Lenin formed a decision-making body, the Political Bureau—known as the Politburo—Stalin was in it. Stalin and Leon Trotsky, the journalist who formed the Red Army, were the only men who could see Lenin without an appointment. When the Red Army suffered setbacks in July 1918, Stalin assumed effective control of it.

Lenin urged Stalin to be ruthless during the civil war. On May 29, 1918, Stalin was given extraordinary powers to relieve the famine in Moscow and in Russia's central provinces. His method was terror. He authorized arrests and shootings by the score. He arrested military officers suspected of obstructing the food transportation system, then packed them on a Volga River barge and sank it.[7]

Stalin clashed with Trotsky, disregarding commands from his Commissariat of War. Stalin's arbitrary military decisions seem to have disrupted the Red Army's campaign on the Southern Front around Tsaritsyn. Trotsky fumed, "I categorically insist that Stalin be recalled."[8]

Stalin's military failures don't seem to have slowed down his quest for power, because he did the grunt work of running the Bolshevik party. He put in long hours handling administrative details other party members either weren't good at or didn't want to be bothered with. In 1920 the Central Committee established a three-person Secretariat to administer the party, and on April 3, 1922, Stalin was chosen as the chief administrator—general secretary.[9]

When appointments were made, naturally he chose people loyal to him. Gradually, imperceptibly, he built a party bureaucracy, a nationwide network that would follow his commands. At the same time, he gave Trotsky's principal allies overseas assignments where they would be out of his way. "[Christian] Rakovsky was sent to the Soviet Legation in London," Robert Conquest explained. "[Nikolai] Krestinsky on a diplomatic mission to Germany, others to similar exile."[10]

For a while nobody seemed to notice what Stalin was doing. Other than affirming basic Marxist dogmas, he seldom expressed his views.[11] He didn't promote grand plans. He concealed his feelings. He had an extraordinary memory, and never forgot or forgave anybody who crossed him. He made a move only when he developed overwhelming advantages. By the time one of his comrades realized he was in danger, it was too late.

Much has been written about how Lenin, in his last days, allegedly became disillusioned with Stalin. Volkogonov, for instance, suggested that Lenin believed Stalin to be "immoral" and therefore not a good choice to run the Communist Party. Yet it was Lenin who established a Bolshevik political monopoly, Lenin who suppressed freedom of discussion, Lenin who established the secret police and ordered the deaths of thousands of people for belonging to the "wrong" class.[12]

Biographer Robert Service observed that "several influential accounts, in the West from the 1960s and in the USSR in the late 1980s, have suggested he was advocating a massive reform of the Soviet political system. They exaggerated Lenin's wish to change things. He did not challenge his own political creation: the one-party state, the one-ideology state, the terrorist state, the state that sought to dominate all social life, economy and culture."[13]

What *did* Lenin want? From December 22 to 29, 1922, Lenin dictated to his two secretaries notes that were to be read before the Twelfth Congress of the Communist Party, April 1923. But he suffered a paralyzing stroke on March 10. His wife, Krupskaya, tried to keep the notes—commonly referred to as Lenin's Testament—secret until read at the Thirteenth Congress, a year after Lenin's death on January 21, 1924. In them, Lenin explained his vision for the future of the Communist Party and his thoughts about possible successors. While he was critical of Stalin, who had been rude to his wife, he was also critical of Trotsky and other party leaders. Biographer Radzinsky observed, "Stalin appears in the most favorable light."[14] Lenin expressed concern about Stalin's "immense power"—that he might not "use it cautiously enough." Yet Lenin never suggested that Stalin be replaced as general secretary. Members of the Congress agreed to keep the notes secret.

Trotsky leaked a copy of the notes to the journalist Max Eastman, an American Communist, who arranged to have them published in the *New York Times,* October 18, 1926. But the publication of the notes was banned in the Soviet Union until the 1950s.

Meanwhile, Stalin proceeded to turn Lenin into a cult figure, with himself as the leader of the cult. Lenin's body was embalmed and put on display in Red Square. Stalin became the official interpreter of Leninism. Stalin promoted his own cult, too, having the city of Tsaritsyn renamed Stalingrad.

As leaders maneuvered for power, there was a bitter debate about how to handle the Soviet economic crisis brought on by civil war and government regulations. The government interfered with free-market pricing.[15] Consequently prices of manufactured goods rose faster than grain prices, and farmers held back grain, potatoes, and milk, hoping their situation would improve. This sparked a bitter debate.

Trotsky, commissar for military affairs, blamed the situation on incompetent government bureaucracy, which meant Joseph Stalin;

Grigori Zinoviev, chairman of the Comintern and Leningrad Soviet chairman; Lev Kamenev, Moscow Soviet chairman;[16] and Nikolai Bukharin, editor of *Pravda*. At the Thirteenth Party Congress, in January 1924, they accused Trotsky of repudiating Lenin's New Economic Policy.[17] Trotsky wanted to promote revolution in Western Europe, but Stalin concluded there wasn't going to be a European revolution anytime soon, so he declared that Bolsheviks should focus on achieving "Socialism in One Country." He won the confidence of many Bolsheviks by efficiently running the Secretariat, which made practical decisions about daily operations.

Trotsky, however, persuaded Zinoviev and Kamenev that Stalin was making too many concessions to the peasants, so they launched an attack on him. But Stalin had been loading the party apparatus with his supporters, and he was joined by Bukharin. At *Pravda,* they saw to it that articles by Trotsky, Zinoviev, and Kamenev were rejected. Stalin's supporters disrupted the speeches by these men. In January 1925, Trotsky was denied his membership in the Politburo, and he was fired as People's Commissar for Military Affairs. Zinoviev was fired as chairman of the Leningrad Soviet and as a member of the Politburo.

After the party had pressured the Chinese Communist Party into a disastrous alliance with warlord Chiang Kai-shek, Trotsky denounced Stalin, and in 1927 Stalin's supporters lined up to expel Trotsky, Zinoviev, and Kamenev from the party. Zinoviev and Kamenev could not bear to be without the party, and they recanted their views, for which Stalin readmitted them. Trotsky, however, remained hostile and had to accept internal exile in Alma-Ata, a town about 1,800 miles east of Moscow.

CATASTROPHIC COLLECTIVIZATION

Although Stalin had consolidated his power in the Communist bureaucracy, it couldn't resist interfering in the economy. In 1927 it introduced taxes on private goods shipped by (government) railroad. Private entrepreneurs were hit with punitive taxes. The government cut the prices it paid for agricultural commodities. The results were that entrepreneurs devised ways to evade taxes, and peasants withheld produce. By 1928, food supplies in towns were half what they had been the previous year.[18]

Bukharin wanted to raise prices that the government offered for agricultural commodities, but Stalin was furious. He decided it was time to scrap the New Economic Policy. Stalin ordered that requisitioning be resumed, and the amounts of grain to be seized were doubled, tripled, even quintupled.[19] Stalin also decided that millions of peasants must be herded into gigantic collective farms where they would be under direct government control.

Peasants, of course, resisted collectivization. Stalin ordered that millions of these peasants, denounced as "kulaks," be deported to the vast, empty, resource-rich Narym region in western Siberia, near the Arctic Circle, where they would be forced to work in mines and on huge industrial projects.

The 1928 crop was even lower than the previous year's, and Stalin's escalating penalties on peasants triggered some 1,300 riots in the countryside.[20] In 1929, Stalin announced a goal of forcing 13 million peasants into collective farms the following year.[21] On December 27, 1929, Stalin called for "the eradication of all kulak tendencies and the elimination of the kulaks as a class."

Communist brigades were organized to carry out these policies. Werth reported, "in certain districts between 80 and 90 percent of those victimized by the dekulakization process were *serednyaki,* or middle-income peasants. The brigades had to meet the required quotas and, if possible, surpass them. Peasants were arrested and deported for having sold grain on the market or for having had an employee to help with the harvest back in 1925 or 1926, for possessing two samovars [urns to boil water for tea], for having killed a pig in September 1929 'with the intention of consuming it themselves and thus keeping it from socialist appropriation.' Peasants were arrested on the pretext that they had 'taken part in commerce,' when all they had done was sell something of their own making."[22]

Peasant resistance intensified—there were 1,992 reported peasant protests in April 1930 alone. According to Werth, "Soviet officials were attacked, and for a few hours or a few days the peasants would try to reclaim the administration of village affairs, demanding the return of confiscated tools and cattle, the dissolution of the

kolkhoz [collective farms], the reintroduction of free trade, the re-
opening of the churches, the restitution of all goods to the kulaks,
the return of peasants who had been deported, the abolition of Bolshevik power, and, in the Ukraine at least, national independence."[23]

The regime continued to impose punitive taxes on peasants. "In
1930," Werth reported, "the state took 30 percent of the agricultural
production of Ukraine, 38 percent in the rich plains of the Kuban in
the Northern Caucasus, 33 percent of the harvest in Kazakhstan.
In 1931, when the harvest was considerably smaller, the percentages
for the same areas were 41.5, 47, and 39.5 percent, respectively. Removing produce on such a scale created total chaos in the cycle of
production."

The GPU's records reportedly show that it executed tens of
thousands of peasants.[24] In 1930, some 700,000 peasants had been
forced off their land,[25] and 140,000 were in concentration camps run
by the GPU (*Gosudarstvennoe Politicheskoe Upravlenie*), successor
to Cheka.[26] In 1931 an estimated 1.8 million peasants were forced off
their land, which was a far larger number than could be accommo-
dated in camp facilities. There was chaos. It isn't known how many
people died because of the bitter cold, the food shortages, and lack
of medical treatment. In 1932, 1.8 million were reported as having
been deported, but a census that year showed only 1.3 million peasants in concentration camps, suggesting that some 500,000 had
died.[27]

On August 7, 1932, the government issued a decree that became
known as the "ear law." Peasants were to be imprisoned or executed
for "any theft or damage of socialist property." This decree figured
in thousands of executions. The government collected even less grain
than before.

Peasants responded to Communist barbarism any way they
could. Werth reported, "Collective farmers tried to hide or steal part
of the harvest every night. A movement of passive resistance took
shape, strengthened by the tacit agreement of almost all concerned,
including collective farm workers, brigadiers, accountants, farm
managers (many of whom had themselves been peasant workers until
their recent promotion), and even local secretaries of the Party."[28]

Increasing numbers of peasants ran away from farms and hoped

to find a better life in cities. To prevent this, the government began issuing identity papers and required that residents register with local
authorities.[29] Moreover, the government stopped selling railway tick-
ets. According to a GPU report, in March 1933, 219,460 peasants
had been caught trying to leave the countryside, and they had been
either escorted back to their collective farms or imprisoned.[30]

Stalin knew what was coming. In August 1932, Vyacheslav
Molotov informed the Politburo about "a real risk of famine even in
areas where the harvest has been exceptionally good."[31]

Famine conditions contributed to the massive dumping of children. An Italian government representative in Kharkiv observed:
"Children are simply brought here and abandoned by their parents
who then return to their village to die. Their hope is that someone in
the town will be able to look after their children. . . . So for a week
now, the town has been patrolled by *dvorniki,* attendants in white
uniforms, who collect the children and take them to the nearest police station. . . . Around midnight they are all transported to the
freight station at Severodonetsk. That's where all the children who
are found in stations and on trains, the peasant families, the old
people, and all the peasants who have been picked up during the day
are gathered together. . . . Anyone who is not yet swollen up and still
has a chance of survival is directed to the Kholodnaya Gora buildings, where a constant population of about 8,000 lies dying on straw
beds in the big hangars. Most of them are children."[32]

There were reports of cannibalism. For instance, this bulletin
about Kharkiv: "Every night the bodies of more than 250 people who
have died from hunger or typhus are collected. Many of these bodies
have had the liver removed, through a large slit in the abdomen. The
police finally picked up some of these mysterious 'amputators' who
confessed they were using the meat as a filling for the meat pies they
were selling in the market."

Robert Conquest reported, "There are scores of stories of particular acts of cannibalism, some eating their own families, others
trapping children or ambushing strangers. Or (as at Kalmazorka,
Odessa Province, this case in connection with the theft of a pig) a
search of the whole village might result in the discovery of children's
corpses being cooked."[33]

Conquest added, "Not all cannibalism, or ideas of cannibalism, were based on despair alone. One activist, who had been working on the collectivization campaign in Siberia came back to the Ukraine in 1933 to find the population of his village 'almost extinct.' His younger brother told him that they were living on bark, grass, and hares, but that when these gave out, 'Mother says we should eat her if she dies.'"[34]

During the famine, a reported 6 million people died.[35] Altogether, from 1929 to 1933—a period about as long as World War I— Conquest wrote, "Though confined to a single state, the number dying in Stalin's war against the peasants was higher than the total deaths for all countries in World War I. There were differences: in the Soviet case, for practical purposes, only one side was armed, and the casualties (as might be expected) were almost all on the other side."[36]

The famine was entirely a creation of the Soviet government. The famine was a consequence of socialism, the core doctrine of which was that political power and economic power must be combined. By seizing assets that had been privately owned, independent of government, socialism made it harder for people to resist oppression. Combining political power and economic power was lethal because nobody, then as now, has found a way to keep bad people out of government where they could harm millions.

Stalin ordered peasants into collective farms not because he thought this would achieve prosperity, but because it would give him more control over the economy. He claimed peasants were going into collective farms voluntarily. He blamed the ensuing disasters on "kulaks," a class that didn't exist. When the magnitude of the famine became apparent, he simply denied it.

Novelist Boris Pasternak wrote in his autobiography, "What I saw could not be expressed in words. There was such inhuman, unimaginable misery, such a terrible disaster, that it began to seem almost abstract, it would not fit with the bounds of consciousness. I felt ill. For an entire year I could not write."[37]

THE GREAT TERROR

The disastrous collectivization policy led many Bolsheviks to criticize Stalin. If he hadn't already filled the ranks of the Communist Party and the Soviet government with people loyal to him, he would surely have been overthrown. In June 1932, Moscow Communist Party official Martemyan Ryutin and several associates drafted their "Appeal to All Members of the All-Union Communist Party," which summarized Stalin's disastrous policies. Stalin viewed this appeal as suggesting that he should be assassinated.[38]

Although Stalin presumably hoped that the OGPU, as the secret police were then known, could arrange to have Ryutin killed, he was concerned this might unify his rivals and spark a revolt—killing Ryutin would be the first execution of an old Bolshevik. Stalin was in a stronger political position than any of his rivals, but he was outnumbered. So he couldn't prevent the Politburo from determining Ryutin's fate.

Sergey Mironovich Kirov, Grigori Ordzhonikidze, Valeryan Kuibyshev, and other Politburo members spoke out against the death penalty being applied to Bolsheviks. A majority voted against the death penalty. All these men supported dictatorship as long as they were in charge. They had enthusiastically supported Lenin's reign of terror following the Revolution, and then had slaughtered Whites during the Civil War. Their moral sensibilities were not to be taken seriously, but Stalin had to maneuver carefully.

Politburo members on the Central Committee agreed that Ryutin and his associates should be expelled from the Communist Party. They were denounced as "enemies of Communism and the Soviet regime, traitors to the Party and to the working class."[39] Ryutin was sentenced to ten years in prison, and twenty-nine of his associates were imprisoned, too.[40]

Purge commissions were set up throughout the Soviet Union. At public meetings they reviewed the life of each party member, focusing on inconsistencies with the party line and unacceptable relatives or associates (such as former czarist army officers).[41] In 1933 some 800,000 members were expelled from the Communist Party. Another 340,000 were expelled in 1934.[42]

During the spring of 1934 Kirov proposed reconciliation among the Communist factions. He suggested releasing from prison those who had opposed Stalin's forced collectivization and industrialization. A majority of the Politburo appeared to support Kirov. Stalin tried to persuade Kirov, who controlled the party organization in Leningrad, to join him in Moscow, where Stalin could more easily monitor his activities, but Kirov declined. He resisted Stalin's control.

Born in 1886, Kirov joined the party before the October Revolution and was arrested for his party activities. After the revolution, he helped extend Bolshevik power in the Transcaucasus region. In 1921 he served as general secretary of the Bolshevik organization in Azerbaijan. Three years later, pleased with his performance, Stalin named him to head the Bolshevik organization in Leningrad. He became a member of the Politburo in 1930.

Kirov was gaining popularity as a Communist leader, but this made him a potential political threat to Stalin. On December 1, 1934, Kirov was assassinated as he entered party offices at the Smolny Institute, the former girls' school that Lenin had used as his headquarters after the February Revolution. The gunman was a young party member, Leonid Nicolayev. Stalin claimed the assassination was the work of a vast anti-Stalinist conspiracy, but there was widespread suspicion that Stalin ordered the assassination. Adding to suspicions was the fact that there weren't any guards on duty the night that Kirov was shot.[43] Stalin had thirteen suspects shot, and this proved to be the beginning of a vast purge of old Bolsheviks who he realized would never accept him as their ruler.

Genrikh Yagoda, head of the GPU, began arresting priests, former landowners, and other familiar targets of the regime. According to Montefiore, Yagoda was "devious, short and balding, always in full uniform, with a taste for French wines and sex toys . . . he boasted that his huge dacha [country house] bloomed with '2,000 orchids and roses,' while spending almost four billion rubles decorating his residences."[44]

Stalin told Yagoda that Nicolayev was a follower of Grigori Zinoviev, who had been critical of Stalin, and so they ought to be arresting "Zinovievites." Yagoda did as he was told, but evidently not with enough zeal to satisfy Stalin. Yagoda was reluctant to go after an old Bolshevik like Zinoviev, so Stalin ordered Nikolai Yezhov, chairman of the Party Control Commission, to work with Yagoda. The sadistic Yezhov, about five feet tall, was known as "the Dwarf." He had a soft voice.[45] The KGB (secret police) files indicated that Yezhov, born in 1895, never completed primary school, and he was classified as a "worker." In 1919 he was sentenced to a year in prison. He subsequently showed himself to be obedient, hardworking, and utterly loyal to Stalin, who recruited him to assist the Central Committee. The official log of visitors to Stalin's offices showed that after Yezhov was appointed to help run the GPU, he was always the last visitor to leave, invariably late at night—so he had become a major behind-the-scenes player in unfolding events.

Yezhov enjoyed a wild life. An enthusiastic bisexual, he reportedly liked to get drunk in the company of prostitutes. According to Marc Jansen and Nikita Petrov, Yezhov's idea of fun was to join a friend, and "the two organized a competition to see who, with their pants off and squatted, was faster and better at blowing away a handful of cigarette ash from a penny by farting."[46]

Montefiore reported that "unstable, sexually confused and highly strung, he was too weak to compete with bulldozers like Kaganovich, not to mention Stalin himself. Yezhov suffered constant nervous illnesses, including sores and itchy skin, TB, angina, sciatica, psoriasis. . . . He often sank into gloomy depression, drank too much and had to be nurtured by Stalin, just to keep him at work."[47]

As far as the public was concerned, Yezhov was the hero of the Great Terror. In 1937 he was awarded the Order of Lenin "for his outstanding success in leading the NKVD organs to their fulfillment of government assignments."[48] There were posters of him displayed everywhere, squeezing a poisonous snake labeled "Enemies of the People."[49] Jansen and Petrov noted that "Yezhov's name was bestowed on everything from a steamship, a factory in the Ukraine, the stadium in Kiev, to a district in Sverdlovsk, the NKVD officers' school, the Krasnodar Higher Agricultural School, and hundreds of other educational institutions, kolkhozes, Pioneers' troops, and so on." Poems were even published in Yezhov's honor.

A week after Kirov's murder, Zinovievites were arrested. Zinoviev and Kamenev themselves were arrested. Zinoviev sent Stalin a letter pleading for his life: "I swear by all a Bolshevik holds sacred, I swear by Lenin's memory . . . I implore you to believe my word of honor. I am shaken to the depths of my being."[50]

Yagoda, however, wasn't able to link Zinoviev and Kamenev with Kirov's murder, because—in Stalin's view—he was too gentle with such old Bolsheviks. Suddenly, on January 14, 1935, Zinoviev signed a statement acknowledging that he had been "criminally negligent." That day, too, Kamenev signed a statement acknowledging his guilt. On January 16, Kamenev was sentenced to five years in prison. Zinoviev got ten years.

Stalin, however, was determined to eliminate his opponents. Since there had been so much debate about executions, he needed a compelling rationale. In 1936, NKVD officials were told that Trotsky, Zinoviev, Kamenev, and their associates were engaged in a vast conspiracy involving terrorists across the country, following Trotsky's instructions to assassinate Soviet leaders. Stalin himself would head the effort to stop this conspiracy, and he would be assisted by Yezhov.

Resistance to Stalin's maneuvers was undermined by extracting "confessions" that implicated his adversaries. A principal method was "the conveyor." Robert Conquest described it as "continual interrogation by relays of police for hours and days on end. As with many phenomena of the Stalin period, it has the advantage that it could not easily be condemned by any simple principle. Clearly, it amounted to unfair pressure after a certain time and to actual physical torture later still, but when? No absolutely precise answer could be given.

"But at any rate, after even twelve hours, it is extremely uncomfortable. After a day, it becomes very hard. And after two or three days, the victim is physically poisoned by fatigue . . . though some prisoners had been known to resist torture, it was almost unheard of for the conveyor not to succeed if kept up long enough. One week is reported as enough to break almost anybody. A description by a Soviet woman writer who experienced it speaks of seven days without sleep or food, the seventh standing up—ending in physical collapse."[51]

Political prisoners from across the country were brought to Moscow to be interrogated.[52] After torture, they agreed to participate in "show trials," confessing to the most preposterous allegations and implicating their friends. Zinoviev agreed to make any statement demanded of him, and when Kamenev was informed about this, he knew he had to do the same.

The show trials took place in the October Room of Moscow's House of Unions. As Edvard Radzinsky explained, "The stage designers had turned the October Room into a revolutionary court, decorated in different shades of red. The judge's desk was covered with bright red cloth. There were monumental chairs embossed with the arms of the Soviet Union. The defendants were near the right-hand wall, behind a wooden barrier. In back of them stood Red Army soldiers with rifles and fixed bayonets. Also behind the defendants was a door, behind which was, shall we say, the 'Wings of His Theater,' with a buffet, restrooms for the defendants, and an area for Yagoda and the prosecutor, Vyshinsky, to hold friendly discussions with the accused in the course of the trial, to criticize their performances and give them instructions. There were additional actors in the body of the hall, NKVD agents in mufti acting the part of 'the people.' If the accused departed from the script as rehearsed, 'the people's' job was to drown their voices with cries of indignation."[53]

In court, Zinoviev testified: "My perverted Bolshevism became anti-Bolshevism, and by way of Trotskyism I arrived at fascism. Trotskyism is a variant of fascism." Kamenev confessed: "I stand before a proletarian court for the third time. My life has been spared twice, but there is a limit to the magnanimity of the proletariat." He asked to be shot.[54] He was dispatched on August 21, 1936.

The fateful shot was fired by a man named Blokhin. Historian Montefiore described him as a "pugnacious Chekist of forty-one with a stalwart face and black hair pushed back, one of the most prolific executioners of the century, killing thousands personally, sometimes wearing his own leather butcher's apron to protect his uniform."[55]

Montefiore reported that "Yezhov himself devised the system of execution. Instead of using the cellars of the Lubyanka or the other prisons, as his predecessors had done, he created a special abattoir. Slightly behind and to the left of the Lubyanka, he used another NKVD building on Varsonofyevsky Lane. The prisoners were driven in Black Crows (trucks used to carry condemned prisoners) across the road from the Lubyanka (there was no tunnel) and into the

courtyard where a low squarish building had been specially con-
structed with a concrete floor sloping towards the far wall built of
logs, to absorb the bullets, and hosing facilities to wash away the flu-
ids. After a shot to the back of the head, the victims were placed in
metal boxes and driven to one of the crematoria in Moscow."[56]

Montefiore added that "the bullets, with their noses crushed,
were dug out of the skulls, wiped clean of blood and pearly brain
matter, and handed to Yagoda, probably still warm. Yagoda labeled
the bullets 'Zinoviev' and 'Kamenov' and treasured these macabre
but sacred relics, taking them home to be kept proudly with his collection of erotica and ladies' stockings."[57]

Stalin enjoyed laughing about the executions. At a dinner honoring heads of the NKVD, Stalin's chief bodyguard, K. V. Pauker, participated in a skit showing Zinoviev being dragged away to be shot.
"Stalin roared with laughter," noted Conquest, "and Pauker gave a re-
peat performance. By this time, Stalin was almost helpless with laughing, and when Pauker brought in a new angle by raising his hands and
crying, 'Hear, Israel, our God is the only God!' Stalin choked with
mirth and had to signal Pauker to stop the performance."[58]

Yuri Pyatakov and Karl Radek, who had been admirers of Trotsky, appeared in show trials implicating a succession of Bolsheviks in
a treasonous scheme purportedly hatched by Trotsky. All, including
Pyatakov, were shot, while Radek seems to have been rewarded for
his stellar performance by being sent to a prison camp—where he
was killed.

Yagoda and Yezhov attended the shootings. Yagoda retrieved the
bullets used to kill old Bolsheviks. Stalin, however, felt that Yagoda
was reluctant to kill these people, so he was shot. Yezhov inherited
the bullet collection.[59]

To ensure the loyalty of NKVD people, Stalin quadrupled their
salaries. They were awarded the most desirable apartments, hospitals, and other benefits.[60] The NKVD expanded to the size of an
army, and there were NKVD units at schools and factories. There
was a nationwide network of informers feeding the NKVD information about suspicious individuals. A special section of the NKVD
spied on members of the Communist Party Central Committee, an-

other special section spied on NKVD agents, and yet another special section spied on those in the special sections.

Stalin spent much of his time deciding who would be executed. Radzinsky wrote, "the Boss was working tirelessly, looking through endless 'lists,' with recommended sentences alongside the names of people who had once run the country, or won fame in the world of the arts. I saw these lists when I worked in the President's Archive. Such lists were regularly submitted to the Central Committee for confirmation by Yezhov. . . . [Stalin] never got tired, reading those thousands of names, and even sometimes adding comments of his own. He had a truly diabolical memory. 'Comrade Yezhov. Pay attention to pages 9-11. About Vardanyan. He is at present secretary of the Taganrog district Party committee. He is undoubtedly a crypto-Trotskyist.' Attention was duly paid, and Vardanyan vanished. He remembered his enemies. Every one of them."[61]

According to Radzinsky, "There were mass arrests every night in the luxurious homes of the NKVD. A ring at the door—the occupant is awakened and a man who only yesterday was master of other people's destinies is led out of his apartment. Knowing what their institution was capable of, many did not open up: the nocturnal ring at the door was answered by a shot within. Gorky's friend Pogrebinsky, head of the NKVD in the city of Gorky, and founder of labor communes for criminals, shot himself, and was followed soon afterward by Kozelsky, a well-known Ukrainian Chekist. Such a listing could be prolonged endlessly. There were innovators in the art of escape. The Moscow Chekist F. Gurov threw himself out of his office window, and jumping was soon all the rage: Chertok, Kamenev's inquisitor, jumped from a twelfth-story balcony as soon as they came for him."[62]

Many Europeans were a bit skeptical about the legitimacy of the show trials, but Stalin was lavishly praised by such European socialists as H. G. Wells, George Bernard Shaw, Emil Ludwig, Henri Barbusse, and Romain Rolland, who had visited the Soviet Union, enjoyed banquets, and apparently noticed nothing amiss.[63]

For a while, in 1936, there was a lull in the show trials, but arrests continued. Every night NKVD agents went out in black cars to arrest party members, especially old Bolsheviks. This came to be known as Soviet "night life." As Radzinsky explained, "The victims were picked up quietly, quickly supplied the testimony required, and were quickly put up against the wall"—usually in Lubyanka prison, where they were shot.

The most privileged party members were the ones who had the most to fear. In the government House on the Embankment, whole families were taken away from their large apartments and executed. Often their apartments went to other party members who suffered similar fates. "The elevator was busy every night," reported Radzinsky.[64]

The pace of arrests was stepped up, and all kinds of people were picked up—including astronomers and children. Many were detained in prison camps, taken there in cattle trucks.

TORTURE, STALIN'S OFFICIAL POLICY

From the very beginning, Lenin and other Bolsheviks had tortured their opponents. Certainly the Cheka had tortured many people. But the Bolshevik regime officially sanctioned "beatings" rather than torture, a distinction that wasn't clear to the victims.

As Robert Conquest explained, Bolshevik victims "were hit in the stomach with a sandbag; this was sometimes fatal. A doctor would certify that a prisoner who had died of it had suffered from a malign tumor. Another interrogation method was the *stoika*. It consisted of standing a prisoner against a wall on tiptoe and making him hold that position for several hours. A day or two of this was said to be enough to break almost anyone.

"Other 'improvised' torture methods," Conquest continued, "included the 'swallow,' which involved tying the hands and feet behind the back and hoisting the victim into the air. One prisoner describes having her fingers slammed in a door. Beating up was usual. Interrogators sometimes had to hand over prisoners to special, heavily built thugs known to the prisoners as 'boxers,' who would carry this out. . . . Needles, pincers, and so on are sporadically reported, and more specialized implements seem to have been in use at the Lefortovo." The distinction between torture and a beating, Conquest noted, was meaningless when a prisoner "came back after such a beating with broken ribs, urinating blood for a week, or with a permanently injured spine and unable to walk."[65]

To get quicker confessions and accelerate the destruction of his rivals, Stalin officially authorized torture in 1937. Radzinsky reviewed Soviet archives and reportedly found this telegram signed by Stalin: "The Central Committee of the CPSU . . . wishes to make it clear that the application of physical pressure by the NKVD has been authorized by the Central Committee. . . . It is well known that all bourgeois agencies use physical pressure on representatives of the proletariat. The question is why should socialist countries have to be more humane with sworn enemies of the working class?"[66]

Radzinsky cited one witness who reported, "The first interrogation often began with a savage beating, to humiliate the prisoner and break his resistance right from the start. Ordzhonikidze's wife was whipped to death. . . . In the NKVD torture chambers in Leningrad, prisoners were made to sit on the cement floor and covered with a box with nails sticking inward from all four sides. Army commander P. Dybenko, a giant of a man, was covered with a box of this kind one cubic meter in size." Radzinsky added, "Depositions of whatever sort were not signed quickly. Women sometimes put up more resistance than men. The wife of Nestor Lakoba, the deceased dictator of Abkhazia, was taken along for questioning every evening, and dragged back to her cell next morning unconscious and covered with blood. But she answered every demand that she could put her name to 'evidence' against her late husband with the same short sentence: 'I will not defile my husband's memory.' She held out even when they thrashed her son, a sixteen-year-old schoolboy, before her eyes and told her that they would kill him if she did not sign the protocol. She still had not signed when she died in her cell."[67]

According to Conquest, "various forms of humiliation were often especially effective on men weakened by torture. An army officer who withstood beating finally broke when the interrogator pushed his head into a spittoon brimful of spittle. Another gave way when an interrogator urinated on his head—an interrogation practice which according to reports became traditional."[68]

Stalin demanded that his adversaries be dispatched faster. Trials were cut to about ten minutes apiece.[69] Death sentences were announced by three-judge panels. Those on the panels were, in turn, executed, as were their successors.

NKVD agents were posted overseas to spy on former czarist generals and officials, as well as leaders of local Communist parties, Soviet diplomats, and the few Soviet officials who traveled abroad. In 1937 Stalin launched a campaign to exterminate Soviet diplomats and intelligence agents.

The last of the show trials involved Nikolai Bukharin. He was arrested in January 1937, displayed on trial in March 1938. He was reminded of his complaints about Stalin, expressed when he had traveled to France in 1936. Bukharin was shot on March 14, 1938.

PURGING THE RED ARMY

Stalin was well aware that although he controlled the government, he was vulnerable to a military coup. He resolved to purge suspicious elements from the army. On July 5, 1936, the NKVD seized Dimitri Schmidt, who commanded a tank unit near Kiev. Schmidt had joined the Bolsheviks in 1915 and served with distinction during the civil war. Conquest called him "a typical though not outstandingly gifted 'natural leader' of partisans—swashbuckling, simple, frightened of nothing."[70] Schmidt was accused of plotting to kill Klementi Voroshilov, who had joined the Bolshevik party in 1903 and performed well as a commander during the civil war. Nobody in the military, however, seemed to believe the charges against Schmidt. There were more arrests against military commanders, and then the pressure eased off. When NKVD head Genrikh Yagoda was arrested on April 3, 1937, this was viewed as a plus for the army.

During his trial, Bukharin had suggested that some top military men were disloyal to the regime. He mentioned Marshal Mikhail Nikolayevich Tukhachevsky, one of the most distinguished men in the Red Army. Tukhachevsky, from an aristocratic family, served in the czar's army during World War I. Following the October Revolution, he joined the Bolsheviks and helped defend Moscow in 1918. He led Bolshevik forces that gained control of Siberia and suppressed the Kronstadt Rising in 1921. A decade later he reformed the Soviet military. Stalin named him a marshal in 1935. Stalin didn't have any evidence that Tukhachevsky was disloyal, but he was well aware that a few military officers could pull off a coup, and Tukhachevsky certainly was capable of being a key player.

On June 11, 1937, eight top army commanders, including Tukhachevsky, were charged with treason and executed. This came as a shock, because there hadn't been a campaign to discredit these individuals, as had been the case before Stalin's political adversaries appeared in the show trials. There wasn't any warning. Stalin didn't provide details of the charges or present evidence against the military commanders. He seems to have calculated that because of the quick executions, most people would assume the military commanders must have been involved in some plot. After all, it wasn't hard to imagine that military commanders, like lots of other Soviet subjects, wanted to get rid of Stalin. In an effort to make the charges more credible, rumors were spread that the allegedly treasonous officers were either German spies or had links to the Germans.[71] Tukhachevsky and undoubtedly the other generals didn't deserve much sympathy, though. As historian Montefiore wrote, Tukhachevsky "was as ruthless as any Bolshevik, using poison gas on peasant rebels."[72]

Stalin soon made it clear he was going after the entire officer corps. Conquest reported, "Brigade Commander Medvedev was tried and shot. . . . Within nine days after the trial, 980 officers had been arrested, including twenty-one Corps Commanders and thirty-seven Divisional Commanders. On 19 June, Yakir's subordinate, Divisional Commander Sablin, was shot. On 1 July, Corps Commanders Garkavi, Gekker, Turovsky, and Vasilenko and Divisional Commander Savitsky perished. Twenty younger generals from the Moscow headquarters alone were also executed. Almost the whole command of the Kremlin Military School was arrested. The Frunze Military Academy, which Kork had headed, was swept by arrests. The Head of its Political Department, Neronov, was arrested as a spy. Not a day passed without the arrest of a member of the staff. Almost all the instructors went to the jails. . . . In the provinces, it was the same: in the Kiev Military District, 600 to 700 officers of the 'Yakir nest' are said to have been arrested at this time. . . . The future Marshall Biriuzov tells in his memoirs of being appointed to be Chief of Staff of the Thirtieth Rifle Division, stationed in Dnepropetrovsk. When he arrived, he found that the entire command had been arrested. . . . A recent Soviet account tells us that in the Chita prison, a number of Air Force pilots were interrogated. One had his collarbone broken. They all had their teeth knocked out. . . . The generals who had just been promoted to fill the vacant places now started to disappear. . . . Almost all the military-intelligence agents were recalled from abroad and shot. . . . In the Navy, the Purge was as sweeping as in the land forces. Of the nine Fleet Admirals and Admirals First Grade, only one (Galler) survived the Purge, to die in prison after the war. . . . With the leaders, their subordinates fell in scores."[73]

Stalin's purge of the military, Conquest reported, wiped out "three of the five Marshals, fifteen of the fifteen Army Commanders, eight of the nine Fleet Admirals and Admirals Grade I, fifty of fifty-seven Corps Commanders, 154 of the 186 Divisional Commanders, sixteen of the sixteen Army Commissars, twenty-five of the twenty-eight Corps Commissars and fifty-eight of the sixty-four Divisional Commissars." Altogether, some 47,000 officers were shot or forced out. Many of these were people who had fought in the civil war and remembered Stalin's limited role. One-quarter of the members of the Soviet Military Council were arrested. Those who didn't commit suicide were shot by the NKVD.

The consequence, of course, was that the Soviet military was critically weakened. Radzinsky, however, suggested that Stalin figured his purge was a fast way of invigorating the military with younger commanders who had better training and experience using newer weapons.[74]

THE KOLYMA DEATH CAMPS

Stalin went after the families, friends, and associates of those on his death lists. They filled the growing system of prison camps—the gulag—many of which were in Russia's frozen north. The most notorious were the more than 140 camps in the Kolyma region, northeastern Siberia near the Arctic, where an estimated 3 million prisoners perished.[75] This compares with some 12 million who perished throughout the gulag. The official purpose of the Kolyma camps was to mine metals, particularly gold, but their real purpose was simply to kill people. Kolyma was the equivalent of Hitler's most notorious death camp at Auschwitz.

The month-long journey to Kolyma was deadly. Trains brought prisoners across Siberia to Vladivostok, and as Conquest wrote, the train was "always one of the worst of the various experiences of the victims, with its fetid wagons, its inadequate water supply, its lack of food and light, its brutal guards."[76] Prisoners were unloaded into transit camps holding an estimated 100,000 at a time. Then they were packed into the holds of ships like the *Nikolai Yezhov* (named, of course, after Stalin's chief executioner). Conquest reported the fate of young girls among the prisoners: "Criminals, who formed the greater part of the human freight aboard this ship, had an absolutely free hand in the hold. They broke through the wall into the room where the female prisoners were kept and raped all the women who took their fancy. A few male prisoners who tried to protect the women were stabbed to death. Several old men had their bread snatched from them day after day, and died of starvation. One of the criminals, who appropriated a woman whom the leader of the band had marked for his own, had his eyes put out with a needle."[77]

Since the camps were cut off from the outside world by the stormy Sea of Okhotsk, prisoners were thoroughly demoralized. The principal method of killing was brutal labor, starvation, and exposure to temperatures reaching almost sixty degrees Fahrenheit below zero. Conquest reported that "in some camps, when communications were restored, it was found that no one was left, not even the dogs. According to one story a convoy lost its way and died, several thousand prisoners with their guards, to a man."[78] During the summers, prisoners were overwhelmed by insects. Conquest: "One specially large type of gadfly can sting through deer hide, and drives horses crazy."

Among the few lucky survivors was general Aleksandr. V. Gorbatov, who wrote a memoir of his experiences, *Years Off My Life*. He had been sent to Kolyma in 1938. Guards encouraged violence among the prisoners, and his boots were stolen—an open invitation to frostbite. Gorbatov slept in a tent covered with snow. Meager rations contributed to deficiency diseases. "My legs began to swell and my teeth grew loose in my gums," he wrote. "My legs went on swelling until they looked like logs, and my knees would no longer bend."[79] Apparently he was saved by the war with Germany, when Stalin realized he needed military commanders.

Franklin D. Roosevelt's vice president, Henry Wallace, spent three days in Kolyma on his way to China. He was accompanied by fellow Soviet sympathizer Owen Lattimore, from the Office of War Information. Wallace subsequently wrote *Soviet Asia Mission*, a book that gushed about how the prisoners were "pioneers of the machine age, builders of cities."[80] He passed along the fiction that "Kolyma miners had gone east to earn more money." He reported on communities "founded by volunteers."[81]

DEATH TOLL

By 1938, though, Stalin seems to have concluded that he had wiped out all potential sources of opposition, and the terror eased off. Yezhov's days were numbered. Soviet newspapers stopped mentioning him. Things named after him were renamed. People sensed that he was trouble, and he ceased to have office visitors. On December 5, 1938, he was ordered to transfer authority over the NKVD to Lavrenty Pavlovich Beria. "The Dwarf" was accused of spying for England, Germany, Japan, and Poland, and he was sentenced to death on February 2, 1940. He appealed, and Stalin declined to review the decision. He was probably shot that same day in the NKVD's execution room on Varsafevsky Lane, which he himself had designed.[82]

Stalin, disassociating himself from the Great Terror, blamed everything on Yezhov. A new biography was issued, reporting that he was a homosexual, an alcoholic, and a spy. Yezhov's writings were banned in the Soviet Union, and his name was no longer mentioned in official circles.[83]

As for Yezhov's successor, biographer Montefiore observed that Beria "was balding, short and agile with a broad fleshy face, swollen sensuous lips and flickering 'snake eyes' behind a glistening pince-nez. This gifted, intelligent, ruthless and tirelessly competent adventurer, whom Stalin would one day describe as 'our Himmler,' brandished the exotic flattery, sexual appetites and elaborate cruelty of a Byzantine courtier in his rise to dominate first the Caucasus, then Stalin's circle, and finally the USSR itself."[84]

Although historians have viewed Beria's appointment as marking the end of the Great Purge, his name came to be associated with torture and terror.[85] Born in 1899, Beria joined the Bolsheviks in 1917. He worked as a revolutionary in Azerbaijan and Georgia until becoming involved with intelligence-gathering operations in 1921. He was party boss in the Transcaucasian republics, where he helped carry out Stalin's purges during the 1930s. He proved himself to be sufficiently ruthless that Stalin made him Yezhov's deputy in 1938. As head of the NKVD, Beria purged the NKVD itself and expanded the gulag into a huge prison camp system. He used prisoners as slave laborers for many projects.

It was Beria who helped plan Trotsky's murder at his Mexican hideaway.[86] Trotsky had his admirers, who sometimes portrayed him as a foe of tyranny, but he had established his credentials as a mass murderer during the civil war—back then, nobody, including Stalin, ordered more executions than Trotsky. He never expressed sympathy for the millions who perished during Stalin's forced collectivization of peasant farms.[87] He didn't seem to care about any other non-Communist victims, either.[88] During the civil war, Trotsky urged that prisoners be sent to concentration camps.[89] Trotsky enjoyed a longer life than he deserved, because purges of the NKVD disrupted the work of those plotting against him.[90]

Beria assigned the task to NKVD agent Leonid Eitingon, whose first scheme failed. The second scheme involved Ramón Mercader, son of a Spanish Communist woman who had been Eitingon's lover. Mercader became romantically involved with the American Trotskyite Sylvia Ageloff and, with her, visited Trotsky at his heavily guarded compound in Coyoacán, near Mexico City. On August 20, 1940, Mercader visited Trotsky, and when Trotsky was reading, Mercader pulled a cut-down ice ax out of his raincoat and plunged it into Trotsky's skull. Trotsky died the next day.

Altogether, Stalin ordered the murder of 70 percent of the members of the Central Committee, some 20,000 NKVD officers, a substantial number of prosecutors, and almost all the old Bolsheviks and their families and associates.[91] Marxist historians have portrayed the

Great Purge as *the* tragedy, assuming the lives of Communist Party members were worth more than the millions of "kulaks" whom Stalin had murdered. One might have more sympathy for purged Communist officials if they hadn't done so much to promote the political monopoly of the Communist Party, the brutal dictatorship, and mass murder of people with different points of view. Stalin did everything Lenin did, only on a bigger scale, and Stalin murdered Communist officials as well as ordinary people. It's hard to avoid the conclusion that what goes around comes around, and purged Communist officials got pretty much what they deserved.

Stalin's purge system demanded escalating numbers of arrests and murders. Increasingly, the NKVD targeted the general population. Anybody who traveled abroad, anybody who had contact with foreigners, members of various nationalities (such as Greeks and Chinese), priests, Jehovah's Witnesses, Jews, Ukrainians, railroad officials, engineers—these and many more people were targets. Stalin's goons tortured children as young as nine years old, extracting confessions of espionage and treason."[92] "By 1937," Conquest remarked, "practically the entire population was potential Purge fodder."[93]

In some cases peasants were brought to a prison, and nobody seemed to know why they were arrested. Nonetheless, prison officials had to have something to show for the arrests, so the peasants were interrogated until they admitted participating in plots to steal horses, poison water, burn barns, or start revolts—even though none of these things had happened.

There are mass burial sites all around the former Soviet Union. Conquest reported, "The one in Vinnitsa . . . where over 9,000 corpses were exhumed . . . one between Khabarovsk and Vladivostok, where some 50,000 seem to have been executed in 1937 and 1938; one at Gorno-Altaisk; one at Bykovnya, near Kiev; one, with over 46,000 bodies, near Leningrad; one near Tomsk; one close to the well-known Polish grave site at Katyn; near Chelyabinsk; near Poltava; in Donetsk; near Voronezh; and, above all, the mass grave at Kuropaty, near Minsk . . . where no fewer than 50,000 victims lie buried. . . . The great majority of the dead were peasants and workers."[94]

Perhaps the best-kept secret—long unknown in the West—was the Soviet system of concentration camps, known as the gulag, for political prisoners who weren't immediately shot. Lenin started the concentration camps in 1918, often with the aim of working prisoners to death. By the 1930s, there were an estimated 2 million to 5 million people in the camps.[95] During the late 1930s, NKVD head Yezhov substantially increased the number of prisoners in the camps. Prisoners were given so little food—as few as 300 calories per day—that deaths from scurvy, pneumonia, and tuberculosis were common. New prisoners were commonly robbed of valuable possessions, such as good shoes and warm coats, soon after arriving in a concentration camp.[96] Since many of the concentration camps were in northern Russia, where the winters were brutal, such robberies increased the likelihood of death.

Criminals ran the Soviet concentration camps. Guards as well as prisoners raped women in the camps. A woman who reportedly refused a guard's advances was turned over to criminals who gang-raped her and pulled out her gold teeth. A teenage girl was scalped. When a criminal gambled and lost his gang's bread ration, his body was cut into pieces.[97] Children seven and eight years old were starved, beaten, and otherwise humiliated.[98] It has been estimated that of all those sent to Soviet concentration camps before World War II, 90 percent died.[99]

Incredibly, none of this was inevitable. Stalin wouldn't have been in power if Lenin hadn't seized power, and Lenin probably wouldn't have been able to do that if Woodrow Wilson hadn't brought the United States into World War I and pressured and bribed Russia's Provisional Government to stay in the war until it and the Russian army disintegrated.

11

WHY IS WORLD WAR II PART OF WILSON'S LEGACY?

B Y 1939, WOODROW WILSON had been dead for fifteen years, but the consequences of his decision to enter World War I were still playing out in Germany and Russia. Both Hitler and Stalin had taken advantage of Wilson's blunder to establish brutal totalitarian regimes. Hitler and Stalin were bitter enemies, but when circumstances brought them together, the result added a world war to Wilson's legacy.

HITLER PREPARES FOR WAR

Hitler, like Wilson, wanted to redraw the map of Europe. His professed aim was to have a powerful German state embrace Germans in Austria, Poland, and Czechoslovakia. All this was consistent with the principle of nationality, or self-determination, that Woodrow Wilson and so many others had promoted. The problem, of course, was that different peoples were so extensively intermingled, it was impossible to draw borders that would include everybody from one nationality and exclude people from other nationalities who might be left to form their own states. A district where Germans were the majority had other peoples as minorities. Consequently, having states fulfill the aspirations of particular nationalities was practically guaranteed to subvert the rights of minority individuals.

Hitler claimed he was seeking *Lebensraum*—"living room"— for future generations of Germans, as if Germany were running out of territory. Germany had plenty of territory, more territory than a lot of other prosperous countries. As the German population increased, people bid up the prices of underdeveloped land, and over time more sites were developed for apartment blocks, office buildings, and other intensive uses. More of the countryside was gradually suburbanized and urbanized. Although some people missed "the good old days" when everything was rural, living standards improved. Then as now, living standards tend to be higher in urban areas than in rural areas.

Hitler looked east for more territory, to Poland and Russia. In essence, he wanted to restore the Treaty of Brest-Litovsk. Hitler coveted territory that General Ludendorff had taken from Russia when he dictated the terms of that treaty, including chunks of Poland and the Ukraine. So his ambitions differed from those of his predecessor, Kaiser Wilhelm II. Hitler didn't demand Alsace-Lorraine from France, and he rejected the idea of a quest for overseas colonies, which had brought Germany into fateful conflict with Britain. He recognized it would have taken Germany a long time to build up enough of a navy to challenge Britain and defend such colonies. He didn't talk about challenging the British navy or toppling the British Empire.[1]

At the time, the German army was still limited to 100,000 men by the terms of the Versailles Treaty. Hitler declared, "My program was to abolish the Treaty of Versailles. It is nonsense for the rest of the world to pretend that I did not reveal this program until 1933, or 1935, or 1937. Instead of listening to this foolish chatter of émigrés, these gentlemen would have been wiser to read what I have written and rewritten thousands of times. No human being has declared or recorded what he wanted more often than I. Again and again I wrote these words—the Abolition of the Treaty of Versailles."[2]

Hitler boldly prepared to rearm, recognizing that if Britain or France wanted to stop him, they could. He had the advantage of knowing what he wanted, while the British and French knew only what they didn't want—more war. Hitler conceived a public relations campaign playing on the guilt of all those who acknowledged that the French, British, and, for that matter, the Americans, had forfeited the moral high ground by insisting on vindictive terms at Versailles.

On May 7, 1933, Hitler went to the Reichstag and delivered

what came to be known as his "Peace Speech," in which he pointed
out that there had been a lot of talk about disarmament, but Germany was the only country to have disarmed. He boldly challenged
the hypocrisy of the British and French by offering to disband Germany's entire military establishment if the British and French disbanded theirs. The French refused to disarm.

On October 14, Hitler announced that because Germany was denied equal rights, it must pull out of the League of Nations. He staged
a plebiscite in which a reported 96 percent of eligible voters cast bal-
lots, and 95 percent supported pulling out of the League of Nations.
How could the Western nations object to a supposedly democratic decision of the people? Neither Britain nor France took action against
Germany following its withdrawal from the League of Nations.[3]

Hitler announced that he would, reluctantly, build up a peacetime army of 550,000 men. The German people had been deceived by
Woodrow Wilson and his Fourteen Points, he said; while Germany
had disarmed, other countries were increasing their armaments.
Britain protested but didn't do anything to stop the German leader.

On February 27, 1936, the French Chamber of Deputies ratified
a mutual defense treaty with the Soviet Union, renewing the alliance
France had had with Russia going into World War I. Hitler expressed
outrage and used the treaty as an excuse to order German troops
into the Rhineland, which had been demilitarized as specified in the
Versailles Treaty. He further ordered that German fortifications be
built in the Rhineland.

Having done so much to provoke bitterness in Germany during
the treaty negotiations at Versailles, the French didn't maintain armed
forces capable of dealing with the consequences of such bitterness.
On their own they could not intervene to prevent German rearmament, and the British weren't interested in an intervention that would
amount to another war. Nor were the United States, whose intervention in World War I had enabled the British and French to humiliate
the Germans; the American people had become disillusioned with
Woodrow Wilson's idea of entering European wars.[4]

Hitler gained further advantages during the Spanish Civil War,
which began in July 1936. By providing supplies and military advis-

ers to General Francisco Franco, the dominant figure in the war, Hitler gained an ally on France's southern border.

In September 1936, Hitler pursued an alliance with Italy's Fascist dictator, Benito Mussolini. Italy wasn't much of a military power, but Hitler apparently figured it was better to have an ally than an enemy on Germany's border, and the alliance meant more pressure on France.

Germany and Japan agreed to exchange information about communism and to "adopt defensive measures," supposedly with the idea of fighting Bolshevism. The resulting Anti-Comintern Pact was signed November 25, 1936.

On January 30, 1937, Hitler gave a speech at the Reichstag, announcing that he was officially withdrawing Germany's signature from the most offensive clauses of the Versailles Treaty, especially the "war guilt" clause that blamed World War I entirely on Germany.

With the *Anschluss* of March 12, 1938, Hitler annexed Austria in the name of self-determination for German-speaking Austrians. The British ambassador protested the *Anschluss* but did nothing.

Hitler also exploited discontent in Czechoslovakia—discontent that resulted from Woodrow Wilson's delusion that political problems could be solved by redrawing political borders. Wilson had participated in cobbling together Czechoslovakia with Slovaks, Hungarians, and Ruthenes, as well as some 3.5 million Germans who resided in about 10,000 square miles of Bohemia, Moravia, and Sudeten Silesia (referred to as Sudetenland).[5] All this would have been fine if Czechoslovakia had a decentralized Swiss-style confederation or a federal system like the United States, with a policy of equal rights, free markets, and toleration. But after Versailles, Czechs gained the power to enforce their culture on everybody, supposedly in the name of self-determination. Czech soldiers shot Germans demonstrating for *their* right of self-determination. The Czech government shut down German schools. Germans were fired from jobs in the government and government-owned enterprises. Hitler had a convenient excuse to seize Czech territory. On September 30, 1938, British prime minister Neville Chamberlain uttered his famously wrong prediction that there would be "peace for our time."

STALIN JOINS HITLER

Concerned about Hitler's aggressive policies, on April 15, 1939, Britain proposed to Soviet foreign minister Maxim Litvinov that the two countries help each other in the event of an attack.

Subsequent diplomatic exchanges showed that the British either didn't give the negotiation a high priority or were trying to drag out the process. As A. J. P. Taylor explained, "The Soviet counter-proposal came two days later, on 17 April. The British took three weeks before designing an answer on 9 May; the Soviet delay was then five days. The British then took thirteen days; the Soviet government answered within twenty-four hours. Thereafter the pace quickened. The British tried again in five days' time; the Soviet answer came within twenty-four hours. The British next needed nine days; the Soviet two. Five more days for the British; one day for the Russians. Eight days on the British side; Soviet answer on the same day. With that the exchange virtually ended."[6]

Moreover, Britain dispatched an attaché—not its foreign secretary—to pursue discussions with the Soviets. As a low-ranking official, the attaché wasn't empowered to make any commitments. It didn't help that the attaché traveled by sea rather than by air, suggesting the British didn't feel there were any urgent matters to talk about.[7] The Munich Agreement had convinced Stalin that the British weren't going to take action against Hitler, and his experiences trying to negotiate a pact with the British confirmed this view.[8]

Hitler recognized an opportunity to pursue an agreement that would enable him to seize Polish territory without risking war with the Soviet Union. What about Hitler's ideological objections to a deal with the Soviets, since a strategy for his career had been to long denounce communism? Hitler had repeatedly shown himself to be a cynical opportunist, and at this time he just wasn't ready to fight the Soviet Union.

German and Soviet officials held discussions through June and July. Karl Schnurre, an official in the German Foreign Office, pointed out that the British could offer the Soviets involvement in a European war; Germany could offer the Soviets neutrality in a European war.[9]

In an effort to move things along, Hitler sent a telegram directly to Stalin on August 20. Stalin offered an encouraging reply and closed with a bit of understated humor: "The Soviet government has instructed me [as if anybody instructed Stalin] to inform you that it agrees to Mr. Ribbentrop visiting Moscow on 23 August."[10]

"Mr. Ribbentrop" was Joachim von Ribbentrop, the German foreign minister. An arrogant, rude, and spiteful man, Ribbentrop hardly fit the profile of the typical diplomat. Born in 1893, the son of a German army officer, he was educated in Switzerland and worked as a clerk in a Montreal bank, as a construction worker on a Canadian railroad, and as a reporter for a New York newspaper. He returned to Canada, where he started a wine importing business that he ran until the outbreak of World War I, when he decided he must serve in the German army. He was wounded and discharged, then worked as a cotton and liquor importer. During the 1920s he made money in the import-export business. Always the social climber, he paid his aunt to adopt him so that he could add the aristocratic *von* to his name. He held lavish parties at his opulent home in Dahlem, a Berlin suburb. Apparently his wife, Anneliese, steered him into the Nazi party—in 1932, after it had gained a substantial following among voters. Hitler attended one of Ribbentrop's parties and was impressed with his knowledge of Britain and France, which led to Ribbentrop's becoming a Nazi adviser on foreign affairs.[11]

When Ribbentrop arrived in Moscow, he found the airport emblazoned with swastikas, and he might have been aware that Stalin removed some prominent Jews from his government. Ribbentrop talked with People's Commissar of External Affairs Vyacheslav Mikhaylovich Molotov, one of Stalin's most trusted comrades. According to historian Simon Sebag Montefiore, Molotov was "small, stocky with a bulging forehead, chilling hazel eyes blinking behind round spectacles, and a stammer when angry (or talking to Stalin)."[12] Born in 1890 in Kukarka, southwest of Kirov, he joined the Russian Social Democratic Workers Party soon after Czar Nicholas II had put down the Revolution of 1905. He was arrested twice for revolutionary activities. In 1917 he was named to the Executive Committee of the Petrograd Soviet. He served as secretary of the Ukrainian Bolshevik party. In 1921 Molotov was a member of the Bolshevik Central Committee. He proved himself to be a hardworking and ruthless man. Early on, he began helping Stalin maneuver his way to supreme power in the Soviet Union. Miraculously, he survived all the purges. He was reportedly the only person to shake hands with Lenin, Stalin, Hitler, Himmler, Göring, Churchill, and Roosevelt.

Ribbentrop, Molotov, and Stalin met twice on August 23, and they agreed on a Nazi-Soviet nonaggression pact. Ribbentrop proposed including a tribute to German-Soviet friendship, but Stalin reportedly replied, "Don't you think we have to pay a little more attention to public opinion in our two countries? For many years now, we have been pouring buckets of shit over each other's heads and our propaganda boys could not do enough in that direction. Now, all of a sudden, are we to make our peoples believe all is forgotten and forgiven?"[13] The pact, without the tribute, was approved by Hitler and signed the next day. Stalin didn't want any photographs taken of the toasts between the Soviet and Nazi representatives.

There were two parts to the pact, one that was made public and the other that was kept secret. Publicly, Germany and the Soviet Union affirmed their determination to avoid war with each other. In the event one of them became involved in war, the other agreed not to help its enemies. The Soviets agreed to buy German machinery, and the Germans agreed to buy Soviet oil and coal. Secretly the Germans and Soviets agreed how they would carve up Eastern Europe. Germany would take western Poland—altogether, most Polish territory. The Soviets would seize eastern Poland. Germany would seize Lithuania. The Soviets would get Finland, Estonia, and Latvia. The secret agreement mentioned but didn't resolve the possibility of an independent Polish state in the future. The Soviet Union didn't acknowledge the secret agreement until 1989.[14]

WAR!

Just one week after the agreement was signed, on Thursday, August 31, at 12:30 P.M., Hitler signed "Directive No. 1 for the Conduct of the War." That night, Reinhard Heydrich led an SS squad to stage an "incident" at a German radio station in Gleiwitz, a town near the

Polish border. One of the men went on the air, proclaiming himself to be a Pole, and broadcast a few words against the Nazis. Some condemned criminals were dressed in Polish army uniforms and shot, as if they had been trying to seize the radio station. Newspapers were notified about these allegedly outrageous anti-Nazi acts.

That night, too, the German government broadcast its demands and emphasized Hitler's patience. The Poles were portrayed as being stubborn and provocative. While the broadcast was going on, German forces were advancing toward the Polish border. On September 1 they marched into Poland.

In the evening, British and French ambassadors warned Ribbentrop that they would come to the defense of Poland if Germany didn't withdraw. Mussolini proposed a conference to find a peaceful solution, but the British refused unless the Germans pulled out of Poland. The befuddled French couldn't figure out what to do. At 9:00 A.M., Sunday, September 3, British ambassador Neville Henderson announced that if the Germans didn't cease hostilities by 11:00 A.M.—in two hours—Britain would be at war against Germany.

The German *Blitzkrieg*—fast, overwhelming, surprise attack— routed the Poles, and Hitler saw no reason to quit. Within two weeks the Polish army was virtually wiped out. The Germans captured Warsaw on September 27. Hitler declared there would never be a Poland as spelled out in the Versailles Treaty.

Meanwhile, on September 17, as agreed on with Hitler, the Soviet army occupied some 111,000 square miles of Poland containing some 12 million Poles, Belorussians, and Ukrainians.[15] The Soviet campaign was led by Nikita Sergeyevich Khrushchev. Born in 1895, the son of a coal miner and the grandson of a serf, he began working in a factory when he was a teenager, and because of this he wasn't conscripted into the Russian army. During the Russian Civil War he joined the Bolshevik party. He worked as a party organizer in Yuzovka, Kharkov, and Kiev. He studied metallurgy in Moscow, handled a variety of party functions there, and became the mayor. He enthusiastically helped Stalin carry out the Great Purge of the 1930s, and was one of only three provincial party secretaries who were spared.

Khrushchev was ruthless in Poland. He arrested, deported, or executed officers, priests, intellectuals, landowners, entrepreneurs, police, and anyone else who might oppose Soviet power in Poland. According to Soviet records, some 381,000 Poles were deported to concentration camps before June 1941. Polish historians claim that as many as 1 million might have been deported.[16] Some 148,000 Polish prisoners of war died in Russian hands. A reported 25,700 Poles were shot, among whom were 4,000 Polish officers whose bodies were dumped in the Katyn forest. In his memoir, Khrushchev described this work as "normalizing the situation in the lands annexed from Poland."[17]

Stalin wanted to revise the terms of the Nazi-Soviet pact, and discussions took place at the Kremlin on September 27 and 28. He was afraid that an independent Polish state, mentioned in the secret pact, would be subject to German influence and might act against the Soviet Union, so he proposed simply splitting Poland. Stalin wanted Lithuania, and in return he agreed Hitler could take Lublin province and part of Warsaw province, in central Poland. The end result was that Poland was carved up fifty-fifty between Hitler and Stalin, and Stalin walked away with the Baltic states, Lithuania, Latvia, and Estonia, affording access to the Baltic Sea and locations for Soviet military bases. Hitler recognized that he faced war in the west, and he wanted to avoid conflict with Stalin to save the Germans from a war on two fronts.

Hitler decided that he must defeat Britain and France, since they had become obstacles to his further expansion in Eastern Europe. He instructed his generals, "The German war aim is a final military settlement with the West, that is, the destruction of the power and ability of the Western Powers ever again to oppose the State Consolidation and further development of the German people in Europe."[18]

Anticipating another British naval blockade, Hitler approved plans to occupy Norway and gain more access to sea routes. The German army invaded Denmark and Norway on April 9, 1940. On May 10, eighty-nine German divisions invaded the Low Countries and France. The French were devastated by the loss of thirty divisions in Belgium. The Germans cornered the British Expeditionary Force near Dunkirk, but some 338,000 British and French soldiers escaped by sea.[19] Nonetheless, Hitler had achieved more gains in a month than the Germans did in four years during World War I—and with a fraction of the losses.[20]

Following the defeat of the French forces, Hitler opted to occupy about three-fifths of the country. He ordered that on June 21, 1940, French representatives surrender in the same railroad car—hauled out of a Paris museum—in the Compiègne Forest, where, two decades before, French general Ferdinand Foch had German representatives sign their armistice on November 11, 1918.

Hitler was there to savor the occasion. He led his associates, including Luftwaffe head Hermann Göring, his personal secretary Rudolf Hess, commander-in-chief of the navy Erich Raeder, field marshal Walter von Brauchitsch, and foreign minister Joachim von Ribbentrop, to a memorial granite monument with a French inscription: "Here on 11 November 1918 succumbed the criminal pride of the German Reich . . . vanquished by the free peoples it tried to enslave."[21]

Journalist William L. Shirer observed Hitler at this gathering: "He steps off the monument and contrives to make even this gesture a masterpiece of contempt. . . . He glances slowly round the clearing. . . . Suddenly, as though his face were not giving quite complete expression to his feelings, he throws his whole body into harmony with his mood. He swiftly snaps his hands on his hips, arches his shoulders, plants his feet wide apart. It is a magnificent gesture of defiance, of burning contempt for this place and all that it has stood for in the twenty-two years since it witnessed the humbling of the German Empire."[22]

TRIUMPH AND TRAGEDY

Hitler, of course, wasn't able to savor revenge for long. He invaded Russia in June 1941 and soon became overstretched. Roosevelt and Churchill found themselves allied with Stalin. Although they defeated Hitler, Stalin grabbed Eastern Europe, and the Cold War began almost immediately.

Woodrow Wilson's tortured legacy would extend for another half-century.

HOW CAN WE AVOID A BLUNDER LIKE WILSON'S?

T HE WORST AMERICAN foreign policy disasters of the past century have been consequences of Wilsonian interventionism. Critics have been dismissed as "isolationists," but the fact is that Wilsonian interventionism has dragged the United States into pointless wars and ushered in revolution, terror, runaway inflation, dictatorship, and mass murder. It's past time to judge Wilsonian interventionism by its consequences, not the good intentions expressed in political speeches, because they haven't worked out.

Surely, one of the most important principles of American foreign policy should be to conserve resources for defending the country. President Woodrow Wilson violated this principle by entering World War I, which didn't involve an attack on the United States.

German submarines sank some foreign ships with American passengers, but they had been warned about the obvious danger of traveling in a war zone. People need to take responsibility for their own decisions and proceed at their own risk. It was unreasonable to expect that because a few adventurers lost their lives, the entire nation had to enter a war in which tens of thousands or hundreds of thousands more people must die.

There never was a serious possibility that Germany might attack the United States during World War I. The German navy was confined to German ports by the British navy, and British convoys dramatically reduced the number of merchant ships sunk by German submarines. The German army was stalemated on the Western

Front, and over a million German soldiers were engaged on the Eastern Front. German boys and older men were being drafted to fill the trenches. There wasn't any armed force available for an attack on the United States. Despite the suggestion, in German foreign minister Arthur Zimmermann's inflammatory telegram, about a possible alliance between Germany, Mexico, and Japan, America was safe.

Wilson claimed that American national security was linked with the fate of Britain, but because the British navy had bottled up the German navy and neutralized German submarines, Germany wasn't capable of invading Britain. In any case, Britain was struggling to maintain its global empire. The settlement following World War I had the effect of adding more territories to the British Empire. Why should American lives have been lost and American resources spent to expand the British Empire?

Why, for that matter, should the United States have defended the French or the Belgians? They were defending their overseas empires, and both had shown themselves to be brutal colonial rulers. The Belgians were responsible for slavery and mass murder in the Congo—the first modern genocide, involving an estimated 8 million deaths.

How could any U.S. president in his right mind have committed American soldiers to defend Britain and France, whose generals squandered lives on a stupendous scale? Britain's General Douglas Haig, for instance, whose blunders figured in the deaths of 95,675 British soldiers and 420,000 total British casualties at the Battle of the Somme (1916). Another 50,729 French soldiers were killed. Haig not only wasn't fired, but he continued to squander lives in battle after battle. It was amazing that a U.S. president would seriously consider conscripting Americans for European killing fields drenched in blood. There were the battles of the Marne (1914, 270,000 French and British soldiers killed), Artois (1915, 100,000 French soldiers killed), Ypres (Second Battle, 1915, 70,000 French soldiers killed), Gallipoli (1915, 50,000 British, Australian, and New Zealand soldiers killed), Verdun (1916, 315,000 French soldiers killed), Arras (1916, 160,000 British soldiers killed), and Passchendaele (1917, 310,000 British soldiers killed).

There would have been massacres even with better generals. As military historian John Keegan observed, "The simple truth of

1914–18 trench warfare is that the massing of large numbers of soldiers unprotected by anything but cloth uniforms, however they were trained, however equipped, against large masses of other soldiers, protected by earthworks and barbed wire and provided with rapid-fire weapons, was bound to result in very heavy casualties among the attackers. . . . The effect of artillery added to the slaughter, as did that of bayonets and grenades when fighting came to close quarters in the trench labyrinths."[1]

Woodrow Wilson didn't need a crystal ball to understand that World War I wasn't our war. He knew how the Europeans, with their entangling alliances, had stumbled into the conflagration. He knew how they stubbornly refused to quit. He knew how the Allied Powers had negotiated their secret treaties to carve up Europe and colonial possessions. He could see how hundreds of thousands of young men were being slaughtered in the mud.

It was claimed that the United States would have been threatened if a single power—Germany—had been able to control the entire European continent. But that was unlikely, since World War I had been stalemated for more than three years. The best the Germans might have hoped for would have been to annex Belgium and northwestern France, where much of World War I had been fought, as well as territories gained from Austria-Hungary and western Russia. If the Germans had won the war, they would have had a hard time holding their empire together because of all the rebellious nationalities—the same nationalities that figured in the collapse of the Austro-Hungarian and Russian empires. The most likely outcome of a German victory: costly civil wars ending in German collapse.

In any event, people have been fighting one another for thousands of years, and America managed to develop despite a succession of empires in Europe and elsewhere. America was in its infancy when Spain was the mightiest power on earth, enriched by precious metals from Mexico and Peru. During the late 1600s, the French king, Louis XIV, dominated Europe, persecuted Protestants, and fought one war after another, but America thrived as a sanctuary. A century later, America broke free from the British Empire. George Washington, as the first president of the United States, wisely counseled his countrymen to stay out of European wars, and this policy was continued by his successor Thomas Jefferson despite French and British interference with U.S. shipping. The United States prospered while the French emperor Napoleon Bonaparte organized the first modern police state, conquered Europe, and marched into Russia.

America's Founders had the humility and wisdom to recognize that the United States couldn't prevent other people from fighting. If the United States had tried forcing "peace" on foreigners, this would have required raising and equipping an army, and fighting adversaries who knew their land much better than we did. We would have had to fight with allies whose motives turned out to be less pure than we had supposed. We would have made enemies we didn't have before. In the end, we would have widened a conflict, and probably more people would have been killed than if we had stayed out.

The arrogant Wilson should have learned a lesson when he tried nation-building in Mexico, and the effort backfired. What could have been simpler than sending some American soldiers across the Mexican border to find a bandit and help install a good ruler down there? Yet Wilson's intervention failed to find the bandit, failed to install a good ruler, but instead only killed people and made enemies.

Preoccupied with his good intentions, Wilson never seemed to have considered the possibility that intervening in Europe might do worse than fail to achieve peace. Because of historic resentments and staggering battlefield casualties, there was a lot of bitterness in Europe. Governments were nearly bankrupt, and people were hungry. They wanted vengeance for their suffering. The political situation was explosive. If one side was able to achieve a decisive victory, the temptation would be strong to seek retribution. So Wilson intervened, enabling the Allied Powers to achieve a decisive victory, and the result was the vindictive Versailles Treaty with its devastating political consequences that played out in Germany and around the world.

Apparently thinking only about what he wanted, he pressured and bribed the Russian Provisional Government to stay in the war, when he ought to have known that country had been falling apart ever since it entered the war in 1914. Wilson ought to have known that millions of Russian peasants weren't going to be affected much one way or the other by what happened on the Western Front, the only thing that Wilson cared about. He ought to have known that

Russian peasants were deserting the Russian army by the thousands, to go home and claim land, and soon there wouldn't be any army to defend the Provisional Government. If Wilson didn't know those things, he didn't have any business trying to play an international war game. Wilson's blunders made it easier for Lenin to seize power on his fourth attempt in 1917, leading to more than seven decades of Soviet communism.

Wilson ought to have known he was playing with fire when, at the Versailles Conference following World War I, he participated in redrawing thousands of miles of national borders. He knew how nationalist hatreds had exploded in the Austro-Hungarian Empire and triggered the Balkan wars and World War I. Turkish nationalists expelled some 100,000 Greeks from the Anatolian Peninsula, where many families had lived for over a thousand years, and large numbers of Greek women were raped and Greek men murdered. Turkish nationalists massacred an estimated 1.5 million Armenians.[2]

Woodrow Wilson's decision to enter World War I had serious consequences in Iraq, too. Because the British and French were on the winning side of the war, the League of Nations awarded "mandates" to Britain and France in the region. If the United States had stayed out of World War I, there probably would have been a negotiated settlement, the Ottoman Empire would have survived for a while, and the Middle East wouldn't have been carved up by Britain and France. But, as things turned out, authorized by League of Nations "mandates," British Colonial Secretary Winston Churchill was determined to secure the British navy's access to Persian oil at the least possible cost by installing puppet regimes in the region.

In Mesopotamia, Churchill bolted together the territories of Mosul, Baghdad, and Basra to make Iraq. Although Kurds wanted an independent homeland, their territory was to be part of Iraq. Churchill decided that the best bet for Britain would be a Hashemite ruler. For king, Churchill picked Faisal, eldest son of Sherif Hussein of Mecca. Faisal was an Arabian prince who lived for years in Ottoman Constantinople, then established himself as king of Syria, but was expelled by the French government, which had the League of Nations "mandate" there. The British arranged a plebiscite purporting to show Iraqi support for Faisal. A majority of people in Iraq

were Shiite Muslims, but Faisal was a Sunni Muslim, and this conflict was to become a huge problem.[3] The Ottomans were Sunni, too,
which meant British policy prolonged the era of Sunni dominance
over Shiites as they became more resentful. During the thirty-seven
years of the Iraqi monarchy, there were fifty-eight changes of parliamentary governments, indicating chronic political instability.[4] All
Iraqi rulers since Faisal, including Saddam Hussein, were Sunnis.
That Iraq was ruled for three decades by a sadistic murderer like Saddam made clear how the map-drawing game was vastly more complicated than Wilson had imagined.

Considering Wilson's global catastrophes, it's remarkable that his
interventionist policies have been adopted by Democratic and Repub-
lican presidents ever since. President Franklin D. Roosevelt followed in
Wilson's footsteps when he maneuvered the United States into World
War II, after promising American voters that he would stay out.
Within five years after Hitler's defeat, more people than ever—some
800 million—suffered oppression from totalitarian regimes, in the
Soviet Union, Albania, Bulgaria, China, Czechoslovakia, Estonia, East
Germany, Hungary, Latvia, Lithuania, Poland, Romania, and Yugoslavia. Millions in Eastern Europe were liberated from Hitler, then
handed over to Stalin. Both Hitler and Stalin murdered Jews. One
might make a case that the war against Hitler was pragmatic, but since
the United States was allied with Stalin, an even worse mass murderer,
World War II couldn't be described as a just war.

President Harry Truman followed in Wilson's footsteps with his
undeclared Korean War, which didn't involve an attack on the United
States, yet killed more than 36,000 Americans. President Lyndon B.
Johnson followed Wilson with his undeclared Vietnam War, still another war that didn't involve an attack on the United States—over
58,000 Americans killed.

Again and again, seemingly easy interventions have become
complicated, starting with Wilson's fiascoes in Mexico and Europe.
The Korean War became a quagmire with its rugged terrain and Chinese hordes, the Vietnam War with its jungles and guerrilla fighters,
and the Middle East with its cities and suicide bombers. We play to
our strengths when we defend our country, and play to our weaknesses when we intervene in the affairs of other countries where

people speak different languages, have different ideas, live in places that are strange to us—and are embroiled in conflicts that have little to do with our national security interests. In some cases, such as the Balkans, the United States intervened in conflicts that had been going on for hundreds of years, before the United States existed.

And, yes, the United States has made enemies by intervening in ancient disputes between Jews and Muslims as well as disputes among Muslim sects in the Middle East. American blood has been shed defending unpopular Saudi kings and the Shah of Iran, and trying to maintain order in Lebanon and build a new Iraqi nation following the overthrow of Saddam. During the past thousand years the Muslim world has produced kings, dictators, and religious fanatics—it's a region largely unfamiliar with religious freedom and constitutional limitations on government power. Yet Wilsonian nation-builders have imagined that they could somehow develop a nice liberal democracy by sending in soldiers and money. What we've seen, of course, has been terror and civil war.

Americans seem surprised when local people have opposed our well-meaning interventions, particularly after we helped get rid of an acknowledged evil like Saddam Hussein. But people don't seem to want somebody else building their nation, even when they've made a mess of it. They might want Americans to send money and sacrifice some lives, then go home. A small but determined terrorist minority can cause a lot of trouble for us.

An interventionist foreign policy requires a president with the highest level of foreign policy expertise, but there isn't any method of ensuring that only such people will occupy the White House. Many factors other than foreign policy expertise influence the outcome of presidential elections, such as a candidate's personality, achievements, and positions on other issues. In any case, the worst foreign policy decisions, such as entering World War I, the Korean War, and the Vietnam War, have tended to involve a consensus among foreign policy experts—"the wise men," as Walter Isaacson and Evan Thomas called them in their book about postwar policy.[5] "The best and brightest" was David Halberstam's phrase in his critique of the Vietnam War.[6]

How could the experts be wrong? Predicting foreign policy outcomes is as difficult as predicting anything else. Intervening in the affairs of other nations means taking sides. It isn't easy to predict which among many personalities and groups might emerge as enemies. Anyway, an outsider has a limited number of options, including support for a sympathetic regime and conquest, both of which would inflame nationalist hatreds.

The catastrophes Woodrow Wilson unleashed ought to serve as a warning that humility is urgently needed in U.S. foreign policy. It is not possible to control what other people do. We can only control what we ourselves do. We will have our hands full making this the best country it can be.

U.S. foreign policy ought to be guided by the following principles:

1. **Defend America.** The focus should be on protecting the national security interests of the United States, not on defending other countries from a wide range of threats. Nor should the United States try to counter political instability elsewhere. There has always been political instability in the world, and most of it doesn't affect the national security of the United States. We should avoid having American forces permanently stationed in other countries. American blood and treasure should be reserved for safeguarding Americans. We should repeal proliferating restrictions on civil liberties that, enacted in the name of fighting terrorism, do little if anything to protect national security.

2. **Stay out of other people's wars.** By definition, these don't involve an attack on the United States. We should phase out alliances that obligate the United States to enter wars unrelated to American national security interests, such as the NATO alliance obligating the United States to enter wars in which any of nineteen member nations might become embroiled. The United States should phase out similar obligations in the Middle East, Korea, and elsewhere. The more American resources are expended in other people's wars, the less are available to protect American national security interests.

3. **Don't try to build other people's nations.** Independent nations cannot be built by stationing U.S soldiers in a territory and giving the government foreign aid. For better or worse, people must build their nations by making their own choices. People don't want

foreigners trying to build their nations, because the foreigners—in particular, a foreign government—would be making the choices. When the United States pursues nation-building, American soldiers are killed enforcing choices that local people don't want. This essentially means American soldiers die in vain.

4. **Be open to the world.** We should maintain freedom of movement for people, goods, and capital, to minimize the risk that economic disputes will escalate into political and military conflicts. We should abolish immigration quotas and welcome immigrants from all nations, except immigrants with known terrorist or other criminal backgrounds. Immigrants should perhaps be excluded from welfare state benefits (which, considering the debilitating effects of welfare, would probably give immigrants an advantage over persons born in the United States). There shouldn't be any tariffs, import quotas, anti-dumping penalties, or other import restrictions. Nor should there be foreign exchange controls or other restrictions on capital flows. The goal should be to minimize government-to-government contacts and facilitate the entire range of peaceful, private contacts around the world.

More emigrants have come to the United States than to all other destinations combined. They have created new technologies, built great companies, enriched American cuisine and the American language itself. This was anything but "isolationism." America became a rich and influential country precisely because of a willingness to learn from everybody.

America cannot save the world by fighting endless wars, but we can set an example. We must protect a flourishing free society that others are welcome to join, or to emulate in their own lands.

NOTES

INTRODUCTION
ARROGANCE AND POWER

1. Bailey, *Woodrow Wilson and the Lost Peace* (New York: Macmillan, 1947), vi.
2. Arthur S. Link, "Wilson and the Great Debate Over Collective Security," in Link, ed., *The Impact of World War I*, 129.
3. John Mosier, *The Myth of the Great War: How the Germans Won the Battles and How the Americans Saved the Allies* (New York: Perennial, 2002), 5.
4. Abraham, *Kerensky*, 92.
5. Tuchman, *The Zimmermann Telegram*, 5.
6. The Versailles Treaty, June 28, 1919, Article 74.
7. Margaret MacMillan, *Paris 1919: Six Months That Changed the World* (New York: Random House, 2001), 283, 284.
8. The Versailles Treaty, June 28, 1919, Articles 156 and 157.
9. Feldman, *The Great Disorder*, vii.
10. Konrad Heiden, *The Fuehrer*, 106.
11. Eric J. Grove, ed., *The Defeat of the Enemy Attack on Shipping 1939–1945* (Brookfield, VT: Ashgate, 1997), Table 1. Published for the Navy Records Society, the focus of the book was World War II experience with convoys, but it reported World War I experience, as well.
12. Mosier, *The Myth of the Great War*, 235.
13. Ibid., 195.
14. Pipes, *The Russian Revolution,* 397, 399, 402, 415, 416, 433, 434.
15. Kennan, *Russia Leaves the War,* 19.
16. Robert Lansing, *War Memoirs* (Indianapolis: Bobbs-Merrill, 1935), 337.
17. Pipes, *The Russian Revolution,* 583.
18. Kennan, *Russia Leaves the War,* 23.
19. Service, *Lenin, a Biography,* 369.
20. Ibid., 342.
21. Rummel, *Lethal Politics,* 1, 2.
22. Pipes, *Three "Whys" of the Russian Revolution,* 3.
23. ———, *The Russian Revolution,* 600, 601, 602.
24. Tuchman, *The Zimmermann Telegram,* 41.
25. Ibid., 46.

1
How Did That Monstrous War Happen?

1. Hajo Holborn, *A History of Modern Germany, 1648–1840* (New York: Knopf, 1964), 382.
2. Thompson, *Napoleon Bonaparte,* 196.
3. Herold, *The Age of Napoleon,* 272.
4. Thompson, *Napoleon Bonaparte,* 345.
5. Herold, *The Age of Napoleon,* 272.
6. Paul Johnson, *The Birth of the Modern, World Society 1815–1830* (New York: HarperCollins, 1991), 70.
7. Antonina Vallentin, *This I Saw: The Life and Times of Goya* (New York: Random House, 1949), 258–59.
8. Herold, *The Age of Napoleon,* 353.
9. Ibid., 357.
10. Ségur, *Napoleon's Russian Campaign,* 159.
11. "De l'esprit de conquête et de l'usurpation," in *Benjamin Constant, Political Writings,* edited by Biancamaria Fontana (Cambridge: Cambridge University Press, 1993), 82.
12. Johnson, *The Birth of the Modern,* 70.
13. Carleton J. H. Hayes, *A Generation of Materialism, 1871–1900* (New York: Harper, 1941), 51.
14. Thomas Sowell, *Conquests and Cultures, An International History* (New York: Basic Books, 1998), 356.
15. Robert Fogel and Stanley Engerman, *Time on the Cross: the Economics of American Negro Slavery* (New York: Norton, 1974), 33, 34; and Thomas J. DiLorenzo, *The Real Lincoln: A New Look at Abraham Lincoln, His Agenda, and an Unnecessary War* (New York: Three Rivers Press, 2003), 49.
16. John Morley, *The Life of Richard Cobden* (London: T. Fisher Unwin, 1906), 677.
17. "The Financial Policy of the Late Government, House of Commons, July 21, 1859," in *John Bright, Speeches on Questions of Public Policy,* vol. 2 (London: Macmillan, 1869), 416–17.
18. Morley, *The Life of Richard Cobden,* 791.
19. David S. Landes, "Technological Change and Development in Western Europe, 1750–1914," in *The Cambridge Economic History of Europe,* vol. 6, edited by H. J. Habakkuk and M. Postan (Cambridge, England: Cambridge University Press, 1978), 428.
20. Alvin Rabushka, *From Adam Smith to the Wealth of America* (New Brunswick, NJ: Transaction Books, 1985), 59.
21. H. C. G. Matthew, *Gladstone, 1875–1898* (Oxford, England: Clarendon Press, 1995), 393.
22. Karl Marx and Friederich Engels, *The Communist Manifesto* (London: Penguin Books, 1967), 222, 237.
23. Sidney Webb, "The Basis for Socialism," in *Fabian Essays in Socialism,* edited by George Bernard Shaw and H. G. Wilshire (New York: Humboldt Publishing, 1891), 48.
24. Taylor, *Bismarck,* 12.
25. "Lord Beaconsfield," Encyclopedia Britannica entry, 11th edition.
26. Hayes, *A Generation of Materialism,* 229.
27. Paul Johnson, *A History of the English People* (New York: Perennial Library, 19785), 326.
28. Hayes, *A Generation of Materialism,* 205.
29. John A. C. Conybeare, *Trade Wars, The Theory and Practice of International Commercial Rivalry* (New York: Columbia University Press, 1987), 183.
30. Hayes, *A Generation of Materialism,* 206.
31. Conybeare, *Trade Wars,* 189.
32. Ibid., 185.
33. Emil Ludwig, *Bismarck, the Story of a Fighter* (Boston: Little, Brown, 1927), 544.
34. Conybeare, *Trade Wars,* 192.
35. Craig, *Germany 1866–1945,* 113.
36. Ibid., 98.
37. David S. Landes, *The Unbound Prometheus, Technological Change and Industrial Development in Western Europe from 1750 to the Present* (Cambridge, England: Cambridge University Press, 1988), 137.

38. Ibid., 258.
39. Charles Kindelberger, *Economic Response: Comparative Studies in Trade, Finance, and Growth* (Cambridge, MA: Harvard University Press, 1978), 186.
40. John H. Clapham, *The Economic Development of France and Germany, 1815–1914* (Cambridge, England: Cambridge University Press, 1951), 322.
41. Hayes, *A Generation of Materialism,* 206.
42. Norman Angell, *The Great Illusion 1933,* 60.
43. Ludwig von Mises, *Omnipotent Government* (New Rochelle, NY: Arlington House, 1969), 2.
44. James L. Stokesbury, *A Short History of World War I* (New York: Perennial, 2002), 75.
45. Ibid., 78.
46. Robert K. Massie, *Dreadnought, Britain, Germany, and the Coming of the Great War* (New York: Random House, 1991), 402–3.
47. Ibid., 403.
48. Ibid., 469.
49. Stokesbury, *A Short History of World War I,* 76.
50. J. F. C. Fuller, *A Military History of the Western World, From the Seven Days Battle, 1862, to the Battle of Leyte Gulf, 1944* (New York: Funk & Wagnalls, 1956), 177. See also Ferguson, *The Pity of War,* 83: "[S]o decisive was the British victory in the naval arms race that it is hard to regard it as in any meaningful sense a cause of the First World War."
51. Quoted in Fuller, *A Military History,* 177.
52. Ida M. Tarbell, *All in the Day's Work: the Autobiography of the Foremost Muckraker of Her Time* (Boston: G. K. Hall, 1985), 383.
53. ———, *A Life of Napoleon Bonaparte* (New York: Macmillan, 1921), 291, 293, 294.
54. Fuller, *A Military History,* 171.
55. Ibid., 172.
56. Massie, *Dreadnought,* 406.
57. Ferguson, *The Pity of War,* 53.
58. Lutz, *Lord Grey and the World War,* 75.
59. Ibid., 80.
60. Quoted in Ferguson, *The Pity of War,* 72.
61. Paul Kennedy, *The Rise and Fall of Great Powers: Economic Change and Military Conflict from 1500 to 2000* (New York: Random House, 1987), 254.
62. Lutz, *Lord Grey and the World War,* 84.
63. Quoted in Ferguson, *The Pity of War,* 77.
64. Churchill, *The World Crisis,* 108, 109.
65. Reed, *How The War Came,* 107, 17, 183.
66. Quoted in Trevelyan, *Grey of Fallodon,* 129.
67. Ferguson, *The Pity of War,* 73.
68. Trevelyan, *Grey of Fallodon,* 130; see also 287.
69. Fay, *The Origins of the World War,* 34.
70. A. J. P. Taylor, *The Habsburg Monarchy,* 173.
71. Arthur J. May, *The Hapsburg Monarchy* (Cambridge, MA: Harvard University Press, 1951), 190.
72. Ibid., 374.
73. A. J. P. Taylor, *The Habsburg Monarchy,* 186.
74. Jászi, *The Dissolution of the Habsburg Monarchy,* 185.
75. Quoted in Fischer, *Germany's War Aims,* 50.
76. Fischer, *Germany's War Aims,* 32.
77. Ferguson, *The Pity of War,* 79.
78. Samuel R. Williamson, Jr., "The Origins of the War," in *The Oxford Illustrated History of the First World War,* edited by Hew Strachan (New York: Oxford University Press, 1998), 9.
79. Strachan, *The First World War,* 7.
80. Charles Seymour, ed., *The Intimate Papers of Colonel House,* vol. 1 (Boston: Houghton Mifflin, 1926), 271.
81. Ferguson, *The Pity of War,* 153.
82. Strachan, *The First World War,* 17.

83. Barnes, *The Genesis of the World War,* 496.

84. Grey, *Twenty-Five Years,* vol. 1, 325.

85. Marshall, *World War I,* 38.

86. Jesse D. Clarkson, *A History of Russia* (New York: Random House, 1968), 418.

87. Marshall, *World War I,* 40.

88. *The Times* (London), 22 December 1920, quoted in Lutz, *Lord Grey and the World War,* 97.

89. Quoted in Ferguson, *The Pity of War,* 67.

90. Tuchman, *The Guns of August.*

91. Fischer, *Germany's War Aims,* 57–72.

2
WHY WAS THE WAR STALEMATED FOR THREE YEARS?

1. Ferguson, *The Pity of War,* 92.

2. Kennedy, *The Rise and Fall of Great Powers,* 243.

3. Ibid., 274.

4. John Terraine, *The Western Front, 1914–1918* (Barnsley, UK: Pen & Sword Books, 2003), 66.

5. Churchill, *The World Crisis,* 519.

6. Marshall, *World War I,* 228.

7. Liddell Hart, *The Real War,* 223.

8. James L. Stokesbury, *A Short History of World War I* (New York: Perennial, 1981), 260.

9. Kolko, *Century of War,* 9.

10. Gilbert, *The First World War,* 299.

11. Quoted in Strachan, *The First World War,* 55.

12. Gilbert, *The First World War,* 296.

13. Karp, *The Politics of War,* 180.

14. Strachan, *The First World War,* 205.

15. Vincent, *The Politics of Hunger,* 44.

16. Hough, *The Great War at Sea,* 28.

17. Craig, *Germany, 1866–1945,* 369.

18. Hough, *The Great War at Sea,* 175.

19. Vincent, *The Politics of Hunger,* 18.

20. Stolper, *The German Economy,* 61.

21. Vincent, *The Politics of Hunger,* 44, 45.

22. Ibid., 137.

23. Gilbert, *The First World War,* xv.

24. Keegan, *The First World War,* 317.

25. Ibid., 137.

26. Vincent, *The Politics of Hunger,* 130.

27. Ibid., 131.

28. Holborn, *A History of Modern Germany,* 435.

29. A. J. P. Taylor, *The Habsburg Monarchy,* 233–51.

30. Gilbert, *The First World War,* 344.

31. David M. Kennedy, from his introduction to Marshall, *World War I,* viii.

32. Stolper, *The German Economy,* 60.

33. Ibid., 64.

34. Kennedy, *The Rise and Fall of Great Powers,* 270.

35. Gilbert, *The First World War,* 287.

36. Kennedy, *The Rise and Fall of Great Powers,* 270.

37. Stolper, *The German Economy,* 71.

38. L. L. Farrar, Jr., "The Strategy of the Central Powers," in *The Oxford Illustrated History of the First World War,* edited by Hew Strachan (New York: Oxford University Press, 1998), 37.

39. Strachan, *The First World War* (New York: Viking, 2004), 291.

40. R. R. Palmer and Joel Colton, *A History of the Modern World* (New York: Knopf, 1983), 679.

41. Hough, *The Great War at Sea,* 175.

42. Strachan, *The First World War,* 292.

43. Liddell Hart, *The Real War,* 311.

44. Kennedy, *The Rise and Fall of Great Powers,* 272.

45. Anthony Livesey, *Great Battles of World War I* (New York: Macmillan, 1989), 112.

46. Marshall, *World War I,* 287.

47. Ibid., 301.

48. Gilbert, *The First World War,* 346.

49. Ibid., 347.

50. Strachan, *The First World War,* 252.

51. Keegan, *The First World War,* 362.

52. Ibid., 368.

53. Kennedy, *The Rise and Decline of Great Powers,* 256.

54. F. R. Bridge, "The Foreign Policy of the Monarchy 1908–1918," in *The Last Years of Austria-Hungary,* edited by Mark Cornwall (Exeter, England: University Press, 2000), 120–23.

55. Margaret MacMillan, *Paris 1919* (New York: Random House, 2001), 245.

56. Douglas Newton, "The Lansdowne 'Peace Letter' of 1917 and the prospect of peace by negotiation with Germany," *Australian Journal of Politics and History,* March 2002, 16–39.

3
WHY DID WILSON DECIDE HE MUST BREAK THE STALEMATE?

1. Margaret MacMillan, *Paris 1919* (New York: Random House, 2001), 6.

2. Alexander L. George and Juliette L. George, *Woodrow Wilson and Colonel House* (New York: Dover Publications, 1956), 120.

3. Ibid., 121.

4. Keynes, *The Economic Consequences of the Peace,* 40.

5. Louis Auchincloss, *Woodrow Wilson* (New York: Lipper/Viking, 2000), 16.

6. Heckscher, *Woodrow Wilson,* 184.

7. George and George, *Woodrow Wilson and Colonel House,* 42.

8. Link, *Wilson: Road to the White House,* 76.

9. Clements, *Woodrow Wilson, World Statesman,* 53.

10. Heckscher, *Woodrow Wilson,* 200.

11. Ibid., 203.

12. George and George, *Woodrow Wilson and Colonel House,* 50.

13. Ibid., 50.

14. Clements, *Woodrow Wilson, World Statesman,* 54.

15. Ibid., 55.

16. Heckscher, *Woodrow Wilson,* 216.

17. George and George, *Woodrow Wilson and Colonel House,* 63.

18. Ibid., 58.

19. Ibid., 103.

20. Ibid., 93.

21. Ibid., 82.

22. Woodrow Wilson letter to Josephus Daniels, quoted in Alexander George and George, *Woodrow Wilson and Colonel House,* 113.

23. George and George, *Woodrow Wilson and Colonel House,* 125.

24. Robert W. Cherny, *A Righteous Cause: The Life of William Jennings Bryan* (Boston: Little, Brown, 1985), 134.

25. Ibid., 136.

26. Eisenhower, *Intervention!,* 4, 11.

27. Ibid., 53.

28. Ibid., 128.

29. Ibid., 127.

30. Ibid., 132.

31. Ibid., 141.

32. Knight, *The Mexican Revolution,* 262.

33. Eisenhower, *Intervention!,* 137.

34. Ibid., 183.
35. Thomas Fleming, *The Illusion of Victory*, 71, 72.
36. Karp, *The Politics of War*, 186.
37. Ibid., 197.
38. Heckscher, *Woodrow Wilson*, 391.
39. Ibid., 391.
40. Ibid., 422.
41. Adam Hochschild, *King Leopold's Ghost, A Story of Greed, Terror, and Heroism in Colonial Africa* (Boston: Houghton Mifflin, 1998), 294.
42. Ibid., 3.
43. Ferguson, *Empire*, 294.
44. Hochschild, *King Leopold's Ghost*, 164.
45. Ibid., 165, 166.
46. Thomas Sowell, *Ethnic America* (New York: Basic Books, 1981), 58, 61.
47. Ibid., 60.
48. Ibid., 65.
49. Walter Laqueur, *Weimar, A Cultural History 1918–1933* (London: Phoenix Press, 1974), 3.
50. Strachan, *The First World War*, 203.
51. Heckscher, *Woodrow Wilson* (New York: Scribner, 1991), 435.
52. Ibid., 437.
53. Ibid., 439.

4
WHY DID WILSON PRESSURE AND BRIBE THE RUSSIAN PROVISIONAL GOVERNMENT TO STAY IN THE WAR?

1. Kennan, *Russia Leaves the War*, 28.
2. Kennan, *Russia and the West*, 5.
3. Ibid., 14.
4. Pipes, *Three "Whys" of the Russian Revolution*, 29.
5. Royle, *Crimea*, 394.
6. W. Bruce Lincoln, *The Romanovs, Autocrat of All the Russias* (New York: Dial Press, 1981), 427.
7. Tolstoy, *Sevastopol Sketches*, 183.
8. Radzinsky, *The Last Tsar*, 379.
9. Ibid., 10.
10. Tuchman, *The Proud Tower*, 236.
11. Lincoln, *The Romanovs*, 638.
12. Ibid., 638.
13. Pleshakov, *The Tsar's Last Armada*, 31, 32.
14. Ibid., 33.
15. Volkogonov, *Trotsky, The Eternal Revolutionary*, xxix.
16. Quoted in Dmitri Volkogonov, *Lenin, A New Biography*, xxxvi.
17. Service, *Lenin: A Biography*, 493.
18. Baron, *Plekhanov*, vii.
19. "What Is To Be Done?" in *Essential Works of Lenin*, edited by Henry M. Christman (New York: Dover, 1987), 161.
20. Radzinsky, *Stalin, The First In-Depth Biography*, 50, 51.
21. Montefiore, *Stalin, The Court of the Red Tsar*, 28.
22. Volkogonov, *Trotsky, The Eternal Revolutionary*, 38.
23. Pipes, *A Concise History of the Russian Revolution*, 59, 60.
24. Gatrell, *Government, Industry and Rearmament in Russia*, 305.
25. Ibid., 306.
26. Norman Stone, *The Eastern Front, 1914–1917* (London: Hodder and Stoughton, 1975), 134.
27. Lincoln, *Passage Through Armageddon*, 56.

28. Ibid., 51.
29. Ibid., 128.
30. Ibid., 128.
31. Pipes, *Three "Whys" of the Russian Revolution*, 29.
32. Gatrell, *A Whole Empire Walking*, 20, 23.
33. Pares, *A History of Russia*, 477.
34. E. Taylor, *The Fall of the Dynasties*, 247.
35. Gatrell, *A Whole Empire Walking*, 33.
36. Stone, *The Eastern Front*, 299.
37. Ibid., 287.
38. Pipes, *The Russian Revolution*, 235.
39. Ibid., 234.
40. Ibid., 235.
41. Stone, *The Eastern Front*, 297.
42. Pipes, *The Russian Revolution*, 237.
43. Stone, *The Eastern Front*, 297.
44. Ibid., 300.
45. E. Taylor, *The Fall of the Dynasties*, 248.
46. Alex De Jonge, *The Life and Times of Grigorii Rasputin* (New York: Barnes & Noble, 1982), 47, 48.
47. Ibid., 48.
48. Pares, *A History of Russia*, 482.
49. E. Taylor, *The Fall of the Dynasties*, 249, 250.
50. Pares, *A History of Russia*, 485.
51. Riasanovsky, *A History of Russia*, 505.
52. Pipes, *A Concise History of the Russian Revolution*, 78.
53. Quoted in Strachan, *The First World War*, 260.
54. Florence Farmborough, *With the Armies of the Tsar: A Nurse at the Russian Front, 1914–18* (New York: Stein & Day, 1975), 254.
55. Figes, *A People's Tragedy*, 326.
56. Pipes, *A Concise History of the Russian Revolution*, 82.
57. Farmborough, *With the Armies of the Czar*, 269, 270.
58. Pipes, *The Russian Revolution*, 302.
59. Abraham, *Alexander Kerensky*, 5.
60. Strachan, *The First World War*, 261.
61. Pipes, *A Concise History of the Russian Revolution*, 84.
62. Nicolas Werth, "A State Against Its People: Violence, Repression, and Terror in the Soviet Union," in Courtois, Werth et al., eds., *The Black Book of Communism*, 43.
63. Quoted in Kennan, *Russia and the West Under Lenin and Stalin*, 17.
64. Heckscher, *Woodrow Wilson*, 435.
65. Kennan, *Russia Leaves the War*, 18.
66. Ibid., 19.
67. Wade, *The Russian Search for Peace*, 37.
68. Quoted in Wade, *The Russian Search for Peace*, 11.
69. Wade, *The Russian Search for Peace*, 37.
70. Ibid., 48.
71. Kennan, *Russia Leaves the War*, 24.
72. Wade, *The Russian Search for Peace*, 80.
73. Ferdinand Grenard, *The Russian Revolution* (1933), quoted in Kerensky, *Russia and History's Turning Point*, 386.
74. Kennan, *Russia Leaves the War*, 25.
75. Service, *Lenin*, 227.
76. Quoted in Service, *Lenin*, 228.
77. Service, *Lenin*, 238.

78. Pipes, *The Russian Revolution*, 387.
79. Ibid., 388.
80. Quoted in Pipes, *The Russian Revolution*, 389.

5

Why Did Wilson Assume His Allies Would Not Demand Vindictive Surrender Terms from Germany?

1. Pipes, *The Russian Revolution*, 669.
2. Craig, *Germany, 1866–1945*, 392.
3. James L. Stokesbury, *A Short History of World War I* (New York: Perennial, 1981), 259.
4. Ibid., 270.
5. Craig, *Germany, 1866–1945*, 392.
6. Gilbert, *The First World War: A Complete History*, 432.
7. Ibid., 441.
8. Keegan, *The First World War*, 409.
9. Gilbert, *The First World War: A Complete History*, 499.
10. Stokesbury, *A Short History of World War I*, 278.
11. Gina Kolata, *Flu: The Story of the Great Influenza Pandemic of 1918 and the Search for the Virus That Caused It* (New York: Farrar, Straus and Giroux, 1999), 7.
12. Ibid., 4.
13. Gilbert, *The First World War: A Complete History*, 437.
14. Richard M. Watt, *The Kings Depart: The Tragedy of Germany, Versailles and the German Revolution* (New York: Simon & Schuster, 1968), 30.
15. Keynes, *The Economic Consequences of the Peace*, 57.
16. Ibid., 57.
17. Strachan, *The First World War*, 324; Toland, *Adolf Hitler*, vol. 1, 76.
18. Quoted in Michael Howard, *The First World War* (New York: Oxford, 2002), 132.
19. Holborn, *A History of Modern Germany*, 511.
20. Ibid., 512.
21. Ibid., 512.
22. Vincent, *The Politics of Hunger*.
23. Ibid., 69.
24. Ibid., 69.
25. Ibid., 70.
26. Quoted in Vincent, *The Politics of Hunger*, 132.
27. Vincent, *The Politics of Hunger*, 134.
28. Owen, *Tempestuous Journey*, 522.
29. Lansing, *The Big Four and Others*, 13.
30. Ibid., 13.
31. Keynes, *The Economic Consequences of the Peace*, 29, 30.
32. Margaret MacMillan, *Paris 1919* (New York: Random House, 2001), 27.
33. Keynes, *The Economic Consequences of the Peace*, 41.
34. Lansing, *The Big Four and Others*, 78.
35. Keynes, *The Economic Consequences of the Peace*, 44.
36. Ibid., 41.
37. Lansing, *The Big Four and Others*, 104.
38. Ibid., 66.
39. Keynes, *The Economic Consequences of the Peace*, 43.
40. Lansing, *The Big Four and Others*, 41.
41. Watt, *The Kings Depart*, 89.
42. Lansing, *The Big Four and Others*, 18, 19.
43. MacMillan, *Paris 1919*, xxix.
44. Quoted in Manfred F. Boemeke, "Woodrow Wilson's Image of Germany, the War-Guilt Question, and the Treaty of Versailles," in Boemeke et al., eds., *The Treaty of Versailles*, 603.
45. Ibid., 604.

46. Ibid., 613.
47. R. J. Rummel, *Death by Government* (New Brunswick, NJ: Transaction, 1995), 1–28.
48. MacMillan, *Paris 1919,* 92.
49. Ibid., 94.
50. The Versailles Treaty, Article 160 (1).
51. The Versailles Treaty, Article 183.
52. The Versailles Treaty, Article 199.
53. The Versailles Treaty, Articles 164, 167.
54. The Versailles Treaty, Articles 185, 190.
55. The Versailles Treaty, Article 169.
56. The Versailles Treaty, Articles 173, 194.
57. The Versailles Treaty, Article 179.
58. Fay, *The Origins of the World War,* 547–58.
59. Ibid., 548, 549.
60. Fritz Fischer, *Germany's Aims in the First World War* (New York: Norton, 1961), 475–509.
61. The Versailles Treaty, Article 235.
62. The Versailles Treaty, Article 244, Annex II, 18.
63. Sally Marks, "Smoke and Mirrors: In Smoke-Filled Rooms and the Galerie des Glaces," in Boemeke et al., eds., *The Treaty of Versailles,* 337, 338.
64. The Versailles Treaty, Article 244, Annex III, 5, 6.
65. The Versailles Treaty, Article 244, Annex IV, 6.
66. The Versailles Treaty, Article 244, Annex V, 2.
67. The Versailles Treaty, Article 244, Annex V. 8.
68. The Versailles Treaty, Article 244, Annex VI, 1.
69. MacMillan, *Paris 1919,* 465.
70. Ferguson, *Empire,* 313.
71. Ibid., 311.
72. Ibid., 311.
73. Ibid., 311.
74. Ibid., 313
75. MacMillan, *Paris 1919,* 460.
76. Ibid., 460.
77. Quoted in MacMillan, *Paris 1919,* 466.
78. Ibid., 466.
79. Manfred F. Boemeke, Gerald D. Feldman, and Elizabeth Glaser's introduction to Boemeke, Feldman, and Glaser, eds., *The Treaty of Versailles,* 3.
80. Burleigh, *The Third Reich: A New History,* 48.
81. Holborn, *A History of Modern Germany,* 529.
82. Burleigh, *The Third Reich: A New History,* 52.
83. Bullock, *Hitler: A Study in Tyranny,* 23.
84. Burleigh, *The Third Reich,* 87.
85. Bullock, *Hitler: A Study in Tyranny,* 33.
86. Ibid., 35.
87. Ian Kershaw, *Hitler, 1889–1936: Hubris* (New York: Norton, 1998), 137.
88. Quoted in Kershaw, *Hitler, 1889–1936,* 148.
89. Kershaw, *Hitler, 1889–1936,* 149.
90. Read, *The Devil's Disciples,* 58.

6

WHY DID WILSON IGNORE THE RISK OF VIOLENT SOCIALIST REVOLUTION IN RUSSIA?

1. Service, *Lenin,* 271.
2. Figes, *A People's Tragedy,* 408.
3. Florence Farmborough, *With the Armies of the Tsar: A Nurse at the Russian Front, 1914–18* (New York: Stein & Day, 1975), 274.

4. Pipes, *The Russian Revolution*, 407.

5. Ibid., 411.

6. Ibid., 414.

7. Ibid., 431.

8. Ibid., 435.

9. Farmborough, *With the Armies of the Tsar*, 287.

10. Figes, *A People's Tragedy*, 408.

11. Pipes, *The Russian Revolution*, 418.

12. Figes, *A People's Tragedy*, 408.

13. Kennan, *Russia Leaves the War*, 164.

14. Kerensky, *Russia and History's Turning Point*, 387.

15. Ibid., 388.

16. Ibid., 386.

17. Ibid., 387.

18. Pipes, *The Russian Revolution*, 463.

19. Ibid., 438.

20. Werth, "A State Against Its People: Violence, Repression, and Terror in the Soviet Union," in Courtois, Werth et al., eds., *The Black Book of Communism*, 53.

21. Ibid., 54.

22. Service, *Lenin*, 309.

23. Pipes, *The Russian Revolution*, 493.

24. Service, *Lenin*, 369.

25. Pipes, *The Russian Revolution*, 505.

26. Service, *Lenin*, 315.

27. Werth, "A State Against Its People," 55.

28. Quoted in Alexander N. Yakovlev, *A Century of Violence in Soviet Russia* (New Haven, CT: Yale University Press, 2002), 53.

29. Figes, *A People's Tragedy*, 523.

30. Pipes, *The Russian Revolution*, 512.

31. Figes, *A People's Tragedy*, 527.

32. Ibid., 530.

33. Yakovlev, *A Century of Violence*, 53.

34. Pipes, *The Russian Revolution*, 521.

35. Werth, "A State Against Its People," 58.

36. Leggett, *The Cheka*, 251.

37. Werth, "A State Against Its People," 58.

38. Quoted in Pipes, *The Russian Revolution*, 553.

39. Pipes, *The Russian Revolution*, 601.

40. Ibid., 572, 573.

41. Service, *Lenin*, 339.

42. Ibid., 341.

43. Ibid., 342.

44. Mawdsley, *The Russian Civil War*, 37.

7

How Did Hitler Exploit Wilson's Blunder to Recruit 50,000 Nazis?

1. Gustav Stolper, *The Germany Economy, 1870 to the Present* (New York: Harcourt, Brace & World, 1967), 57.

2. Gerald D. Feldman, *The Great Disorder: Politics, Economics, and Society in the German Inflation, 1914–1924* (New York: Oxford University Press, 1997), 27.

3. Ibid., 28.

4. Ibid., 32.

5. Stolper, *The German Economy*, 60.

6. Feldman, *The Great Disorder,* 33.

7. Burleigh, *The Third Reich: A New History,* 54.

8. Webb, "Fiscal News and Inflationary Expectations," 779.

9. Margaret S. Gordon, *Barriers to World Trade* (New York: Macmillan, 1941), 16.

10. Frank W. Taussig, *The Tariff History of the United States* (New York: G. P. Putnam's Sons, 1931), 447–88.

11. Paul A. Buran, "The U.S.S.R. in the World Economy," in *Foreign Economic Policy for the United States,* edited by Seymour E. Harris (Cambridge, MA: Harvard University Press, 1948), 171. Soviet exports, in thousand metric tons, were 24,112.8 in 1913 and 2,160.8 in 1922–1923. Soviet imports, in thousand metric tons, were 15,342.8 in 1913 and 907.5 in 1922–1923.

12. V. I. Lenin, *Collected Works,* vol. 36 (Moscow: Foreign Languages House, 1960), 529.

13. Mikhail Heller and Aleksandr M. Nekrich, *Utopia in Power: The History of the Soviet Union from 1917 to the Present* (New York: Summit Books, 1986), 117.

14. Feldman, *The Great Disorder,* 558.

15. Ibid., 545.

16. Ibid., 568.

17. Ibid., 526.

18. Quoted in Feldman, *The Great Disorder,* 682.

19. Cited in Feldman, *The Great Disorder,* 516.

20. Burleigh, *The Third Reich: A New History,* 54.

21. Bullock, *Hitler: A Study in Tyranny,* 90.

22. Burleigh, *The Third Reich: A New History,* 55.

23. Feldman, *The Great Disorder,* 706.

24. Bullock, *Hitler: A Study in Tyranny,* 90.

25. Heiden, *The Fuehrer,* 107.

26. Quoted in Feldman, *The Great Disorder,* 680.

27. Heiden, *The Fuehrer,* 107.

28. Feldman, *The Great Disorder,* 707.

29. Heiden, *The Fuehrer,* 107.

30. Feldman, *The Great Disorder,* 693.

31. Ibid., 700.

32. Ludwig von Mises, "The Great German Inflation," in *Money, Method, and the Market Process,* edited by Richard Ebeling (Norwell, MA: Kluwer Academic Publishers, 1990), 98.

33. Feldman, *The Great Disorder,* 760.

34. Ibid., 763.

35. Ibid., 766.

36. Padfield, *Himmler,* 59.

37. Bresciani-Turroni, *The Economics of Inflation,* 5.

38. Bullock, *Hitler: A Study in Tyranny,* 92.

39. Ian Kershaw, *Hitler, 1889–1936: Hubris* (New York: Norton, 1998), 132.

40. Ibid., 188.

41. Ibid., 190.

42. Bullock, *Hitler: A Study in Tyranny,* 109.

43. Feldman, *The Great Disorder,* 778.

44. Bullock, *Hitler,* 115.

45. Kershaw, *Hitler, 1889–1936,* 217.

46. Bullock, *Hitler: A Study in Tyranny,* 118.

8
HOW DID LENIN TAKE ADVANTAGE OF WILSON'S BLUNDER AND SECURE POWER?

1. Nicolas Werth, "A State Against Its People: Violence, Repression, and Terror in the Soviet Union," in Courtois, Werth et al., eds., *The Black Book of Communism,* 67.

2. Ibid., 70.

3. Ibid., 76.
4. Ibid., 78.
5. Ibid., 88.
6. Ibid., 90.
7. Ibid., 92.
8. Ibid., 93.
9. Ibid., 95.
10. Ibid., 97.
11. Ibid., 101.
12. Quoted in Werth, "A State Against Its People," 105.
13. Malle, *The Economic Organization of War Communism*, 160. And on p. 161, Lenin is quoted as saying, on March 4, 1918: "It is a rare week when I do not receive a complaint about money not being paid out."
14. Pipes, *The Russian Revolution*, 685.
15. Ibid., 697.
16. Malle, *The Economic Organization of War Communism*, 204.
17. Ludwig von Mises, *Socialism: An Economic and Sociological Analysis* (Indianapolis: Liberty Classics, 1979), 104.
18. Pipes, *The Russian Revolution*, 674.
19. Ibid., 701.
20. Ibid., 723.
21. Ibid., 729.
22. Quoted in Pipes, *The Russian Revolution*, 737.
23. Pipes, *The Russian Revolution*, 735.
24. Ibid., 737.
25. Alexander N. Yakovlev, *A Century of Violence in Soviet Russia* (New Haven, CT: Yale University Press, 2002), 87, 88.
26. Ibid., 88.
27. Ibid., 89.
28. Ibid., 90.
29. Pipes, *The Russian Revolution*, 791.
30. Quoted in Werth, "A State Against Its People," 66.
31. Pipes, *The Russian Revolution*, 796.
32. Ibid., 803.
33. Ibid., 816.
34. Applebaum, *Gulag: A History*, 9.
35. Yakovlev, *A Century of Violence*, 34.
36. Quoted in Pipes, *The Russian Revolution*, 824.
37. Quoted in Yakovlev, *A Century of Violence*, 64.
38. Ibid., 64.
39. Pipes, *The Russian Revolution*, 836.
40. Werth, "A State Against Its People," 109.
41. Yakovlev, *A Century of Violence*, 15.
42. Bunyan, *The Origin of Forced Labor in the Soviet State*, 159.
43. Quoted in Bunyan, *The Origin of Forced Labor in the Soviet State*, 93.
44. Ibid., 96.
45. Bunyan, *The Origin of Forced Labor in the Soviet State*, 66.
46. Quoted in Bunyan, *The Origin of Forced Labor in the Soviet State*, 76.
47. Bunyan, *The Origin of Forced Labor in the Soviet State*, 164.
48. Ibid., 171.
49. Werth, "A State Against Its People," 115.
50. Service, *A History of Twentieth Century Russia*, 125.
51. Ibid., 126, 127.
52. Werth, "A State Against Its People," 117.
53. Ibid., 114.

54. Ibid., 122.
55. Ibid., 122.
56. Mawdsley, *The Russian Civil War*, 287.
57. Phillip Cagan, "The Monetary Dynamics of Hyperinflation," in *Studies in the Quantity Theory of Money*, edited by Milton Friedman (Chicago: University of Chicago Press, 1956), 26.
58. Mawdsley, *The Russian Civil War*, 286.

9

How Did Wilson's Fateful Decisions
Pave the Way for the Nazi Regime?

1. Heiden, *The Fuehrer*, 203.
2. Bullock, *Hitler: A Study in Tyranny*, 125.
3. Ian Kershaw, *Hitler, 1889–1936: Hubris* (New York: Norton, 1998), 239.
4. Bullock, *Hitler: A Study in Tyranny*, 133.
5. Kershaw, *Hitler, 1889–1936*, 133.
6. Ibid., 396.
7. Heiden, *The Fuehrer*, 205.
8. Read, *The Devil's Disciples*, 126.
9. Padfield, *Himmler*, 92.
10. Kershaw, *Hitler, 1889–1936*, 268.
11. Bullock, *Hitler: A Study in Tyranny*, 141.
12. Kershaw, *Hitler, 1889–1936*, 293.
13. Ibid., 299.
14. Bullock, *Hitler: A Study in Tyranny*, 157.
15. Ibid., 165.
16. Ibid., 189.
17. Kershaw, *Hitler, 1889–1936*, 324.
18. Stolper, *The German Economy*, 117.
19. Kershaw, *Hitler, 1889–1936*, 324.
20. Ibid., 333.
21. Bullock, *Hitler: A Study in Tyranny*, 162.
22. Stolper, *The German Economy*, 113.
23. Charles P. Kindleberger, *Manias, Panics, and Crashes: A History of Financial Crises* (New York: Basic Books, 1978), 197.
24. ———, *The World in Depression, 1929–1939* (Berkeley: University of California Press, 1986), 144–47.
25. Ibid., 152.
26. Margaret S. Gordon, *Barriers to World Trade: A Study of Recent Commercial Policy* (New York: Macmillan, 1941), 67.
27. Ibid., 66.
28. The original insight was Henry George's: "What protection teaches us, is to do to ourselves in time of peace what enemies seek to do to us in time of war." See his *Protection or Free Trade* (New York: Robert Schalkenbach Foundation, 1980), 47. The book originally appeared in 1886.
29. Stolper, *The German Economy*, 119.
30. Bullock, *Hitler: A Study in Tyranny*, 168.
31. Kershaw, *Hitler, 1889–1936*, 362.
32. Ibid., 362.
33. Fest, *Hitler*, 318.
34. Kershaw, *Hitler, 1889–1936*, 363.
35. Ibid., 365.
36. Bullock, *Hitler: A Study in Tyranny*, 213.
37. Kershaw, *Hitler, 1889–1936*, 368.
38. Bullock, *Hitler: A Study in Tyranny*, 201.

39. Fest, *Hitler,* 320.
40. Bullock, *Hitler: A Study in Tyranny,* 201.
41. Kershaw, *Hitler, 1889–1936,* 364.
42. Ibid., 363.
43. Ibid., 364.
44. Bullock, *Hitler: A Study in Tyranny,* 183.
45. Kershaw, *Hitler, 1889–1936,* 370.
46. Bullock, *Hitler: A Study in Tyranny,* 217.
47. Fest, *Hitler,* 340.
48. Bullock, *Hitler: A Study in Tyranny,* 220.
49. Kershaw, *Hitler, 1889–1936,* 388.
50. Bullock, *Hitler: A Study in Tyranny,* 233.
51. Quoted in Kershaw, *Hitler, 1889–1936,* 394.
52. Kershaw, *Hitler, 1889–1936,* 395.
53. Wilhelm Röpke, "End of an Era," in *Against the Tide* (Chicago: Henry Regnery, 1969), 79.
54. Bullock, *Hitler: A Study in Tyranny,* 259.
55. Ibid., 263.
56. Ibid., 268.
57. Ibid., 275.
58. Stolper, *The German Economy,* 129.
59. Gordon, *Barriers to World Trade,* 289.
60. Ibid., 82, 83.
61. Bullock, *Hitler: A Study in Tyranny,* 285.
62. Kershaw, *Hitler, 1889–1936,* 514.
63. Bullock, *Hitler: A Study in Tyranny,* 305.
64. Kershaw, *Hitler, 1889–1936,* 517.
65. Ibid., 518.
66. Fest, *Hitler,* 471.
67. Bullock, *Hitler: A Study in Tyranny,* 309.

1 0
HOW DID WILSON MAKE POSSIBLE STALIN'S TERROR?

1. Conquest, *Stalin: Breaker of Nations,* 13.
2. Walter Laqueur, *Stalin: The Glasnost Revelations* (New York: Scribner's, 1990), 9.
3. Roy Medvedev, *Let History Judge: The Origins and Consequences of Stalinism* (New York: Columbia University Press, 1989), 32.
4. Montefiore, *Court of the Red Tsar,* 30.
5. Laqueur, *Glasnost Revelations,* 9.
6. Montefiore, *Court of the Red Tsar,* 31.
7. Medvedev, *Let History Judge,* 57.
8. Ibid., 58.
9. Volkogonov, *Triumph and Tragedy,* 69.
10. Conquest, *The Great Terror,* 9.
11. Ibid., 64.
12. Volkogonov, *Triumph and Tragedy,* 72.
13. Service, *Lenin: A Biography,* 467.
14. Radzinsky, *Stalin: The First In-Depth Biography,* 208.
15. Service, *A History of Twentieth Century Russia,* 155.
16. Ibid., 158.
17. Ibid., 156.
18. Ibid., 164.
19. Nicolas Werth, "A State Against Its People: Violence, Repression, and Terror in the Soviet Union," in Courtois, Werth et al., eds., *The Black Book of Communism,* 142.
20. Ibid., 145.

21. Ibid., 145.
22. Ibid., 148.
23. Ibid., 149.
24. Ibid., 150.
25. Ibid., 151.
26. Ibid., 151.
27. Ibid., 155.
28. Ibid., 161.
29. Ibid., 164.
30. Ibid., 164.
31. Ibid., 163.
32. Ibid., 165.
33. Conquest, *Harvest of Sorrow,* 258.
34. Ibid., 258.
35. Werth, "A State Against Its People," 159.
36. Conquest, *Harvest of Sorrow,* 4.
37. Quoted in Conquest, *Harvest of Sorrow,* 10.
38. Conquest, *The Great Terror,* 24.
39. Ibid., 26.
40. Ibid., 26.
41. Ibid., 26.
42. Ibid., 26.
43. Radzinsky, *Stalin,* 321.
44. Montefiore, *Court of the Red Tsar,* 95.
45. Radzinsky, *Stalin,* 325.
46. Marc Jansen and Nikita Petrov, *Stalin's Loyal Executioner: People's Commissar Nikolai Ezhov, 1895–1940* (Palo Alto, CA: Hoover Institution Press, 2002), 19.
47. Montefiore, *Court of the Red Tsar,* 169.
48. Quoted in Jansen and Petrov, *Stalin's Loyal Executioner,* 113.
49. Jansen and Petrov, *Stalin's Loyal Executioner,* 115.
50. Radzinsky, *Stalin,* 327.
51. Conquest, *The Great Terror,* 123.
52. Radzinsky, *Stalin,* 338.
53. Ibid., 343.
54. Ibid., 344.
55. Montefiore, *Court of the Red Tsar,* 197.
56. Ibid., 246.
57. Ibid., 198.
58. Conquest, *The Great Terror,* 146.
59. Radzinsky, *Stalin,* 345.
60. Ibid., 347.
61. Ibid., 400.
62. Ibid., 393.
63. Ibid., 351.
64. Ibid., 396.
65. Conquest, *The Great Terror,* 121.
66. Radzinsky, *Stalin,* 354.
67. Ibid., 354, 355.
68. Conquest, *The Great Terror,* 122.
69. Radzinsky, *Stalin,* 392.
70. Conquest, *The Great Terror,* 188, 189.
71. Ibid., 188.
72. Montefiore, *Court of the Red Tsar,* 222.
73. Conquest, *The Great Terror,* 206, 207, 209, 210, 211.
74. Radzinsky, *Stalin,* 374.

75. Conquest, *Kolyma: The Arctic Death Camps,* 228.
76. Ibid., 20.
77. Ibid., 33.
78. Ibid., 42.
79. Gorbatov, *Years Off My Life,* 130, 131.
80. Henry A. Wallace, *Soviet Asia Mission* (New York: Reynal & Hitchcock, 1946), 89.
81. Ibid., 90.
82. Jensen and Petrov, *Stalin's Loyal Executioner,* 188.
83. Ibid., xi.
84. Montefiore, *Court of the Red Czar,* 75, 76.
85. Conquest, *The Great Terror,* 432.
86. Radzinsky, *Stalin,* 437.
87. Conquest, *The Great Terror,* 412.
88. Ibid., 412.
89. Applebaum, *Gulag: A History,* 8.
90. Conquest, *The Great Terror,* 417.
91. Ibid., 179, 180.
92. Ibid., 274.
93. Ibid., 258.
94. Ibid., 288.
95. Ibid., 311.
96. Ibid., 312.
97. Ibid., 314.
98. Ibid., 316.
99. Ibid., 339.

11
WHY IS WORLD WAR II PART OF WILSON'S LEGACY?

1. A. J. P. Taylor, *Origins of the Second World War,* 69, 70.
2. Quoted in Bullock, *Hitler: A Study in Tyranny,* 315.
3. A. J. P. Taylor, *Origins of the Second World War,* 76.
4. A. J. P. Taylor, *Origins of the Second World War,* 73.
5. A. J. P. Taylor, *Origins of the Second World War,* 151.
6. A. J. P. Taylor, *Origins of the Second World War,* 231.
7. Service, *A History of Twentieth Century Russia,* 255.
8. Montefiore, *Court of the Red Tsar,* 303.
9. Bullock, *Hitler: A Study in Tyranny,* 516.
10. Montefiore, *Court of the Red Tsar,* 308.
11. Read, *The Devil's Disciples,* 397.
12. Ibid., 39
13. Ibid., 311.
14. Nicolas Werth, "A State against Its People: Violence, Repression, and Terror in the Soviet Union," in Courtois, Werth et al., eds., *The Black Book of Communism,* 208.
15. Ibid., 209.
16. Ibid., 209.
17. Nikita Khrushchev, *Khrushchev Remembers* (Boston: Little, Brown, 1970), 143.
18. Bullock, *Hitler: A Study in Tyranny,* 557.
19. Ibid., 585.
20. Ibid., 587.
21. Ibid., 590, 591.
22. Shirer, *Berlin Diary,* 422.

CONCLUSION
How Can We Avoid a Blunder Like Wilson's?

1. Keegan, *The First World War,* 293.
2. R. J. Rummel, *Death by Government* (New Brunswick, NJ: Transaction, 1995), 236.
3. See Christopher Catherwood, *Churchill's Folly: How Winston Churchill Created Modern Iraq* (New York: Carroll & Graf, 2004), 129, 153, 156.
4. Catherwood, *Churchill's Folly,* 217.
5. Isaacson and Thomas, *The Wise Men.*
6. David Halberstam, *The Best and the Brightest* (New York: Random House, 1972).

BIBLIOGRAPHY

ARTICLES

Ballard, Robert D. "The Riddle of the *Lusitania*." *National Geographic*, April 1994, 68–85.

Berger, Henry. "A Conservative Critique of Containment: Senator Taft and the Early Cold War Program." In *Containment and Revolution*, edited by David Horowitz, 125–39. Boston: Beacon Press, 1967.

Bernstein, Richard. "Honor the Uprooted Germans? Poles Are Uneasy." *New York Times*, 15 October 2003.

Burdekin, Richard C. K., and Paul Burkett. "Money, Credit, and Wages in Hyperinflation: Post–World War I Germany." *Economic Inquiry*, July 1992, 479–95.

———. "Hyperinflation, the Exchange Rate and Endogenous Money: Post–World War I Germany Revisited." *Journal of International Money and Finance*, August 1996, 599–621.

Cowan, Tyler. "The Marshall Plan: Myths and Realities." In *U.S. Aid to the Developing World*, edited by Doug Bandow, 61–74. Washington, DC: Heritage Foundation, 1985.

Gottfried, Paul. "Wilsonianism: The Legacy That Won't Die." *Journal of Libertarian Studies*, Fall 1990, 118–26.

Hayes, Michael T. "The Republican Road Not Taken: The Foreign-Policy Vision of Robert A. Taft." *Independent Review*, Spring 2004, 509–25.

Hetzel, Robert L. "German Monetary History in the First Half of the Twentieth Century." *Federal Reserve Bank of Richmond Economic Quarterly*, Winter 2002, 1–32.

Higgs, Robert. "No More 'Great' Presidents." In *The Free Market*, March 1997, http://www.mises.org/freemarket_detail.asp?control=141&sortorder=authorlast.

Holborn, Hajo. "Diplomats and Diplomacy in the Early Weimar Republic." In *The Diplomats, 1919–1939*, edited by Gordon Craig and Felix Gilbert. Princeton, NJ: Princeton University Press, 1953.

Kennan, George F. "The Sources of Soviet Conduct." *Foreign Affairs*, July 1947.

Kindelberger, Charles P. "The Great Disorder: A Review of the Book of That Title by Gerald D. Feldman." *Journal of Economic Literature* 3 (1994): 1216–25.

Marshall, George C. "Against Hunger, Poverty, Desperation and Chaos." *Foreign Affairs*, May–June 1997, 160.

Mises, Ludwig von. "The Great German Inflation." In *Money, Method, and the Market Process: Essays by Ludwig von Mises*, edited by Richard M. Ebeling, 96–103. Norwell, MA: Kluwer Academic Publishers, 1990.

Morley, Felix. "American Republic or American Empire." *Modern Age*, Summer 1957, 20–32.

Moser, John. "Principles Without Program: Senator Robert A. Taft and American Foreign Policy." *Ohio History*, September 2001, 177–92.

Newton, Douglas. "The Lansdowne 'Peace Letter' of 1917 and the Prospect of Peace by Negotiation with Germany." *Australian Journal of Politics and History*, March 2002, 16–39.

Raico, Ralph. "The Case for an America First Foreign Policy." In *The Failure of America's Foreign Wars*, edited by Richard M. Ebeling and Jacob Hornberger. Fairfax, VA: Future of Freedom Foundation, 1996.

Rothbard, Murray N. "The Foreign Policy of the Old Right." *Journal of Libertarian Studies* 2, no. 1 (1978): 85–96.

———. "World War I as Fulfillment: Power and the Intellectuals." *Journal of Libertarian Studies*, Winter 1989, 82–125.

Sennholz, Hans F. "Hyperinflation in Germany." *The Freeman*, October 1970.

Stromberg, Joseph R. "'Mere' Isolationism, the Foreign Policy of the Old Right." *The Freeman*, February 2000.

Sunic, Tomislav. "Woodrow Wilson's Defeat in Yugoslavia: The End of a Multicultural Utopia." *Journal of Libertarian Studies*, Fall 1994, 34–43.

Taylor, A. J. P. "The War Aims of the Allies in the First World War." In *Essays Presented to Sir Lewis Namier*, edited by Richard Pares and A. J. P. Taylor, 475–505. London: Macmillan, 1956.

Tooley, T. Hunt. "The Hindenburg Program of 1916: A Central Experiment in Wartime Planning." *The Quarterly Journal of Austrian Economics*, Summer 1999, 51–62.

Tullio, Giuseppe. "Inflation and Currency Depreciation in Germany, 1920–1923: A Dynamic Model of Prices and the Exchange Rate." *Journal of Money, Credit & Banking*, May 1995, 350–62.

Webb, Steven B. "Fiscal News and Inflationary Expectations in Germany after World War I." *Journal of Economic History*, September 1986, 769–94.

West, W. Reed. "Senator Taft's Foreign Policy." *Atlantic Monthly*, June 1952, 50–52.

BOOKS

Abraham, Richard. *Alexander Kerensky: First Love of the Revolution*. New York: Columbia University Press, 1987.

Acheson, Dean. *Present at the Creation: My Years in the State Department.* New York: Norton, 1969.

Alexander, Bevin. *How Hitler Could Have Won World War II: The Fatal Errors That Led to Nazi Defeat.* New York: Crown, 2000.

Ambrose, Stephen E. *Rise to Globalism: American Foreign Policy Since 1938.* New York: Penguin, 1983.

Amis, Martin. *Koba the Dread: Laughter and the Twenty Million.* New York: Miramax, 2002.

Andrew, Christopher, and Vasili Mitrokhin. *The Sword and the Shield: The Mitrokhin Archive and the Secret History of the KGB.* New York: Basic Books, 2000.

Apostal, Paul N., Michael W. Bernatzky, and Alexander N. Michelson. *Russian Public Finance During the War.* New Haven, CT: Yale University Press, 1928.

Applebaum, Anne. *Gulag: A History.* New York: Doubleday, 2003.

Arendt, Hannah. *The Origins of Totalitarianism.* New York: Harcourt, Brace & World, 1951.

Ascher, Abraham. *The Revolution of 1905: Authority Restored.* Palo Alto, CA: Stanford University Press, 1992.

Bailey, Thomas A. *Woodrow Wilson and the Lost Peace.* New York: Macmillan, 1947.

Bandow, Doug. *Tripwire: Korea and U.S. Foreign Policy in a Changed World.* Washington, DC: Cato Institute, 1996.

Bandow, Doug, ed. *The U.S.–South Korea Alliance: Time for a Change.* New Brunswick, NJ: Transaction Publishers, 1992.

Barnes, Harry Elmer. *The Genesis of the World War: An Introduction to the Problem of War Guilt.* New York: Knopf, 1929.

———. *Revisionism, a Key to Peace and Other Essays.* San Francisco: Cato Institute, 1980.

Baron, Samuel Haskell. *Plekhanov: The Father of Russian Marxism.* Palo Alto, CA: Stanford University Press, 1966.

Barraclough, Geoffrey, ed. *The Times Atlas of World History.* Maplewood, NJ: Hammond, 1978.

Becker, Jasper. *Hungry Ghosts: Mao's Secret Famine.* New York: Free Press, 1996.

Beesly, Patrick. *Room 40: British Naval Intelligence, 1914–1918.* New York: Harcourt Brace Jovanovich, 1982.

Beevor, Antony. *The Spanish Civil War.* New York: Penguin, 2001.

Bell-Fialkoff, Andrew. *Ethnic Cleansing.* New York: Palgrave Macmillan, 1996.

Blackwell, William L. *The Industrialization of Russia: A Historical Perspective.* Arlington Heights, IL: H. Davidson, 1994.

Blair, Clay. *The Forgotten War: America in Korea, 1950–1953.* New York: Times Books, 1987.

Boemeke, Manfred, Gerald D. Feldman, and Elizabeth Glaser-Schmidt, eds., *The Treaty of Versailles: A Reassessment After 75 Years.* Cambridge, England: Cambridge University Press, 1998.

Brent, Jonathan, and Vladimir Naumov. *Stalin's Last Crime: The Plot Against the Jewish Doctors, 1948–1953.* New York: HarperCollins, 2003.

Bresciani-Turroni, Costantino. *The Economics of Inflation.* London: George Allen & Unwin, 1937.

Bretton, Henry L. *Stresemann and the Revision of Versailles.* Palo Alto, CA: Stanford University Press, 1953.

Brinkley, Douglas, ed. *Dean Acheson and the Making of U.S. Foreign Policy.* New York: St. Martin's, 1993.

Brownell, Will. *So Close to Greatness: A Biography of William C. Bullitt.* New York: Macmillan, 1987.

Bruck, W. F. *Social and Economic History of Germany from William II to Hitler, 1888–1938.* New York: Russell & Russell, 1962.

Buchanan, George. *My Mission to Russia and Other Diplomatic Memories.* Boston: Little, Brown, 1923.

Bullock, Alan. *Hitler and Stalin: Parallel Lives.* New York: HarperCollins, 1993.

———. *Hitler: A Study in Tyranny.* New York: Harper & Row, 1962.

Bunyan, James. *The Bolshevik Revolution, 1917–1918: Documents and Materials.* Palo Alto, CA: Stanford University Press, 1961.

———. *Intervention, Civil War, and Communism in Russia: Documents and Materials.* New York: Octagon Books, 1976.

———. *The Origin of Forced Labor in the Soviet State, 1917–1921.* Baltimore: Johns Hopkins University Press, 1967.

Buranov, Yuri. *Lenin's Will, Falsified and Forbidden.* Amherst, NY: Prometheus Books, 1994.

Burk, Kathleen. *Britain, America and the Sinews of War, 1914–1918.* Boston: George Allen & Unwin, 1985.

Burleigh, Michael. *The Third Reich: A New History.* New York: Hill & Wang, 2000.

Calvocoressi, Peter, Guy Wint, and John Pritchard. *Total War: Causes and Courses of the Second World War.* New York: Pantheon, 1989.

Carpenter, Ted Galen. *Beyond NATO: Staying Out of Europe's War.* Washington, DC: Cato Institute, 1994.

———. *Collective Defense or Strategic Independence: Alternative Strategies for the Future.* Lexington, MA: Lexington Books, 1989.

———. *Delusions of Grandeur: The United Nations and Global Intervention.* Washington, DC: Cato Institute, 1997.

———. *NATO at 40: Confronting a Changing World.* Lexington, MA: Lexington Books, 1990.

———. *Peace and Freedom: Foreign Policy for a Constitutional Republic.* Washington, DC: Cato Institute, 2002.

Chace, James. *1912: Wilson, Roosevelt, Taft and Debs—The Election That Changed the Country.* New York: Simon & Schuster, 2004.

———. *Dean Acheson: The Secretary of State Who Created the Modern World.* New York: Simon & Schuster, 1998.

Chamberlin, William Henry. *The Russian Revolution, 1917–1921.* 2 vols. New York: Macmillan, 1935.

Chang Kia-ngau. *The Inflationary Spiral: The Experience of China, 1939–1950.* Cambridge, MA: MIT Press, 1958.

Chen, Jian. *Mao's China and the Cold War.* Chapel Hill, NC: University of North Carolina Press, 2001.

Chickering, Roger, Stig Forster, Christof Mauch, and David Lazar, eds. *Great War, Total War: Mobilization on the Western Front, 1914–1918.* Cambridge, England: Cambridge University Press, 2000.

Churchill, Winston S. *The World Crisis: An Abridgment of the Classic Four-Volume History of World War I.* New York: Scribner's, 1992.

Clements, Kendrick A. *Woodrow Wilson, World Statesman.* Chicago: Ivan R. Dee, 1999.

Cohen, Warren I. *The American Revisionists: Lessons of Intervention in World War I.* Chicago: University of Chicago Press, 1967.

Coletta, Paolo Enrico. *William Jennings Bryan.* Lincoln, NE: University of Nebraska Press, 1964–69.

Conquest, Robert. *The Great Terror: A Reassessment.* New York: Oxford University Press, 1990.

———. *The Great Terror: Stalin's Purge of the 1930s.* New York: Macmillan, 1973.

———. *Harvest of Sorrow: Soviet Collectivization and the Terror Famine.* New York: Oxford University Press, 1986.

———. *Inside Stalin's Secret Police: NKVD Politics, 1936–1939.* Palo Alto, CA: Hoover Institution Press, 1985.

———. *Kolyma: The Arctic Death Camps.* New York: Viking Press, 1978.

———. *The Nation Killers: The Soviet Deportation of Nationalities.* New York: Macmillan, 1970.

———. *Stalin and the Kirov Murder.* New York: Oxford University Press, 1989.

———. *Stalin: Breaker of Nations.* New York: Viking, 1991.

Cooper, John Milton. *Breaking the Heart of the World: Woodrow Wilson and the Fight for the League of Nations.* Cambridge, England: Cambridge University Press, 2001.

Cornwall, Mark, ed. *The Last Years of Austria-Hungary: Essays in Political and Military History, 1908–1918.* Exeter, England: University of Exeter Press, 2000.

Courtois, Stéphane, Nicolas Werth, Jean-Louis Panne, Andrzej Paczkowski, Karel Bartosek, and Jean-Louis Margolin. *The Black Book of Communism: Crimes, Terror, Repression.* Cambridge, MA: Harvard University Press, 1999.

Cowley, Robert, ed. *The Great War: Perspectives on the First World War.* New York: Random House, 2003.

Craig, Gordon A. *The Germans.* New York: Putnam, 1982.

———. *Germany, 1866–1945.* New York: Oxford University Press, 1978.

Crankshaw, Edward. *Bismarck*. New York: Viking, 1981.
―――. *The Fall of the House of Habsburg*. New York: Viking, 1963.
Crocker, George N. *Roosevelt's Road to Russia*. Chicago: Regnery, 1959.
Dallin, David J., and Boris I. Nicolaevsky. *Forced Labor in Soviet Russia*. New Haven, CT: Yale University Press, 1947.
Davis, Belinda J. *Home Fires Burning: Food, Politics, and Everyday Life in World War I Berlin*. Chapel Hill, NC: University of North Carolina Press, 2000.
Denson, John V., ed. *The Costs of War: America's Pyrrhic Victories*. New Brunswick, NJ: Transaction Books, 1988.
Deutscher, Isaac. *The Prophet Outcast: Trotsky, 1924–1940*. New York: Oxford University Press, 1970.
―――. *The Prophet Armed: Trotsky, 1879–1921*. New York: Oxford University Press, 1954.
―――. *The Prophet Unarmed: Trotsky, 1921–1929*. New York: Oxford University Press, 1959.
Dolot, Miron. *Execution by Hunger: The Hidden Holocaust*. New York: Norton, 1987.
Dyakov, Yuri, and Tatyana Bushuyeva. *The Red Army and the Wehrmacht: How the Soviets Militarized Germany, 1922–33, and Paved the Way for Fascism*. Amherst, NY: Prometheus Books, 1995.
Eisenhower, John S. D. *Intervention! The United States and the Mexican Revolution, 1914–1917*. New York: Norton, 1993.
Ekirch, Arthur A. *Progressivism in America: A Study of the Era from Theodore Roosevelt to Woodrow Wilson*. New York: Franklin Watts, 1974.
Epstein, Klaus. *Matthias Erzberger and the Dilemma of German Democracy*. Princeton, NJ: Princeton University Press, 1959.
Evans, Richard J. *The Coming of the Third Reich*. New York: Penguin, 2003.
Eych, Erich. *A History of the Weimar Republic*. 2 vols. Cambridge, MA: Harvard University Press, 1963.
Farnsworth, Beatrice. *William C. Bullitt and the Soviet Union*. Bloomington, IN: Indiana University Press, 1967.
Fay, Sidney Bradshaw. *The Origins of the World War*. New York: Macmillan, 1928.
Fehrenbach, T. R. *This Kind of War: A Study in Unpreparedness*. New York: Macmillan, 1963.
Feldman, Gerald D. *Army, Industry and Labor in Germany, 1914–1918*. Princeton, NJ: Princeton University Press, 1966.
―――. *German Imperialism, 1914–1918: The Development of a Historical Debate*. New York: Wiley, 1972.
―――. *The Great Disorder: Politics, Economics, and Society in the German Inflation, 1914–1923*. New York: Oxford University Press, 1993.
―――. *Iron and Steel in the German Inflation, 1916–1923*. Princeton, NJ: Princeton University Press, 1977.
Feldman, Gerald D. et al., eds. *The Adaptation to Inflation*. New York: de Gruyter, 1986.

Feldman, Gerald D., Manfred F. Boemeke, and Elizabeth Glaser, eds. *The Treaty of Versailles, 75 Years After*. New York: Cambridge University Press, 1998.

Ferguson, Niall. *Empire: The Rise and Demise of the British World Order and the Lessons for Global Power*. New York: Basic Books, 2002.

———. *The Pity of War: Explaining World War I*. New York: Basic Books, 1998.

Fergusson, Adam. *When Money Dies: The Nightmare of the Weimar Collapse*. London: Kimber, 1975.

Fest, Joachim. *Hitler*. New York: Harcourt, Brace, 1973.

Figes, Orlando. *A People's Tragedy: A History of the Russian Revolution*. New York: Viking, 1997.

Fischer, Fritz. *Germany's War Aims in World War I*. New York: Norton, 1967.

Fleming, D. F. *The Cold War and Its Origins, 1917–1960*. 2 vols. Garden City, NY: Doubleday, 1961.

Fleming, Thomas. *The Illusion of Victory: America in World War I*. New York: Basic Books, 2003.

Flynn, John T. *The Decline of the American Republic*. New York: Devin-Adair, 1955.

Foot, Rosemary. *The Wrong War: American Policy and the Dimensions of the Korean Conflict, 1950–1953*. Ithaca, NY: Cornell University Press, 1985.

Francis, David R. *Russia from the American Embassy*. New York: Scribner's, 1921.

Friedrich, Otto. *Before the Deluge: A Portrait of Berlin in the 1920s*. New York: Perennial, 1995.

Fussell, Paul. *The Great War and Modern Memory*. New York: Oxford University Press, 1975.

Gaddis, John Lewis. *The Long Peace: Inquiries into the History of the Cold War*. New York: Oxford University Press, 1987.

———. *Russia, the Soviet Union and the United States: An Interpretive History*. New York: Wiley, 1978.

———. *Strategies of Containment: A Critical Appraisal of Postwar American National Security Policy*. New York: Oxford University Press, 1982.

———. *The United States and the Origins of the Cold War*. New York: Columbia University Press, 1972.

———. *We Now Know: Rethinking Cold War History*. New York: Oxford University Press, 1997.

Gardner, Lloyd C. *Architects of Illusion: Men and Ideas in American Foreign Policy, 1941–1949*. New York: Quadrangle, 1970.

Gardner, Lloyd C., ed. *The Korean War*. New York: Quadrangle, 1972.

Gardner, Lloyd C., Walter F. LaFeber, and Thomas J. McCormick. *Creation of the American Empire: U.S. Diplomatic History*. Chicago: Rand McNally, 1973.

Gardner, Lloyd C., Arthur M. Schlesinger Jr., and Hans J. Morgenthau. *The Origins of the Cold War*. Waltham, MA: Ginn-Blaisdell, 1970.

Gatrell, Peter. *Government, Industry and Rearmament in Russia, 1900–1917*. New York: Cambridge University Press, 1994.

————. *The Tsarist Economy, 1854–1917*. New York: St. Martin's, 1986.

————. *A Whole Empire Walking: Refugees in Russia During World War I*. Bloomington, IN: Indiana University Press, 1999.

Gatzke, Hans W. *Stresemann and the Rearmament of Germany*. Baltimore: Johns Hopkins University Press, 1954.

George, Alexander L., and Juliette L. George. *Woodrow Wilson and Colonel House: A Personality Study*. New York: Dover, 1964.

Gilbert, Martin. *The First World War: A Complete History*. New York: Henry Holt, 1994.

————. *The Second World War: A Complete History*. New York: Henry Holt, 1989.

Goldman, Emma. *My Disillusionment in Russia*. Mineola, NY: Dover, 2003. Reprint of 1922 edition.

Gorbatov, A. V. *Years Off My Life: A Soviet General's Experiences of the Stalinist Purges*. New York: Norton, 1964.

Graham, Frank D. *Exchange, Prices and Production in Hyper-Inflation: Germany 1920–1923*. Princeton, NJ: Princeton University Press, 1930.

Grey, Edward. *Twenty-Five Years, 1892–1916*. New York: Frederick A. Stokes, 1937.

Grossman, Vasily. *Forever Flowing*. Evanston, IL: Northwestern University Press, 1997.

Hackworth, David H., and Julie Sherman. *About Face: Odyssey of an American Warrior*. New York: Simon & Schuster, 1989.

Hardach, Gerd. *The First World War, 1914–1918*. Berkeley, CA: University of California Press, 1977.

Heckscher, August. *Woodrow Wilson*. New York: Scribner's, 1991.

Heiden, Konrad. *The Fuehrer: Hitler's Rise to Power*. Edison, NJ: Castle Books, 2002. Reprint of 1944 edition.

Herold, Christopher. *The Age of Napoleon*. Boston: Houghton Mifflin, 1963.

Hickey, Michael. *The Korean War: The West Confronts Communism*. Woodstock, NY: Overlook Press, 2000.

Higgs, Robert. *Crisis and Leviathan: Critical Episodes in the Growth of American Government*. New York: Oxford University Press, 1987.

Hill, Richard. *War at Sea in the Ironclad Age*. New York: Sterling, 2000.

Hitler, Adolf. *Mein Kampf*. Boston: Houghton Mifflin, 2001.

————. *My New Order*. New York: Octagon Books, 1973.

Hochschild, Adam. *The Unquiet Ghost: Russians Remember Stalin*. New York: Viking, 1994.

Hogan, Michael J. *Cross of Iron: Harry S. Truman and the Origins of the American National Security State, 1945–1954*. New York: Cambridge University Press, 1998.

Höhne, Heinz. *The Order of the Death's Head*. London: Pan Books, 1969.

————. *The Order of the Death's Head: The Story of Hitler's SS*. New York: Penguin, 2000.

Holborn, Hajo. *A History of Modern Germany, 1840–1945*. New York: Knopf, 1969.

Holtfrerich, Carl-Ludwig. *The German Inflation 1914–1923: Causes and Effects in International Perspective.* Berlin: Walter de Gruyter, 1986.

Horn, Martin. *Britain, France and the Financing of the First World War.* Montreal: McGill-Queens University Press, 2002.

Hough, Richard. *The Fleet That Had to Die.* New York: Viking, 1958.

———. *The Great War at Sea, 1914–1928.* Edinburgh: Birlinn, 2000.

Iakovlev, Alexander N. *A Century of Violence in Soviet Russia.* New Haven, CT: Yale University Press, 2002.

Isaacson, Walter, and Evan Thomas. *The Wise Men: Six Friends and the World They Made.* New York: Simon & Schuster, 1986.

Jakobson, Michael. *Origins of the Gulag: The Soviet Prison Camp System, 1917–1934.* Lexington, KY: University Press of Kentucky, 1992.

Jászi, Oszkár. *The Dissolution of the Habsburg Monarchy.* Chicago: University of Chicago Press, 1961.

Johnson, Eric A. *Nazi Terror: Gestapo, Jews and Ordinary Germans.* New York: Basic Books, 2000.

Johnson, Paul. *Modern Times: The World from the Twenties to the Eighties.* New York: Harper & Row, 1983.

Johnson, Paul. *Napoleon.* New York: Viking, 2002.

Jones, Thomas. *Lloyd George.* Cambridge, MA: Harvard University Press, 1951.

Kaes, Anton, Martin Jay, and Edward Dimendberg, eds. *The Weimar Republic Sourcebook.* Berkeley, CA: University of California Press, 1995.

Kahan, Arcadius. *Russian Economic History, the Nineteenth Century.* Chicago: University of Chicago Press, 1989.

Kann, Robert A. *History of the Habsburg Empire, 1526–1918.* Berkeley, CA: University of California Press, 1974.

Karnow, Stanley. *Vietnam: A History.* New York: Viking, 1991.

Karp, Walter. *The Politics of War: The Story of Two Wars Which Altered Forever the Political Life of the American Republic, 1890–1920.* New York: Harper & Row, 1979.

Katzenellenbaum, S. S. *Russian Currency and Banking, 1914–1924.* London: P. S. King, 1925.

Kazmer, Daniel R. *Russian Economic History: A Guide to Information Sources.* Detroit: Gale Research, 1977.

Keegan, John. *The First World War.* New York: Knopf, 1999.

———. *The Second World War.* New York: Viking Penguin, 1990.

Keep, John L. H. *The Russian Revolution: A Study in Mass Mobilization.* New York: Norton, 1977.

Kennan, George F. *The Decision to Intervene: The Prelude to Allied Intervention in the Bolshevik Revolution.* Princeton, NJ: Princeton University Press, 1958.

———. *Russia and the West Under Lenin and Stalin.* Boston: Little, Brown, 1960.

———. *Russia Leaves the War: The Americans in Petrograd and the Bolshevik Revolution.* Princeton, NJ: Princeton University Press, 1956.

Kennedy, Paul. *The Rise and Fall of Great Powers: Economic Change and Military Conflict from 1500 to 2000.* New York: Random House, 1987.

Kerensky, Alexander. *The Catastrophe: Kerensky's Own Story of the Russian Revolution.* New York: D. Appleton, 1927.

———. *The Crucifixion of Liberty.* New York: John Day, 1934.

———. *Russia and History's Turning Point: The Russian Revolution and Its Aftermath.* New York: Duell, Sloan & Pearce, 1965.

Kershaw, Ian. *The Nazi Dictatorship: Problems and Perspectives of Interpretation.* London: Hodder Arnold, 1989.

Kessler, Harry. *Walter Rathenau: His Life and Work.* New York: Harcourt, Brace & Co., 1930.

Keynes, John Maynard. *The Economic Consequences of the Peace.* New York: Penguin, 1995.

Kissinger, Henry. *Diplomacy.* New York: Simon & Schuster, 1994.

Knight, Alan. *The Mexican Revolution: Counter-Revolution and Reconstruction.* Lincoln, NE: University of Nebraska Press, 1990.

———. *The Mexican Revolution: Porfirians, Liberals and Peasants.* Lincoln, NE: University of Nebraska Press, 1990.

Kocka, Jurgen. *Facing Total War: German Society 1914–1918.* Leamington Spa, Warwickshire, England: Berg Publishers, 1984.

Kofsky, Frank. *Harry S. Truman and the War Scare of 1948: A Successful Campaign to Deceive the Nation.* New York: St. Martin's, 1993.

Kolko, Gabriel. *Century of War: Politics, Conflict, and Society Since 1914.* New York: New Press, 1994.

Kostyrchenko, Gennadi. *Out of the Red Shadows: Anti-Semitism in Stalin's Russia.* Amherst, NY: Prometheus, 1995.

Kramer, Alan. *German Atrocities, 1914: A History of Denial.* New Haven, CT: Yale University Press, 2001.

Krauss, Melvyn. *How NATO Weakens the West.* New York: Simon & Schuster, 1986.

Kruedener, Baron Jurgen von, ed. *Economic Crisis and Political Collapse: The Weimar Republic 1924–1933.* Oxford, England: Berg Pub Ltd., 1990.

LaFeber, Walter. *America, Russia, and the Cold War, 1945–1990.* New York: McGraw-Hill, 1991.

Lansing, Robert. *The Big Four and Others of the Peace Conference.* Boston: Houghton Mifflin, 1921.

———. *The Peace Negotiations: A Narrative.* Boston: Houghton Mifflin, 1921.

Laursen, Karsten, and Jorgen Pedersen. *The German Inflation, 1919–1923.* Amsterdam: North Holland, 1964.

Lederer, Ivo J., ed. *The Versailles Settlement: Was It Foredoomed to Failure?* Boston: Heath, 1960.

Leggett, George. *The Cheka: Lenin's Political Police.* New York: Oxford University Press, 1986.

Leonhard, Wolfgang. *Betrayal: The Hitler-Stalin Pact of 1939.* New York: St. Martin's, 1989.

Liddell Hart, Basil Henry. *The Real War, 1914–1918*. New York: Little, Brown, 1930.

———. *History of the Second World War*. New York: Putnam, 1971.

Lincoln, W. Bruce. *In War's Dark Shadow: The Russians Before the Great War*. New York: Oxford University Press, 1994.

———. *Passage Through Armageddon: The Russians in War and Revolution, 1914–1918*. New York: Simon & Schuster, 1986.

———. *Red Victory: A History of the Russian Civil War*. New York: Simon & Schuster, 1989.

Link, Arthur S. *Wilson the Diplomatist: A Look at His Major Foreign Policies*. Baltimore: Johns Hopkins University Press, 1957.

———. *Wilson: Road to the White House*. Princeton, NJ: Princeton University Press, 1965.

———. *Woodrow Wilson: Revolution, War and Peace*. Arlington Heights, IL: AHM Publishers, 1979.

Link, Arthur S., ed. *The Impact of World War I*. New York: Harper & Row, 1969.

Link, Arthur S., and William B. Catton. *The Progressive Era and the First World War, 1900–1920*. New York: Knopf, 1973.

Link, Arthur S., and William M. Leary Jr., eds. *The Progressive Era and the Great War, 1896–1920*. New York: Appleton Century Crofts, 1969.

Link, Arthur S., and Richard L. McCormick. *Progressivism*. Arlington Heights, IL: Harlan Davidson, 1983.

Lutz, Hermann. *Lord Grey and the World War*. New York: Knopf, 1928.

MacDonald, Callum. *The Killing of SS Reinhard Heydrich*. New York: Free Press, 1999.

Malia, Martin E. *The Soviet Tragedy: A History of Socialism in Russia, 1917–1991*. New York: Free Press, 1994.

Malle, Silvana. *The Economic Organization of War Communism, 1918–1921*. Cambridge, England: Cambridge University Press, 1985.

Mann, Robert. *A Grand Delusion: America's Descent into Vietnam*. New York: Basic Books, 2000.

Mantoux, Etienne. *The Carthaginian Peace, or The Economic Consequences of Mr. Keynes*. London: Oxford University Press, 1946.

Martel, Gordon, ed. *The Origins of the Second World War Reconsidered: The A. J. P. Taylor Debate After Twenty-Five Years*. Boston: Allen & Unwin, 1986.

Marshall, S. L. A. *World War I*. Boston: Houghton Mifflin, 2001.

Massie, Robert K. *Nicholas and Alexandra*. New York: Ballantine, 2000.

Mawdsley, Evan. *The Russian Civil War*. Boston: Allen & Unwin, 1987.

McCullough, David. *Truman*. New York: Simon & Schuster, 1992.

McNeill, William H. *The Pursuit of Power: Technology, Armed Forces and Society Since 1000*. Chicago: University of Chicago Press, 1982.

Melgunov, Sergei. *Red Terror in Russia*. Westport, CT: Hyperion Press, 1975. Reprint of 1926 edition.

Miller, Donald L. *The Story of World War II*. New York: Simon & Schuster, 2001.

Millis, Walter. *Road to War, 1914–1917*. Boston: Houghton Mifflin, 1935.

Mombauer, Annika. *Helmuth von Moltke and the Origins of the First World War*. New York: Cambridge University Press, 2001.

———. *The Origins of the First World War: Controversies and Consensus*. New York: Longman, 2002.

Montefiore, Simon Sebag. *Stalin: The Court of the Red Czar*. New York: Knopf, 2004.

Morgenthau, Hans J. *Politics Among Nations: The Struggle for Power and Peace*. New York: Knopf, 1962.

Moynahan, Brian. *Rasputin: The Saint Who Sinned*. New York: DaCapo Press, 2000.

Murray, Gilbert. *The Foreign Policy of Sir Edward Grey*. Oxford, England: Clarendon Press, 1915.

Offner, Arnold A. *Another Such Victory: President Truman and the Cold War, 1945–1953*. Palo Alto, CA: Stanford University Press, 2002.

Overy, Richard, and Andrew Wheatcroft. *The Road to War: The Origins of World War II*. New York: Random House, 1989.

Owen, Frank. *Tempestuous Journey: Lloyd George, His Life and Times*. New York: McGraw-Hill, 1955.

Owen, Louisa Lang, and Charles M. Barber. *Casualty of War: A Childhood Remembered*. College Station, TX: Texas A&M University Press, 2003.

Padfield, Peter. *Himmler*. New York: Henry Holt, 1991.

Pares, Barnard. *A History of Russia*. New York: Knopf, 1953.

Payne, Robert. *The Life and Death of Adolf Hitler*. New York: Praeger, 1973.

Pearce, Brian. *How Haig Saved Lenin*. New York: St. Martin's, 1987.

Pearson, Michael. *The Sealed Train*. New York: Putnam, 1975.

Pipes, Richard. *Communism: A History*. New York: Modern Library, 2003.

———. *A Concise History of the Russian Revolution*. New York: Knopf, 1995.

———. *Russia Under the Bolshevik Regime*. New York: Knopf, 1993.

———. *The Russian Revolution*. New York: Knopf, 1990.

———. *Struve: Liberal on the Right, 1905–1944*. Cambridge, MA: Harvard University Press, 1980.

———. *Three "Whys" of the Russian Revolution*. New York: Vintage, 1997.

Pleshakov, Constantine. *The Tsar's Last Armada: The Epic Voyage to the Battle of Tsushima*. New York: Basic Books, 2002.

Pool, James. *Hitler and His Secret Partners: Contributions, Loot and Rewards, 1922–1945*. New York: Pocket Books, 1997.

———. *Who Financed Hitler: The Secret Funding of Hitler's Rise to Power, 1919–1933*. New York: Dial Press, 1978.

Possony, Stefan. *Lenin, Compulsive Revolutionary*. Chicago: Regnery, 1964.

Powaski, Ronald E. *The Cold War: The United States and the Soviet Union, 1917–1991*. New York: Oxford University Press, 1998.

Quigley, Carroll. *The Anglo-American Establishment*. New York: Books In Focus, 1981.

———. *Tragedy and Hope: A History of the World in Our Time*. New York: Macmillan, 1966.

Radosh, Ronald. *Prophets on the Right: Profiles of Conservative Critics of American Globalism.* New York: Simon & Schuster, 1975.

Radzinsky, Edvard. *The Last Tzar: The Life and Death of Nicholas II.* New York: Anchor, 1993.

———. *The Rasputin File.* New York: Nan A. Talese, 2000.

———. *Stalin: The First In-Depth Biography Based on Explosive New Documents from Russia's Secret Archives.* New York: Doubleday, 1996.

Raimondo, Justin. *Reclaiming the Right: Lost Legacy of the Conservative Movement.* Burlingame, CA: Center for Libertarian Studies, 1993.

Read, Anthony. *The Deadly Embrace: Hitler, Stalin and the Nazi-Soviet Pact.* New York: Norton, 1988.

———. *The Devil's Disciples: Hitler's Inner Circle.* New York: Norton, 2004.

———. *Kristallnacht: The Nazi Night of Terror.* New York: Times Books, 1988.

Reed, Robert Threshie, First Earl of Loreburn. *How the War Came.* London: Methuen, 1919.

Reed, Thomas C. *At the Abyss: An Insider's History of the Cold War.* New York: Ballantine, 2004.

Reitlinger, Gerald. *The SS: Alibi of a Nation, 1922–1945.* New York: Viking, 1968.

Riasanovsky, Nicholas V. *A History of Russia.* New York: Oxford University Press, 1969.

Roberts, Geoffrey. *Unholy Alliance: Stalin's Pact with Hitler.* Bloomington, IN: Indiana University Press, 1989.

Röpke, Wilhelm. *Against the Tide.* Chicago: Regnery, 1969.

Rosenberg, Tina. *Haunted Land: Facing Europe's Ghosts After Communism.* New York: Random House, 1995.

Royle, Trevor. *Crimea: The Great Crimean War, 1854–1856.* New York: St. Martin's, 2000.

Rummel, R. J. *Lethal Politics: Soviet Genocide and Mass Murder Since 1917.* New Brunswick, NJ: Transaction, 1990.

Rutherford, Ward. *The Russian Army in World War I.* London: Gordon Cremonsi, 1977.

Schmitt, Bernadotte.E., and Harold C. Vedeler. *The World in the Crucible, 1914–1919.* New York: Harper & Row, 1984.

Ségur, Count Philippe-Paul de. *Napoleon's Russian Campaign.* Alexandria, VA: Time-Life Books, 1985.

Service, Robert. *A History of Twentieth-Century Russia.* Cambridge, MA: Harvard University Press, 1998.

———. *Lenin: A Biography.* Cambridge, MA: Harvard University Press, 2000.

———. *Russia: Experiment with a People.* Cambridge, MA: Harvard University Press, 2003.

Seton-Watson, Hugh. *The Russian Empire, 1801–1917.* Oxford: Clarendon Press, 1967.

Shamalov, Varlam. *Kolyma Tales.* New York: Penguin, 1995.

Sheehan, Neil. *A Bright and Shining Lie: John Paul Vann and America in Vietnam.* New York: Random House, 1988.

Shirer, William L. *Berlin Diary: The Journal of a Foreign Correspondent, 1934–1941*. Boston: Little, Brown, 1988.

———. *The Collapse of the Third Republic: An Inquiry into the Fall of France in 1940*. New York: Da Capo Press, 1994.

———. *The Nightmare Years, 1930–1940*. Edinburgh: Birlinn, 2001.

———. *The Rise and Fall of Adolf Hitler*. New York: Random House, 1961.

———. *The Rise and Fall of the Third Reich: A History of Nazi Germany*. New York: Simon & Schuster, 1960.

Simpson, Colin. *The Lusitania*. Boston: Little, Brown, 1973.

Sinclair, David. *Hall of Mirrors*. London: Random House, 2001.

Smith, Daniel M. *Robert Lansing and American Neutrality, 1914–1917*. Berkeley, CA: University of California Press, 1958.

Smith, Gene. *When the Cheering Stopped: The Last Years of Woodrow Wilson*. New York: Morrow, 1964.

Solzhenitsyn, Aleksandr I. *The Gulag Archipelago: An Experiment in Literary Investigation*. 2 vols. New York: Harper, 1974.

Spence, Jonathan D. *The Search for Modern China*. New York: Norton, 1990.

Stalin, Joseph. *Speeches Delivered at Meetings of Voters, Stalin Election District, Moscow, on December 11, 1937 and February 9, 1946*. Moscow: Foreign Languages Publishing House, 1950.

Stevenson, David. *Cataclysm: The First World War as Political Tragedy*. New York: Basic Books, 2004.

Stolper, Gustav. *The German Economy 1870–1940*. New York: AMS Press, 1984.

Strachan, Hew. *The First World War*. New York: Viking Penguin, 2004.

———. *The First World War: To Arms*. Oxford, England: Oxford University Press, 2001.

Strachan, Hew, ed. *The Oxford Illustrated History of the First World War*. New York: Oxford University Press, 1998.

Taft, Robert A. *A Foreign Policy for Americans*. Garden City, NY: Doubleday, 1951.

Talmon, J. L. *The Origins of Totalitarian Democracy*. New York: Frederick Praeger, 1961.

———. *Political Messianism: The Romantic Phase*. New York: Praeger, 1968.

———. *The Myth of the Nation and the Vision of Revolution*. London: Secker & Warburg, 1981.

Taylor, A. J. P. *Bismarck: The Man and the Statesman*. New York: Knopf, 1955.

———. *English History, 1914–1945*. New York: Oxford University Press, 1965.

———. *The Origins of the Second World War*. London: Penguin, 1965.

———. *The Habsburg Monarchy, 1809–1918*. Chicago: University of Chicago Press, 1976.

Taylor, Edmond. *The Fall of the Dynasties: The Collapse of the Old Order, 1905–1922*. Garden City, NY: Doubleday, 1963.

Thompson, J. M. *Napoleon Bonaparte*. New York: Barnes & Noble Books, 1996.

Toland, John. *Adolf Hitler*. Garden City, NY: Doubleday, 1976.

———. *In Mortal Combat: Korea 1950–1953*. New York: Morrow, 1991.

———. *No Man's Land: 1918, the Last Year of the Great War.* New York: Ballantine, 1980.

Tolstoy, Leo. *The Sevastopol Sketches.* New York: Penguin, 1986.

Tooley, Hunt. *The Western Front: Battleground and Home Front in the First World War.* New York: Palgrave Macmillan, 2003.

Trevelyan, George Macaulay. *Grey of Fallodon: The Life and Letters of Sir Edward Grey.* Boston: Houghton Mifflin, 1937.

Tuchman, Barbara W. *The Guns of August.* New York: Macmillan, 1962.

———. *The Proud Tower: A Portrait of the World Before the War, 1890–1914.* New York: Macmillan, 1966.

———. *The Zimmermann Telegram.* New York: Ballantine Books, 1994.

Tucker, Robert C. *Stalin as Revolutionary, 1879–1929: A Study in History and Personality.* New York: Norton, 1973.

———. *Stalin in Power: The Revolution from Above, 1928–1941.* New York: Norton, 1990.

Turner, Henry Ashby. *Stresemann and the Politics of the Weimar Republic.* Princeton, NJ: Princeton University Press, 1963.

Viereck, George Sylvester. *The Strangest Friendship in History: Woodrow Wilson and Colonel House.* New York: Liveright, 1932.

Vincent, C. Paul. *The Politics of Hunger: The Allied Blockade of Germany, 1915–1919.* Athens, OH: Ohio University Press, 1985.

Volkogonov, Dimitri. *Lenin.* New York: Free Press, 1994.

———. *Stalin: Triumph and Tragedy.* New York: Grove Weidenfield, 1991.

———. *Trotsky, the Eternal Revolutionary.* New York: Free Press, 1996.

Wade, Rex. *The Russian Search for Peace, February–October 1917.* Palo Alto, CA: Stanford University Press, 1969.

Warner, Dennis Ashton, and Peggy Warner. *Tide at Sunrise: A History of the Russo-Japanese War, 1904–1905.* New York: Charterhouse, 1974.

Watt, Donald Cameron. *How War Came: The Immediate Origins of the Second World War, 1938–1939.* New York: Pantheon, 1989.

Webb, Steven B. *Hyperinflation and Stabilization in Weimar Germany.* New York: Oxford University Press, 1989.

Weinberg, Gerhard. *A World at Arms: A Global History of World War II.* New York: Cambridge University Press, 1994.

Weitz, John. *Hitler's Banker: Hjalmar Horace Greeley Schacht.* Boston: Little, Brown, 1997.

Wheeler-Bennett, John W. *The Forgotten Peace: Brest-Litovsk, March 1918.* New York: William Morrow, 1939.

———. *The Nemesis of Power: The German Army in Politics, 1918–1945.* New York: St. Martin's, 1954.

Wheeler-Bennett, John W. *Wooden Titan: Hindenburg in Twenty Years of German History, 1914–1934.* New York: Morrow, 1936.

Widdig, Bernd. *Culture and Inflation in Weimar Germany.* Berkeley, CA: University of California Press, 2001.

Williams, Joyce G. *Colonel House and Sir Edward Grey: A Study in Anglo-American Diplomacy.* Lanham, MD: University Press of America, 1985.

Wilson, A. N. *Tolstoy*. New York: Norton, 1988.

Wilson, Woodrow. *The Public Papers of Woodrow Wilson*, edited by Ray Stannard Baker and William E. Dodd. New York: Harper, 1925–1927.

Li Zhisui. *The Private Life of Chairman Mao*. New York: Random House, 1994.

ACKNOWLEDGMENTS

This book traces the explosive consequences of an American policy long ignored in American history books. The consequences were long ignored because they played out elsewhere, on other continents. By the time Americans were affected, connections with the original American policy had been lost or forgotten.

I want to thank David Boaz and Ed Crane (Cato Institute), Robert Higgs (Independent Institute), and Leonard Liggio (Atlas Economic Research Foundation) for encouraging me on this project.

I have had helpful conversations with historians Thomas Fleming, Richard Pipes, and Robert Conquest.

Harvard University, Stanford University, the Hoover Institution, and the Library of Congress proved useful in providing research material, as did Internet out-of-print booksellers around the world.

I'm grateful to be working with such a fine editor as Jed Donahue at Crown Forum. The project couldn't have gone more smoothly.

I want to thank Andrea Millen Rich and Kathleen Hiserodt (Laissez Faire Books) for their patience and support.

And thanks to Madeline, Marisa, Justin, Kristin, and Rosalynd for making it all worthwhile.

INDEX

ABOUT THE AUTHOR

Historian Jim Powell is the author of *FDR's Folly: How Roosevelt and His New Deal Prolonged the Great Depression* and *The Triumph of Liberty: A 2,000-Year History Told Through the Lives of Freedom's Greatest Champions*. He has given talks at Harvard University, Stanford University, and other universities across the United States, as well as in England, Germany, Japan, Argentina, and Brazil. He has written for the *New York Times*, the *Wall Street Journal*, the *Chicago Tribune*, *Money* magazine, *Reason*, *Barron's*, *Esquire*, the *Christian Science Monitor*, and numerous other national publications. A senior fellow at the Cato Institute since 1988, Powell served as editor of Laissez Faire Books for eleven years. He studied history at the University of Chicago under Daniel Boorstin and William McNeil. Powell lives with his family in Westport, Connecticut.